Warning: This book, if loaned, may never be returned.

THE COMPLETE JOY

O · F

# HOME BREWING

## FOURTH EDITION

*FULLY REVISED AND UPDATED*

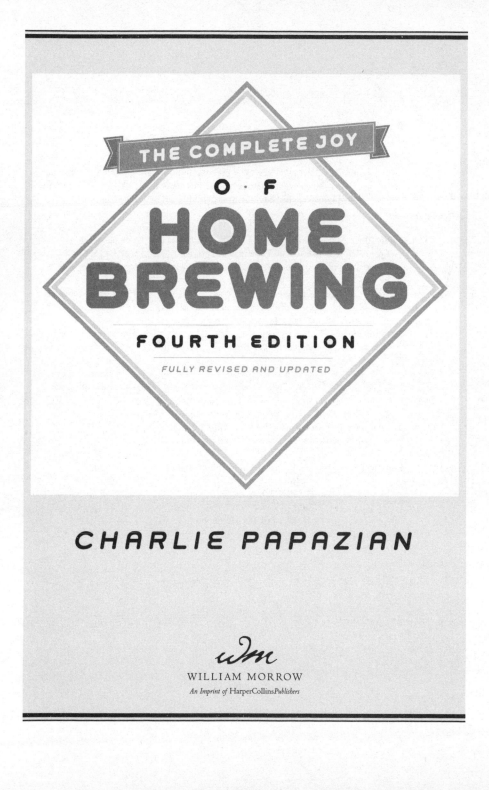

# THE COMPLETE JOY

## O·F

# HOME BREWING

## FOURTH EDITION

FULLY REVISED AND UPDATED

# CHARLIE PAPAZIAN

WILLIAM MORROW
An Imprint of HarperCollins Publishers

*The Complete Joy of Homebrewing, Fourth Edition,* is dedicated to all of my students, both young and old. You have taught me much more than I have taught you. I thank you for the inspiration given to me.

I especially thank my wife, Sandra, and daughter, Carla, who are the real joys in my life.

And finally, thank you to the hundreds of Brewers Association staff whom I've had the pleasure to work with since 1978. You have been the foundation that has helped create the positive change we enjoy as American beer culture.

*"Whatever suits you, tickles me plum to death."*
—W. JENSEN

*"You never know 'til you check it out."*
—C. L. MATZEN

*"A beer with balls!"*
—J. A. "ESPO" ESPOSITO

*"Oh, my soul's on fire."*
—J. A. STONER

*"You never know."*
—L. PRINCE

*"Are you kidding me?"*
—J. TELISCHAK

*"Charlie's here."*
G. CONNER

*"Relax. Don't worry. Have a homebrew."*
—ANON.

*"What's this?"*
—C. A. CARLSON

*"Just right, but getting better."*
—M. L. ALLMON

*"The best beer you've ever made."*
—A. AVILA

*"P.F.G."*
—T. G. TEAGUE

*"Zymurgy!"*
—M. F. MONAHAN

*"Mmmm, Bom."*
—S. R. R. PAPAZIAN

# CONTENTS

**MAKING HONEY MEAD**                                                        **381**

What is mead? • But first . . . about honey • Traditional meads •
Mead recipes • Resources for 13 mead recipes

# PREFACE

## A WORD FROM THE REAL MICHAEL JACKSON*

How Charlie Papazian can change your life
*(With help from his friend Michael—that's me)*

Possession of this book means you are in for a good time. If you don't actually own it yet, buy it immediately. The secrets of good beer are within, but we are talking more than recipes. This is a lifestyle manual, a philosophical tract, and a work of subversive literature. This book is based on the many explorations of Charlie Papazian. Before I met Charlie, I had been told that he was a remarkably resourceful, practical man. When he picked me up at the airport for the first time, more than 20 years ago, I saw a man who clearly did not believe in wasting money on a new car. I have on one occasion seen Charlie ride a hired elephant, but he looks like a man who might usually travel by magic carpet. Or perhaps a genie who emerges from a bottle of beer to make your wishes come true.

The author should be called Good Time Charlie. To think, this man graduated with a degree in nuclear engineering. The world had a narrow escape. He could have blown us all into Outer Space, judging from some of the beers he brews. It's just as well that he removed himself from his native New Jersey, where his experiments might have endangered heavily populated metropolitan areas. He has for many years lived out of harm's way in Boulder, Colorado. He has a tepee there. I have wondered why, but some questions yield no answer.

It has been argued that the pre-Columbian Native Americans did not brew, preferring to relax with a pipe of peace. Some homebrewers have tried to combine the two approaches, but Charlie has a peaceful nature already. Rather than putting his engineering degree to some Strangelovian misuse, he became an elementary school teacher, and a very good one at that. I have seen past pupils greet him with what I can best describe as affectionate awe. You will, too, once he has taught you to brew.

Brewing, like cooking, can be enjoyable at any level. You can stick to favorites,

---

*Michael Jackson was the world's most widely published writer on beer. His books included* The Great Beer Guide. The World Guide to Beer, Ultimate Beer, Beer Companion, Great Beers of Belgium, *and many others. He passed away in his London home in 2007.*

or go for gold. The choice is yours, and you can stop where you like. Home-brewers everywhere have fun, and enjoy saving money, but their real motivation in the United States is usually to make a style of beer that is a challenge to them, or one that is not readily available in their state.

Can homebrews match commercial beers? I have occasionally commented that many homebrewers in the United States are more knowledgeable than some of the professionals. The analogy I would make is with sports-car buffs and line managers in Detroit. The hobbyist has encountered every kind of engine or gear-box, and knows how to improvise and be creative. The line manager may in some instances know only the model to which his plant is dedicated.

Homebrewers are sociable, gregarious. They have clubs with witty names: the vulgar acronym BURP (Brewers United for Real Potables; Washington, D.C.); the plain punny Foam Rangers (Houston, Texas); the literary Maltose Falcons (San Francisco). I seem forever to be going to their parties, often in odd locations. I particularly remember one in a hangar full of microlite aircraft, while another involved a side trip to Cape Kennedy.

Being around homebrewers means being drawn into their many enthusi-asms. For some years, I was enlisted to the support of a softball team called The Boulder Brewers, despite their games being about five thousand miles from my home in London. On another occasion, I found myself speaking at a fund-raising dinner for a modern dance group. More recently, Charlie introduced me to the Slow Food movement, at whose Salone de Gusto he and I found ourselves promoting beer and American cheese to an audience of Italians. Faced with a challenge like that, he wore a coat and tie; quite a change for a man I once saw dressed as a blueberry pie.

Because we beer activists have a good time, we try to be tolerant when people suggest that our passion is misspent. "It's only beer. How can it be that important to you? Isn't all beer the same?" Do people put the same questions to a lover of fine wines? I don't think so. It is understood that wines are complex and varied, and that a devotee would grievously miss these pleasures if they were removed.

Beer is the most civilized of drinks. It was man as the hunter-gatherer, yet to civilize, who invented wine. How did civilization begin? With a beer, of course, at least six thousand years ago. Mr. Hunter-Gatherer collected fruits, most of which have only a short season. When he attempted to store what he had gath-ered, the fruits rotted—became wine, which is not very nutritious. Perhaps in search of something with a longer season, and more nutrition, humans began to farm the land. Their first crop was grain, and their first recipe was for beer. This happened in the Fertile Crescent of the ancient world.

The first brewers grew the grain and made the beer. Yes, they were home-brewers. Beer was made on farms, at country mansions, castles, monasteries, and inns as the art of brewing spread west through Europe. These people were homebrewers, too. What kind of beer did they make?

That depended upon the time and place. Not only malted grain, but also raw; not only barley but also wheat and rye were used, each providing its own taste and texture. The agents of aroma, flavor, and preservation have included not only hops but also juniper berries, cherries and a wide variety of roots, barks, and flowers. Even today, a handful of winy-tasting beers are fermented by wild yeasts; an acidic few by mixed cultures; a substantial group by fruity ale yeasts; and the majority by more thorough lager strains.

Every valley had its own raw materials and climate, every brewer his own recipes and methods. Almost all beer was sold only in its own village. What a delight that must have been. In Europe, only in Belgium does a hint of that diversity survive.

What happened to diversity? With the emergence of mass-marketed golden lager as a national brand, beginning in America in the 1870s, almost every other style of beer has been in jeapordy of being washed away.

The first defiance of this tide came from two men on opposite sides of the Atlantic. In Scotland, Peter Maxwell Stuart inherited his family's castle, restored its brewery, and started to market his Traquair House Ale. In California, Fritz Maytag gave a new life to Anchor Steam, the only brewery in America at that time not making a golden lager.The tide began to turn in the 1970s. I would draw your attention to the following: Senator Alan Cranston, of California; President Carter; Charlie Papazian; the four founders of the Campaign for Real Ale; Michael Jackson (that's me); Charlie Finkel; and Jack McAuliffe.

Ever since Prohibition (which played its own part in destroying traditional breweries and beers) homebrewing had been banned. It was finally made legal in a bill introduced by Senator Cranston and signed by President Carter. No one used this new freedom to greater effect than Charlie Papazian.

In Britain, four beer lovers had begun CAMRA, a consumerist movement to defend the traditional beers of the United Kingdom. Inspired by this, brewpubs and small breweries began to open in Britain. (Small breweries had been closing throughout Europe and the Americas since World War I.)

Heartened by this reversal, I turned my thoughts to vulnerable specialty breweries and beers that I had encountered elsewhere in the world, in my travels as a journalist. I wrote *The World Guide to Beer*, the first book seriously to document the world's specialty beer styles: national, regional, and local. This book was modeled on Hugh Johnson's *World Atlas of Wine*.

My book caught the eye of Charles Finkel, who had established a company called Merchant du Vin with a view to importing wines. He decided instead to import beers, basing his range on those I had most highly praised. Imported beer at the time was all mainstream golden lager. Finkel brought in specialties from Britain, the Nordic countries, Belgium, and Germany. Rather than advertising, or price-cutting, he used "beer education" as his selling tool.

If imported specialty beers, some highly unusual, could sell in the United

States, couldn't America brew its own examples? Traquair House and Anchor Steam were both inspirational for Jack McAuliffe, who had spent time in Scotland while in the U.S. Navy. He moved to Northern California and started the first new micro, New Albion.

More soon followed. American homebrewers were turning professional. I wrote about them in further books and magazine articles, calling them "boutique brewers." Some brewers loved this sobriquet, borrowed from the Californian winegrowers; other beer lovers thought it sounded ephemeral.

The term "microbrewery" came from the American Homebrewers Association in its magazine *Zymurgy* from Boulder, Colorado. American homebrewing became a training ground for micros and brewpubs. The American Homebrewers Association gave rise to a separate organization for small commercial brewers. Technical journals were produced for both. An annual competition for homebrewers gained a bigger brother for brewpubs and micros. Better yet, the professionals' competition was (and still is) part of the Great American Beer Festival, an annual public event. This attracts 25,000 people each year, offering them 1,300 beers, in sixty-odd styles, from over 300 American breweries.

Many a young man or woman I first knew as a homebrewer I now see collecting medals at the GABF for the beers they make in their brewpub or microbrewery. Whether their products are India Pale Ales, Russian Stouts, Bohemian pilsners, Oktoberfest lagers, Belgian spiced beers, Scottish ales, or American honey wheats, these are some of the most distinctive, skillfully composed beers in the world.

Even today, there is a widespread view that Europe has all the best beers. Many European brewers are busily dumbing down their beers, in the mistaken belief that this will endear them to drinkers of international-style lagers. Nor are the classics widely available. Germany's classic styles barely penetrate Belgium or Britain, and vice versa. No European city has the diversity of beer styles available in New York or Boston, Chicago or Denver, San Francisco or Seattle.

Even in the days when this country was being settled, the English ales and porters were found in Massachusetts or New Hampshire; the Dutch or Flemish beers in and around Manhattan; the Bohemian and German lagers in Pennsylvania or Wisconsin. Today, I can readily find all of those styles, and many more, in State College, Pennsylvania; Madison, Wisconsin; or Portland, Oregon.

When I travel in the United States, which I seem to do constantly, I delight in the diversity and quality of the country's beers—whether they be homebrews or specialties from brewpubs or micros. Even the big national and international brewers have specialties these days.

When I first visited the United States it was very difficult indeed to find anything but golden lagers, light and neutral in body and taste. Today, there are more than 1,500 breweries in the United States and five or ten times as many beers.

Charlie cannot take the credit for all this, but his writings and ideas—and the organizations deriving from them—have done much to help brewers get started as amateurs, and sometimes as professionals.

Dip into this book and your life will never be the same again.

Michael Jackson
London, 2003

# A WORD ABOUT THIS FOURTH EDITION

It is now the spring of 2014 and I'm close to completing this fourth revised edition of *The Complete Joy of Homebrewing*. I take pause in writing this introduction, the last piece of a long six months spent reviewing, revising, editing, adding, updating, researching, changing, correcting, deleting, and improving this book. I have a homebrew, sip, and think.

I dwell on how much people's attitudes toward beer have changed. There has been a profound and extraordinary shift in the paradigm outlining our ideas about what we want in a beer and how we enjoy it.

But what is even more profound to me is the impact that beer and brewing—and particularly homebrewing—have had on people's lives. I think about this book as my journey and the beginning of your journey. By the time this new edition is released, all editions will have sold more than 1.3 million copies. I have met tens of thousands of homebrewers over these years, but I'm still awed every time someone says to me, "Charlie, you've probably heard this a thousand times, but your book has changed my life." It never gets old. Yes, this beer thing we've all found our way to get involved in has changed our lives. Not only with the quality of the beers we enjoy, but as they contribute to the quality of our lives.

I am dumbstruck when I realize how many people who started learning how to brew with this book now have careers in the beer business or own a brewery. Well over 90 percent of the craft breweries in America were started by homebrewers. As this book goes to print, there will be about three thousand small breweries in the United States, and those breweries employ about 120,000 people—and that's not including the extended businesses that supply or provide services to the craft beer industry.

My head starts spinning when I consider what homebrewing has done for so many people. You will find that making, sharing, and enjoying your own homebrew is powerful stuff. There is nothing like a glass of my own beer to reflect and get myself centered on the most important things in life. You may be surprised to hear this from me, but the most important thing is not beer or homebrew. It's about creating, sharing, family, and friendship.

To you, the homebrewer: Enjoy life and homebrew responsibly and continue your journey wherever it may take you.

# FOREWORD

BY PROFESSOR CHARLES BAMFORTH,

UNIVERSITY OF CALIFORNIA, DAVIS

I am often asked if I brew at home. A typical reply would be, "I don't–and if I was a brain surgeon I wouldn't relax by operating on my wife."

Truth is, for the longest time I could never understand why people would want to brew at home, any more than they would change their own engine oil, make their own furniture, or rewire the house. "Leave it to a professional" was always my mantra.

And then I was invited to speak at an American Homebrewers Association (AHA) Conference. Wow. I finally got it. What passion. What thirst—for knowledge as well as for well-crafted beverages. What energy.

These were impassioned brewers, just as much as any brew master for a multinational behemoth company. The ones I especially admired were those recognizing that *all* brewers are part of the same fellowship. No matter if the brewhouse is a bucket or a building, they are all using the same science to deliver beers of excellence. And they respect one another. And, for my part, I realized how committed most of these folks are to achieving the very best by the application of as much as they can possibly glean about the wonders of malting and brewing.

My eyes were further opened on two other occasions, both through participation in a reality television series aired in the Bay Area a year or two ago.

First off, I was invited to judge beers that had been brewed using setups that the contestants had been obliged to cobble together from a pile of junk unveiled for their perusal a couple of weeks earlier. I don't remember exactly what was in the mound of garbage, though I do remember the terra-cotta pots. Truth be told, the beers I sampled and commented on were remarkable. I remember saying that I had a million dollars' worth of brewery within a $10 million building and I would be delighted if all the brews were as good as these. The lesson of course is obvious: if you know what you are doing and apply the practices founded upon a thorough understanding of the essentials of brewing, then you can indeed make a silk purse using something that looks like a pig's ear.

A few weeks later the three finalists were filmed for the grand finale in my brewery. They were instructed by the producers to deliver their own little brew houses to Davis and set them up with the university facility as the backdrop. The wort they were told to produce for subsequent fermentation in their own homes was targeted at 20°Plato and 100 IBU. There was a lot of boiling, I can tell you! The final contestant headed out the door at 1 AM, and not before my team and I had realized just how zealous, capable, and, to use the word in admiration if not exactitude, "professional" these guys were. These weren't cobbled-together breweries, and these were individuals who totally knew their stuff.

And who did more than anyone else to lay the groundwork that has allowed homebrewing to become vastly more than a mechanism for producing cheaper beer for personal consumption? Charlie Papazian. Charlie was a nuclear engineering student at the University of Virginia who realized that malt, hops, yeast, and water and the joy of turning them into quaffable ales and lagers were altogether more satisfying than quarks and uncertainty principles (although there is always an element of the latter in brewing). So Charlie began homebrewing in the 1970s and, having started a teaching career in Boulder, Colorado, he evangelized in courses on his hobby at the Community Free School and wrote a pamphlet to spread the joy. In 1978, two months after President Jimmy Carter signed into legislation the freedom for people to brew beer at home, Charlie founded the AHA and launched the *Zymurgy* publication. In due course he gave us the Craft Brewers Conference, the Great American Beer Festival, the Association of Brewers, and the *New Brewer*. And, of course, he wrote *The Complete Joy of Homebrewing*. The first edition came in 1984. This is its fourth rendition—and millions of eager brewers have feasted upon it. Charlie Papazian, through this and all his works, is a genuine champion of all beer and is a prime exponent of how to get it right. I admire him and his achievements enormously. Equally, I know he will forgive me for still not having a brewery of my own at home.

—Charlie Bamforth, Professor of Malting and Brewing Sciences, UC Davis

*Dr. Charles Bamforth has been part of the brewing industry for more than thirty-four years and has been described as the world's top beer researcher. He was formerly in senior research, quality, and managerial positions with Brewing Research International and Bass Brewers and, in addition to his role as the lead professor of brewing at UC Davis, is an honorary professor at the University of Nottingham, England, and was previously Visiting Professor of Brewing at Heriot-Watt University in Scotland. Charlie is editor in chief of the* Journal of the American Society of Brewing Chemists *and has published innumerable papers, articles, and books on beer and brewing. In 2011 Charlie was honored with the Award of Distinction from the American Society of Brewing Chemists.*

# INTRODUCTION TO *THE COMPLETE JOY OF HOMEBREWING*

I've had plenty of time to reflect on my forty-four years of continued homebrewing—all that has changed, and so much that has been sustained. I've learned to recognize two constants: 1) Traditions of beer brewing are always evolving, and 2) the best thing you can do for yourself and your homebrewing is to relax, not worry, and have a homebrew.

Why do I know these truths? I brewed my first beer in 1970. Those early homebrews inspired such wonderful times that my friends begged me to teach them how to make beer. I've been teaching beermaking ever since. In the earlier days I discovered how intimidating homebrewing could be to the uninitiated; how nervous and anxious people were about entering into the mystic world of beermaking. After all, how many things can one actually create that result in such satisfaction and enjoyment? Beermaking seemed out of the boundaries of possibilities to most people. Fact is, these same feelings exist today among people who have never brewed, just as they did in the early 1970s. "Relax. Don't worry. Have a homebrew." This became the mantra in my early teachings. Homebrewers and friends welcomed and embraced that attitude. The word spread that homebrewing quality beer was easy.

I know homebrewing your first batches of beer, like doing anything totally new and "risky," creates anxiety. Supporting each other with a simple offering of homebrew and "Relax. Don't worry. Have a homebrew" is just the formula you need to go on and succeed by doing. Knowing there are hundreds of thousands creating their first batch of beer each year with the same shared values comforts each batch of beer. It is also a window on how we look at life.

Thousands of people come up to me and express their appreciation that I have kept a tone of humor throughout the book, while conveying reassurance and technically accurate and informative information. I realize a book like this can easily overwhelm the beginner. It is with great and deliberate purpose I emphasize a good dose of humor and lightness throughout, in order to keep you engaged while minimizing your anxiety.

Some of the humor may seem personal and mysterious. It is. Mystery and personality is what each of our lives is about. Beermaking is about life and living it well. By reading this book and engaging in the process of creating beer you will be creating things very personal and mysterious. With this book and its "attitude" you will find your own humor between the lines. You will learn how to approach the mysterious with accomplished confidence.

During my early days of homebrew crusading, popularity slowly grew and I found myself founding the American Homebrewers Association in Boulder, Colorado, with my good friend Charlie Matzen in 1978. The attitude and principles of homebrewing we pursued with the association are the same as what inspired the pages of this book. I am still involved on a daily basis as president of the Brewers Association, of which the American Homebrewers Association is part.

As you will discover, there are so many things to learn about beermaking and beer culture. The American Homebrewers Association's magazine, *Zymurgy*, became and still is the vehicle for conveying some of the most up-to-date information about our hobby, while at the same time creating a sense of worldwide community among homebrewers. You can feed your passion and learn more at the AHA's Website www.homebrewersassociation.org.

With the 1980s and 1990s came a revival of appreciation for beer in America. Homebrewers put the pride back into American beer culture. The American Homebrewers Association and tens of thousands of homebrewers just like you brewed one pot of brew at a time and inspired the microbrewing/brewpub, craft brewing, and craft beer movements throughout the world. Furthermore, the American Homebrewers Association initiated the network that provided the founding of so many other association events and services, perhaps one of the most famous being the Great American Beer Festival. All of this, I believe, is a testament to what quality homebrew and a great attitude can achieve.

Traditional beer styles go in and out of favor with consumers. When they are rediscovered, homebrewers tend to be their champions. While there is still a commercial market for simply refreshing, lighter, and less flavorful beer, homebrewers are the beer world's saviors, maintaining the enthusiasm for the classic traditions of beer and nurturing the emergence of new flavors and traditions. I don't know whether creative people are drawn to homebrewing or homebrewing helps develop creative people. It really doesn't matter which it is. It is probably both and that is why creativity with a reverence toward tradition has been the personality of almost every single homebrewer I've met.

My travels have taken me all over the world visiting professional and amateur brewers, and after more than four decades of involvement with this fantastic hobby, I am still learning and still inspired by the brewers I meet. People like you offering me your beers or your experience is what drives the enjoyment of this hobby. Hundreds of homebrew clubs meet monthly—probably in your area, too—offering the camaraderie, great beer, and information that continue to improve our beers and our hobby.

The principles and techniques behind making great homebrew have not changed dramatically in the past few decades, but quality and innovation have. New homebrewers have always been the driving force behind the excitement of the hobby. While there are hundreds of thousands of veteran homebrewers making excellent beer, the element of discovery provides the energy that drives all of us to brew better beer with each new batch. There are few things more satisfying in the world than to be involved with instilling a sense of discovery, happiness, and satisfaction in others. This is what homebrewing does.

Providing a means to help new homebrewers develop a love of beer and homebrewing is what every edition of *The Complete Joy of Homebrewing* has been about. Every single recipe has been reviewed and improved based on the availability of ingredients and new, evolved information. There are several new recipes, most of which are favorites that I continue to brew today. Every procedure, chart, and guideline has been reviewed for accuracy, updated, and revised.

I was always tempted to add new charts, data, and techniques—there's so much more great information I'd like to share with you. But as this is a first book for most homebrewers, I have not added too much to the technical side of the brewing process. If you get hooked and are ready to take your hobby to the next level, then check out the advanced discussions in the companion to this book, *The Homebrewer's Companion, Second Edition: The Complete Joy of Homebrewing, Master Edition*. It is packed with loads of additional information, recipes, data, valuable charts, and techniques that will take you beyond this first book on homebrewing. Whether you continue to brew with extracts or are looking to improve your all-grain beers, *The Homebrewer's Companion* will certainly help you continue to develop your skills and provide additional beer and brewing knowledge.

And beyond that there is a list of additional resources at the end of this book to take you on your own personal journey while making the best beers you have ever had in your life. I think I'll have a homebrew; my own. And of course relax and not worry.

Thank you for what you've given back to me. A smile, a laugh, a cheer, and good brew.

# READY, SET . . . GO!

## THE HOMEBREWER AND THE JOY OF BREWING

This book is written for the "will-be" homebrewer: a homebrewer who will be able to relax and consistently make good beer time after time. It is for you who want to jump right in and brew a batch of beer today! And why not? Ales and lagers; pilseners, stouts, pale ales, India Pale Ales, Oktoberfests, bock beers, Belgian ales, porters, bitters, milds, strongs, fruity, quirky, innovative specialty beers, and meads . . . they are all easy to make. Many of these styles are even ready to enjoy within three weeks! This book is for you, the will-be homebrewer who wants to enjoy the creative process of doing and learning what beer is all about. Relax.

The three sections of this book are written with the homebrewer in mind: the beginner, the intermediate, the advanced, and the appended. Each section stands on its own, providing a complete "itinerary" for each part of your beer journey with homebrewing. The beginner need not be anxious about the more advanced recipes in this book, because superb beer can be made just by following the fundamental principles of brewing outlined in the beginner's section. Those of you who have become infected with the homebrew bug can easily pursue the fundamentals of both intermediate and advanced brewing. Wherever your homebrewing journey takes you, you will find this book valuable from any point of view.

Making quality beer is *easy*! Don't let anyone tell you any differently. At the same time, making bad beer is easy, too. The difference between making good beer and bad beer is simply knowing those little things that make a big difference and can ensure success every time. Above all, the homebrewer should remember not to worry, because worrying can spoil the taste of beer faster than anything else. Relax. Don't worry.

So now you've decided to brew your own beer. In essence, you've given yourself the opportunity to make the kind of beer that *you* like. Reading this book and learning the fundamentals will give you a foundation to express yourself unendingly in what you brew.

Remember, the best beer in the world is the one you brewed.

You may wonder whether you really need to read another book after coursing through this one. You don't, but there are lots of great tips, insights, and much more information available in my continuation of the "Joy" in *The Home-brewer's Companion, Second Edition.* I couldn't possibly have fit all the great information and insight I've experienced in forty-plus years of homebrewing in one book, so that's why *The Homebrewer's Companion* came to be.

## IS IT LEGAL?

Every state in the United States has statutorily recognized homebrewing or winemaking. The last two holdout states, Alabama and Mississippi, finally legalized homebrewing in 2013. Homebrewing beer is *not* a criminal activity. George Washington and Thomas Jefferson were homebrewers. . . . Now even President Barack Obama's kitchen staff brews homebrew for special occasions and enjoyment.

In November 1978, a bill passed by Congress repealed federal restrictions on the homebrewing of beer. In February 1979, President Carter signed the bill into law. What is the law, and why was homebrewing ever illegal in the first place? It all dates back to that "Noble Experiment"—Prohibition. In 1920, it became illegal to make beer, period! In those dark ages the only kind of beer that was available was clandestine homebrew. Millions of Americans got into the act of making homebrewed *alcohol.* Quality was not important; it didn't seem to matter how good homebrew tasted as long as what Grandpa made had a kick to it and the bottles didn't explode under the bed (there were a lot of wet beds in those days—from the bottoms up). Prohibition finally ended and the commercial production of beer was legalized. The homebrewing of wine and/or beer should

*The "Mother of all homebrews." Lena was an icon gracing every can of Blue Ribbon malt extract during Prohibition and post-Prohibition through the 1980s.*

have been legalized as well. Homemade wine was legalized, but unfortunately, through a stenographer's omission, the words "and/or beer" never made it into the Federal Register.

Since homebrewing became federally legal any adult age twenty-one years or older is permitted to brew "not more than one hundred gallons of beer in a year." If there is more than one adult in a household, then two hundred gallons of beer can be brewed in one year. That's a lot of beer!

Because the Twenty-first Amendment of the U.S. Constitution gives states precedent in governing most beverage alcohol laws, each state had to officially legalize homebrewing; some states immediately legalized homebrewing while others resisted until 2013, when the fiftieth state decriminalized homebrewing.

The beer you brew is intended for your personal use. It is illegal to sell your homebrew—so don't! The law in most states does provide for removal of home-brew from the "home brewery" for organized tastings, competitions, and so on. No registration forms are required to brew homebrew, nor are there any permit fees. The point to remember is that your homebrew is meant for your own per-sonal enjoyment. Don't sell it, and no one will bother you except friends and neighbors who want to drink your beer.

## WHY IS TODAY'S HOMEBREW BETTER?

Before the legalization of homebrewing in the United States, good information and quality ingredients were very difficult to find. Times have changed. Now, the best is available to anyone who seeks it. The technology of homebrewing ingredi-ents, kits, and malt extracts has progressed to an advanced state of the art. Initial credit must be given to the British. Homebrewing was legalized in Great Britain in 1963. As popularity grew over the years, manufacturers of homebrew supplies took more interest. There was money to be made and money to be spent on devel-oping more perfect homebrew products. In the United States we have seen the development and availability of quality ingredients and equipment of British, Australian, Canadian, Belgian, and German import as well as American origin.

Americans have inspired the quality manufacturing and growing of both domestically produced and imported ingredients. Driven by a passion for qual-ity, homebrewers have become so innovative that the quality and design of homebrew equipment and processes have exceeded our wildest expectations! Furthermore, the brewing industry in the United States has discovered that, as homebrewers, we like good beer. There are more than three thousand small breweries in the United States, with breweries in every state. Many of the early microbreweries and brewpubs of the 1980s have been so successful that they have grown too large to be called microbreweries, yet they continue to make the same quality beer that defines "good beer." Now the name "craft brewery" is used in the United States to describe all these great small and independent breweries making the specialty products we used to call "microbrews" but now call "craft beers." Sierra Nevada, New Belgium, Samuel Adams, Boulder Beer, Full Sail, Deschutes, Boulevard, Bell's, Saint Arnold, and New Glarus are some of the many pioneer craft beer brands familiar to beer enthusiasts throughout America. The worldwide commercial craft-brewing phenomenon is a direct extension of the passion, efforts, and quality of American homebrewers. And now you are about to become a part of the passion—one five-gallon batch at a time.

## WHY BREW YOUR OWN?

### IF YOU LIKE BEER—YOU DESERVE IT!

There are many reasons to brew your own beer. The first thought that comes to most people's minds is economy. Certainly, it can be less expensive to brew your own, and that's why many begin. But if you embark on the road to home-brewing because you like beer ("Go yeast, young man!"), you soon discover that *quality, variety,* and *independence* are the reasons you continue to brew. The taste of fresh beer can't be beat, and the opportunity to brew any style of beer makes this "hobby" irresistible.

As a homebrewer, you will find that your interest in beer will grow, perhaps exponentially. You certainly will become a beer enthusiast. I guarantee it. Brewing beer will change your life—in a very good way. You will begin to understand what beer is all about. You will find yourself appreciating all kinds of beer, both your own and commercially available beer.

Discovering the real joy of brewing is something you deserve, especially if you like beer.

Pass it on.

Relax. Don't worry. Have a homebrew!

# BEER, HISTORY, AMERICA, AND HOMEBREW

America's beer roots lead back to the brewing traditions of the "European Old World." Whether the beer is homebrewed, commercially craft-brewed, or large brewery–brewed, beer drinkers can be confident that American beer is quality-brewed with attention to technical details and to beer drinkers' desires. Between 1980 and as of this writing, the varieties and flavors of beer available here in the United States have gone through a dramatic evolution. Nevertheless, the fundamental factors that have influenced the taste of American beer and that of beer throughout the world haven't changed in more than 4,500 years!

In the beginning of beer history, the household was the primary source of beer, followed by the small-town brewery. Eventually today's large breweries evolved. Much has been gained, much has been lost, and now we are in the midst of regaining a national beer heritage.

There continues to be a groundswell of interest in America, beginning with a surge in homebrewing, in rediscovering, perhaps, the lost truths about beer.

Let's take a closer look at some of the things that had been lost and regained and reasons that trends in beer taste and culture influence the popular views about beer.

## A LONG, LONG TIME AGO

It all began at home.

Historians have surmised that long, long ago, in the early days of the Mesopotamian and Egyptian cultures, the first beer was brewed. It was homebrew!

Barley was one of the staple grains of the various Mediterranean cultures. It grew well in the climate that prevailed at the time and was used as the main ingredient in various breads and cakes. People soon discovered that if barley were wetted, allowed to germinate, and subsequently dried, the resulting grain would taste sweeter and be more nutritional and less perishable. This was probably discovered quite by accident when some inattentive member of a household left

a basket of grain out in the rain and then tried to salvage the mess by drying it. Inadvertently, they had made malted barley. It wasn't such a mistake after all. As a matter of fact, it made for more pleasant-tasting breads and porridges.

It was inevitable that someone would leave their porridge, malted barley flour, or bread in the rain. The dissolved sugars and starches were fair game for yeasts in the air. Soon, the yeasts began to ferment the "malt soup." When the mysteriously bubbly concoction was consumed, it was with pleasant surprise that the household felt a mysterious inner peace with their surroundings. Furthermore, the fermentation process added nutritional benefits to the diet. However crude the process may have been, the first "beer" had been brewed.

This mildly alcoholic beverage soon became a significant part of the culture of the Egyptians and Mesopotamians, while civilized societies in other parts of the world were also discovering the joy of naturally fermented grain-based beverages. Alcohol was not understood. Neither was yeast. But magically these beverages bubbled and made people feel, perhaps, godlike. It is not surprising, then, that religious significance became attached to these gifts of visions. One can easily imagine the ceremonial significance that fermented beverages played in such cultures as the Egyptian, Aztec, and Incan. Rice beers, millet beers, barley beers, honey beers, corn beers . . . even the Eskimos had a mildly alcoholic fermented reindeer's milk.

It all began at home, and throughout the world households brewed their own for thousands of years. But as towns and cities developed, homebrewing activity began to diminish, especially in Western cultures.

As towns developed, good drinking water became scarcer. Beer, with its mild alcoholic content, was one of the few liquids safe to drink and thus in great demand. At the same time small-town brewers began to relieve the household of the essential task of making beer.

## VARIETY AND STYLE

Because of the development of the small-town brewery, distinctive beers became indigenous to a region, rather than to every household. Slowly, the variability of climate, agriculture, economy, and other human activity began to express itself more profoundly. During this transition from household to small brewery, modern-day beer came into historic perspective. The centralization of brewing served to consolidate regional trends.

Let's take a look at some of the factors that influence the taste of beer. To a great extent, indigenous ingredients, social attitudes, religion, and climate give beers throughout the world much of their distinctive regional character. Different strains of barley and the availability of other grains influence the character of each region's beer. Yeast strains indigenous to an area greatly affect the product brewed. The availability of herbs or hops also characterizes regional beers. For example, beers brewed in those areas with an abundance of hops historically have had a more pronounced hop character. The delicate style of the original Pilsner Urquell from the Czech Republic may be attributed to the character of the water as well as to the native ingredients. There are literally hundreds of styles of Belgian beer, and for many "it's *not* the water" but a variety of yeasts that are allowed to naturally introduce fermentation to each brewery's beer. The result? Distinctive flavors that are difficult to reproduce elsewhere in the world. Agricultural and climatic conditions surely must have influenced a style of beer called wheat beer, brewed in Germany and now (thanks to homebrewers) in the United States.

Human activity has a significant influence on beer styles. For example, bock beer is a strong beer that originated in the German town of Einbeck. It was a beer that gained favor with royalty and was transported great distances for their pleasure. Its high alcohol content prevented the beer from spoiling. It was very different from the low-alcohol beverages often brewed for local consumption. Likewise, India Pale Ale was a style of strong ale brewed in Great Britain for the purpose of providing the British troops with good ale while they occupied India. It was and still is a beer that is high in alcohol and hop content, both contributing preservative qualities to beer. Consequently, human endeavors warranted the brewing of stronger beers, in order to help preserve it during long transports.

Throughout history, other human factors, such as economics and shortages of ingredients, have influenced styles of beer. When wartime priorities were given to feeding troops, a shortage of grain resulted in a shortage of beer and/or a more diluted product. Especially evident today in various parts of the world is the effect of high taxation on brewing styles. Of course, beer contains alcohol and in most countries alcohol is taxed. So, naturally, the more alcohol in the beer the more it is taxed, and the more it costs not only the brewery but the beer drinker. This situation can be seen most clearly in Ireland, where the world-famous Guinness Stout is brewed. Without a doubt, the locally available stuff is delicious, but upon investigation one discovers that the alcoholic content often does not exceed 3 percent. Over 60 percent of the price of a pint of Guinness in Ireland is tax! The Guinness "Export" Stout that is made for export is taxed at a lower rate; therefore, it is higher in alcohol and a very, very different beer. Draught Guinness, however, is now exported at the same low alcohol level, due to its growing popularity.

## AMERICAN BEER

What is American beer? Today's most popular style of "American beer" is still a light-colored, lightly flavored, light-bodied lager beer, a style very different from the American beer of yesteryear and perhaps different from the American beer of tomorrow. Through the years, American beer has been very much influenced by agricultural, climatic, economic, political, and cultural factors. Because of the economic efficiencies of mass production and the impact of multimillion-dollar mass media advertising, light-tasting lager has been successful and copied all over the world.

Before Prohibition, thousands of breweries existed in America, each supplying their local communities and respective regions with distinctive styles and freshly made beer. There were, as well, millions of people homebrewing quality beers. The healthy diversity of beer styles must have been wonderful to experience. One imagines that there was a genuine sharing of kinship among brewers, whether they were homebrewers or professionals. It must have been that important feeling that went into the beer that made all the difference.

Between January 1920 and December 1933, the United States suffered through Prohibition and the dark ages of beer. When it was over, only the larger breweries had survived by making malt products for the food industry. Low-budget operations combined with equipment left idle and in disrepair for over a decade contributed to the demise of the smaller, local breweries.

What emerged was an industry of larger breweries. They were still somewhat anxious about the prevailing attitude toward alcohol. As incredible as this may seem, many of the richer styles of American beer were not brewed, in an attempt by the breweries to market beer that would appeal to women. One thing that Prohibition changed for women was the acceptance of their company, sharing with men a beer or other beverages at illicit speakeasies throughout America. It helped set a new paradigm for the American beer market.

Mass marketing began to rear its foaming head in search of the perfect beer that would appeal to the most people. Never mind diversity. Never mind variety. Never mind the traditional ideals that American brewers had developed for more than 150 years. Never mind choice.

Then came World War II. A shortage of war material necessitated the scrapping of steel, some of which was idle brewery equipment. A shortage of food diminished beer production. The beer that was made had less malt in it. Many men were out fighting a war, and the beer drinkers back home were mainly women.

A lighter style of beer was thus beginning to gain popularity in the United States—and justifiably so. With the warm climate that we in the States enjoy for half a year, a lighter beer can be a refreshing experience. With the agricultural abundance of corn and rice here, these ingredients have found their way

more and more into American beer, lightening the taste and body. If it's well brewed and you enjoy it, there is absolutely nothing wrong with this kind of beer. But it is only one type of beer brewed in the world among hundreds of other different types of beer.

What we were missing until the homebrewing revival and the emergence of small and independent craft brewers and their craft beers was, sadly, choice. The economics of mass marketing had indeed influenced what was offered.

Now we see an incredible variety of beer available throughout the United States: American-made craft beer from craft brewers, specialty beers made by the larger brewers, and a growing diversity of beers imported from around the world.

## THE SPIRIT OF HOMEBREWING CONTINUES

As a homebrewer you not only maintain the spirit of local, fresh, and quality-made beer that *you* like, but you also give yourself and the people who you know the opportunity to feel and understand what beer is all about. Personal feeling is exactly what's lacking in most mass-marketed beer brewed and consumed these days. Make no mistake about it—our beer world is so much better than it was in the 1980s and early 1990s. But don't forget for a moment that the large brewing companies of the world continue to "squeeze" the market with their lighter-flavored products, always trying to minimize choice. Developing your skills as a homebrewer is the best insurance you can have to ensure that you will always have the beer you like. In addition, you will realize that your brewing skills provide valuable insight into the world of beer and are revered and respected wherever you roam.

American homebrewers are roofers, museum curators, mental health directors, truck drivers, geneticists, Air Force pilots, film directors, farmers, secretaries, mortgage bankers, doctors, longshoremen, beauticians, engineers, teachers, lawyers, plumbers, electricians, dentists, policemen (and policewomen), tax collectors, housewives, journalists, elected officials, regulators, mothers, fathers, sons, daughters. . . . There is no one type of American homebrewer. There is no one type of beer.

In all our diversity, we homebrewers choose to brew for our own reasons. The tradition and craft of homebrewing are nothing new, but these days they have special significance. At least for now, it is only the homebrewer who can really understand why beer tastes the way it does and share that "special feeling" of beer quality with the world's small and independent commercial craft brewers.

# ESPECIALLY FOR THE BEGINNER

## GETTING STARTED

Brewing your own beer is as easy as opening a can of ingredients and boiling water.

## INTRODUCTION

There is an extraordinary variety of homebrew supplies available to the homebrewer. When you are a beginner, it's nice to be able to walk into a homebrew supply store and know that there are dozens of malt extracts and beer kits from which to choose. A conscientious homebrew supplier will stock only quality products, so most of the time you can be assured that the products on the shelf are going to help you make great beer—even your first time.

But for you, the beginner, the choices may be a bit overwhelming. Where to start?

The place to start is with good advice, quality ingredients, and a simple, absolutely foolproof recipe for your first batch of beer, which you can enjoy within three weeks. Are you on the edge of your seat yet? If so, I don't blame you.

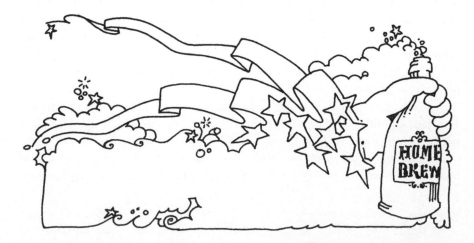

This beginner's section is written especially for the first-time brewer. Maybe you're a bit anxious and wonder whether it is possible to be able to make good beer. You may not even know what good beer is, but with all that's happening today in the world of craft-brewing, you are already quite primed and ready to take the plunge.

This section is written to assure you that brewing fantastic beer is easy and can be done simply, without compromising quality. Many of you may even find yourselves lingering as a "beginner" for quite some time, reveling and enjoying the results.

So RELAX . . . DON'T WORRY . . . AND BEGIN!

## THE BASICS

### *Ingredients*

Beer is made from four essential ingredients: water, fermentable sugars (traditionally malted barley), hops, and yeast. These ingredients are processed and combined according to a recipe. Given the right conditions, the yeast will convert (ferment) the fermentable sugars to alcohol, carbon dioxide, and the taste we know as beer. The beer is then bottled and aged anywhere from a week to several months (depending upon the style one chooses to brew).

*Malted barley* is a naturally processed form of barley. Barley is a grain that is similar to wheat in appearance. In order to malt the barley, a "maltster" will steep the barley in water under carefully controlled conditions until it begins to sprout, after which the germinated barley is dried. After drying, the barley is said to have been malted. This process develops sugars, soluble starches, and other characteristics in the barley desirable for brewing beer.

The malted barley is further converted to sugars through a process called mashing, whereby the malted barley is immersed in water at controlled temperatures that allow enzymes in the malted barley to convert starches to sugars. These sugars are subsequently converted through yeast fermentation into alcohol, carbon dioxide, and the flavor of beer.

Many breweries often will substitute corn, rice, wheat, rye, or other grains for a portion of the malted barley. The breweries will process these starches into fermentable sugars. These other grain-derived sugars will ferment as the malt sugars do, imparting their distinctive fermented character to the beer. Often these other forms of fermentable sugars are used for "lightening" the flavor of

the beer. Some forms and types of grain can brighten and contribute interesting and desired character to beer.

*Hops* are green flowerlike cones that grow on perennial vines, emerging each spring from the rootstock of the hop plant. They have been popularly used in beer-making for about 250 years. Hops impart a degree of bitterness and floral and fruity flavors to beer, providing a balance when combined with the sweetness of malt. The addition of hops to beer also inhibits spoilage and enhances head retention.

Over 90 percent of beer is *water*. The water you use will lend its character to the beer. Most drinking water supplies in the United States are fine for making quality homebrew. If your water supply is known to have a significant amount of dissolved sulfur, iron, carbonates, or bicarbonates, then you should use low-mineral bottled water for your brewing water. If your water is high in chlorine taste, it would be to your advantage to use a household filter to remove chlorine. If the water tastes good, then brew with it.

*Yeasts* are responsible for converting the bittersweet tea (called "wort") of fermentable sugars and hops to the bubbly, alcoholic beverage we call beer. Yeasts are living microorganisms that use sugar as food for their life cycle. Thousands of different kinds of yeasts can be found everywhere in our lives. For a brewer, it is a bit disconcerting to discover that most of them are wild yeasts. The unintended introduction of these wild yeasts can result in some pretty wild brews, usually not to one's liking. The kind of yeast used for beermaking can, for now, be generally classified as "beer yeast," that is, yeast specially cultured for the purpose of brewing beer. (Bread yeast is cultured and designed for making bread. Wine yeast is cultured and designed for making wine.)

Generally, there are two types of beer yeast: lager yeast and ale yeast. They are used to brew different styles of beer. Their differences will be discussed later.

### The Fermentation Process

A brewer's job is to combine ingredients and pursue fermentation. This fermentation will last from ten days to several months (again depending on the style of beer being brewed). During this period, yeasts reproduce and disperse themselves throughout the fermenting beer, converting sugars to alcohol, carbon dioxide, and a variety of flavors. After the initial five to fourteen days, the yeast will have exhausted most of its sugar supply and will begin to settle to the bottom of the fermentation vessel. At this point brewers often will transfer the clearing beer to a second tank in order to help separate the beer from the sediment that forms on the bottom of the first fermenter. When fermentation activity has been completed, the brewer will package the beer in bottles, cans, or kegs. Most large breweries will take the beer from aging tanks, filter it, artificially carbonate it, and then pasteurize it before bottling. Pasteurizing is accomplished by heating the beer to kill off yeast and other microorganisms and is done by many large breweries for economic reasons and as a means of helping preserve the beer. Pasteurization can affect the perceived flavor, aroma, and mouthfeel of the beer.

As a homebrewer, you have the option of starting from scratch and brewing exactly as commercial breweries do, using the same raw ingredients.

But unlike the breweries, you are brewing on a tiny scale and have the choice of embracing simplicity. You don't have to go through the ritual of malting

*Can you do the cancan? A sampler display of the more than one hundred varieties of malt extracts and beer kits from which a homebrewer may choose.*

your own barley, nor do you have to get involved in mashing your own grains. The ready-to-go main beer ingredient takes the convenient form of malt extract.

Malt extract is simply malted barley that has been processed into a sweet malt "soup." Then, 75 to 80 percent of the water is carefully evaporated, reducing the liquid to a concentrated syrup (or in the case of dry malt extract, in which all the water is evaporated, a dry powder).

Even simpler for the homebrewer are the many malt extracts and homebrew kits that are hop flavored. In other words, the hops have already been added. All you need to do is add water (perhaps boil for a brief period) and yeast (often supplied with the kit).

The only difference between the potential quality of homebrewed beer and commercially brewed beer is the vast amounts of money spent on consistency and quality control. Big breweries want their beer to turn out exactly the same every time. As a homebrewer, you will come to know your beer intimately and understand the variables that are involved in beermaking. You will make superb beer, but it will vary slightly from batch to batch. That is the nature of beermaking, and it makes your new endeavor exciting and more rewarding.

## GETTING YOUR HOMEBREWERY TOGETHER

A note on units of measurement. All units are expressed in American measurements, with metric units in parentheses. The abbreviations for the metric units are l (liters), g (grams), kg (kilograms), cm (centimeters), and so on.

### EQUIPMENT

The following list of special brewing equipment will be adequate for making 4 to 5 gallons (15 to 19 l) of beer at a time.

1  3- to 4-gallon (11.5 to 15 l) pot (an enameled or stainless steel pot is best)
1  6½-gallon (25 l) glass carboy *or* 5-gallon (19 l) glass *or* food-grade plastic carboy (these are large jugs with a small opening to which a fermentation lock can be affixed). NOTE: A 6½-gallon carboy is recommended and more convenient for fermenting 5-gallon batches. If purchasing a 6½-gallon carboy, mark the outside at the 5-gallon level as a convenient indicator.
1  5- to 10-gallon (19 to 38 l) new plastic fermenter "bucket" or food-grade plastic trash pail
1  6-foot (2 m) length of ⅜-inch (.95 cm) inside-diameter clear, food-grade plastic hose
1  plastic hose clamp to fit a ⅜-inch (.95 cm) hose

1  fermentation lock
1  rubber stopper (size 6.5) with hole to fit fermentation lock
1  3-foot (1 m) length of 1¼-inch (3.2 cm) outside diameter, 1-inch
   (2.5 cm) inside diameter, clear, food-grade plastic hose
1  large plastic funnel
1  thermometer (range: freezing to boiling)
1  beer hydrometer and measuring "cylinder"
1  bottle washer (optional but highly recommended)
Lots of bottle caps, new and unused
1  bottle capper
60  returnable 12-ounce (355 ml) beer bottles (anything other than
   screw-top bottles will do) or 25 champagne bottles (most champagne
   bottles can be capped)

You also will need a container of unscented liquid household bleach in order to sanitize your equipment.

You can find all of this equipment at your local homebrew supply shop. Explore Internet-based online homebrew shop directories (for example, www.homebrewers association.org), or take a look in the Yellow Page directories under "Beermaking Supplies" or "Winemaking Supplies." New beer bottles can be bought at homebrew supply shops or used bottles can be found at recycling centers and bars. Champagne bottles are also usable and can be found at restaurants and hotels that regularly serve champagne for brunch, or anyplace that has just hosted a wedding reception.

## EASY BREW 101: INGREDIENTS

*Enough for your first 5-gallon (19 l) batch of beer*

I start you off with a recipe for a type of beer called an ale rather than a lager. Ales ferment more quickly and are consequently ready to enjoy and drink more quickly. The distinction between ales and lagers is discussed later.

5 to 6 pounds (2.3 to 2.7 kg) hop-flavored malt extract or "beer kit"*
*or*
3 to 4 pounds (1.4 to 1.8 kg) hop-flavored malt extract or beer kit* plus
   1 to 2 pounds (.5 to .9 kg) plain unhopped light dried malt extract
   (or corn sugar may be substituted; see chart on page 28)

*Malt extracts and beer kits come in a variety of "flavors." The major distinction is their color: extra pale, pale, light, amber, brown, and dark cover the range of choices for the homebrewer. If you desire a lighter beer for your first batch, naturally choose a lighter malt extract. Likewise, for your darker bock beers and stouts, choose a darker malt extract. Only with experience and experimenting will you begin to discern the various characteristics of the brands of malts available. For now, don't worry about the perfect malt extract for your palate. You will be more than adequately pleased with your initial efforts. *Relax.*

*Quite a spread, the homebrewery from brewpot to mug! From left to right: funnel
siphon hose, brewpot, hydrometer (and flask), charismatic spoon, lever-type
bottlecapper, plastic closed-fermenter (with fermentation lock), one liter of stout,*

5 gallons (19 l) water
1 package ale yeast
¾ cup (175 ml) corn sugar

## WHAT YOU ARE GOING TO DO

### *Going for Greatness!*

1. Combine and dissolve your malt extract (and sugar if used) in
   1½ gallons (5.7 l) of water and bring to a boil for 60 minutes.
2. Sanitize your fermenter with a weak household (chlorine) bleach and water
   solution. Later in the process, sanitize and then thoroughly rinse with hot
   tap water all equipment that comes into contact with the unfermented and
   fermenting beer: funnel, thermometer, hydrometer, hose, cork, fermentation
   lock, and all other equipment that touches the beer.
3. Add 3 gallons (11.5 l) of clean cold water to your clean and rinsed
   fermenter.

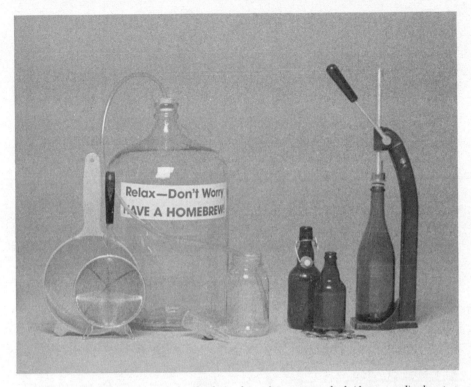

*strainers, glass (carboy) fermenter with plastic hose, fermentation lock (foreground), glass jar (to collect overflow during fermentation), bottles, bottlecaps, and bench-type bottlecapper.*

4. Add your boiled and hot hop-flavored malt extract and water mixture to the cold water in your fermenter.
5. When the temperature is ideally between 68 and 75 degrees F (20 to 24 C*), measure the specific gravity with your beer hydrometer and then add the yeast.
6. Attach the fermentation hose, and after initial fermentation has subsided, attach the fermentation lock.
7. Ferment for 8 to 14 days.
8. Bottle and cap.
9. Age for 7 to 10 days.
10. *Drink the beer!* Have a homebrew.

Sound simple? It is. But let's go over each point step by step in order to further clarify the recipe, procedures, and equipment.

*All references to temperature will be in degrees Fahrenheit with degrees Celsius in parentheses.

**1. Combine and dissolve your malt extract (and sugar if used) in 1½ gallons (5.7 l) of water and bring to a boil for 60 minutes.**

The list of ingredients gives you some flexibility. The Beginner's Chart (extract vs. corn sugar) on page 28 will help you determine the kind of beer you would prefer to brew.

Beer kits and hop-flavored malt extracts come in a variety of sizes. One of the more common sizes is a 3½-pound (1.6 kg) can of hop-flavored malt extract syrup. For your first batch of beer use one can of syrup with only one pound of plain light dried malt extract. If you desire a richer flavor in your beer, use two cans of syrup, no matter what the size, as long as it is 2½ to 3½ pounds. (1.2 to 1.6 kg). Sugar is not recommended.

*First, have a homebrew! Then making good beer is as easy as adding a can of malt extract syrup to water in a brewpot. Stir, add heat, and have another homebrew. It gets easier with each step.*

Most beer kits come with instructions. Many of them will recommend the use of sugar equal to the amount of malt extract. But remember: You will always make a far superior beer by eliminating and substituting or minimizing the amount of any refined sugar.

Many beer kits do not instruct the homebrewer to boil their ingredients; however, your beer will always be *much* better if your ingredients are boiled for at least 45 minutes.

So open your can of hop-flavored malt extract (it helps to immerse the can in hot water prior to opening in order to make the thick syrup more manageable) and add it to a pot of 1½ gallons (5.7 l) of water. If you are using dried malt extract or corn sugar, add these ingredients as well. Stir to dissolve all of the ingredients and bring to a boil for 60 minutes.

**2. Sanitize your fermenter with a weak household (chlorine) bleach and water solution. Later in the process, sanitize all equipment that comes into contact with the unfermented and fermenting beer: funnel, thermometer, hydrometer, hose, cork, fermentation lock, and all other equipment that touches the beer.**

SANITIZING YOUR EQUIPMENT IS ONE OF THE EASIEST AND MOST FUNDAMENTALLY IMPORTANT THINGS THAT YOU WILL DO.

If you do not take care to clean your equipment, the best recipe in the world will result in disappointment.

The thing to remember is to relax and not worry . . . do what must be done. It is easy. It's no big deal.

Anything that will come in contact with the fermenting beer should be sanitized. This can be easily achieved by making up a solution of 1 to 2 ounces (30 to 60 ml) of household bleach to every 5 gallons (19 l) of cold water. Rinse, fill, or soak your fermenter (you will use your 5- or 6½-gallon glass carboy as your fermenter) in this solution, then rinse away all traces of chlorine odor with hot water.

Caution: Do not mix any other cleaning agent or chemical with chlorine bleach.

Safety first: Never handle a glass carboy when it is wet on the outside or with wet hands. The risk of slippage and breakage is serious and should be minimized.

**3. Add 3 gallons (11.5 l) of clean cold water to your clean and rinsed fermenter.**

Remembering that anything that comes in contact with your beer should be sanitized, measure out approximately 3 gallons (11.5 l) of cold water and add it to your carboy. Your sanitized funnel will aid you.

*Relax! When using hop-flavored malt extracts and kits, the boiled ingredients can be poured directly into the cold water in the fermenter. When cool, simply add yeast and let ferment for 5 to 10 days.*

**4. Add your boiled and hot hop-flavored malt extract and water mixture to the cold water in your fermenter.**

Carefully pour your hot water and ingredients through the funnel and into the glass carboy. The carboy will not break from the shock of the hot water because you have previously added cold water to absorb the thermal shock. If you are using a plastic fermenter, the risk of hot shock to the vessel is irrelevant.

*If using a glass or plastic carboy:* Screw the sanitized cap onto the carboy at this point. If there is no cap, use a sanitized rubber cork. Turn the carboy on its side and agitate the contents in order to evenly mix the cold water with the warm ingredients. Then, if there is any remaining space in the carboy, add enough cold water to fill the carboy to within 3 or 4 inches (7 to 10 cm) of the top or to the 5-gallon (19 l) level if using a 6½-gallon (25 l) carboy. Shake the contents once again to mix the cold water evenly. Warning: If you stray from these beginning instructions and use any kind of hops, strain the hot ingredients (wort) before adding to the fermenter.

*If using a plastic "bucket"-type fermenter:* Use a sanitized long-handled stainless steel or new plastic spoon to stir and aerate the contents of your unfermented brew. If you add additional cold water, stir well so that the liquid contents are evenly mixed.

**5. When temperature is ideally between 68 and 75 degrees F (20 to 24 C), measure the specific gravity with your beer hydrometer and then add the yeast.**

Take a temperature reading of your beer with your sanitized thermometer. If the temperature is between 68 and 75 degrees F (20 to 24 C), you are ready to add the yeast—but first measure and record the specific gravity (density) of your "soon-to-be-beer." This is as easy as reading a thermometer, but instead of using your thermometer you will use your beer hydrometer. Measuring specific gravity before and after fermentation will give you an indication of the alcoholic content of your beer and will also help tell you when to bottle.

**What's a hydrometer?** A hydrometer is an instrument that measures the density (thickness) of liquids relative to the density of water. This measure of density is known as the specific gravity. Once upon a time someone proclaimed that the specific gravity (density) of pure water at a certain temperature would be exactly the number 1.000. So, if we add dissolvable solids such as sugar to water, the solution begins to get denser and the specific gravity rises from 1.000 on up. For example, when you put 1 cup dry sugar into 1 quart water the volume hardly changes. The sugar has dissolved into solution and there's more "stuff" in the volume of liquid, making it more dense; more weight for equivalent volume.

# Beginner's Chart

The Flavor Characteristics of Homebrewed Beer
With and Without Using Corn Sugar
FOR 5 GALLONS (19 l)

| LBS. OF MALT EXTRACT | 50% MALT EXTRACT 50% CORN SUGAR | 75–90% MALT EXTRACT 10–25% CORN SUGAR | NO SUGAR ADDED. I.E., 100% MALT EXTRACT |
|---|---|---|---|
| 2½ to 3½ (1.1 to 1.6 kg) | (3 lbs. [1.4 kg] sugar) thin, light body, dry, 3–4% alcohol content | (³⁄₈–1 lb. [110–450 g] sugar) good real beer flavor, light body, low alcohol (2½–3%) | excellent real beer flavor, yet very light in flavor, body, and alcohol (2–2½%); a good lower-calorie beer |
| 4 (1.8 kg) | (4 lbs. [1.8 kg] sugar) dry, light body, very alcoholic | (½–1 lb. [230–450 g] sugar) good real beer flavor, light body, up to 3% alcohol | excellent real beer, medium–full flavor, low alcohol, light body |
| 5 (2.3 kg) | NOT RECOMMENDED | (½–1³⁄₈ lb. [230–570 g] sugar) good real beer flavor, high in alcohol (4–5%) | excellent real beer, full flavor low–medium alcohol (3–3½%), medium body |
| 6 (2.7 kg) | NOT RECOMMENDED | (1½–1½ lbs. [230–680 g] sugar) good real beer full flavor, very high in alcohol, robust, full body; longer fermentation time required, not recommended for beginners | excellent real beer, full flavor, medium alcohol content, medium–full body |
| 7 (3.2 kg) | NOT RECOMMENDED | (¾–1¾ lbs. [340–800 g] sugar) same as above | excellent real beer, full flavor, high alcohol, full body, sweeter palate |

The combination of 4½ to 5 gallons (17 to 19 l) of water with 5 pounds (2.7 kg) of malt extract and/ or corn sugar will result in a specific gravity of about 1.035 to 1.042. As the yeast ferments the dissolved sugars into alcohol and carbon dioxide, the density of the liquid drops because of the lack of sugar in the solution and because alcohol is less dense than water.

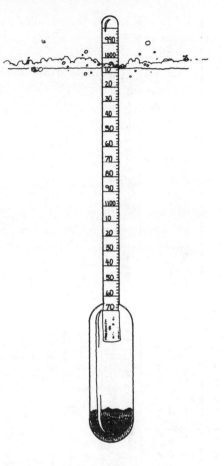

Take a good look at your hydrometer instructions and note the temperature at which your hydrometer measures accurately. Most hydrometers read accurately at 60 degrees F (16 C). Therefore, if you are measuring the specific gravity at, let's say, 80 or 90 degrees F (27 or 32 C), you will get an inaccurate reading. Why? Well, let's look at it this way: If you take something like honey and heat it, it becomes thinner and less dense. Therefore, its specific gravity is less. The same thing happens with your brew, but more subtly. For every 10 degrees F (5.6 C), your measurements will be off by .002 to 003. So, if at 80 degrees F (27 C) your brew measures 1.038, you've got to add .004 to .006 points to know that the real specific gravity is about 1.043, *or* wait until your brew cools and take a specific gravity reading, *or* take a small sample and read it at 60 degrees F (16 C).

Whatever happens . . . don't worry.

To take a hydrometer reading of the contents of your fermenter, carefully pour and fill your hydrometer flask. Place your hydrometer in the flask and read the specific gravity scale. Record this number, as well as the temperature, in a recipe journal. DO NOT RETURN THE UNFERMENTED BEER TO THE FERMENTER! Taste it and then discard it. The loss is a small price to pay to make sure that your unfermented beer remains free of unwanted microcritters.

Once the temperature is below 75 degrees F—70 to 75 degrees (21 to 24 C) is ideal—add the ale yeast. If using dried yeast, rehydrate the package of yeast in 1 cup (250 ml) preboiled and cooled water at 90 degrees F (32.5 C). Rehydrate for 15 minutes and add to your brew.

## 6. Attach a fermentation hose or fermentation lock for closed fermentation.

If using a 5-gallon (19 l) carboy, attach the fermentation hose and, after the initial fermentation has subsided, attach the fermentation lock.

If using a 6½-gallon (25 l) carboy or larger than a 5-gallon plastic "bucket" fermenter for your 5-gallon batch, simply affix the fermentation lock into the opening.

The fermentation of your beer will be a "closed fermentation." This term indicates that it will be closed off from the air and the environment. You can be 99-plus percent assured that your beer will not become contaminated with wild yeasts or other microorganisms that may produce off-flavors. (NOTE: There are no known pathogens, deadly microorganisms, that can survive in beer . . . so don't worry about disease.)

For the 5-gallon carboy "blowoff" configuration, first sanitize the 3-foot

*Blowing bubbles! Within 24 hours, active fermentation will expel excess yeast, excessively bitter hop resins, and a small amount of fermenting beer; a small price to pay for smooth, clean-tasting homebrew. The overflow is collected in a small jug and later discarded.*

(1 m) length of 1¼-inch (3.2 cm) outside diameter clear plastic hose. If you've strayed from my initial recipe by adding grains or hops to your recipe (you'll learn how to do this in the next section called "Betterbrew—Intermediate Brewing), be sure to strain out all hop and grain ingredients from your brew and only after straining fit the hose into the carboy's opening.

For the initial 2 or 3 days of fermentation, this configuration will serve as a "pipe" that will direct the overflow of fermenting foam out and into an awaiting container. This method of fermentation has the extra advantage of "blowing off" excessively bitter hop resins, excess yeast, and other things that may contribute to slightly more assertive flavors and aromas.

If you are using a 6½-gallon glass carboy to ferment 5 gallons (or a 5-gallon carboy to ferment 4 gallons) of beer, it is not necessary to affix a blow-off hose to the carboy. Don't worry about not being able to "blow off" excess yeast and hop resins. You aren't likely to be able to perceive the difference in your beginning endeavors. Attaching a rubber cork and fermentation lock configuration is adequate, because fermentation foam will usually not reach the top of the carboy.

REMEMBER: Handle glass carboys with care and never with wet hands.

You will notice a great deal of activity during the first 2 or 3 days of fermentation. It is quite impressive to observe. After those first 3 days, the activity will diminish and you will want to place a fermentation lock atop the carboy for the remainder of the fermentation. Affix the fermentation lock into the sanitized rubber cork.

Your fermentation lock is a simple device that allows fermentation gases to escape from the fermenter but will not allow air to enter the fermenter. Sanitize the fermentation lock in your household bleach and water solution. Then place the fermentation lock atop the carboy. Be sure to fill the lock with about ¾ inch (2 cm) of water. YOU MUST FILL IT WITH WATER. You will soon notice that the gas produced by fermentation bubbles merrily through and out the fermentation lock.

## 7. Ferment for 8 to 14 days.

The style of beer you are brewing is ale. It is brewed at temperatures generally ranging from 60 to 75 degrees F (15 to 24 C). For this recipe and at these fermentation temperatures, you don't need to age or lager the fermented brew for great beer. If quality ingredients are used, visible fermentation will subside within 5 to 14 days. At this time, you also will notice that the beer seems to be darker; this is due to the yeast settling out (as bottom sediment), making the beer appear more clear. This change in appearance will start at the top of the fermenter and move down. If you choose to do so, or if necessity dictates, you may store the beer in the carboy with an active fermentation lock for one month without any risk of significant deterioration of flavor. But your beer will be at its

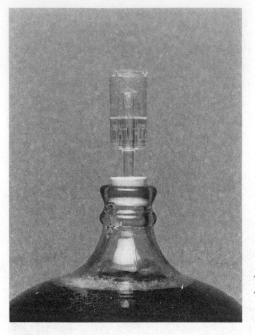

*All quiet on the yeastern front! After 2 to 3 days of vigorous fermentation, activity will subside and the yeast will begin to fall (sediment) to the bottom of the fermenter. If you use a "blow-off" hose, it can be replaced with a fermentation lock, allowing fermentation gases to escape, yet "locking" the still-fermenting beer from the outside air.*

best if bottled when visible signs of fermentation are negligible. You should assure yourself that it is bottling time by taking hydrometer readings on 2 or 3 consecutive days. If the readings remain unchanged, your brew is certainly ready to bottle. REMEMBER: Pour a small amount (about 1 cup) of beer into your hydrometer flask, take a reading, and either drink it or discard it, but do *not* return it to the fermenter. NOTE: Your beer may be hazy or even cloudy at the time of bottling. It will clear in the bottle.

## 8. Bottle and cap.

First of all relax . . . don't worry . . . and have a homebrew (if you haven't made your first batch yet, store-bought craft beer may do) . . . and get a friend or two to help you. That shouldn't be too difficult.

Once again: Sanitize all of the equipment and apparatus that will come in contact with your beer with a bleach and water solution—¼ cup (60 ml) household bleach to 5 gallons (19 l) cold water. It is easiest to sanitize your beer bottles in a tub or large, clean plastic pail. If you have invested in a bottle washer, you will find that rinsing bottles, carboys, and buckets will be safer and more effective and conserve hot water. A bottle washer is a worthwhile investment!

During the bottling process you will be adding a small amount of "priming" sugar to the now flat, inactive beer after it has been transferred out of the fermenter. Once in the bottle, this small amount of sugar will be fermented by

*The warehouse! Fermenting beer is content to sleep in the quietest of corners.*

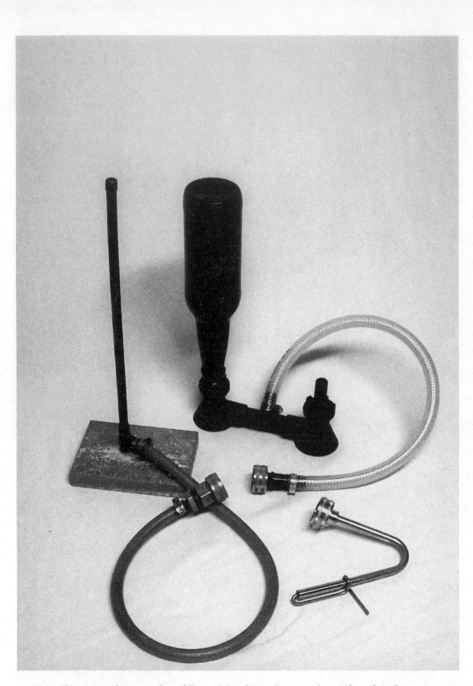

*Water wonders—making life easy! Bottle washers can be made or bought at local homebrew supply shops. They save time, hot water, effort, and money; not a bad combination. You'll never regret the small investment.*

the still-living yeast and create the perfect amount of carbonation. It is very important not to exceed the recommended sugar dosage of ¾ cup (175 ml) corn sugar per 5 gallons (19 l); by no means should you ever exceed 1 cup (240 ml) per 5 gallons (19 l). And note that it is a measure of *cups,* not pounds.

**Simple precaution and warnings:** Adding an excessive amount of priming sugar will result in overcarbonation and the possibility of exploding bottles. The Prohibition period of homebrewing left a legacy of poor methods. Here are two to avoid: 1) Priming the beer by adding ½ to 1 teaspoon of sugar to each bottle will result in inconsistent carbonation and bacterial contamination, which may result in overcarbonation and excessive foaming. 2) Waiting for the specific gravity to drop to a certain point is undependable because the final gravity of today's quality homebrew will vary with each recipe.

The following steps will help you organize your bottling procedures:

1. Sanitize your bottles.
2. Sanitize your 5- to 10-gallon (19 to 38 l) plastic bucket.
3. Sanitize your 6-foot (2 m) length of clear plastic (siphoning) hose.
4. Boil your bottle caps for 5 minutes (or disinfect in cheap vodka).
5. Boil ¾ cup (175 ml) corn sugar in 12 ounces (350 ml) water for a few minutes.

NOW, THEN

6. Place the carboy or plastic fermenter of finished beer on top of a table or counter. Remove the fermentation lock.
7. Position the sanitized plastic pail or plastic fermenter "bucket" on the floor (below the carboy) and add the dissolved and boiled solution of corn sugar. NOTE: If you have fermented in a plastic fermenter "bucket" you will be transferring your beer for bottling either into a glass or plastic carboy or a second plastic fermenter "bucket" (which you will need to have purchased).
8. Wash your hands. Take hold of the sanitized plastic hose and fill it completely full with water (no air bubbles allowed!). Put your clean thumbs over the ends, walk over to the carboy of beer, and quickly insert one end into the beer. No sucking necessary.
9. Your siphon is ready. Don't be intimidated—it's only beer. Relax. Lower the other end of the hose to the bottom of the plastic bucket (which should be on the floor), let loose, and gently transfer the beer into the plastic pail. Be aware of two things: a) Don't splash the beer or create a lot of bubbles—siphon quietly, and b) siphon all of the beer out of the carboy *except* the last ½ inch (1.2 cm) of sediment . . . BUT DON'T WORRY!
10. Take a hydrometer reading to confirm that fermentation is complete and

*Giving you more time to have a homebrew, bottle washers make quick work of fermenter- and bottle-washing chores.*

then record the final gravity in your recipe journal for future reference. NOTE: Contrary to what you may have led yourself to believe, your beer is *not* going to have an ending specific gravity equivalent to water: 1.000. There will be some residual, unfermentable malt "sugars" that will give your beer body and roundness to the flavor. The presence of these "sugars" will result in a final specific gravity of from 1.005 to 1.017 (even higher for your very heavy, all-malt beers). The important thing to remember is that if the hydrometer readings remain unchanged for 2 or 3 consecutive days, your beer is ready to bottle.

11. Place the "sugar-primed" beer on a table or counter and proceed to siphon the beer quietly (again without a lot of splashing) into each bottle. Leave about 1 inch (2.5 cm) of air space. You will find that you can control the

*It takes four hands and a homebrew! Anyone can siphon beer in preparation for bottling. The completely fermented beer is transferred to a sanitized plastic brewing pail, leaving the sediment of yeast behind. A measured amount of sugar is added and then the beer is bottled.*

*Keep your beer within arm's distance! The flow of finished beer from the bucket can be restricted by simply finger-squeezing the hose clamp. Careful, don't aerate the beer; put that hose all the way to the bottom of the bottle and leave about an inch (2.5 cm) of air space at the top of the bottle.*

*Easy does it! Bottling is easy and enjoyable with a homebrew.*
*Clean bottle caps are gently secured with the aid of a bottlecapper.*
*From this point it is only 7 to 14 days before you'll be enjoying your new efforts.*
*It's always time to enjoy your past efforts.*

flow of the beer with the hose clamp or by pinching the hose back on itself to constrict the flow when necessary.

12. Place the sanitized caps atop the bottles and cap with your bottle capper.
13. Label or mark your bottle caps to indicate what kind of beer is in the bottle. After all, you *will* be brewing more beer.
14. Store the bottles upright and out of sight in a quiet, dark corner of your home at room temperatures above 65 degrees F (18.5 C) and preferably below 75 degrees F (24 C).

## 9. Age for 7 to 14 days.

Now comes the hard part: waiting.

Within 5 or 6 days, your beer will show signs of clearing. The yeast that is in suspension will slowly drop to the bottom of the bottle and form sediment. At the same time, over a period of 7 to 14 days, the yeasts will carbonate the beer, at which point your beer will be ready to drink. Now you can store the beer at cooler temperatures if you wish.

*Some people collect butterflies! Ever since bottles were invented there have been
hundreds of types of bottlecappers patented. You'll only need one.*

## 10. Drink the beer!

*Hot damn!* It's ready.

But wait a minute: First, you should know that there is unavoidable yeast
sediment on the bottom of each bottle. It won't filter out and it won't hurt you

(it's actually rich with B vitamins), but you probably don't want it in your glass of beer; it will impart a yeasty character to the flavor. So be careful that you don't disturb it by doing something like turning the bottle upside down to see if it was made in China.

All you have to do is uncap a lightly chilled bottle of brew and pour all but the last ½ inch (1.2 cm)—about an ounce (30 ml)—of beer continuously into a glass pitcher (forget the plastic . . . this is *your* beer, so use the best). Now serve it in your favorite clean beer glass (please—no paper or plastic cups).

To drink, slightly part the lips as they touch the glass. Let the beer flow into the quonchologus and swallow. And be sure to smile when you drink your beer.

## APPENDIX TO THE BEGINNER'S SECTION

There are various schools of thought in homebrewing technique. All of them have a justified place when taken in proper perspective.

### AGING (LAGERING AND ALE STORAGE "CELLARING") VS. QUICKLY MATURING BEERS

The temperature of fermentation and quality of yeast are significant in determining when a beer will taste its best. Ale yeast and fermentation at temperatures

above 65 degrees F (18.5 C) will result in a beer that will be ready to bottle within 2 weeks. Stronger ales or ales using yeasts that don't sediment quickly can gain benefit from what is known as "cellaring." After warm-temperature fermentation is complete (no signs of fermentation activity), the temperature of ale is usually not dropped below 55 degrees F (13 C). At temperatures lower than 55 degrees F (13 C), ale yeast becomes very slow or completely inactive and more rapidly drops out of suspension as sediment. This cellaring step can improve clarity and reduce yeast sediment and yeast flavors in bottles.

Only with the use of very high-quality lager yeast, fermenting below 55 degrees F (13 C), and lagering below 45 degrees F (7 C) is there any justification or advantage for cold lagering and aging beer. Excessive aging of lager beers after bottling will not be advantageous unless temperatures are below 40 degrees F (4 C)—and often as low as 33 degrees F (1 C)—and a quality lager yeast must be used. Ultimately, the determining factor is: Drink it when you like it, as you like it, and when you *feel* it's the right time.

When you desire to really keep it simple, some mild and lower alcohol styles of beers can undergo a short maturation period and taste excellent. In other words you can ferment and finish your beer in the same fermenter at a constant temperature. Robust and stronger ales and lagers may have a "young" character that is less desirable to most beer drinkers, but may be of preference to some.

## TO BOIL OR NOT TO BOIL?

Malt, hops, yeast, and water—that is what it all boils down to, and boil you must. Many beer kits do not advise boiling the ingredients with water at all. Others advise boiling for only 10 to 15 minutes. Ignore that advice. Some beginning brewers minimize boiling times in an attempt to simplify or shorten the brewing process. Please don't. By avoiding or reducing boiling times, you are eliminating time to relax and have a homebrew.

Boil your wort for a minimum of 60 minutes. An active and rolling boil will help stabilize the flavor of your beer once it has reached its peak. The chemical reactions taking place between hops and malt during a good rolling boil will help clarify your beer and reduce chill haze (that tasteless haze that forms when you chill your beer). It will also help minimize the possibility of contamination from microorganisms that can detrimentally affect the character of your beer.

A good rolling boil of hops, malt, yeast, and water is essential for fully utilizing hops and helping to predict bitterness.

In some cases a short or no-boil regime can result in a sweet cornlike flavor and aroma in beer that, when evident, usually detracts from your enjoyment.

## SINGLE-STAGE VS. TWO-STAGE FERMENTATION

Single-stage fermentation is a method in which all fermentation resides in one vessel. Two-stage fermentation is a method of fermenting your beer in two different containers. Using this latter method, the brewer or homebrewer observes the initial fermentation closely during the first several days. After the initial activity has subsided, the beer is siphoned into another fermenter and a fermentation lock is attached. The sediment of spent yeast cells is left behind in the first fermenter.

The purpose of two-stage fermentation is to isolate the beer from prolonged contact with an inordinate amount of inactive yeast cells. For the homebrewer, this is a matter of concern *only* if you plan to ferment your beer for more than 2 or 3 weeks, because after this period of time the spent yeast will begin to break down and may impart a degree of yeastlike flavors to your beer. But remember: There is really no advantage in keeping your beer sitting around for more than 3 weeks unless you are brewing at cold temperatures and with quality lager yeast.

Homebrewers may brew with lager yeasts at room temperatures and lager in a second fermenter with good results when care is taken in sanitation. But you don't have to wait if you don't want to, because the beer will be freshest and taste its best within 3 or 4 weeks from starting. A second fermenter is convenient for brewers, such as myself, who never know when they are going to have time to bottle. Quite honestly, for one reason or another, I often don't get around to bottling or kegging for 4 to 6 weeks. So it is important for me to use closed fermentation and a second fermenter. I started brewing in 1970 and still homebrew 5-gallon (19 l) batches 12 to 18 times a year and am absolutely ecstatic with my results.

## OPEN VS. CLOSED FERMENTATION

Open fermentation is a method of fermenting your beer in a loosely covered, cleaned, and sanitized plastic container.

When considering that the number one concern in making clean, fresh-tasting homebrew is sanitation, open fermentation should only be considered in the brewing of fast-maturing and quickly bottled ales (and room temperature "lagers"). Open fermentation can be followed by secondary fermentation in a closed container (locked away from the air with a fermentation lock) for a brief period of 1 or 2 weeks maximum. If the beer is "clean" and free of contaminants, the beer will survive for extended periods of time—BUT, with initial open fermentation you add an element of risk. This risk is minimized with sanitation.

When your interest in homebrewing leads you to cold-brew, lager-type beers, you will ensure a much greater degree of success with closed fermentation because the longer it takes you to bottle your beer, the cleaner your beer must be.

One advantage of open fermentation is its apparent simplicity for the beginner;

*Having a strained relationship? Then why not have a homebrew? When hops or grains are added to the brewpot they should be separated from the wort (unfermented beer) before entering the fermenter. Here, the hot boiling wort is strained into cold water that has already been added to the fermenter. NOTE: If a plastic fermenter is used, it is essential that it be fitted with a lid and fermentation lock during fermentation.*

also, the equipment (plastic fermenters) may be more accessible. There should be no problem in brewing this way as long as sanitation is emphasized.

## OPEN FERMENTATION AND BREWING IN PLASTIC

If you have purchased a beer kit that comes complete with a 5- to 10-gallon (19 to 38 l) plastic bucket or brewing pail (often a food-grade trash pail), you can brew beer that is every bit as good as beer brewed in a closed fermenter. However, there are a few points to consider:

1. Care should be taken to sanitize the container and everything that comes in contact with the beer.
2. Do not use scratched or stained plastic containers. This type of surface is extremely difficult to sanitize because contaminating microorganisms can hide and resist even household bleach.
3. Brew only room-temperature ales and "lagers" that will be ready to bottle within 2 or 3 weeks.
4. Do not leave the fermenting beer in an open fermenter more than 7 days; either bottle it if ready (stable hydrometer readings over a period of 2 or 3 days indicate that fermentation is complete) or carefully transfer it by siphoning it into a second fermenter and lock it away from the air with a fermentation lock.

All other brewing, fermenting, and bottling procedures are the same as previously described.

## SUGAR AND BEER KIT INSTRUCTIONS— TO FOLLOW OR NOT TO FOLLOW

Beer kits, packaged in cans with all manner of beer styles to choose from, are a welcome introduction to homebrewing for many. They are simple to use and require minimal processing. They are designed so that they do not intimidate a new homebrewer with overwhelming procedures or concerns. A good beer can be made from many of them.

However, if you want to make better beer or you want to help others improve upon their own kit beers, here's some advice that will result in major improvements in beer flavor.

Whenever a beer kit calls for the addition of sugar in a recipe, substitute light dry malt extract (except where it calls for sugar for priming carbonation). You will end up with a beer that tastes like something you would want to pay money for.

REMEMBER: Don't be intimidated. Brewing good beer is *easy*. Relax. Don't worry. Have a homebrew.

# BETTERBREW—
# INTERMEDIATE
# BREWING

## BREWING OUR BEST FROM MALT EXTRACTS

## INTRODUCTION

Don't ever believe for even one instant that you know all that you will ever want to know. Now that you've brewed and tasted your first batch of beer, you know what I've been trying to tell you all along. Relax, don't worry, and have a homebrew. Certainly you have that great feeling of accomplishment and satisfaction. Word is out on the streets. Your friends are knocking on your door.

But your first batch of beer is only the beginning. An indeterminable amount of experience awaits you—beyond what you have accomplished and beyond the pages of this book, perhaps eventually leading to *The Homebrewer's Companion, Second Edition: The Complete Joy of Homebrewing, Master Edition.*

This section will further develop your appreciation and awareness of the process of brewing beer, introducing you to the unlimited versatility of brewing with malt extracts. You will learn how to combine malt extracts with traditional ingredients such as grains, hops, water, and yeast, as well as with unusual ingredients such as honey, fruit, and various herbs and spices.

Brewing with kit beers and hop-flavored malt extracts is often so rewarding that many homebrewers continue with their convenience, quality, and incomparable character. But for many the intrigue of formulating and using recipes beckons.

Learning about and understanding the varieties of ingredients that go into beer will give versatility in achieving very specific character and flavor in homebrewed beer, perhaps even those perfect flavors that are unavailable to the beer drinker any other way. You will be giving yourself more choice.

This section introduces you to additional procedures, concepts, and the language of the brewer (a complete glossary is in Appendix 1). The information provided in this section and from here forward is for you to grow and create

your own experience. No one can tell you exactly how your beer is going to taste; only you can determine that.

Following recipes will not necessarily improve upon what you do and what you are able to accomplish, but understanding the process and what it is you are dealing with will. Listening, seeing, learning, doing, and *feeling* are what brewing better beer is all about.

With this in mind and homebrew in hand you are ready to "Go for Greaterness."

## TIPS FOR BEER KIT HOMEBREWERS

Before diving into Betterbrews, here's a tip for you contented beer kit homebrewers.

Most kit beers are designed to have relatively low bitterness. Many are flavored with hop extract, which contributes bitterness but none of the other often desirable hop characteristics to beer. Along with substituting light dried malt extract for the sugar that many kit instructions call for, adding a small amount of fresh whole or pelletized hops in a knowledgeable manner can immensely improve the quality of your beers. It is relatively inexpensive and the procedures are virtually worry-free.

For those who choose to continue their brewing endeavors with simple kit beers, here are a few simple examples of how to enhance the quality of your homebrew. These next three options may provide the complexity and satisfaction you will want in your homebrewed beer.

For a 5-gallon (19 l) batch, ½ ounce (14 g) of low- to medium-bitter hops such as Hallertau, Mt. Hood, Vanguard, Cascade, Goldings, or Willamette boiled for a *full 60 minutes* will make a positive and noticeable contribution to your kit beers.

Adding ½ ounce of low- to medium-bitter hops that are noted for their flavor during the *final 5 to 10 minutes* of the boil will contribute a complex hop flavor that will otherwise always be lacking if hop extract is listed as an ingredient of the kit. Fuggles, Centennial, Amarillo, Nelson Sauvin, Hallertau, Mt. Hood, Cascade, Goldings, Tettnang, and Saaz are just some of the more popular aroma and flavor hops.

Finally, to add aromatic finesse to any beer, add ½ ounce of aroma hops during the final 2 minutes of the boil, then immediately strain, sparge, and transfer to the fermenter. By including this step in your brewing process, you will create a balance, complexity, and depth of character in your beer that is missing from most kit beers.

## EQUIPMENT

The equipment that you will use as an intermediate homebrewer is identical to that listed in the Beginner's Section with the exception that you may need additional glass carboys and fermentation locks for brewing more than one batch of beer at a time. For those larger batches you may need a larger pot.

You will also need the following additional equipment:

1 small kitchen strainer, approximately 6 inches (15 cm) across
1 large strainer, at least 10 inches (25 cm) across
1 extra refrigerator (only if you decide to brew cold-fermented lager beers)
1 bottle washer*

### *Thermometers*
You will want a thermometer that reads temperatures from freezing to boiling. This range is expressed as 32 degrees F (0 C) (freezing) to 212 degrees F (100 C). Boiling is 212 degrees F at sea level and about 200 degrees F (93.5 C) at 5,000 feet (1,500 m) elevation.

A conversion formula and table is available in Appendix 11.

A good thermometer for homebrewing is one that will read degrees Fahrenheit

---

*This piece of equipment is listed in the Beginner's Section as "optional." While it is optional here also, it is a highly recommended piece of brewery equipment. Available at most homebrew supply shops, it is a simple device that not only conserves hot water but also is a convenience and a time-saver. Once you have one, you will never figure out why you were ever without it.

from freezing to boiling and that will be sensitive enough to accurately indicate temperatures within 10 seconds. A good thermometer will cost between $8 and $15 and is well worth the investment, particularly if you plan on trying your hand at some advanced brewing techniques.

*References to temperature in this book are expressed in degrees Fahrenheit with degrees Celsius/Centigrade in parentheses.*

### Hydrometers

Your hydrometer is a useful tool in determining the status of fermentation activity. It also helps indicate the amount of ingredients and alcohol percentage in your brew.

As previously explained, hydrometers are simple devices that measure the density of liquids. You immerse a hydrometer in liquid, allowing it to float. Note how deeply it sinks into the liquid. When floating, the hydrometer displaces its own weight of the liquid and will therefore sink down deeper in a light liquid than in a heavier liquid (a liquid that may have dissolved sugars, such as unfermented beer).

Your hydrometer will have a specific gravity scale calibrated to read accurately at 60 degrees F (16 C). Hydrometers often have two other scales useful to the homebrewer. These hydrometers are called "triple-scale hydrometers." In addition to the specific gravity scale (explained in the Beginner's Section), there is a scale for determining the potential alcohol content of your beer and a scale called a "Balling scale," which can be read as degrees Plato. All of these scales coincide and are used to determine different types of information from the density of your brew.

*The Balling (or Plato) Scale*—This is the scale commonly used by professional brewers in the United States and Continental Europe. It is also directly proportional to the specific gravity scale popularly used by homebrewers and British brewers. The numbers that represent this measurement, expressed in degrees Plato, are about equal to one-fourth the value of the last three numbers that indicate specific gravity (e.g., 1.040 is equal to 10 degrees Plato; one-fourth of 40 is equal to 10). When your beer begins at gravities greater than 1.064, this method of conversion is less accurate. Refer to the table in Appendix 11.

A density that measures one degree Plato means that 1 percent of the weight of the measured liquid is dissolved sugar. In other words, a density of 10 degrees Plato indicates that there would be 10 pounds of dissolved sugars in enough water to make 100 pounds of solution.

*The Potential Alcohol Scale*—This is a very easy scale for homebrewers to use. In order to determine the alcohol content of your beer, simply record the initial reading that you get from this scale before you add your yeast. From this number subtract the reading that you take at bottling time. For example, if your original reading was 6 percent and your final reading indicates 2 percent, your approximate alcohol content is 6 minus 2 = 4 percent by volume.

The alcohol content of your beer can also be determined in a similar manner by using the specific gravity scale or Balling (or Plato) scale.

Multiplying the difference between initial Balling (or Plato) and final Balling by the number .42 will give you an approximate measure of the alcohol content of your beer by percent weight. For example, if your initial Balling was 15 and your final Balling was 7, the difference would be 8, and $8 \times .42 = 3.36$ percent by weight.

To determine alcohol content by means of the specific gravity scale, likewise subtract the final specific gravity from the original specific gravity and multiply by 105 to get percent alcohol by weight. For example: 1.040 minus 1.010 = 0.030; thus, $0.030 \times 105 = 3.15$ percent.

Because alcohol is lighter than water, a measured volume of water is not equal by weight to an equal volume of alcohol. To convert percent alcohol by weight (abw) to percent alcohol by volume (abv) multiply by 1.25. Likewise, to convert percent abv to abw multiply by 0.80.

Whew. That was more math than beer, but I know that figuring out the strength of homebrew is of interest to nearly every homebrewer. It's time to take a breath and have a homebrew, isn't it?

## COLOR

As anyone knows who enjoys variety, the colors of beer can seem as wondrous as a rainbow. Instead of a pot of gold imagine there is a pot of hot wort at one end of the rainbow and a frothy mug of brew at the other.

From the very pale straw colors of American light lagers to the midnight mysteriousness of Irish stouts, there are hues of gold, orange, amber, brown, red, copper, and yellow that enhance our enjoyment of each style of beer. With such variety of colors and intensity it is difficult to assess the "color" of beer in terms of a common language embodied in one system. A system for all styles of beers has never been worked out because beers may be darkened by brown, black, red, or copper-colored malts; added fruit; caramelization during the boil; and other factors, all contributing a unique visual effect that cannot be measured by a specific wavelength (color) of light passing through.

But something is better than nothing in this case; so brewing scientists have developed standards that measure the intensity of light and dark on a scale that ranges roughly from pale straw to black. Until recently a measuring system called the Lovibond scale was used to describe the color intensity of beer. Beer was compared to a defined set of colored samples of liquid. A vial of beer would be compared to vials of the color samples and assigned a degree Lovibond. It's worth noting that beer samples cannot be compared to printed colors. Why? Because the intensity of beer color will vary depending on the size and shape of the glass it is in. A test tube of your favorite stout may look brown because light doesn't have very far to go passing through a test tube of beer, while it appears opaque in your favorite pint mug. That's why liquid samples had to be used in standardized vials.

Modern brewers use a system called the Standard Reference Method (SRM) to measure color intensity. This is a more sophisticated method involving the use of light meter-analyzers to assign a number (degrees SRM) to light intensity. Degrees SRM and degrees Lovibond are approximately the same and certainly can be used interchangeably by homebrewers to approximate the color intensity of their beers.

To make things even more fascinating, European brewers have their own color scale reference called EBC (European Brewers Convention) units. There's no exact conversion formula from SRM to EBC, but it suffices to simply multiply $SRM \times 2 = EBC$. Let's keep it that simple, because generally it works for most light- and amber-colored beers.

Certainly sophisticated equipment and worried concern about exacting color are beyond the interest of most homebrewers. However, we can use the

SRM system to approximate references to color intensity to learn more about beer and brew different styles more accurately.

Here are a few standards that can serve as a guideline to help you interpret the SRM system.

## Color Based on Standard Reference Method (SRM)

| | | |
|---|---|---|
| Budweiser,<br>German Pils<br>Pilsner Urquell | 2.0 degrees<br>3.0 degrees (average)<br>4.2 degrees | yellow/straw/gold |
| Anchor Steam Beer | 9 degrees | light amber |
| Michelob Classic<br>Dark | 17 degrees | brown |
| Stout | 35 degrees and higher | black |

## BREWING BETTERBREW

What follows is an outline of a typical recipe for 5 gallons (19 l) of beer made with a malt extract base.

Ingredients for 5 gallons (19 l):

4 to 7 pounds (1.8 to 3.2 kg) plain malt *extract*: syrup or dried powder

Plus one or any combination of the following specialty malts (grains)*:

0 to 1 pound (0 to 454 g) crystal malt (or caramel malt)
0 to ½ pound (0 to 227 g) black malt
0 to ½ pound (0 to 227 g) chocolate malt
0 to ½ pound (0 to 227 g) roasted barley

Plus:

0 to 2 pounds (0 to 0.9 kg) corn sugar (though not recommended)
1 to 2 ounces (28 to 56 g) boiling hops (whole hops or pellets)
¼ to ½ ounce (7 to 14 g) finishing hops
1 to 2 packages beer yeast or liquid yeast culture

*There are dozens of other malted and unmalted grains that may be used in malt extract brewing, but these require advanced brewing techniques that will be discussed later.

The procedure for preparing 5 gallons (19 l) of Betterbrew is almost as easy as brewing kit beers; the only difference is that you add your own hops and personal choice of specialty grains, thus gaining more variety in the beers you make.

From the above ingredients, you will prepare a *wort* (pronounced "wert"). The term *wort* is universally used by all brewers to describe the "concoction" of unfermented beer. To make 5 gallons (19 l) of beer using the Betterbrew method and ingredients, first crush the specialty grains with a mill often available at your local homebrew shop or crush them yourself with a rolling pin using firm pressure. The grains should be crushed into small pieces but not pulverized to flour. Mill grinding is described in more detail in the Advanced Homebrewing section of this book. Add the crushed specialty grains to 2 gallons (7.6 l) water. The grain-water mash is heated and just before the mash begins to boil, strain out the used grains, retaining the 2 gallons (7.6 l) of "specialty malt tea" you've just made. Add to it any sugar, the malt extract, and the boiling hops and boil for 1 hour. Three gallons (11.4 l) of cold water are added to the fermenter. The hops are then removed from the concentrated wort by passing the wort through a sanitized strainer and into the cold water in the fermenter, bringing the total volume to 5 gallons (19 l). Add cold water if needed. Once the wort has cooled to below 78 degrees F (26 C), a hydrometer reading is taken and the yeast pitched (*pitching* is the term used to describe the inoculation of the wort with yeast).

From this point a homebrewer with any amount of experience could skip the following sections about ingredients and head straight for the recipes later in this book. You'll be able to make some pretty good-tasting beer. But being able to continually make better beer with each new batch takes more than just using somebody's recipe.

This book is about learning and being able to understand your beer. It is about feeling your beer and letting your beer feel you. This is where the rewards of homebrewing come from.

The following sections describe the ingredients that are available for use by the homebrewer. The information is presented here for you to understand the fundamentals of brewing ingredients and for future reference.

## KEY INGREDIENTS

### MALTED BARLEY AND MALT EXTRACT

Malted barley is one of the four essential ingredients of beer. From it are derived the fermentable sugars that contribute to the condition (carbonation), alcohol content, and fermented flavor of beer.

#### *What Is Malted Barley and How Is It Made?*
Essentially, barley is germinated to a certain degree, at which point it is then dried. This delicate process of germination and drying develops sugars, soluble starch, and starch-to-sugar-converting enzymes (called *diastase*), all of which are valuable to the subsequent brewing process.

The malting process begins by choosing the appropriate variety of barley. Some varieties of barley are more suitable for the production of malt whiskey or food sweeteners. Others are more appropriate for making beer. When the choice of barley has been made, the kernel quality is tested for moisture, nitrogen (protein content), and viability (ability to germinate).

After barley is accepted for malting, it is taken from storage and cleaned, sorted, and conveyed to steep (water) tanks. The procedure from the steep tank to the finished malt varies depending on the type of malt desired. Generally, the barley spends about 40 hours in tanks of fresh clean water with three intervals (eight hours each) during which the water is allowed to drain. Once moisture content reaches about 40 to 45 percent, the wet barley is conveyed to the germination room. Here it is allowed to germinate at temperatures carefully stabilized at about 60 degrees F (16 C). Over the approximate 5-day germination period, air is blown up through the bed of grain. In addition, the grain is occasionally turned to prevent the rootlets from forming a tangle.

After 5 days, the wet malt becomes what is referred to as "green malt." Subsequent kilning (drying) of the green malt over a period of perhaps 30 to 35 hours and a gradual raising of temperatures to 122 degrees F (50 C) for lager malts or 221 degrees F (105 C) for more strongly flavored malts result in finished malt—a product of sugars, soluble starches, and developed enzymes.

From the germination and drying room, the malt is conveyed to machines that separate the rootlets from the malted barley. From here the malted barley is ready for the brewer. Malting barley is a natural process that has been utilized by man. Normally, barley plants produce barleycorn seeds in order to reproduce. Remember, barley is a seed and is designed by nature to germinate and provide food for itself during its initial growth. The starch in barley is stored food. Upon natural germination a sprouting plant develops enzymes. These enzymes convert the stored food (starch) to usable plant food (plant sugars) for growth. As the growing plant is able to manufacture chlorophyll it will then be self-sufficient; chlorophyll will manufacture food for the plant from the sun's energy.

*Forever waves of grain! Temperature, air flow, and the mechanical turning of the green malt are carefully controlled in the malt house. A germination and kilning room is shown here.*

### How Is Malted Barley Used in the Brewing Process?

From malted barley, sweet liquid can be made through a process called *mashing*. To this sweet liquid are added ingredients such as hops to complete the process of making wort.

The first step in mashing involves the milling or grinding of the malt to remove the husks and break the kernels into granular-size pieces. A measured amount of water is mixed with the ground malt to dissolve sugars, starches, and enzymes. This is called the mash. When the temperature of the mash is raised to 150 to 160 degrees F (66 to 71 C), the diastatic enzymes that are present in the malt become most active and convert soluble starches to sugars. The liquid mash becomes sweet. After conversion, the "spent" grains are separated from the sweet liquid. The sweet liquid is called "malt extract."

In a brewery (or with advanced homebrewing techniques), the sweet liquid is transferred to the brewing kettle and the brewing process is continued with the addition of hops and the boiling of what is now called the wort.

### How Is the Malt Extract That Homebrewers Use Made?

The malt extract that homebrewers use comes in the form of syrup or dried powder. Using sophisticated equipment, malt extract manufacturers condense the malt extract by carefully evaporating much of the water.

The evaporation of water from malt extract takes place in a vacuum. Under a vacuum, these special evaporators allow liquid to boil at lower temperatures because of lower air pressure. Similarly, water boils at lower temperatures at higher altitudes (blood will literally boil in outer space, where there is no atmospheric pressure). This procedure is more economical as well as less harmful to the flavor of the malt extract. The pressures at which malt extract syrups and powders are made evaporate water at temperatures usually between 105 and 160 degrees F (41 to 71 C).

If the final product is syrup, the water content is usually about 20 percent, the other 80 percent being sugar and unfermentable solids that are important to beermakers.

If the final product is a dried powder, the malt extract has undergone a complete evaporation process by means of "spray-drying," thus removing almost all of the water.

When you use a malt extract syrup or powder, you add water again, thus reconstituting the original malt extract. With clean brewing techniques and quality ingredients, beers made from malt extracts will be every bit as good as similar styles of all-grain (no malt extract) beers.

Many beer kits in the form of canned syrups have undergone an additional step. Before condensing by evaporation, hops may have been added to the malt extract. The wort is boiled and then condensed to syrup by an evaporation process. Thus, these kits are promoted as "no-boil" beer kits.

## Are All Malt Extract Syrups and Powders the Same?
No!

More than a hundred varieties of malt extract syrups and powders are available to the homebrewer. They vary quite a bit. All of the variables of making malted barley and malt extract manifest themselves in the final beer. Furthermore, some malt extract products contain additives (which may or may not be desirable) such as corn syrup, sugar, caramel, minerals, preservatives, etc.

The variables of the malting and mashing process determine the final character of the beer being brewed. Those variables are things such as variety of barley, kilning time, and temperature of the kiln during the malting process. Variables in the mashing process have a great influence on flavor, head retention, body, sweetness (or dryness), aroma, and fermentability of the wort. Most malt extracts for homebrewing are of excellent quality, but they will vary according to the character of beer that was intended by the individual malt manufacturer. The light malt extract made by one malt manufacturer will make a beer distinctively different from that made by another. Likewise, the amber, dark, pale and so on will all vary.

As a homebrewer, you can begin to realize the tremendous variety that awaits you.

## Specialty Malts (Grains) for the Malt Extract Brewer
Specialty malts are used by homebrewers to add special and desirable character to beer. Color, sweetness, body, and aroma are a few of the characteristics that can be controlled and emphasized. Some styles of beers such as stout and bock cannot be made without specialty malts being an ingredient at some stage of the process. Sometimes beer kit manufacturers will use specialty malts in their malt extract to create a particular style of beer.

Specialty grains are prepared by crushing them. A small amount of pressure can be applied to a rolling pin as it passes over the grains. For those brewers who have a malt or flour mill (grinder), the grinding plates may be adjusted to allow a slight crushing of the grain as it passes through. Grinding of any malt to powder is undesirable and should be avoided. Most local homebrew supply shops have a malt mill that can crush your malt. That's convenient!

*Go for greatness! Specialty malts add character to beer.*

### When Are Specialty Malts Added to the Homebrewing Process?

Many homebrewers and many homebrewing books have debated this question. The fact is that when any whole grain is boiled in wort, the wort will absorb certain flavors that are extracted from the husks of the grain, such as a certain amount of tannin and other substances. The flavor of tannin can be described as astringent or noticeably dry or grainy. Also, in the case of crystal malt, a very small amount of unconverted starches will be extracted that contribute to a haze (that does not affect the flavor) in the beer when it is chilled.

Some malt extract homebrewers boil specialty grains with their wort, while others prepare a preliminary extract from these specialty grains, then remove the grains from the "soup" before adding malt extract and hops and commencing the boil.

To boil or not to boil, that is the question. . . .

For simplicity, boiling cannot be beat and satisfactory beer will result. Chill haze will not detract from the flavor, and the astringency of the tannin will mellow somewhat with age; sometimes the astringency may be so subtle that you won't even detect it.

But a far Betterbrew can be made if you avoid boiling grains by using a simple preboiling procedure. If grains are used, crush and add them to your brewpot along with 1½ gallons (5.7 l) of cold water. Then bring the water to a boil. When boiling commences, remove the grains with a small strainer. This method will extract the goodness of the specialty grains over the 15 to 25 minutes it takes to achieve boiling. This procedure also decreases the sharp and potential astringency that grains can contribute if boiled along with the malt extract. Aging time will be significantly reduced.

After you have removed the grains, add the malt extract and carry on. REMEMBER: Don't worry! Do the best that you can manage. Relax and have a homebrew.

## Specialty Malts

BLACK MALT—Black malt is produced from malted barley. Its production involves roasting the malted barley at temperatures so high that they drive off almost all of the aromatics (malt flavor).

Its use in brewing is chiefly for coloring the beer. Black malt will color the foam on beer but to a lesser degree than roasted barley (see Roasted Barley). In excess, black malt will contribute a dry burnt flavor to the beer that may be perceived as a bitterness different from that derived from hops. This may or may not be desirable, depending on the desired flavor character.

There are no enzymes in black malt.

DEBITTERED BLACK MALT—This malt is similar to black malt, but processed differently to minimize harsh astringent bitterness. The maltster uses the trick of removing the husk from the grain before it is roasted. Recall, the husk has lots of astringent tannins that contribute to an assertive and burnt flavor, desirable in some types of beer. Debittered black malt is a very dark roasted malt that contributes very dark colors and a strong roast, almost cocoalike character, with minimal astringent bitterness.

CHOCOLATE MALT—No, this is not the chocolate malt you may have enjoyed as a kid (or still do as an adult). Chocolate malt is a dark brown malt that has been produced by the roasting of malted barley. It is not roasted quite as long as black malt; consequently, it is lighter in color and retains some of the aromatics and flavor of malt's sweetness.

It will impart a nutty, cocoalike toasted flavor to the beer.

There are no enzymes in chocolate malt.

CRYSTAL MALT (CARAMEL MALT)—Crystal malt is made from green malt (that is, malted barley that has not been kiln dried yet) and is produced by drying the wet germinated barley at controlled temperatures. It is first gently dried for a short time; then during a period of 45 to 60 minutes the malt is "mashed" in the grain as temperatures rise to 212 degrees F (100 C). Most of the starch is quickly converted to sugar and while warm remains in a liquid state. Upon cooling, the sugars set to a hard crystal.

Because of the "mashing" process that the crystal malt has undergone, some of the soluble starches and sweet character will not ferment. Its addition

*Some like it dark! Roasted barley, black, and chocolate malts add color and distinctive
character to stout, porter, bock, and other dark beers.*

to wort will enhance the sweetness of the beer and often add a caramel, toffee,
and/or freshly baked cookie character to the beer. Adding crystal malt will also
increase the body of the beer as well as aid in head retention. Because of its
darker color, it will enrich the color, lending a gold or even reddish glow to
the beer. Crystal malts come in light, medium, and dark color varieties. Color
is designated on the Lovibond scale: Light 10; Medium 40; Dark 90+.

There are no enzymes in crystal malt.

ROASTED BARLEY—Roasted barley is not made from malted barley. It
is made by roasting unmalted barley at high temperatures. During the process,
the temperature is gradually increased to in excess of 392 degrees F (200 C). The
barley is carefully and frequently sampled in order to avoid charring. Roasted
barley is not black in appearance, but a rich dark brown.

Tasted as a grain, it has an assertive, roasted flavor, similar to roasted coffee
beans. Especially when used in the making of stout, it lends a distinctive roasted
flavor as well as pleasant bitterness. Its flavor is very distinct from black malt. It
contributes significantly to the color of the beer and creates a brown head of foam.

There are no enzymes in roasted barley.

DEXTRINE (CARA-PILS) MILD, VIENNA, AND MUNICH
MALTS—These specialty malts are also available to the homebrewer. They
can be used with malt extract but need to undergo a mashing process. Mashing
will be explained later.

*A body builder! Crystal malt lends a copper color as well as sweetness and full body to beer.*

There are no enzymes in dextrine malt. It must be mashed in the presence of enzymes supplied by other malts. Its use will lend a fuller body to the beer and aid in head retention.

Mild malt is very lightly toasted malt in the British style that contains enzymes. It will contribute an amber color to beer.

Vienna malt is lightly toasted malt in the German style that contains enzymes. It will contribute an amber color and some degree of what is called full body to beer.

Munich malt contains enzymes. It contributes an amber color to the beer and a malty sweetness.

OTHER SPECIALTY MALTS—There are dozens of other kinds of malts you'll want to check out if you get immersed in grain brewing: sour malt, peat-smoked malt, beechwood-smoked malt, brown malt, a wide range of colors and flavors of crystal and caramel malts, special Belgian malts, 2-row, 6-row, English, Canadian, American, German, Australian malts, wheat malts, roasted wheat malts, rye malts, biscuit and aromatic malts, and many more. Check them out at your local homebrew supply shop. The selection will inspire beer dreams.

For detailed information on these malts and many more types of malt, see the "Malt" section of *The Homebrewer's Companion, Second Edition.*

### Getting to Yes: German Styles, English Styles, American Styles, Belgian Styles . . .

If you're like most homebrewers, you have had quite a variety of beer experiences, both homebrewed and commercially made. Sometimes there is a desire to duplicate a world classic or, more generally, the quality of beer from Germany, Holland, Belgium, England, Canada, or even the United States. Specific beer qualities derive from the artful blending of ingredients and the skilled execution of process. There are dozens of important variables that need to be considered.

If you are a malt extract brewer, one of the easiest variables to look at is your choice of malt extract. When brewing German-style beers, use extracts produced in Germany; likewise, if you wish for a more authentic character in your British-style ales, use extracts of British origin. Homebrew supply shops offer varieties of malt extract naturally produced from no fewer than the following countries: Australia, Belgium, Canada, Germany, England, Ireland, the Netherlands, New Zealand, Scotland, and the United States. It would be too simplistic to attribute all of the final character of your beer to the origin of the malt extract used, but different barley varieties and malting techniques do have an influence on beer's character. Purchasing malt extract made in the same country as the beer style you are making will be a step in the right direction.

The same principle holds true for those who brew from grains. It is easier to make an authentic-tasting English-style pale ale when you use English-made pale ale malt. Make German lagers with German malt, Belgian ales with Belgian malt, and American lagers with American lager malt. The proper processing of malts of known origin is but one step toward achieving the finesse many advanced all-grain brewers eventually strive for.

## HOPS

Hops are the flowerlike cones of the hop vine. Their bitterness, flavor, and aroma are the primary considerations of the brewer. But their importance to the beer-brewing process goes beyond their contributions to flavor and aroma. To an important extent they inhibit the growth of certain beer-spoiling bacteria. The use of hops also aids in flavor stability and head retention.

### History

Brewers first used hops in making beer more than a thousand years ago, but only since the early part of the 1800s have they been used with any regularity. Hops gained favor with brewers and beer drinkers because of their antiseptic and preserving qualities—no small concern before the age of refrigeration. Spoiled, sour batches of beer occurred all too frequently.

Other plants and herbs were used to preserve beer. According to Sanborn C. Brown in his book *Wine and Beers of Old New England: A How-to-Do-It History,* spruce, ginger, ground ivy (also called cat's foot, alehoof, alecost, alehove, fieldbalm), sweet mary, tansy, sage, wormwood, and sweet gale were often used. See "Herbs and Spices" on page 105 for more on hops versus herbs. A terrific and complete resource for a history of herbal beers is Stephen Buhner's book, *Sacred and Herbal Healing Beers* (Brewers Publications, 1998).

Hops became the most popular preserving agent because of the plant's tenacity, ease of cultivation, and flavor. As science advanced it was discovered that, in addition to preservation, hops can also help to coagulate and eliminate undesirable malt proteins in the brew kettle, aid clarification, promote good head retention, and stabilize beer flavors as well as clean the beer drinker's palate of what was traditionally a sweeter, stickier, more cloying brew. Hops are now an important and essential agricultural product, primarily used for brewing. As the demand increases, new varieties are forcing out older breeds in order to grow hops that are less susceptible to disease, yield a good harvest per acre, retain freshness longer, have a desirable flavor or aroma character, have a high bitterness value per weight, and are capable of being processed for shipment throughout the world.

Although hops can grow well in many regions of the world, the major commercial hop-producing areas are Germany, the south of England, southern

*A very special elegance! Whole hop flowers make beer bitter—not to mention giving it its very special bouquet and flavor—while also serving as a natural preservative.*

Australia, Tasmania, New Zealand, and the U.S. (Washington State, Oregon, and some in Idaho). See Appendix 5: "Growing Your Own Hops."

Hops that homebrewers obtain come from the same crops that supply major breweries and are available to the homebrewer in four forms: compressed whole hops, pelletized hops and, less commonly, hop extract and hop oil.

### Hops and the Homebrewer

The most important thing to remember about hops is that they appear and behave like a flower, though in actuality they are the flowerlike cones of fruit that harbor tiny sacks of oils and resins and sometimes seeds. We'll refer to these cones as whole hops in this book. If you understand this much, then all the complexities of the hop and its involvement in the brewing process will be much more easily understood.

Hops can be infused into the brewing process at various stages in much the same way as various teas are made. As in tea, the results vary with preparation. Results will also vary with the freshness of the ingredient, variations in the quality of year-to-year crops, and length of growing season. It is an ingredient in beer that is temperamental and moody and involves itself with every aspect of the brewing and tasting process.

There are hundreds of cultivated varieties of hops, just as there are many varieties of apples. Each variety has its own spectrum of characteristics. Varieties of hops are chosen for the properties of bitterness, flavor, and aroma that they lend to the beer. Different varieties possess varying degrees of these characteristics. By choosing to use different varieties of hops, the brewer can decide what character his or her beer will have.

Because hops are of plant origin they are perishable. Some varieties are more perishable than others. Once they are picked from the vine they are gently dried. Then they are physically processed and packaged in a manner that will reduce exposure to excessive heat and oxygen. Heat and oxygen are the deteriorating factors that will eventually spoil hops. As a homebrewer, understanding why oxygen and heat spoil hops will enhance your ability to recognize quality hops and make better beer.

The bittering, flavoring, and aroma-enhancing powers of hops come from oils and resins in the whole hop. The tiny capsules of resin are called *lupulin* and can easily be seen at the base of the whole hop's petals; they look like yellow pollen. These resinous glands protect the essential oils but only for a given amount of time. As time, heat, and oxygen work their effect on these oils they become rancid, just as any vegetable oil will. The perishability of vegetable oils is, to a large degree, attributable to the reaction of oxygen with the oil—a process called oxidation. Cold or even freezing temperatures and the removal of oxygen inhibit oxidation.

Regional styles of beer are influenced to a significant degree by the hops

*Swollen glands! Tiny lupulin oil glands coat the base of the whole hop's petals. The lupulin contributes to the bitterness and aromatics of the hop.*

that are used. It is not peculiar for breweries that are situated in hop-growing countries to be more highly hopped than in areas where hops must be "imported." For example, beers that are significantly more bitter and more aromatic are quite popular in Oregon, Washington State, and the south of England; these are hop-growing areas. Elsewhere, styles of beer emerge in areas where only certain varieties can be grown; such is the case with the original pilsener beer from the Czech region, called Pilsner Urquell, which once was brewed exclusively with the distinctive Saaz hop. Interestingly, as brands sometimes grow and become internationally distributed they don't maintain the distinctive characters that originally defined their success. On the contrary, small brewers and homebrewers embrace and thrive on imparting and maintaining distinctive characters to their beers, especially characters derived from hops.

Hops offer quite a bit of variety, and their use will depend on preferences of taste. Some will enjoy very bitter beers while others will prefer milder hop rates. Some (actually very few) disdain the aroma of hops while others will celebrate the euphoric and aromatic attributes of hops. Brewers who like a lot of hops are often called "hopheads." Whether or not you are a hophead, you have the opportunity to choose the right hop for your type of beer. There is no one-hop-fits-all. As a homebrewer, you will be able to experiment to a degree that is not practical

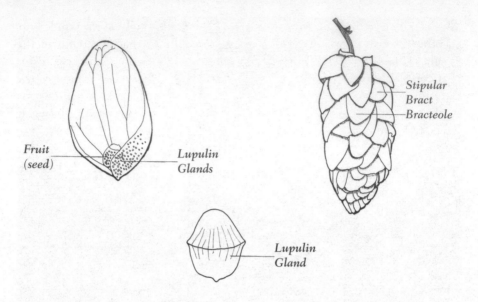

Fruit (seed)

Lupulin Glands

Stipular Bract

Bracteole

Lupulin Gland

for the large commercial breweries. You will have more opportunity for choice and experimenting. Enjoy this opportunity.

## What Makes Hops Bitter? Where Do the Hop Flavor and Aroma Come From?

The biochemistry of hops and its interaction with the beermaking process can become quite involved. Yet in all of its wonderful complexity, the basics can be easily understood and effectively utilized as a foundation for the homebrewing of all beers.

As mentioned previously, hops produce lupulin glands containing resins and oils that are the major contribution to beermaking. They appear as bright yellow-gold, powdery balls located at the base of the whole hop's petals (bracteoles). In reality, these yellow balls are not powdery at all but are tiny natural packages of oils and resins. When rubbed between the fingers, the packages will burst, releasing aromatic oils (which you can smell) as well as sticky resins. If these lupulin glands are orange, do not feel sticky, or do not smell aromatically fruity, herbal, or floral, they have been oxidized and are not suitable for brewing most kinds of beer.

There are many other components of hops, but homebrewers are most concerned with the aromatic hop oils and two types of resins. The hop oils contribute to the hop flavor and aroma in the finished beer. The resins contribute only to the bitterness of the beer.

BITTERNESS—The two types of hop resins that are significant in contributing to beer's bitterness are called alpha acid and beta acid. Their presence is measured by their weight relative to the dried weight of the whole hop. In other words, 6 percent alpha acids would indicate that 6 percent of the weight of the dried whole hop is alpha acid resins. It is the alpha acid resins that contribute most significantly to the bitterness of beer; consequently, the bittering capability of hops is expressed in terms of alpha acid percentage.

In order to give you some idea as to the amount of hops used in bittering beers, the following table is presented as a guideline.

## Hop Bittering Character for 5 Gallons (19 l) of Light- to Medium-Bodied Pale Beer

### Percent Alpha Acids

| OUNCES OF HOPS | 3 TO 5% | 6 TO 7% | 8 TO 9% | 10 TO 12% |
|---|---|---|---|---|
| ½ ounce | | | mildly bitter | mild to medium bitterness |
| 1 ounce | very mildly bitter | mild to medium bitterness | medium bitterness | very bitter |
| 2 ounces | mildly bitter | medium bitterness | very bitter | extremely bitter!! |

NOTE: Lighter beers use less hops to be bitter. Heavier beers can stand to be more highly hopped.

**BITTERING YOUR BEER: UTILIZATION OF ALPHA AND BETA ACIDS**—In order to utilize the bittering acids of the hops you *must* boil the hops with the wort. This "bitterness" boiling is done in your brewpot for 30 to 90 minutes. A rolling boil is necessary in order to physically and actively mix the alpha and beta acids with the sweet wort.

The reason hops must be boiled in order to extract their bittering qualities is that the hop resins are not very soluble in water; in other words, they will not dissolve into solution. The intense heat and turbulence of boiling water creates a condition that allows a chemical reaction (called isomerization) to occur that makes the alpha acid resins soluble in water. In contrast, beta acids become soluble only when oxidized, the small amount of bitterness the beta acids contribute being the consequence of this oxidation. As a homebrewer you may be able to get some reasonable bitterness from old and oxidized hops, but off-flavors and inconsistency contribute negatively to the quality of the finished beer. Don't fool yourself.

REMEMBER: The alpha (and beta) acid resins contribute *only* to the bitterness of the beer.

HOW BITTER IS BITTER?—The Hop Bittering Character chart on page 67 will give you a rough idea of the relation of the amount of hops used and the perceived bitterness of a light- to medium-bodied beer. But really, how bitter is bitter, and how is it measured?

Brewing scientists have developed a method by which they measure what they call International Bitterness Units (IBUs—or, more commonly, BUs for short). One BU is equal to 1 milligram of a specific compound called iso(merized) alpha acid in 1 liter of wort or beer. More BUs in a given beer mean more bitterness perceived. But there is an enigma here, because 20 BUs in a rich, full-bodied, malty stout will be perceived by the tongue as having far, far less bitterness than 20 BUs in a light American-style lager beer. Both have the same amount of bittering substance, but the perception will be different. *The lesson here is that a given amount of BUs (i.e., hops used for bitterness) in a beer does not always equal the same amount of bitterness perceived.*

BITTERNESS UNITS—TO WHAT DEGREE DIFFERENTIATION?—Do you want to talk beer bitterness with the beginning beer enthusiast? Here are some generalized guidelines that provide an understandable sense of bitterness levels for anyone who likes beer.

0 to 10 BU are not generally perceived as bitterness in international light lagers and not at all perceived in other stronger-flavored beers.

12 to 20 BU give a mild and pleasant bitterness in 4 to 5 percent pale ales, amber lagers, and ales.

20 to 30 BU will be perceived as mild and pleasant in more robust ales, stouts, porters, red ales, and stronger lagers.

40 to 50 BU will be assertive in most any type of lager or ale; especially intense in lower alcohol beers below 5.5 percent and balanced for maltier stronge pale ales and India Pale Ales.

Beyond 50 BU is reserved for hop-emphasized beers.

More information about International Bitterness Units is included later in this book in the "Advanced Homebrewing and Hops" section on page 301. Many more details about hops and bitterness can also be found in *The Homebrewer's Companion, Second Edition.*

HOW CAN A HOMEBREWER KNOW HOW MUCH HOPS TO USE TO ACQUIRE A DESIRED BITTERNESS?—By knowing the percentage of alpha acids in the hops you use, you can accurately match the desired bitterness levels in a given style of beer or recipe.

You may use some simple mathematics to predict BU levels in any beer you brew (see "Advanced Homebrewing and Hops" on page 301). Or you may make a few assumptions and simply base your final beer bitterness on Homebrew Bitterness Units—a factor of the ounces and alpha acid content of the hops you use.

HOMEBREW BITTERNESS UNITS (HBU)—Another method with which homebrewers can determine how much hops to use involves the convenient and easy-to-use concept of Homebrew Bitterness Units (HBUs). In metric units it is expressed as Metric Bitterness Units (MBUs).

Homebrew Bitterness Units = % alpha acid of hops × ounces of hops. This is a very useful concept when a recipe for a given volume of beer calls for, say, 2 ounces of 5 percent alpha acid Hallertau hops, which is equal to 10 HBUs. It is important to note the volume of beer being brewed when using Homebrew Bitterness Units as a measurement of hops.

1. If your Hallertau hops are only 4 percent alpha acid, you will know to use:

$$10 \text{ HBU} \div 4\% = 2.5 \text{ ounces of Hallertau hops}$$

OR

2. If you wish to use another variety of hops, say Chinook hops at 10 percent alpha acid, you know to use:

$$10 \text{ HBU} \div 10\% = 1 \text{ ounce of Chinook hops}$$

Similarly for metric units, MBU = % alpha acid of hops × grams of hops. If 280 MBUs are called for in a recipe, then:

1. If your Hallertau hops are only 4 percent alpha acid you will know to use:

$$280 \text{ MBU} \div 4\% = 70 \text{ g of Hallertau hops}$$

OR

2. If you wish to use another variety of hops, say Chinook hops at 10 percent alpha acid, you know to use:

$$280 \text{ MBU} \div 10\% = 28 \text{ g of Chinook hops}$$

HOP FLAVOR AND AROMA: "FINISHING" WITH FINISHING HOPS—Utilizing the flavor and aromatic constituents of hops has become tremendously popular among homebrewers and craft beer enthusiasts. These hop characters can be quite pleasing. If overdone, they can blow you away, which may be what you intended, or maybe not. Regardless, understanding how to manage the addition of hops can dramatically enhance hop characters. Hop flavors and aromas are not for every beer drinker, but done with purposeful consideration, hops can provide quite an exciting variety to the character of beer. The process of adding hops for flavor and aroma is called *finishing*; the hops used are called *finishing, flavor,* or *aroma hops*.

The flavor of the hop and its associated aroma come from the hop oils within the lupulin gland. These hop oils are not the same as the bittering resins. Hop oils are soluble in water and very volatile—that is, their essence will quickly dissipate with the steam vapors during the boil. Remember, hops are like flowers. If you desire to impart flavor and aroma to your beer, the addition and preparation are similar to brewing a pot of well-made tea. Gently boiling or steeping the freshest hops during the final 1 to 15 minutes in the brewpot will impart varying degrees of flavor and aroma (while not contributing much bitterness to the brew).

Dry hopping is another method brewers use to impart aroma, flavor, and some perception of bitterness (but not Bitterness Units) to the finished beer. It is a simple procedure involving the addition of clean, dry hops to the secondary fermenter for 3 to 7 days prior to bottling. One-quarter to one-half of an ounce (7 to 14 g) for 5 gallons (19 l) will contribute evident to assertive character in beer. These hops must be removed before bottling. There is little risk that the hops you are using are contaminated with beer-spoiling microorganisms. Generally, if hops are packaged well and look clean, the presence of harmful beer spoilage bacteria is minimal or nonexistent. However, in order to reduce the possibility of contamination, I recommend that the dry hopping be done only after all, or the majority, of the fermentation is complete. For convenience and minimum of worry and fuss, hop pellets are excellent for dry hopping. The alcohol content and the natural acidity of fermented beer will inhibit bacterial growth. Keep in mind that unfermented wort is the perfect place for bacteria to grow.

I'm a hophead, though I don't always enjoy extreme additions of hop bitterness, flavor, or aroma. It all depends on the kind of beer I feel like and the mood I happen to be in. Besides dry hopping in the fermenter, as described above, I often introduce hop flavor and/or hop aroma to beer by adding proportions of my best and freshest hops at the end of the boil—no longer than 5 to 15 minutes for deriving hop flavor and no longer than 1 to 5 minutes (steeping) at the end of the boil for hop aroma. You must be ready to transfer and cool your hot wort immediately when using this method. This method works, and it works well, without the hassle of removing hops from the fermenter.

## What Are Hop Oils?

By definition, hop oils are the volatile oils in the hop cone. They are a very complex combination of chemical compounds. The addition of hop oils in parts per billion to beer can have a dramatic effect on the hoppy aroma and flavor of beer. Not usually carried by homebrew supply stores, they can be ordered by special request. Hop oils and their use is discussed in *The Homebrewer's Companion, Second Edition.*

## What Are Hop Pellets?

Hop pellets are nothing more than whole hops mechanically processed by what is called a hammer mill. This machine pulverizes the whole hop. The pulverized hop and ruptured lupulin glands are then forced into a pelletizing machine to be compressed and extruded into pellets. Their own sticky oils and resins hold the pellets together naturally.

The disadvantage of pelletizing hops is debatable. It has been argued that the rupturing of the lupulin glands will detract from the subtle flavor and bittering ability of the hop. The most significant disadvantage of hop pellets is that they are not easily removed from the wort. For homebrewers, the removal of hop pellets from the wort can be done using a stainless weave strainer and is essential if the blow-off hose method of fermentation is used. The other significant

*It's not what you think it is! These hop pellets are the result of a mechanical transformation of whole hops. Whole hops are milled, then compressed into pellets. They are convenient space savers and resist spoilage.*

disadvantage of hop pellets is that a natural "filter bed" (used to create clear worts for fermentation) cannot be created during the hop straining and sparging process.

Hop pellets are perishable over a period of time. Oxygen will diffuse into the pellet, and heat will enhance the process.

The advantages of pelletizing hops are fourfold. First, very little storage space is needed. Second, the freshness of the hops is more easily controlled; oxygen can only easily reach the surface layer of resins and oil, and the rest of the hop oils and resins are more protected within. Third, pellets are convenient to use when dry hopping in your secondary fermenter. Finally, blends of hops can be processed into one pellet.

### What Are Hop Extracts?

Hop extract is the liquid bittering essence of hops and is used for convenience in the brewing industry. Some liquid hop extracts are processed with a wide variety of chemical solvents that dissolve the hop resins into solution and chemically "isomerize" these resins so that they are soluble in beer wort. New methods of extraction involving liquid (supercold) carbon dioxide have been developed to extract both the bittering resins and the volatile oils. These hop extracts and oils are available to the homebrewer, but are difficult to find.

Non-$CO_2$ hop extracts have no flavor or aromatic value. Their use by homebrewers is minimal. If you choose to use hop extract, do so with care and knowledge of how powerfully bitter it is. Also, be sure to always boil the hop extract in the wort or at least a small amount of water unless specifically told that it is unnecessary. Some (very few) hop extracts are processed with toxic chemical solvents that are still present in very small amounts. Boiling will volatize (evaporate) them.

### Hopped Malt Extract and Hopped Beer Kits

If you purchase malt extract that is hop flavored and you are wondering about the character of the hop flavor in the malt, reading the label will begin to give you some indication of what to expect.

Hop-flavored malt extracts are hopped with whole hops, pellets, or hop extract. If hop extract is used, there will be no hop flavor or aroma, only bitterness. If you desire hop flavor or aroma, you will have to add it yourself. Some beer kits and malt extracts are hopped with whole or pelletized hops. The boiling of worts made from these malt extracts will dissipate much of the hop flavor and aroma unless done for a shorter period of time.

Beer kits promoting themselves as "wort concentrates" or "concentrated wort" imply that the syrup is not simply concentrated malt extract but malt extract to which hops have been added, boiled, and then concentrated to syrup—ready to brew without boiling. If in doubt ask your homebrew supply shop owner, who can find out the details for you.

*Take your pick—but go for freshness! One-quarter ounce of whole hops (left) contrasts with three ounces of hop pellets (right).*

## How to Recognize Quality Hops

It is very important for you, the homebrewer, to get fresh or well-cared-for hops. You are not doing yourself any favors or saving any money by buying old hops. It isn't too difficult to recognize the difference between good and bad hops.

Look, feel, smell—listen to all your senses. Whole hops and pellets should be green in appearance. Oxidation will turn them an unappealing dry brown color. The lupulin glands in whole hops should be a recognizably bright yellow color. Lupulin will turn orange when oxidized. When rubbed between the fingers, quality whole hops will feel sticky due to the rupturing of the lupulin glands; also, the aromatic oils can be smelled. Nonsticky, dusty feeling, and/or cheesy aroma suggest oxidation.

The packaging of whole hops and hop pellets is extremely important.

Oxygen-barrier plastic bags or metal foil bags from which oxygen has been removed and replaced with nitrogen are the best ways of preserving hops for the homebrewer. Refrigeration prolongs the life of packaged hops even longer and is absolutely essential for hop pellets or whole hops not packaged in oxygen-barrier plastic bags. If you are able to smell hops through a plastic bag, the bag is not an oxygen-barrier bag. Freezing your hops in sealed packages will retain freshness for years and is the best method of storage. Hop quality can actually improve with age and proper cold storage—up to a certain point.

Well-cared-for hops are important. Homebrewers use many varieties that will deteriorate and lose 50 to 70 percent of their brewing value within weeks if not packaged and stored appropriately.

## What Varieties of Hops Are Available to the Homebrewer?

The chart beginning on page 76 is a compilation of varieties of hops with brief descriptions regarding alpha acid content (bitterness), stability (perishability), origin, and miscellaneous comments. Often the name of a hop indicates both the region where it is grown and the variety. For example, Czech Saaz would indicate that the variety is Saaz and the country in which it was grown was the Czech Republic. Similarly Hersbrucker Hallertau would indicate Hallertau hops grown in the Hersbrucker region of Germany; Kent Goldings, Goldings hops grown in Kent, England.

There are various methods that brewing scientists and hop growers use to determine the "percent alpha acid." Some methods will give higher numbers than others. It is important to know which method to use if you are brewing commercial batches of beer and consistency is important. For the homebrewer these differences do not drastically affect the overall quality of small-batch brewing because there are so many other variables in homebrewing systems that also affect the final bitterness contributed. For a matter of consistency the ASBC (American Society of Brewing Chemists) methods reflect the percent alpha acid range in the Hop Variety Guide chart.

REMEMBER: Whole hops are like flowers that come from plants. Their average alpha acid content as delineated in this chart is a generalization and will vary from year to year, crop to crop, and with handling. Your source for hops should be able to obtain accurate information about the hops that are being offered. A rating of 2 to 4 percent alpha acid content indicates very low bittering value; 4 to $5\frac{1}{2}$ percent alpha acid content indicates low bittering values; $5\frac{1}{2}$ to 9 percent alpha acid indicates an assertive medium range of bitterness; while 9 to 15-plus percent alpha acid indicates a very powerful bittering value—with these hops, be careful not to overhop in the boil!

## Nobility and Naming Rights of Hops

Worldwide there are several hundred varieties of commercially grown and available hops. During research and development, there are tens of thousands of hop hybrids under observation and consideration. So who gets naming rights? If they are privately bred and developed, hop varieties often get trademarked names. If the hybrids are developed with government funding, names are chosen by the government-funded breeding project and the breed is made available to all farmers. But there are a few particular varieties of hops that are somewhat sacred: the original "Noble Hops."

What are Noble Hops? There are only five varieties of hops that are considered "noble" and they're only considered "noble" if grown in their own region. They are Hallertauer Hallertau, Spalter Spalt, Tettnanger Tettnang, Hersbrucker Hersbruck, and (Czech) Saazer Saaz. These five varieties are considered "original" breeds and they have been grown for a long time. The first part of the name is the region in which the hop is grown and the second part is the name of the hop. For example Hallertauer Hallertau represents Hallertauer as the region and Hallertau as the actual name of the hop. If a Hersbruck hop were grown in the Hallertauer region, it would be called Hallertauer Hersbruck, but would not be considered a Noble Hop. Most other varieties of German-grown hops are either hybrids of German hops or hops of other national origins.

All five Noble Hops are considered "flavor/aroma" hops. They are relatively low in bitterness compared to hybrids that are grown for higher yields and higher bittering values. Hops that are flavor/aroma or bittering varieties can be used in any manner the brewer chooses. In other words, a "flavor/aroma" hops can be used to bitter a beer, and likewise a "bittering" hop can be used for flavor and/or aroma.

In the United States, generally speaking, if the varietal description is only one word, it's grown in the United States. If the first of two words is a country or region, then of course the hops should have been grown in that region.

It need not be mentioned that varieties of hops have their own unique characters. Furthermore, where hops are grown also has a huge impact on quality, flavor, and aroma. The amount of sunlight, humidity, soil type, and temperature, as well as picking method and time and drying and storage methods further impact hop qualities. All these variables offer distinctive choices to brewers worldwide.

The stability rating in the chart lets you know how much care hops need. Ratings of "Poor" or "Fair" indicate the importance of refrigeration/freezing or proper packaging; hops are capable of losing 50 percent of their brewing value within 2 to 3 weeks at room temperature. "Good" or "Very Good" stability indicates that these hops will last a very long time with proper packaging.

As I've mentioned, there are no set rules for using hops. Any variety may be used as a bittering hop in both ales and lagers; likewise, any variety of hop may be used for flavor and aroma (finishing hop). Generally the higher the alpha acid content of the hop, the more aggressive and sharp the perception of bitterness

# Hop Variety Guide

See important notes at the end of the guide on page 87.

## American-Bred Hops Often with Floral-Citrus-Like Character

| VARIETY | AVERAGE ALPHA ACID CONTENT (PERCENT) BASED ON ASBC METHOD* | STABILITY OF WHOLE HOPS† | ORIGIN | COMMENTS |
|---|---|---|---|---|
| Amarillo | 8–10 | Good | USA | A Cascade-type hop; citrusy, floral. Popular in American pale ales, especially IPA and barley wines, but popular in several other types of beer. |
| Cascade | 4.5–7.5 | Fair | USA | Very popular American all-purpose bittering and aroma hop. Floral and citrusy character. |
| Centennial | 9–11.5 | Fair | USA | "Supercharged" Cascade type; fine aroma hop, citrusy. Popular in American pale ales, especially IPA. |
| Chinook | 12–14 | Fair | USA | Intense bittering hop with excellent citrus, floral character. American hoppy ales. |
| Citra | 11–13 | Fair | USA | Good bittering hop but best used in late hopping for aroma and flavor. Grapefruit/citrus with some passion fruit character. |

| VARIETY | AVERAGE ALPHA ACID CONTENT (PERCENT) BASED ON ASBC METHOD* | STABILITY OF WHOLE HOPS† | ORIGIN | COMMENTS |
|---|---|---|---|---|
| Delta | 5.5–7 | Very good | USA | Hybrid of Cascade and Fuggle. Relatively mild with spicy and citrus flavor/aroma character. Similar to U.S. Fuggles, Willamette. |
| Galena | 12–14 | Fair to Good | USA | Very good bittering hop. A bit more floral than other high alpha hops. |
| Horizon | 11–13.5 | Fair to Good | USA | Very good hop for bittering and flavor/aroma; floral/spicy. |
| Sorachi Ace™ | 12–14 | Good | USA | Nonaggressive bittering as well as a good flavor/aroma hop. |
| *High Alpha Bittering Hops, Many with Excellent Flavor and Aroma Qualities* | | | | |
| Apollo | 15–19 | Very good | USA | Late/finishing hopping - grapefruit+ ; similar to Nugget, CTZ. |
| Bravo | 14–17 | Fair | USA | Fruity, floral flavor and aroma; as bittering hop, similar to CTZ. |
| Chelan | 12–14.5 | Good | USA | Similar to Galena as bittering. |

(continued)

## Hop Variety Guide

| VARIETY | AVERAGE ALPHA ACID CONTENT (PERCENT) BASED ON ASBC METHOD* | STABILITY OF WHOLE HOPS† | ORIGIN | COMMENTS |
|---|---|---|---|---|
| Columbus/ Tomahawk™/ Zeus (CTZ) | 14–18 | Fair to Poor | USA | Intense bittering hop with assertive and distinctive flavor and aroma; sulfurlike earthy and very pleasing. Popular IPA hop. |
| Galaxy | 13.5–15 | Info not found | Australia | Distinctive citrus + passion/tropical fruit characters, especially when used as flavor and aroma hop. |
| Magnum | 12–14 | Very good | USA, Germany | Popular and one of the most mellow high alpha hops lending itself to less aggressive perception of bitterness. |
| Mosaic | 11.5–13.5 | Very good | USA, Germany | Hybrid hop; Simcoe mother and Nugget father. |
| Nelson Sauvin | 12–13 | Info not found | New Zealand | Distinctly strong passion fruit and winey sauvignon aromas, especially with late hopping for flavor and aroma quality. Excellent for dry hopping. |
| Newport | 13.5–17 | Fair | USA | Hallertau-grown Magnum is the mother; similar to Magnum, Galena, Nugget. |

| VARIETY | AVERAGE ALPHA ACID CONTENT (PERCENT) BASED ON ASBC METHOD* | STABILITY OF WHOLE HOPS† | ORIGIN | COMMENTS |
|---|---|---|---|---|
| Nugget | 12–14 | Good | USA | An aggressive bittering hop with moderate herbal aroma. |
| Pacific Gem (New Zealand) | 11–15 | Fair to Poor | New Zealand | High alpha hop popular in New Zealand for bitterness. Known to have delicate blackberry and floral oak character. |
| Pride of Ringwood | 7–10 | Poor | Australia | High alpha hop. Quite assertive in bitterness. Not recommended as flavor or aroma hop. |
| Simcoe™ | 12–14 | Good | USA | Nonaggressive bittering as well as a good flavor/aroma hop. Distinctive flavor and aroma; sulfurlike earthy and very pleasing. Popular IPA hop. |
| Summit | 16–19 | Good | USA | Can contribute sulfur compound character similar to onions, garlic, also pleasant spicy, earthy grapefruit citrus. Skillful use required. |
| Tillicum | 12–14.5 | Good | USA | Similar to Galena, Chelan. |
| Warrior™ | 16–20 | Good | USA | Aggressive bittering hop with acceptable aroma and low Co-Humulone content. |

(continued)

# Hop Variety Guide

## Goldings, Fuggles, Hybrids of or Traditional English Ale Hops

| VARIETY | AVERAGE ALPHA ACID CONTENT (PERCENT) BASED ON ASBC METHOD* | STABILITY OF WHOLE HOPS† | ORIGIN | COMMENTS |
|---|---|---|---|---|
| Admiral | 13.5–16.2 | Info not found | UK | Neutral UK bittering hop. |
| Bramling Cross | 5–7 | Info not found | UK | Particularly spicy with black currant aroma, used as a late finish hop. |
| Challenger | 6.5–9 | Good | UK | Traditional English ale dual-purpose bittering and flavor hop; related to Northern Brewer. |
| First Gold | 6–9.5 | Fair to Good | UK | Similar to Goldings but with higher bittering value. Not common. Very good all-purpose hop for English ales. |
| Fuggles | 3.5–6 | Good | USA, UK | English Fuggles has seed content. Excellent traditional English ale hop. Excellent aroma and flavor. |
| Glacier | 5.5–7.5 | Fair to Good | USA | Character is a combination of Fuggles and Willamette. Good all-around hop. |

| VARIETY | AVERAGE ALPHA ACID CONTENT (PERCENT) BASED ON ASBC METHOD* | STABILITY OF WHOLE HOPS† | ORIGIN | COMMENTS |
|---|---|---|---|---|
| Goldings | 4–7 | Fair to Good | USA, UK (Kent), Slovenia (Styrian—see Fuggles) | Character varies greatly depending on where it is grown. USA: Earthy overtones are largely absent, but a good mellow all-around hop. UK: East Kent grown considered premium pale ale hop—earthy and very desirable contribution to light ale character. Styrian: Actually a Fuggle grown in Slovenia |
| Northdown | 7.5–10.5 | Good | UK | Good English ale bittering hop. Acceptable flavor hop. |
| Palisade™ | 5.5–9.5 | Good | USA | Some floral/fruity; earthy flavors/aroma. Similar to Willamette. |
| Progress | 6.5–7.5 | Good | UK | Less commonly available. Robust hop aroma with moderate bittering. Traditional for English ales. |
| Target | 10.5–13.5 | Fair to Poor | UK, Belgium, Germany | English ale hop primarily used for bittering; acceptable "English" aroma hop. |

(continued)

# Hop Variety Guide

| VARIETY | AVERAGE ALPHA ACID CONTENT (PERCENT) BASED ON ASBC METHOD* | STABILITY OF WHOLE HOPS† | ORIGIN | COMMENTS |
|---|---|---|---|---|
| WGV (Whitbread Goldings Variety) | 5–8 | Info not found | UK | Mild bitterness; aroma sweet, with herbal English character. |
| Willamette | 4–6 | Fair | USA | A hybrid of Fuggle, but more floral and citruslike than English Fuggles; ale or lager. |
| German "Noble Hops": Hallertauer, Hersbrucker, Tettnanger, Spalter, or Hybrids of | | | | |
| Crystal | 3.5–5.5 | Poor | USA | A U.S. Hallertauer hybrid with excellent European hop flavor and floral/spicy aroma. |
| German Tradition | 5–7 | Very Good | Germany | Similar to a German Hallertauer but with a higher alpha acid content. |
| Hallertau | 3.5–5.5 | Fair to Poor | Germany, USA, New Zealand | Flavor and aroma vary tremendously depending on where grown. Germany: wonderful earthy tones. USA: relatively neutral flavor and aroma, yet quite acceptable for traditional lagers—mild/floral/spicy. New Zealand: all organic—very sweet, floral, and berrylike; not a true Hallertauer/unlike classic European Hallertauer. |

| VARIETY | AVERAGE ALPHA ACID CONTENT (PERCENT) BASED ON ASBC METHOD* | STABILITY OF WHOLE HOPS† | ORIGIN | COMMENTS |
|---|---|---|---|---|
| Hersbruck | 2.5–5.5 | Fair to Poor | Germany | Regional variety of Hallertauer. Wonderful, classic flavor/aroma hop. Earthy and sweet–floral. |
| Liberty | 3–5 | Fair | USA | U.S. Hallertauer hybrid. Distinctive good flavor and aroma hop. |
| Mittelfrueh | 3.5–5 | Poor | USA, Germany | A classic type of Hallertauer hop; herbal, spicy, earthy, sweet–floral. German lagers. |
| Mt. Hood | 4.5–8 | Poor | USA | A U.S. Hallertauer hybrid. Very good flavor and aroma hop for lagers. Less herbal than German Hallertauer. |
| Opal | 5–8 | Fair | Germany | Known to be fruity, floral and/or herbal in character with late hopping. Smooth bitterness. |
| Santiam | 5–7 | Fair | USA | A Tettnanger hybrid with excellent sweet and floral flavor and aroma. Similar to German Tett. Great for lagers. |
| Saphir | 3.5–5 | Fair | Germany | Earthy, herbal and sweet floral notes in aroma and flavor. Excellent qualities. Can be assertive in bitterness if overdone. |

(continued)

## Hop Variety Guide

| VARIETY | AVERAGE ALPHA ACID CONTENT (PERCENT) BASED ON ASBC METHOD* | STABILITY OF WHOLE HOPS† | ORIGIN | COMMENTS |
|---|---|---|---|---|
| Smaragd (Emerald) | 4–6 | Fair | Germany | Herbal and floral as a late hop addition. |
| Spalt Classic | 4–5 | Poor | Germany | Similar to Spalt Select; mild, slightly spicy. |
| Spalt (German) Select | 3.5–5.5 | Good | USA, Germany | Traditional German lager-style hop for bittering, flavor, and aroma. Similar to Saaz and Tettnang. |
| Strisselspalt | 3–5 | Fair to Good | France | Similar to a German Hersbrucker hop; earthy with a sweet floral and slight citrus character; non-aggressive bitterness. |
| Tettnang | 3–5 | Fair to Poor | USA, Germany | USA: mild and sweetly floral almost honeylike. Flavor/aroma hop. Germany: herbal, spicy. |
| Ultra | 2–3.5 | Good | USA | Sister of Mt. Hood. Similar to Liberty and Crystal hops. |

| VARIETY | AVERAGE ALPHA ACID CONTENT (PERCENT) BASED ON ASBC METHOD* | STABILITY OF WHOLE HOPS† | ORIGIN | COMMENTS |
|---|---|---|---|---|
| Vanguard | 5–6 | Good | USA | Midrange alpha acid. Good all-around hop similar to U.S. Hallertauer. |
| *Saaz or Hybrids of* | | | | |
| Lublin | 3–5 | Poor | Poland | Saaz-type hop grown in Poland. Very favorable character for pilseners. |
| Saaz | 3–5 | Poor | USA, Czech Republic | Flavor and aroma commonly referred to as "herbal/spicy." A great "soft" bittering hop, with excellent flavor and aroma character for classic pilsener lager. |
| Sterling | 4.5–7.5 | Good | USA | A combination of Saaz and Mt. Hood character. Excellent flavor and aroma hop. |
| *Traditional Hops Used Interchangeably in Lagers and Ales* | | | | |
| Brewers Gold | 5.5–7 | Fair | Germany | Traditional ale hop and full-bodied lagers. |

(continued)

## Hop Variety Guide

| VARIETY | AVERAGE ALPHA ACID CONTENT (PERCENT) BASED ON ASBC METHOD* | STABILITY OF WHOLE HOPS† | ORIGIN | COMMENTS |
|---|---|---|---|---|
| Northern Brewer | 6.5–10 | Good | USA, Germany, UK | Very good hop for both lagers and ales. Generally a bittering hop. U.S. crop usually on the low end alpha range. |
| Perle | 7–10 | Excellent to Good | USA, Germany | Versatile as a high alpha flavor hop; similar to Northern Brewer. |
| **Other Hops Used in Brewing Ales and Lagers** | | | | |
| Ahtanum | 5.5–6.5 | Fair to Good | USA | Relatively new aroma and mild bittering hop. |
| Bullion | 6.5–9 | Poor | USA | Old cultivar popular in former times, less commonly used today, may or may not be available in future. Found in many old brewing recipes. Good bittering hop, but not preferred for its aroma or flavor. Brewers Gold is a good substitute. |
| Cluster | 5.5–8.5 | Excellent | USA | Once the most popular heritage bittering hop; now not a very popular aroma and flavor character. |

| VARIETY | AVERAGE ALPHA ACID CONTENT (PERCENT) BASED ON ASBC METHOD* | STABILITY OF WHOLE HOPS[†] | ORIGIN | COMMENTS |
|---|---|---|---|---|
| Millennium | Very high | Good | USA | Grown mostly for producing hop extract; not generally available to homebrewers. |
| Mouteka | 6.58–7.5 | | New Zealand | Lemon/lime citrus, passion fruit, mango character likely emerges if used as flavor/aroma hop. |
| Riwaka | 4.5–6.5 | | New Zealand | Said to have a very distinctive and strong grapefruit character as flavor/aroma hop. |
| Wild Hops | 2–7 | Varies | Wild | If they smell good use them. Dry, cold storage and use in small batches if quality is doubtful. |

*ASBC Method refers to Method of Analysis by the American Society of Brewing Chemists.

[†]About stability: Stability is influenced by crop, weather, storage, harvest time, compression, drying methods, and other factors. These ratings are generalized guidelines only for whole compressed hops. These ratings are not applicable to pelletized hops because they are all very stable. Very good: 90% of bitterness remains after 4 months of storage at 70 degrees F (21 C); Good: 80–90%; Fair: 60–80%; Poor: less than 60% and some will suffer dramatic loss within a month. NOTE: Stability of whole compressed hops is extended when stored at cold or freezing temperatures and in an oxygen-free environment.

will be. Lower alpha hops when used on an equal bitterness unit basis will lend a "softer" perception to the bitterness. This is an important generality for home-brewers who desire hop flavor, aroma, and nonaggressive bitterness in their beer.

The "no rule" statement is especially true for homebrewers, though it should be recognized that certain varieties of hops are used to impart distinctive types of bitterness, flavors, and aromas to traditional styles of lagers and ales. The chart offers some comments on traditional uses of each variety, but feel free to experiment on your own.

Both low and very high alpha acid hops can be used in late and dry hopping and can contribute many types of flavor and aroma to beer without an aggressive increase in hop-induced bitterness. For more hop insight, detail, and information on flavor and hop aroma, see *The Homebrewer's Companion, Second Edition*.

Some informative hop-oriented Websites include:

www.hopunion.com, www.yakimachief.com, www.freshops.com, www.nzhops.co.nz, www.hopsteiner.com, www.barthhaasgroup.com, www.hopsfromengland.com, www.indiehops.com.

For more information, see the "Advanced Homebrewing and Hops" section that starts on page 301 and the "Hops" section of *The Homebrewer's Companion, Second Edition*.

Many classic styles of beer in the world lay claim to the use of special hops, but hops alone do not make for the duplication of a classic style of beer. It is a combination of all of the other ingredients, brewing style, and attitude that truly makes for distinctive and world-classic beers—and your homebrew.

As a homebrewer, your affair with hops should be an enjoyable one. If there is ever any doubt in your mind, remember: *Relax. Don't worry. Have a homebrew.*

## WATER

Beer is 90 to 95 percent water. The flavor and mineral content of water is important in the brewing of beer. However, the importance of water is relative to all of the other ingredients and processes that are involved with the brewing of quality beer. The best brewing water in the world cannot make good beer without good malt, yeast, sanitation, and brewing attitudes.

Water and its properties interact with every process of beermaking; malting, mashing, boiling, fermentation, cleaning, and tasting all derive their efficiency and character, in part, from the water that is used. The chemistry of water and its interaction with the brewing process can become quite involved. But as a homebrewer you don't need a degree in organic chemistry to appreciate its value in brewing.

If the water you use for brewing tastes good and is considered suitable for drinking in the United States, then there is only one thing you as a beginner or intermediate brewer might consider doing to improve it. Some municipal water supplies have chlorine content that is excessive for brewing the absolute best beer. Using an under-the-counter or countertop activated-charcoal-type water filter will remove chlorine. You can also consider boiling your water before brewing to rid the water of free available chlorine, thus minimizing the reactions between chlorine and beer ingredients that can result in a perceptible harshness in flavor and aroma.

The addition of minerals to your brewing water for malt extract brewing is a very minor consideration compared to the importance of sanitation and quality brewing ingredients.

## What Determines Water Quality?

Water quality is determined by its flavor, its suitability for human consumption, and the related organic and mineral content. Potable and good-tasting water is almost always suitable for use in homebrewing of malt extract beers; however, it is the mineral content that determines ideal suitability in many phases of the brewing process.

Chemically, water is measured in terms of its hardness (or softness) and acidity or alkalinity—pH or parts per million (ppm) of certain minerals.

Some of the more common brewing "salts" (minerals) that are added or measured in brewing water are calcium sulfate ($CaSO_4$, commonly known as gypsum) and sodium chloride (common salt, $NaCl$). When these or any mineral salts are dissolved in water they go through a process called dissociation, that is, the calcium (ion) separates itself from the sulfate ($SO_4$) ion; likewise, the sodium ion separates itself from the chloride ion. The presence of each of these ions or any other ion will not only contribute characteristic flavors to the beer but may have the potential to react with other minerals and ions that are present in the other beer ingredients.

## How Does Water Quality Influence the Brewing Process?

Let it suffice, here, to say that the most important mineral reactions in the brewing process occur during the mash, when the enzymes convert starches to fermentable sugars. Understanding water chemistry becomes important in the brewing of all-grain beers. A discussion of all-grain brewing and related water chemistry will come later in this book and is discussed in more detail in the *The Homebrewer's Companion, Second Edition*.

For a malt-extract homebrewer, all of the mashing reactions have taken place and the addition of minerals is unnecessary. *In fact the minerals that the malt extract manufacturer may add in its mashing process remain in the malt extract.*

For the malt-extract homebrewer, the only mineral ions that contribute significantly to the brewing process are the ions of gypsum ($CaSO_4$) and common salt (NaCl). The calcium ion will help the clarification process during fermentation; the yeast will more easily sediment. Also, calcium ions will aid in removing proteins, tannins, and husk flavors from the boiling wort, which, if not removed to some degree, will lend a haze as well as a harsher flavor to the finished beer. Sulfates ($SO_4$) will lend a dry, crisp palate to the finished beer.

However, if sulfates are added in excess, poor hop utilization will result (bitterness will not easily be extracted). Also, in extraordinary and unpalatable excess, a harsh, salty, and laxative nature will characterize the finished beer. The sodium ion (Na) will contribute to the perceived flavor of beer by enhancing other flavors. In excess, it will contribute to a harsh, sour, or metallic flavor. Chlorides (Cl) will tend to lend a soft, round, full, sweet flavor to beer.

Any mineral in excess will ruin your beer. As a general rule, all of these minerals are present in malt extracts and to varying degrees in your own water source (information about the contents of your drinking water is usually available at no cost from your local water department). The addition of these minerals to any great degree is not necessary. As a matter of fact, when brewing with malt extracts, distilled or deionized (mineral-free) water is perfectly suitable for brewing.

If you do choose to add gypsum or salt to your water, do so knowing the original mineral content of your water. For water that has very little mineral content (soft), the addition of 1 to 4 teaspoons (4 to 16 g) of gypsum per 5 gallons (19 l) is within reason. The addition of salt should not exceed ½ teaspoon (2.5 g) per 5 gallons (19 l).

## Advanced Water Chemistry and Duplication of World-Classic Brewing Waters

Water chemistry begins to get very complex when minerals begin to react with each other and the other ingredients that are used in the brewing process; consequently, not only are the hardness, acidity, and alkalinity actively affected by brewing ingredients, but the actual mineral content fluctuates as well. The possible outcomes are characterized by terms such as *permanent* and *temporary hardness*, and *permanent* and *temporary alkalinity*, expressed in terms of parts per million of certain minerals or a measurement of pH, respectively.

Adding your own minerals to achieve a desired effect is complicated and requires an effort on your part to understand the chemistry of water. You are only asking for problems by simply following water recipes without at least having a feel for what reactions are taking place. You don't need to be an expert. Learning the fundamentals of brewing chemistry is not an unreasonable challenge if you have the desire. A more involved section on brewing water is presented in this book's "Advanced Homebrewing and Water" section (page 304) and the "Water" section of *The Homebrewer's Companion, Second Edition*.

## YEAST

The type of yeast that you use in brewing is as important as any other ingredient in your beer. Yeast is biologically classified as a fungus. It is a living microbiological organism, metabolizing, reproducing, and living off the ingredients and breathing off the conditions that you have concocted in order to make beer. Yeast is the thing that finally determines what the flavor of the beer will be.

There are literally hundreds of varieties and strains of yeasts. They are present everywhere as "wild yeast." Only cultivated strains of beer yeast should (normally) be used in the brewing of beer. If other strains or wild yeasts contaminate your beer, the result will often be strange flavors, gushing, overcarbonation, haze formation, and all kinds of unexplainable fermentation characteristics.

Exceptions? Yes, there are always exceptions, and wild yeasts can be introduced into certain types of fermentation to create unusual, "wild," sour, "funky," eccentric, and "innovative" beer. Sometimes brewers (including yourself) may want to introduce commercially available unusual yeasts and souring bacteria. These microcritters can create varying degrees of acidity, flavors, and aromas often described as wild yeast and/or bacterial character. Brewers can also introduce their own "captured" wild yeasts (and bacteria) from used wooden barrels and yeast sediment in bottles of "wild" beer. The really adventurous expose—literally—their fermentation to the winds of nature in their own backyard, usually with unpredictable results, sometimes favorable and sometimes not. But these are not the yeasts used to make traditional German, British, or American styles of beer.

## What Are the Main Types of Beer Yeast?

There are two main types of beer yeast that are used by brewers. They are classified as *ale yeast* ("top-fermenting" type, *Saccharomyces cerevisiae*) or *lager yeast* ("bottom-fermenting" type, *Saccharomyces uvarum*, formerly known as *Saccharomyces carlsbergensis*). These two varieties of beer yeast are further broken down into categories of specific strains. In the world of brewing today there are hundreds of strains of both ale and lager yeasts, all of which will offer variety to the finished beer.

## Varieties of Yeasts and Concerns of the Homebrewer

You can make absolutely excellent beer at room temperatures from either ale yeast or lager yeast. Understanding some basic principles of yeast behavior will help you answer some of the questions arising when using different yeasts.

*Ale yeast* is a variety of yeast that is best used in fermentations and bottling conditioning at temperature ranges of 55 to 75 degrees F (13 to 24 C). Lower temperatures tend to inhibit fermentation; some strains will not actively ferment below 50 degrees F (10 C). Some strains of ale yeast exhibit a tendency to flocculate (gather) at the surface of the fermenting beer during the first few days of fermentation; that is why the term *top-fermenting* is associated with all ale yeasts. Eventually, ale yeast will settle and create sediment on the bottom of the fermenter. Fermentation by ale yeasts at these relatively warmer temperatures produces a beer that many regard as having a distinctive ale character. It should be remembered that other ingredients play an equally important role in the flavor of ale.

*Lager yeast* is a variety of yeast that is best used at temperatures ranging from an initial 55 degrees F (13 C) down to 32 degrees F (0 C). Beer can be fermented by lager yeasts at warmer, alelike temperatures with very good results; however, the desired traditional "smoothness" of lager beers can only be achieved with lagering at temperatures usually below 45 degrees F (7 C) for anywhere from three weeks to many months. Some strains of lager yeast are better than others at producing acceptable lagerlike character at warmer fermentations. The final flavor of the beer will depend a great deal on the strain of lager yeast and the temperatures at which it was fermented. All strains of lager yeast will flocculate and then settle as sediment to the bottom of the fermenting vessel; that is why they are called bottom-fermenting yeasts.

## Where Can Good Brewing Yeasts Be Found and How Are They Packaged?

Good beer yeasts can be found at any homebrew supply shop.

Most beer yeasts used by homebrewers come in the form of dried or liquid yeast cultures. Dried yeast is packaged in sealed foil packages. Liquid cultures are widely available in refrigerated vials or special packaging and are very popular and easy to use. There are hundreds of quality yeast strains available to homebrewers. Quality yeast makes quality beer. Numerous strains of both lager and ale yeasts are available from several companies.

The advantages of dried beer yeast are that it is simple to use, usually very active, and foolproof. The quality of certain brand names of dried lager and ale yeasts has improved dramatically in the last decade, offering convenience, but relatively limited choice. Consult your local homebrew supply shop for up-to-date assessments and what is popular in your area.

One can significantly maximize the performance of dried yeasts (and consequently the flavor of your beer) by properly rehydrating it. Do this by boiling 1½ cups (355 ml) of water for 5 to 10 minutes, pour into a sanitized glass jar (washed and boiled for about 15 minutes), cover with clean foil, and let cool to 100 to 105 degrees F (38 to 41 C). Do not add any sugars. Add dried yeast and let it rehydrate for 15 to 20 minutes, and then bring the temperature of the rehydrated yeast close to that of the wort and pitch.

True cultures of dried lager yeasts were once very hard to find because of the difficulty in packaging and maintaining the true lagering characteristics. Homebrewers used to have to determine whether or not the dried lager yeast would ferment at low temperatures and experiment and observe. Because small brewers demanded better quality, modern manufacturing techniques now produce quality dried ale and lager yeast. Use only dependable name brands of dried lager yeast that your homebrew supply shop recommends. If you find that fermentation is not active at lower temperatures, then you are doomed to ferment those dried lager yeasts at room temperature or use the more dependable liquid lager yeast cultures. The brand Saflager is one example of true dried lager yeast.

Most lager yeasts can dependably be propagated from liquid cultures. Their use and care are more involved than the simplicity of using very active dried beer yeast. More about liquid yeasts and their culture is discussed later in this book in "Culturing Yeast or Yeast Herding" on page 310. A more thorough discussion on yeast can be found in the "Yeast" section of *The Homebrewer's Companion, Second Edition*.

Fermentation and the behavior of yeasts is a most interesting part of beer brewing. Remember that yeast is a living microorganism that may be as temperamental as you are. Understanding what makes yeast do its thing will help make your beer better, because it appreciates knowing that you care.

# TRADITIONAL AND INNOVATIVE INGREDIENTS USED BY HOMEBREWERS

## SUGARS

Sugar is the ingredient in beer that lends sweetness to the finished product or becomes fermented by yeasts into alcohol, carbon dioxide, and the flavor of beer. There are many, many different kinds of sugar that can be introduced into the brewer's wort. Some are naturally introduced with malted barley or other grains, while others may be introduced as an adjunct by the brewer for economic rea-

sons or to achieve some very distinctive flavor characteristics.

Sugars are scientifically classified by names such as sucrose, glucose, maltose, etc., according to their molecular configuration. The sources of sugar are very numerous; for example, sucrose is naturally present in malt, honey, maple syrup, molasses, corn syrup, and more.

In order to help you understand the classifications of sugar and the forms that they take, let's look at the basic molecules of sugar.

Sugars are made from various configurations of carbon, hydrogen, and oxygen atoms. The general configuration of these atoms is called a carbohydrate. The way these carbohydrates are linked determines the type of sugar.

The sugars homebrewers encounter most often are dextrose, fructose, glucose, lactose, maltose, and sucrose. These sugars are often derived naturally from malt or other starches. Another kind of carbohydrate, starch, is long chains of sugar molecules linked together by chemical bonds. The chemical bonds of starch can be broken by enzymes and chemical reactions, thus reducing the long carbohydrate chains of starch to shorter chains of sugar.

Are you still with me? It is helpful to know that some sugars are sweeter than others; likewise some sugars are more easily fermented by yeast and others are not fermentable at all. Although there are dozens of types of sugars involved in the brewing process, some are more significant than others. Following are sweet and short descriptions of the main types of sugars most often encountered by homebrewers. Their availability is discussed later.

## Classifications of Sugars

*Dextrose*—See "Glucose."

*Fructose* (or *levulose*)—Fructose is one of the most rapidly fermentable sugars. It is also the sweetest tasting. Besides occurring naturally in malt and fruit, it may be derived from a variety of starches and processed to a syrup form. The term *high-fructose syrup* does not mean 100 percent fructose, rather more likely a combination of 40 percent fructose and 60 percent glucose and other sugars. Fructose crystals are derived from cane or beet sugar.

*Glucose* (or *dextrose*)—Glucose is another very rapidly fermentable sugar. As a purchasable form of sugar it has usually been derived from starch. It can be processed into chips, crystals, or syrups. The name "dextrose" is an industrial term for glucose. Glucose and dextrose are molecularly one and the same. The distinction is that dextrose is glucose that has been derived from a chemical conversion of starch (usually corn) to sugar. Dextrose is often referred to as "corn sugar."

*Lactose*—Lactose is a sugar that is not fermentable by beer yeast (it is fermentable by certain types of wild yeasts). It is derived from milk and can be bought as crystals. Its flavor is minimally sweet.

*Maltose*—Maltose is fermentable by beer yeasts but relatively more slowly than are sucrose, glucose, and fructose. It occurs naturally in malt, as well as in a wide variety of other natural sweeteners. It consists of two glucose molecules linked together.

*Sucrose* (and *invert*)—Sucrose is rapidly fermentable by beer yeasts. It occurs naturally in malt. Commercially it is available in crystalline form, usually as common white table sugar. Invert sugar is a type of sugar that is made from an acid treatment of sucrose. The name "invert" refers to the optical effect that a solution of invert sugar has on light.
Like sucrose, invert sugar is a combination of one glucose and one fructose molecule. Pure invert sugar is as fermentable as sucrose; but because of byproducts that are produced during the acid treatment, invert sugar may be 5 to 10 percent less fermentable than sucrose and can contribute unusual (both desirable and undesirable) flavor characteristics.

## Availability and Use of Various Sugars in Homebrewing

### White Sugars

*Candi sugar*—Used by Belgian brewers in several traditional strong ales, Candi sugar is nothing more than slowly crystallized pure sucrose. The crystals are large and clear, coming in white, amber, and brown colors. The darker colors are the crystallization of caramelized sugar and add a degree of flavor to beer. These sugars are commonly used to lighten the body of stronger beers while producing more alcoholic strength.

*Cane and beet sugars*—These common white table sugars are nearly 100 percent sucrose. There is virtually no difference between pure grades of beet and cane sugars. Impure grades can lend distinctively unpleasant flavors to beer. In homebrewing they may be used for economy, to boost the alcohol content or to lighten the flavor and body of the beer. If cane or beet sugar is used in excess of 20 percent of the fermentable sugar, a characteristic "cidery" flavor may develop. The selection of certain strains of yeast or controlling fermentation conditions can help reduce these "cidery" characters. The addition of white sugar is not generally recommended unless a lighter-bodied beer is desired or an effort is being made to "brighten" the character of hops.

Cane or beet sugar may be converted to invert (sucrose) sugar by boiling in water with a small amount of citric acid; however, this process is unlikely to eliminate the flavor associated with the excessive addition of sucrose and is a needless process. If sugar is something you want to add to your beer, use corn sugar (dextrose, glucose). The partial or complete inversion of sucrose may occur while being boiled in the naturally acidic wort of malt extract.

For sanitation purposes all common white table sugars should be boiled in water or in the wort.

*Corn sugar*—Corn sugar is a commonly used sugar "adjunct" in homebrewing. Processed from refined corn, it is referred to as dextrose; technically it is more accurately classified as glucose and is readily fermentable. Purer grades of corn sugar should be used by the homebrewer. Corn sugar can be easily bought at any homebrew supply store.

The addition of corn sugar to homebrew recipes will lighten the body and flavor of the beer and at the same time contribute to the alcohol content. Its use in excess of 20 percent of the total fermentable sugars will often contribute to the flavor characteristic of the finished beer, lending what most homebrewers will refer to as a dry "cidery" flavor. While some desire this character, it does not contribute to a true malt beer character. Its use, although economical, should be carefully considered by the homebrewer who values the time spent brewing and waiting for beer to mature and be fully enjoyed.

The addition of corn sugar as a "priming" sugar at bottling or kegging time is the most versatile use of corn sugar. A ratio of ¾ cup (250 ml) of corn sugar dissolved and boiled in 1 pint (0.5 l) of water is a standard rate for 5 gallons (19 l) of beer. For kegging 5 gallons (19 l) of beer, ⅓ cup (80 ml) of sugar should be used.

In order to easily mix and prevent foaming from the addition of dry sugar, corn sugar should be boiled with wort or water before its addition to the fermenter or finished beer.

*Lactose*—Lactose can be added to fermenting or finished beer in order to achieve slight sweetness and additional body. It can be purchased at many homebrew specialty shops or health food stores as white crystals. Because it is not fermentable by beer yeasts, its character will remain unchanged. It is not a very sweet-tasting sugar; therefore its contribution to sweetness is minimal. Some commercial British breweries will add it to "sweet stouts" in order to contribute to the body of the beer. In the case of British sweet stouts, sucrose is added for sweetness to a pasteurized and conditioned (carbonated) product at bottling time.

Lactose is not easily dissolved in beer; therefore, it should be boiled with small amounts of water before its addition to the beer.

## Brown Sugars and Molasses

*Candi sugar*—See entry under "White Sugars."

*Demerara sugar*—Difficult to find in the United States, this is a popular damp, golden-amber sugar often used by homebrewers and some British breweries to add a bit of caramel-like character and lighten the body of beer.

*American light to dark brown sugars*—These American household sugars are nothing more than refined white (sucrose) table sugar with a very small amount of molasses added. Current U.S. regulations require that all cane or beet sugar be refined. The addition of brown sugar is no different from the addition of white table sugar with a small amount of molasses (see "Molasses"). Ten percent or less (of the total amount of fermentable sugar) of these types of sugars can contribute a personal touch to your homebrewed beers with favorable and interesting flavors.

Brown sugars should be boiled in wort or water before adding to the fermenter.

*Palm sugars*—The sap from certain tropical palms is collected and reduced to a crystalline cake form often yellowish in color. Often available in specialty

Asian food markets, this is the sugar that popular palm wines are made from and drunk fresh and still fermenting in the area that they are homebrewed. This sugar is not very refined and its flavor will vary depending upon the sugar's source. Its flavor contribution can be imagined from tasting it in its sugar form. It's probably fermentable with some residual body left over.

*Molasses*—Molasses syrups are the uncrystalized sugars and impurities that are removed during the refinement of sugars. They are fermentable to a variable degree, depending on the type of molasses. Their addition to beer will certainly lend a great deal of color and flavor. Because of the strong flavor associated with the unfermentable portion of molasses, its use should be limited. For example, an amount of 1 cup (355 ml) per 5 gallons (19 l) will certainly be discernible by most people. Its contribution to homebrew is likened to a rich, toffeelike and "buttery" flavor. It can contribute certain pleasantness to beer, but in excess satiates the palate and detracts from the drinkability.

There are three common grades of molasses: light, medium, and blackstrap. All molasseses contain a varying degree of aromatics that contribute to flavor. The lighter molasses contains a higher sucrose (with some fructose and glucose) content while the darker blackstrap molasses contains less sugar (about 65 percent sucrose) but more aromatics.

NOTE: Sorghum molasses is a special kind of molasses (see "Syrups: Sorghum syrup").

Molasses should be boiled with the wort or water before introducing it to fermentation. For carbonating purposes, 1 cup of molasses may be substituted for ¾ cup of corn sugar (for 5 gallons [19 l] of beer) at bottling time.

*Raw sugar* (or *turbinado*)—In the United States, raw sugar is similar in character to a very light brown sugar. A small amount of molasses contributes to its color. Its character is no different from that of cane or beet sugar.

*Rapadura (dried and crystallized sugarcane juice)*—This is a natural and unrefined sweetener popular in Brazil and now quite available in specialty food stores. It is simply dried juice squeezed from sugarcane. There are various grades, and some are quite dark and flavorful. One-half pound to 1 pound (227 to 454 g) to a 5-gallon (19 l) batch can add a pleasant caramel-toffeelike character to a pale beer.

*Date sugar*—Derived from dates, this sugar may be worth experimenting with. It is actually ground-up dried date with no further processing. I have never used it, but it should contribute uniqueness to your beer. Be aware that because it is literally ground dates it will not dissolve completely.

*Syrups*

*Agave syrup*—Agave is a succulent plant grown in the deserts of Mexico. The sweet juice from the harvested plant is condensed to form a syrup. Agave syrup used as a sweetener is derived from a different type of agave plant than what is fermented and distilled to make tequila. It contributes a slight caramel character to the flavor and aroma of beer. Agave syrup should not be added in amounts of more than 20 percent of the total amount of fermentable sugars. Homebrewers have found that sluggish or stopped fermentation occurs when an excessive amount of agave syrup is used. It is available from your local homebrew supply store by special order or sometimes in the "alternative" sweetener section of supermarkets.

*Golden syrup*—A British sucrose-based syrup that lends a butterscotch-caramel character to beer. It increases alcohol and lightens body.

*Corn syrup*—There is a wide variety of corn syrups available, ranging from "brewers-grade" to common household corn syrup. Consequently, the sugar content of these syrups will vary tremendously. Some corn syrups are highly fermentable while others leave unfermentable residual sweetness and character in the finished beer. Brewing grades of corn syrup are usually a mixture of glucose and maltose. It is difficult for the homebrewer to obtain these syrups except when already added to certain varieties of malt extracts. Household corn syrups are available in most grocery stores; however, care should be taken to read the label in order to discern the addition of flavoring (vanilla, and so on) and yeast-inhibiting preservatives, neither of which are desirable in beer. Dark household corn syrup is nothing more than the lighter variety with coloring added (usually caramel).

Corn syrups may be used in homebrewing. Depending on the type used, they will contribute to the alcohol content and various degrees of residual sweetness, flavor, and body. As with any sugar adjunct, an excess of 20 percent will detract from a real beer character.

Corn syrups should be boiled with the wort or with water before their addition to the fermentation.

*Sorghum syrup*—Sorghum is a dark, sweet syrup similar in character to molasses and sometimes called sorghum molasses. It is derived from the pressed juices of sweet sorghum grown in warmer temperate climates. Its use should be similar to molasses (see "Molasses") and it lends a unique flavor to beer.

*Maple syrup*—Yes, it can be used as a beermaking ingredient. It is mostly sucrose, water, and trace minerals. In the first edition of this book I confessed I had never used nor tasted beer made from maple syrup. Now, thanks to many readers who have shared their maple-syrup-flavored beer, I feel very confident when I say, "Yes, please do." I enjoyed the samples when maple syrup was used liberally, and only when the beer was a sweeter, fuller-flavored style did the maple flavor shine through. I'd recommend at least 1 gallon (3.8 l) (oh, how that hurt$) per 5 gallons (19 l) of beer.

I also have had the pleasure of tasting beer made from maple sap instead of water. Fantastic—the beer had a subtle woodiness to it; dry and crisp.

I'm still game and would enjoy the pleasure of tasting your maple beer should we ever have the opportunity to share a brew together.

*Rice syrup* (or *rice powder*)—Rice syrup is a combination of sugars derived from a modified natural malting process. Sugars are developed by malting a portion of rice in order to develop enzymes. This "malted" rice is added to cooked white rice with an additional amount of malted barley (necessary for the required amount of starch-converting enzymes) and allowed to undergo a mashing process by which rice starches are converted to a spectrum of sugars, including glucose and maltose. The subsequent sweet mash is processed to a syrup much the same way as malt extract would be.

Rice syrup is available at many homebrew supply shops and some health food stores. It can be used in brewing lighter-flavored American-style lager beers. Rice powder is completely evaporated rice syrup.

*Treacle*—Treacle is British-style molasses, and has a tendency to taste a bit like butterscotch-caramel. It is sometimes used in specialty dark ales.

### Honey

Honey is in a class of sugar by itself and should not be ignored for use by the homebrewer. Its contribution to the flavor of homebrew is wonderfully unique. Many an award-winning flavorful beer has been made with a combination of malts and honey.

There are dozens of sugars that are found in honey. Glucose and fructose are present in the most significant amounts, with traces of sucrose and maltose attributable for less than 5 percent. The "stuff" of honey is not only sugar but a variety of sugar-ripening enzymes (secreted by the bees), wild yeast spores, pollen, beeswax, water (usually less than 17 percent in order to inhibit fermentation), bees' legs, antennae, stingers, eyebrows, and various other body parts.

Honey is derived from the nectar of flowers, processed and ripened by honeybees. Because the source of nectar can vary, so does the honey. There are hundreds of varieties of honey. The color, aroma, and flavor are the most recognizable differences.

For beermaking purposes, lighter honeys such as clover and alfalfa are often considered to be safe choices because of the minimal contribution of unusually strong flavors. If you are "honey-smart" and know your honey, some prized honeys can really "up" the finesse and quality of your homebrew. The floral character of orange blossom honey, the desert aroma of mesquite honey, the deep and dark character of buckwheat honey, the super floral romance of linden honey, and many other varietals all can be excellent choices.

Honey has a high degree of fermentability and subtly pleasant fermented flavor. It can contribute to a dry crispness, lighter body, and a high alcohol content without the off-flavors associated with refined white sugars. In order to maintain real beer character, it should be used in amounts of less than 30 percent. Amounts greater than this are not unpleasant but do detract from what might be considered a traditional beer flavor.

It should be noted that honey lacks yeast nutrients, yet the addition of nutrients is not necessary if honey is combined with malt extract. Barley malt will provide adequate nutrients for healthy fermentation.

Because of the presence of extraneous matter (beeswax, body parts, and wild yeast spores) in raw unfiltered honey, it should always be boiled with the malt extract wort or added at the end of the boil in order to pasteurize it. If

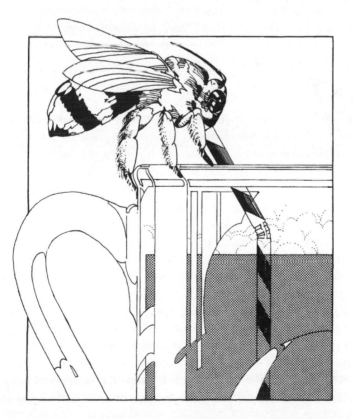

filtered honey is used, it is still a reassuring practice to add the honey to the boil. During boiling, extraneous matter may be skimmed and removed from the surface.

Honey can be fermented (with water) by itself or with various fruits, spices, or herbs. These fermentations are called mead. Their character can vary from a sweet winelike beverage to a dry sparkling champagne type. Recipes for making mead are discussed in "Making Honey Mead" on page 381.

### Miscellaneous Sweeteners

*Caramel*—Caramel is not a sweetener. It is derived from sugar either by a heating process or by chemically treating sugars in order to yield a brown bitter-like substance called caramel. Its use in beer is primarily as a coloring adjunct. It is not generally available for homebrewers but is used in commercial brewing and some malt extracts.

*Malto-dextrin*—Dextrin cannot be fermented by beer yeast. It is a chain of three glucose molecules that cannot be broken by the fermentation or respiration cycles of beer yeast. The presence of these "unfermentables" in beer lend body, foam stability, and a residual sweetness to the finished beer. Dextrin is naturally present in varying degrees in malt extract. Its addition to homebrew recipes as a powder increases the body of the beer. It is a convenience and a means of controlling the character of the finished beer by the malt extract homebrewer.

## FRUITS

Any fruit that is fit for human consumption may be used in flavoring beer. Some fruits lend a more favorable character than others. Because of the pioneering spirit of homebrewers, fruits are now used in flavoring commercially brewed beers. The most well-known and traditional fruit-flavored beers come from Belgium and are fermented with cherries, raspberries, peaches, or currants (cassis).

Cherries, raspberries, apples, pears, peaches, grapes and grape juice, red or black currants, mangoes, pomegranates, blackberries, cranberries, cactus fruits, passion fruits, kiwifruits, blueberries, chokecherries, and wild cherries are just a few of the fruits currently popular with homebrewers. Ripe, fresh, whole fruit will have the most intense flavor.

There are two methods for adding fruit to your beer. Each seeks to minimize the risk of contaminating your beer with microorganisms that may take the flavor and aroma of your beer in the wrong direction. The first method is to add the fruit to the boiling hot wort in order to pasteurize it. The second method is to wait until the beer is almost completely fermented before adding fruit. At this point of the fermentation, there is enough alcohol and unfriendly environment to inhibit most beer spoilage organisms. The details for both of these methods are as follows:

**Method 1:** To be on the side of sanitary, fresh or fresh frozen fruits should be pasteurized before their introduction to the fermentation. This creates somewhat of a paradoxical situation, since the most practical and effective way to pasteurize is by heat. But fruits should not be boiled because of their pectin content. If boiled, the pectin will "set" and create some problems with the beer's clarity. Also, boiling may extract or accentuate some of the undesirable flavor characteristics of seeds and pits, not to mention boiling away some of the more desirable delicate flavor of the fruit.

In order to pasteurize the fruit, I recommend its addition at the end of the boiling of the wort, turning the heat off and allowing the fruited wort to steep for 15 to 20 minutes at a temperature of 150 to 180 degrees F (66 to 82 C).

If small fresh fruit is used (especially berries or cherries), break the skin by crushing. Crushing is not necessary with frozen fruit, as the freezing process has already broken the skin, allowing juices to flow. When using large fruit, devise a means of crushing it so that the juice and flesh are readily exposed during fermentation.

The fruit can be left in the wort and fermented in the primary fermentation, but should be removed after initial fermentation. Take special care if fermenting fruit in a narrow-necked glass carboy. Leave adequate space so that the foam of fermentation never reaches the outlet of the carboy. Clogging can result, pressure may build to excessive levels, and a dangerously explosive and extremely messy situation will most certainly result. If fruit juice is used, straining is, naturally, unnecessary.

**Method 2:** After primary fermentation is complete, siphon the beer into a secondary fermenter with extra headroom available. Use clean and washed fruit. Add crushed and prepared fruit to the secondary fermentation. The acidic environment and alcohol content of fermented beer will inhibit the growth of most beer spoilage organisms. The sugars in the fruit will instigate a second fermentation that may take a longer period of time than beer without fruit. Usually if there is any bacterial contamination that affects your beer, it is in the form of acid-creating lactobacillus. A slight amount of acidity is often pleasant and accentuates the flavor of the fruit.

If fruit flavor is desired, there are other options available to homebrewers, such as fruit extracts and essences. Read the labels very carefully and know what you are getting. Is it natural? Are there additives? How much should you use?

In general, reduce your hopping rates when making fruit-flavored beers. Often the combination of high bitterness and certain fruit flavors clash. Excessive hop bitterness often detracts from the delicate and aromatic characters of the fruit you are using, so be conservative with your hops when you are first experimenting.

Ahhh, the joys of being a homebrewer.

## VEGETABLES

Hot damn. You can let your imagination go wild here, but don't think that you're the first to brew with vegetables.

*Chili peppers*—Anaheim, Hatch, jalapeño, Ghost, serrano, cayenne, habanero, Thai, and many other varieties offer different flavors and different heat sensations, used in skillful and artful quantities. Chili-flavored beer is often a real crowd pleaser. Surprised? So was I the time I sprung my first batch on an unsuspecting crowd. They loved it.

For controlled and best results, add to a secondary fermenter measured quantities of roasted (with the skin on if you like the aromatic character of roasted chilies) green chilies, chopped serrano, Thai, or jalapeño peppers, or dried cayenne, or any hot chili pepper. After a few days of steeping in the finished beer, the beer is ready for tasting. Add more chili if the heat is not to your satisfaction. If you're not a hothead, be careful and start conservatively.

*Pumpkin*—The Pilgrims may have been the first Americans to brew pumpkin-flavored beer. Use cooked pumpkin and add it to a mash with active enzymes. Do not use canned pumpkin to which preservatives have been added. Feel free to throw in some pumpkin pie spices (ground ginger, cinnamon, allspice, nutmeg, cloves—maybe even a chili pepper to make your pumpkin beer grin). Many small commercial brewers brew this as a seasonal treat. It's terrific! See page 281 of *The Homebrewer's Companion, Second Edition,* for a recipe detailing the processing and brewing of pumpkin ale.

*Red beets*—This idea may come in handy next time you want red beer. Two tennis ball–size raw red beets washed and peeled, sliced or chopped, added to your secondary fermenter will contribute a magnificent brilliant red color to your otherwise light-colored beer or mead. If you're making a pale-colored beer flavored with cherries, raspberries, strawberries, cranberries, or any other red fruit, you can add beets to intensify the color. Beets contain sugar, so you may see a slight increase in fermentation activity for a while, but it's really not significant. Virtually no flavor is contributed. Beets in your beer can't be beat for being reddy. I'll be rooting for your beer.

*Peas, beans, parsnips, carrots, Jerusalem artichokes, zucchini, potatoes, and the "thing" that grew in the neighbor's yard*—I've heard tales of all of these, but can't say I've had the pleasure of sampling many. Maybe I'm setting myself up in the wrong way, but if anyone out there would like to send me a bottle, please do.

## GRAINS

The use of whole or processed grains or the starch derived from grains is an option many homebrewers utilize. Wheat, rye, oats, rice, barley, sorghum, corn, millet, teff (a grain of Ethiopian origin), quinoa, and triticale (a hybrid grain produced by crossing durum wheat and rye) are a few of the many grains suitable for brewing.

The brewing process that utilizes the starches from these grains is a bit more involved than the methods that have so far been outlined. The main thing to remember is that the starch must undergo processing in order to convert starches to sugars that are fermentable by beer yeast. These grains should not simply be thrown into the boiling pot. The resulting beer may be okay, but simply knowing how to properly utilize the goodness of these grains will dramatically improve the results.

What follows is a brief outline of the procedures that should be undertaken by you, the homebrewer, should you choose to experiment with grains; there's a more complete discussion in the "Advanced Homebrewing and the All-Grain Homebrewer" section on page 286 and a thorough discussion in *The Homebrewer's Companion, Second Edition.*

The starches that you want to utilize in grains must be converted to sugars. In order to do this, they must be introduced to the starch-to-sugar-converting enzymes present in malted barley. But even before the enzymatic process can be efficiently carried out, the enzymes must have an easier way to "get at" the starches. So, the first step is to coarsely crack or grind the whole grain and then boil it for at least ½ hour. After boiling is complete, the cooked grain may be introduced to an enzyme-active "mash" of malted barley or diastatic malt extract (an enzyme-active malt extract). Simply speaking, if the "soupy" mash is held at temperatures of 150 to 160 degrees F (66 to 71 C), the enzymes will actively convert starch to sugars. NOTE: "Flaked" grains have been precooked and need not be boiled. Also, modified starch such as household cornstarch need not be cooked.

The use of grains in homebrew will provide for much more variety and an opportunity to experiment with your beermaking. Step-by-step procedures are explained in detail starting on page 286.

## HERBS AND SPICES

### *Beer and the Protestant Reformation*

Throughout beer history, hops were just one ingredient among many used in formulating beer. In fact, hops were a very controversial ingredient that involved religion, politics, power, and taxes.

Only in the last one to two hundred years has beer emerged as a refreshment beverage. For centuries beer was a vehicle for herbal medicine. Beer was healing. It was as mainstream in olden times as it is today, but it was controlled by another set of corporations.

The Catholic Church controlled the herbs most commonly used in "gruit." Gruit was the formulation of herbal mixtures responsible for flavor and actually controlling the degree of beer's intoxicating effects. By intoxication I mean to imply that alcohol was not the only thing that would make one howl at the moon or slumber into stress-free mindscapes.

Scurvy grass and spruce tips were added to beer to help prevent scurvy. Did you need to liven up your libido? The combination of herbs such as yarrow, sweet gale, and marsh rosemary when added to beer have highly inebriating and "stimulating" effects.

For male sexual dysfunction, ginger would be prescribed in beer gruits. Licorice was used to help reduce stress and was quite a popular additive, still used today, but without medicinal pretext.

St. John's wort (an actual name of an herbal plant) is very well known for its antidepressant effects. Its name has roots in beermaking.

Yarrow, bog myrtle, rosemary, licorice, elderberry, nettle, and coriander were among hundreds of herbs commonly used in brewing. The right herbal beer provided not only a setting for socializing, but it also satisfied nutritional needs, offered remedies, and improved disposition.

Where did the city of Pilsen and its Pilsner beer get its name? Pilsen refers to the psychoactive herb henbane, which was commonly used before the *Reinheitsgebot* (1516 German Beer Purity Law) as an intoxicating ingredient in beer. I didn't dig up this and other herbal facts; Stephen Buhner did in his 500-page book, *Sacred and Herbal Healing Beers* (Brewers Publications, 1998). In this thoroughly researched book, Stephen reveals the pre-hop traditions used by brewers throughout the world. His insight makes you seriously think about the changing world of beer.

The history of herbs and beer can get really fascinating. Consider the significance of the year 1516—the year of the German *Reinheitsgebot*. You could say that the *Reinheitsgebot* was the equivalent of America's politically charged "just say no to drugs" campaign.

Hops became a hot religious and political ingredient, especially during the time of the Protestant Reformation. The German Beer Purity Law of 1516 was enacted in favor of the more soporific and less licentious qualities and use of hops. The law many of us regard as a "purity" code was in essence a political and Protestant installation to oppose the Catholic Church's control of pleasurable and healing substances.

My own research revealed that in the days before hops were used, many different herbs or spices were employed to add zing to the brew. Two of the more popular flavorings were capsicum and coriander. Capsicum is a botanical name for peppers, usually hot peppers. Capsicum was said to be added for the warm glow it created while indulging. It was also said to "disperse the wind and crudities of indigestion." Wonderful! Just what every beer party needs.

Today, sacred, herbal, and spiced beers are not necessarily going to sweep the beer world, but the spirit of creative thinking and the examination of beer's origins are certainly healing, rejuvenating, and thirst provoking.

### More Innovative Spices of Life for Your Beer

As a homebrewer, you have the freedom to choose your ingredients . . . anything you so desire. But don't get too cocky about your "new," bright ideas, because a look back into the history and traditions of beermaking will indicate that whatever bright idea you've concocted to add to your beer—well, someone somewhere probably has beat you to it. Here are a few spices that homebrewers have found to be popular flavor additions to beer. If you can imagine enjoyment from these flavors, try them, but be cautious and don't overdo it the first time. Have patience—you can always add a little bit more the next time, but you can't remove anything if you've overdone it.

*Cinnamon*—Two teaspoons (8 g) of ground cinnamon or 3 to 4 inches (7 to 10 cm) of the whole bark (cinnamon stick) may be added during the final 10 to 15 minutes of the boil. This can be a very refreshing addition to darker beers. If added in small amounts, its flavor is not quite identifiable, yet its presence is noticed by all.

*Coriander (cilantro) seed*—This aromatic seed, often used in curries, was a popular beer ingredient in colonial America and eighteenth-century Europe. It is very assertive, so be sure you enjoy its flavor before adding it to your brew. Use freshly crushed coriander seed and add 1 or 2 teaspoons (4 to 8 g) at the end of the boil for a subtle hint in light beers. For easily identified character, trying boiling 1 or 2 ounces (28 to 56 g). There are different qualities of flavor and aroma of coriander seeds depending on where they are grown; explore the different coriander character found in seeds bought in Indian, Mexican, Latino, African, and Asian ethnic markets.

*Ginger*—The grated fresh root of the ginger plant has grown to be a favorite adjunct for many homebrewers. It goes well in both light and dark beers. The refreshing flavor it contributes to beer is appreciated by even those who claim they don't usually like beer. It is a winner unless you have an aversion to the flavor of ginger.

Fresh gingerroot has a character much different than that of dried ginger. Both will work, though keep in mind the character of dried ginger is more aggressive. Fresh ginger can be found in the produce section of most supermarkets. Grated on any cheese grater, it can be added during the final 10 to 15 minutes of the boiling of the wort or added to the secondary fermentation for a more fragrant and intensive experience. One ounce (28 g) for 5 gallons (19 l) will add considerable character to any beer. I have used amounts varying from ½ ounce to 4 ounces (14 to 110 g) for 5 gallons (19 l) of beer, all of which were enjoyed by many.

Many varieties of ginger are grown throughout the world. Galangal is one variety from Thailand that offers a refreshingly unique character to beer. Fresh or dried, add grated or sliced galangal during the last 10 to 20 minutes of the boil for maximum flavor and aroma or in the secondary fermenter for more aromatics.

*Heather*—A common plant of the Scottish countryside, heather was popularly used as an ingredient in ale. The top 2 inches (5 cm) of the flowering plant should be used to add a floral and aromatic character to beer. For a very traditional ale of old Scotland, use about 3 quarts (3 l) of freshly picked heather tips for 5 gallons (19 l). Dried heather can sometimes be found at homebrew supply stores.

*Juniper berries and boughs*—A traditional ingredient of certain types of Scandinavian ales, the freshly cut boughs with fruit are boiled with water to create an amber juniper-flavored water with which the beer is brewed. In grain brewing, the boughs are also placed in the bottoms of vessels to filter out grains and/or hops. The type of juniper used is not a tree but a low-lying bush common in high mountain areas and in Scandinavia. The character is refreshing and a bit fruity, with hints of herbal woodiness.

*Kaffir lime leaves*—Available at Asian food stores specializing in Thai cuisine, the whole fresh leaves add a delightful zest and unique limelike character to beer. They are potent, so use sparingly, adding them at the very end of the boil; preferably steeping without boiling. Adding them into the secondary fermenter will liven up the freshness of the character. These lime leaves go particularly well with refreshing styles of lighter summer ales and lagers.

*Licorice*—The hard woody root of the licorice plant is often used in beermaking. A 4- to 6-inch (10 to 15 cm) piece of root will contribute some licorice character to the beer and aid in head retention. Licorice is naturally sweet, but the amount of sugar present is insignificant to affect fermentation. Homebrew supply shops often carry "brewer's licorice," made from the extract of licorice root. A 2- to 5-inch (5 to 13 cm) piece in 5 gallons (19 l) will contribute character to the finished beer. Brewer's licorice is easily dissolved in the boiling wort. Licorice root must be shaved or chopped into pieces and boiled in the wort for at least 15 minutes; longer is better. In reasonable amounts, licorice can contribute some pleasant qualities to beer, particularly dark beers.

*Orange peel*—There are sweet and bitter versions of this dried product available at most homebrew supply stores. They are used in several types of Belgian specialty beers, most commonly Wit (or white) Belgian wheat ale. About ½ ounce (14 g) will do for 5 gallons (19 l). The peel lends an overall refreshing but subtle orange citrus character to beer. If you are using fresh orange peel, use only organic oranges to avoid contamination with insecticides.

*Spruce tips*—The new spring growth from evergreen spruce trees or processed spruce essence is popular among many homebrewers as a flavoring. Spruce was quite popular in colonial America, when hops were not available. Its addition to beer provides a refreshing flavor as well as vitamin C (which helps the stability of finished beer). You may add spruce flavor to your beer by harvesting the tips of new growth on spruce trees, stems, and needles. A pint jar loosely filled with spruce twigs will provide adequate character to 5 gallons (19 l) of brew. I once helped brew a batch of spruce beer in the Queen Charlotte Islands off the west coast of British Columbia, Canada. There, the Sitka spruce provided an abundance of tasty needles. The resulting malt-extract-based brew was astoundingly good. I can describe it very accurately as having a flavor similar to Pepsi-Cola but without the sweetness, and a beer flavor, to boot.

If fresh spruce needles aren't available in your neck of the woods, spruce essence is often available in many homebrew shops. Two to 5 teaspoons (14 to 35 ml) for 5 gallons (19 l) will be adequate.

Warning: Pine tar is not the same thing as spruce essence. I once heard of a homebrewer who thought otherwise. Incredibly, he poured half a pint of the stuff into his wort. The beer tasted like the road surface of the Brooklyn Bridge. (No, I've not licked the bridge—I'm being humorous.)

*Yarrow*—An indigenous flowering plant of both America and Europe whose flowers and leaves were commonly used in ales before the advent of hops. They can be substituted for hops at a rate of about 4 ounces (112 g) per 5 gallons (19 l) of beer. They impart an herbal and floral character to beer that is quite pleasant and balanced. See the yarrow ale recipe on page 252.

*Other spices*—Cardamom, cloves, allspice, nutmeg, horseradish, horehound, walnut leaves, nettles, Szechwan peppercorns, sweet basil, root beer extract flavors (sassafras bark, sarsaparilla shavings, wintergreen, vanilla bean, teaberry, deerberry, checkerberry, boxberry, spiceberry, and others), and anise are a few other spices I've tried in beer or that continue to intrigue me.

## MISCELLANEOUS INGREDIENTS

There's no doubt that your imagination will surpass anything that this book could ever address. Hundreds of different ingredients have been used by homebrewers since the original edition of this book was published. The long list is deserving of its own essay and indeed entire issues of the American Homebrewers Association's bimonthly magazine *Zymurgy* have been devoted to this subject (see *Zymurgy Special Issue 1994* and *Zymurgy,* September–October 2002). In the original edition of this book, honey, coffee, and chocolate were suggested probably for the first time in the twentieth century. Now honey, coffee, and chocolate beers are popularly available from many small craft and large brewers. Traditional smoked beer from Germany was outlined as it is here, but since then homebrewers and commercial craft brewers have been adding smoked malt to dozens of styles of lagers and ales with great flavor success. The chicken beer—well, we haven't seen too many cock ales in homebrew stashes or on the grocery store shelves. You win some and gladly lose some.

*Chocolate*—Unsweetened baker's chocolate or bittersweet chocolate can be a wonderful addition to beer. Read the ingredients of whatever chocolate you buy to avoid undesirable additives. There you are, brewing a batch of dark beer, and perhaps having a few in the process. And there it is, just sitting there in the cupboard, staring you in the face—a 1- to 6-ounce (28 to 170 g) chunk of chocolate. "I wonder . . . ," you think and take another sip of homebrew. And before you know it, in it goes. Voilà, chocolate beer. And it doesn't turn out badly. In fact you brew one special batch once a year, to celebrate love and your impulse. Unsweetened cocoa powder will do even better!

*Smoke*—This is not so strange as it seems. There is a traditional lager beer brewed in Bamberg, Germany, called Rauchbier, where they actually kiln-dry and smoke malted barley by burning beechwood. The result is a delicious, albeit unusual, beer tasting of smoke. German beechwood-smoked malt is available through your homebrew supply shop. Homebrewers and small professional craft brewers have popularized other types of smoked ale and lager. Cherrywood-smoked malt is commercially made in the United States, while more creative brewers are making their own smoked malt. You can smoke a portion of your grains in your barbecue pit (deciduous tree wood such as apple, mesquite, oak, maple, cherry, alder, and hickory work well). German smoke-flavored beers in the 1980s and '90s were traditionally pale to light brown in color, but now the demand for smoked beers has grown enough that it is common to see German-brewed smoked bocks, Helles, and wheat beers. In the U.S., creative brewers are adding smoked malt to several styles of ales and lagers, both dark and light. They are a wonderful treat with smoked foods. The people who live on Gotland

Island, Sweden, brew a birch-smoked malt and juniper beer that is very popular in that part of the world. The Alaskan Brewing Company currently brews a wonderful award-winning alder wood–smoked porter.

*Coffee*—Ahhh, what coffee and stout lover wouldn't consider a formulation of Blue Mountain, Kona, Colombian, or espresso stout, made from the most exotic of coffee beans? The word is spreading and the stout is shared. More and more homebrewers are trying their hand at formulating coffee-flavored beers. Both caffeinated and decaffeinated are options you can explore.

I love the flavor of good coffee, and in order to preserve the fine flavor and aroma use only freshly ground beans and steep (never boil) them in the hot wort after the boil is done and during the final 5 minutes before straining and sparging. Another great option would be to add freshly ground coffee to the secondary and "cold extract" the coffee essence. How much to use? Give it a shot with ¼ pound (115 g) or a double shot with ½ pound (225 g) for your first 5 gallons (19 l) and progress from there.

*Chicken*—I saved this one for last. The recipe for Cock Ale is an authentic one, taken from a book by Edward Spencer published in 1899 titled *The Flowing Bowl: A Treatise on Drinks of All Kinds and of All Periods, Interspersed with Sundry Anecdotes and Reminiscences.* Here is the recipe:

### Cock Ale

In order to make this, the Complete Housewife instructs us to take 10 gallons of ale and a large cock, the older the better. Parboil the cock, flea [flay?] him, and stamp him in a stone mortar till his bones are broken (you must craw and gut him when you flea him), then put the cock into 2 quarts of sack [16th-century dry Spanish white wine], and put to it 3 pounds of raisins of the sun stoned, some blades of mace, a few cloves; put all these into a canvas bag, and a little before you find the ale has done working, put the ale and bag together into a vessel; in a week or 9 days bottle it up, fill the bottles but just above the neck, and give it the same time to ripen as other ale.

Holy Moses! What a drink! I have frequently read of the giving of "body" to ale and stout by means of the introduction of "horseflesh," but to put the rooster into the ale cask smacks somewhat of barbarism.

The addition of a whole chicken to your beer is very unusual, but to find someone who has actually tried it is even more unusual. "It wasn't all that bad," said he.

## YEAST NUTRIENTS

Beer yeast requires an adequate supply of nutrients and trace minerals for healthy fermentation. These nutrients are naturally present in malted barley or developed by enzymes during the malting or mashing process. The addition of extra prepackaged yeast nutrients to all malt extract beers is unnecessary. The only time that you as a homebrewer need to consider the addition of extra yeast nutrients is if you've used more than 40 percent adjuncts—that is, ingredients other than malt extract.

Yeast nutrients are recommended when brewing honey meads, but more on that later.

There are different types of yeast nutrients and energizers available in homebrew supply shops. If you find the need to use them or think it will make you feel better if you do so, go ahead, use them, but follow the instructions provided and do not overdose your brew.

## CLARIFYING AIDS

Here's a some background about what's going on.

During the brewing and fermentation process there will be different kinds of suspended matter in the brew. If good ingredients are used and attention has been given to sanitation of equipment, then most types of beer will clear naturally, with patience, to a sparkling, bright, enjoyable transparency.

If it makes you feel better and you want to encourage clear beer, clarifying aids are available for use in beermaking. There are four kinds of suspended matter that naturally involve themselves in the brewing and fermenting process: coagulated proteins developed during the boiling of the wort, yeast that becomes suspended for a period of time during fermentation, hop oils and related compounds that result from extravagant dry hopping, and haze caused by undesirable bacteria.

Let's consider coagulated proteins. Some batches of beer that you make may be perfectly clear at first but will later develop a haze when chilled in the refrigerator. This "chill haze" is nothing to get anxious about. It is mostly a visual phenomenon and will not affect the flavor. Chill haze is a result of a precipitation of compounds produced by tannin-protein reactions that are invisibly soluble and in solution at room temperatures. At cold temperatures they are no longer soluble and precipitate as a haze.

Chill haze can be minimized by controlling the malting and mashing process more closely, but at the same time this control results in the sacrifice of other aspects that the brewer wishes to achieve. It's often a trade-off.

If the chill haze really annoys you, I could recommend that you drink out of a stone jar or wooden mug, but that would be facetious, so I won't. There are some additives discussed below that can be introduced into your brew to help eliminate chill haze.

Yeast in suspension can create a haze. Some yeasts flocculate better than others. Flocculation describes the ability to settle to the bottom and create a firm sediment more readily. Some yeasts have a tendency to remain in suspension longer than others. Brewers who desire yeast in suspension, particularly for certain styles of wheat beer, will not filter their beer before packaging. Filtration and yeast clarifying aids are available if you want to address your yeast haze concerns.

Introducing a lot of dry hops in the secondary aging stage can add oil and other hop compounds that will create a hop haze. You could filter that haze out, but that would also filter out the flavors and aromas you introduced in the first place. Hop haze? It's delicious and you may have to live with some degree of hop haze if you are heavily dry hopping.

You might enjoy the unique character that haze-producing bacteria create, but I'm really being hopeful when I say this. Having unintentional haze-producing bacteria is not a common occurrence, in fact it is rare. The remedy is to be more attentive with your sanitation techniques. Relax. Don't worry. Have a homebrew. You will get over it, if it happens. At the very least it's a humbling experience.

The ingredients that are added in the brewing process to help clarification are called *finings* (pronounced "fine-ings"). These ingredients attract suspended matter by the use of their molecular electrical charge, in much the same way as a magnet works. Positive electric charges attract negative ones and vice versa. Now, this wouldn't be so important to know except that the different types of suspended matter in beer have different electrical charges, and different types of finings likewise have different electrical charges.

*Irish moss*—The precipitated and coagulated proteins that make for cloudy wort in the boiling cauldron upon your stove are positively charged. The addition of vegetable-derived finings, such as Irish moss (a seaweed sometimes called carragheen), during the final 10 minutes of the boil will aid in settling out the proteins. The negatively charged Irish moss attracts the positively charged proteins; the process takes place in the brewpot. One-quarter to one-half teaspoon of Irish moss powder added during the final 10 minutes of boiling will accomplish the desired effect.

Yeast will naturally settle to the bottom after it has completed most of its fermentation. In order for this to happen, proper yeast nutrition is essential. It should be noted that different yeast strains and how they are handled will influence the sedimentation process. Particularly helpful is the addition of positively charged animal-derived finings. Most beer yeasts are negatively charged, so the attraction will be active.

*Gelatin*—Derived from the hooves of horses and cows, gelatin has a positive charge that will aid in attracting and settling suspended yeast. Dissolved and prepared gelatin is added just before packaging the beer. It is best used when kegging homebrew, as there is a longer distance for the yeast to settle through. To prepare the gelatin, add 1 tablespoon to 1 pint (225 ml) of cold water and gently heat until dissolved. Do not boil the gelatin solution, as this will break down the gelatin to uselessness. Add the solution to the beer at the same time you add your priming (bottling) sugar. Or don't add it at all, and have a homebrew.

*Isinglass*—Isinglass is a gelatinous substance derived from the internal membranes of fish bladders. Its use is very popular in Great Britain and wherever "real ale" is served from the cask. This style of beer benefits from the forty-eight-hour clarification induced by the addition of isinglass at kegging time. Isinglass is positively charged but its effectiveness in settling yeast will vary with the strain of yeast being used. Its preparation is time-consuming; it involves weak acid solutions and must be done with care over a period of days. Improper preparation will render these finings useless. Its use in American homebrewing is superseded by the more appropriate settling qualities of drinking a glass of homebrew and having patience. But if it is isinglass you wish to use, refer to the instructions that should accompany it.

*Papain*—Papain is known as a protelytic enzyme that is extracted from the skin of the papaya. It is used as the active ingredient in meat tenderizer. This enzyme achieves some of the same effect as the "protein rest" during the mashing process of malted barley or during the malting process. Proper malting or mashing techniques are usually employed by all malt extract manufacturers in order to achieve minimal protein levels, thus minimizing chill haze formation.

If papain is used, it should be used sparingly: $\frac{1}{2}$ gram of papain for 5 gallons (19 l) will react with the proteins and prevent them from combining with tannin. The enzyme is active at temperatures below 122 degrees F (50 C) and takes several days to complete its reaction. Since it is deactivated with boiling, it must be added to cooled wort. It normally would be added during the latter part of secondary fermentation or maturation. The downside of using papain is that it also breaks down foam-enhancing proteins, and though it is deactivated by boiling, it will survive the lower pasteurization temperatures.

Papain is difficult to find in an unadulterated state. Some homebrew shops may carry it, but you will more likely find papain at specialty food shops that carry an extensive line of herbs and spices.

*Gallotannin*—Produced primarily from gall nuts (the "gall" growth found on trees, particularly oak trees), this tannin is remarkably useful in helping clarify worts and beer. Its molecular tannic structure is unique, and unlike many other types of tannin, gallotannin is soluble in water (and thus beer and wine) and can be used to precipitate out proteins and help clarify beer. There are several stages in the brewing process when gallotannins can be added at a rate of 1.2 grams per 5 gallons (19 l) (7 grams per U.S. barrel; or 6 grams per hectoliter). In the mash it is effective during the duration of the mash, however the gallotannins, and what precipitates during the 1 to 2 hours of the mashing process, get filtered out. They can be added at the end of the boil or during late hopping, dry hopping, or during maturation—but gallotannins create quite a bit of protein precipitate as sediment, which needs to be removed from the beer.

*Ground cinnamon* and *coriander seed*—These have similar behaviors to gallotannin due to their tannin content, but are not as dramatic in clarifying as gallotannin. Some urge caution when using coriander seed too early and too much in the brewing process because it may contribute to an unusual mouthfeel and flavor, but this "unusualness" could be considered desirable by some.

*PVP (polyvinylpyrdlidone)/Polyclar*—Plastic! This substance is an insoluble white plastic powder that, like a statically charged balloon clinging to the ceiling, will electrostatically attract tannin molecules as it drifts to the bottom. This process is called adsorption. It is a physical phenomenon. There is no chemical reaction of the plastic with the beer. After the Polyclar has settled, the beer is drawn off, leaving the sediment behind. Because there are no longer any tannins in the beer, its combination with protein is prevented—no chill haze.

Polyclar should be added to the beer after the yeast has sedimented. The addition of 2 teaspoons (2 g) of Polyclar for every 5 gallons (19 l) of beer should effectively remove tannins within a few hours.

Polyclar is available at many homebrew supply stores.

*Activated silica gel*—Although not available to homebrewers, this substance is worth mentioning because it is used by many commercial brewers. It does the same thing as Polyclar except that it adsorbs protein molecules rather than tannin.

## ENZYMES

Enzymes can be described as molecules that are triggered and ready to react with other substances to help create a new substance. They are formed by living things and are activated or deactivated by certain conditions.

The creation and utilization of enzymes in beermaking are essential and occur naturally during the malting and starch-to-sugar mashing conversion.

Diastatic enzymes, as they are called in the brewing process, are adequately developed during the malting stage. There are many naturally occurring enzymes in malt. The use of these in the all-grain brewing process is detailed in the "Advanced Homebrewing" section, page 288.

If enzymes are added to malt extract brews or during the mashing process, they will certainly influence the balance of fermentable sugars and unfermentable dextrins that give body and aid in head retention.

Generally speaking, the addition of enzymes by a homebrewer is not very controllable; however, if your curiosity leads you to experiment, here are explanations of two enzymes that are sometimes accessible to homebrewers. It is more than likely that your use of them will result in beer that will have less sweetness, less body, less head retention, and more alcohol, as you will convert what is normally unfermentable into sugars that are. Your beers will have a flavor characteristic of super-light American beer.

*Alpha-amylase*—The powder that can sometimes be found in homebrew shops that is labeled "Alpha-amylase" should be of fungal origin (*Aspergillus niger*). Its addition to beer wort, mash, or liquefied starch will enzymatically convert starches to the simplest and completely fermentable forms of sugar (glucose) at temperatures less than 140 degrees F (60 C). Temperatures above 140 degrees F will permanently "denature" (deactivate) the enzymes. Fungal alpha-amylase (sometimes called *gluco-amylase*) is processed for different levels of enzymatic activities; therefore, the amount that should be used will vary with the strength of the powder. Generally, for homebrewing purposes, about 1 teaspoon of enzymes used for 5 gallons (19 l) of beer should suffice to markedly influence conversion. At temperatures close to 140 degrees F (60 C), conversions should be complete within 3 hours. When used in commercial brewing, alpha-amylase is usually added during secondary cold storage and maturation. In 1 week, reactions will be complete: the conversion of unfermentable dextrin carbohydrates to fermentable sugars that will in turn be fermented by yeast.

Alpha-amylase is often used in the production of barley syrup from unmalted barley. It is sometimes an ingredient in malt syrups that are not 100 percent malt extract. Bacterially derived *beta-amylase* is not recommended for use by the homebrewer. It liquefies starches to dextrins, is heat resistant, and will survive boiling temperatures. It will result in beer that is unstable and difficult to control.

*Koji*—The biological name for this enzyme is *Aspergillus oryzae*. Of fungal origin and best known for its use in making Japanese rice wine (sake), koji is actually impregnated rice or barley. Koji concentrate, an enzyme powder, is sometimes available to the homebrewer. Koji seed (tane) is not yet developed into enzymes and is not useful to the brewer. Koji enzymes will convert starches to sugars most efficiently at temperatures between 100 and 120 degrees F (43 to 49 C) in about 10 to 20 minutes. It is deactivated at temperatures above 130 degrees F (54 C). One teaspoon of koji concentrate (enzymes) added to ingredients for 5 gallons (19 l) should aid in the conversion of liquefied starches (dextrins) to fermentable glucose sugar. *Aspergillus oryzae* enzyme is sometimes used in the commercial brewing of American light beers. It is added during cold secondary storage and allowed at least a week to react with the beer. Time of conversion is very variable and is affected by temperature and strength of the enzyme. As a homebrewer you will need to experiment.

*Diastatic malt extract*—Manufactured in a way that does not denature the enzyme during the evaporation process, DME or diastatic malt syrup (DMS) can be used by brewers who wish to convert lots of adjuncts (such as corn, rice, wheat, etc.) but do not have adequate enzyme content in their malted barley.

During homebrewing, this syrup may be added to a mash of cooked starch for proper conversion to sugar at temperature ranges between 150 and 160 degrees F (66 to 71 C). Three pounds (1.4 kg) of diastatic malt extract should be adequate to convert 1 pound (450 g) of grain or starch.

## MISCELLANEOUS BREWING AIDS

*Ascorbic acid (vitamin C)*—Ascorbic acid, commonly known as vitamin C, is used in many foods as an antioxidant preservative. Oxidation is the process through which oxygen will react and combine with just about anything. When oxygen reacts with finished beer, it will produce off-flavors and instability. The more that a brewer can do to eliminate oxygen from coming in contact with beer once fermentation begins, the better the beer will be.

When ascorbic acid is added to beer, oxygen reacts with it, rather than with the beer. Oxidized vitamin C is less harmful to the stability and flavor of the beer than oxidized beer.

One-half teaspoon of ascorbic acid crystals dissolved in boiled water will help prevent oxidation of 5 gallons (19 l) of beer. It is not recommended that vitamin C tablets be used, because of other ingredients added to these tablets. Vitamin C crystals are available at all homebrew supply stores.

NOTE: Ascorbic acid is not a necessary ingredient in beermaking. If care is taken not to splash and aerate beer during siphoning and bottles are filled to within 1 inch of the top, oxidation problems will be minimal. Whatever you do, *don't worry*; if adding ascorbic acid will prevent worrying, do it—otherwise, it is an unnecessary option.

*Citric acid*—I used to think that the addition of citric acid was important in beermaking. Now, because I think I understand beer ingredients and the brewing process more, I can't imagine why one should use it. Its addition increases the acidity of the already acidic wort. Malt extracts and all-grain mashes are acidic by their very nature. The use of citric acid in malt extract brewing is simply not necessary.

The addition of citric acid in honey meads or wine may be justified, in order to create a desirable acid "fruity" flavor.

*Brewing salts*—Sometimes called Burton water salts, minerals such as non-iodized table salt (NaCl), gypsum ($CaSO_4$), and Epsom salt ($MgSO_4$) can be added to beer wort in an attempt to duplicate the brewing water in Burton-on-Trent, famous for its pale ales. It is extremely difficult to duplicate world-famous brewing water unless you start with distilled or deionized water. A more complete discussion of water and brewing salts can be found in the "Advanced Home-brewing and Water" section of this book (page 304) and in the "Water" section of *Homebrewer's Companion, Second Edition*.

Briefly, brewing salts are more important when brewing an all-grain beer. The addition of gypsum to malt extract wort will be helpful, especially if you know that your water supply is soft. You can ask your city or county water department for a mineral analysis of your water supply. If your water contains less than 50 ppm (parts per million) of calcium, then the addition of 1 to 4 teaspoons (4 to 16 g) of gypsum will aid the fermentation process.

Food-grade gypsum is available at all homebrew supply shops.

Other brewing "salts" such as calcium chloride ($CaCl_2$) and potassium chloride (KCl) may be cautiously considered as brewing ingredients, but not before a more thorough understanding of their effects on brewing chemistry has been established.

*Heading liquids*—Heading liquids are extracts of odd roots, barks, and other things that will have a "detergent effect" on the beer; bubbles will last longer. Their use in homebrewing is not necessary if sanitary procedures are combined with good ingredients. I have been able to get the best heads on the simplest of malt extract beers, as good as the famed Guinness Stout head—really! Don't let anyone tell you otherwise.

If your beer is having problems keeping its head, the problem is more likely the glass you are drinking from. Grease, oils, or detergent residues left on glasses will destroy a head. The corn chip and potato chip oils on your lips will also destroy a head, let alone ChapStick or lipstick.

If you do use heading liquid, follow the instructions on the container.

When you make homebrew, you are dealing with a living organism. It is alive—and because it is alive, it feels. Every person's brew has its own distinctive characteristics that carry through each batch. The entire process of beermaking depends on one's thoughts and attitude and equally on the lives of millions of tiny organisms called yeasts.

The magic of making homebrew can only come from the magic given it: magic as simple as the space you occupy.

## THE SECRETS OF FERMENTATION

### HOW YEASTS BEHAVE

Beer yeast is a single-cell living organism. In its microbial world it is classified as a fungus. The activity during its life cycle offers to the brewer the gift of beer. The "living" part of your beer should never be overlooked or taken for granted. Yeast is not simply some "thing" that is added as an ingredient and quickly forgotten. Sure, left on its own accord it will indeed take it upon itself to make beer. But I can assure you that merely thinking about yeasts as living organisms and involving your own common sense in understanding what they are doing will make your beer better.

The intricacies of the life cycle of yeast are still not fully understood by microbiologists and may never be. There are simply some secrets that are never unraveled. But quite a bit is known about what yeasts like and how they behave. The purpose of this discussion is to convey to you, the homebrewer, a foundation that will enable you to begin to appreciate and understand yeasts and how they make beer.

As with any living organism, there is a tremendous variety of behavior among the species. The facts and descriptions that follow are accurate but are often generalizations. When dealing with yeast, one must be flexible enough to allow the individualities of yeast to express its own character.

During the brewing cycle, yeast will progress through its entire life cycle. In a matter of days, the population will increase three to five times. While it is tending to the activity of reproduction it is also involved at one time or another with three main activities during its life cycle:

1. *Respiration:* The process through which yeast gains and stores energy for future activities and reproduction.
2. *Fermentation:* The process through which yeast expends energy, converting sugars to alcohol, carbon dioxide, and beer flavor. During this period of time, yeast is mostly in suspension, allowing itself dispersal and maximum contact with the liquid beer wort.
3. *Sedimentation:* The process through which yeast flocculates and drifts to the bottom of the fermenter. With fermentation almost completed, the activity of the yeast is "shut down" for lack of food and energy. The yeast begins to undergo a process that will preserve its life as it readies itself for dormancy.

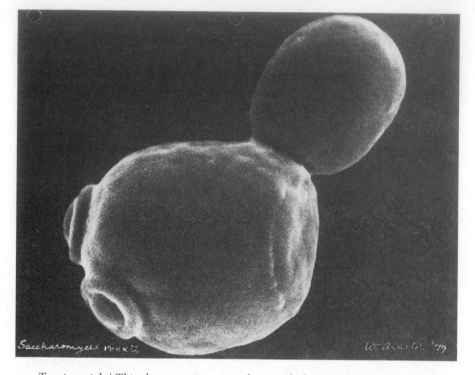

*Turning tricks! This electron microscope photograph shows a typical yeast cell in a budding (reproductive) stage. Scars can be seen lower left and right where other buds have separated. When fermentation is most active, there are 50 million of these cells in 1 milliliter of wort! Beer will appear clear to the naked eye when concentrations of 100,000 cells per milliliter are reached.*

It is important that yeasts do what they do quickly and in good health. There are many other microorganisms, such as bacteria and wild yeasts, that can live and propagate themselves in beer wort but they will be inhibited if your brewing yeast can get a good head start in its own life cycle.

In order for brewing yeast to ferment quickly, there are certain nutritional and environmental conditions that are favorable. They involve:

1. Temperature
2. pH (acidity or alkalinity); physical condition of its surroundings
3. Nutrients and food
4. Oxygen
5. Good initial health

In essence, these conditions for life are no different than those for all other forms of life, including our own.

These conditions are not difficult to understand. When you make the small effort to appreciate the simplicity of these basics, you will be able to answer many questions before you ask them.

Let's take a quick look at the conditions that yeasts favor.

1. *Temperature*—Depending on the variety, yeast can have an active life cycle and ferment in the temperature range of 33 to 90 degrees F (1 to 32 C). Most ale yeast (top-fermenting type, *Saccharomyces cerevisiae*) works best at 60 to 75 degrees F (16 to 24 C). Lager yeast (bottom-fermenting type, *Saccharomyces uvarum*) works best and produces the most desirable beer flavors at 35 to 55 degrees F (2 to 13 C).

   If yeasts are in an environment that is too cold, their activity will be significantly lower or stop altogether.

   If the temperature of the beer wort is excessive, the yeast will die, usually at temperatures in excess of 120 degrees F (49 C), or its activity will be greater. Warmer temperatures increase the risk of bacterial contamination and propagation. For a number of reasons, including elevated temperatures, yeast may also produce some very undesirable off-flavors in the beer. These off-flavors can generally be characterized as fruity, butterscotchlike (diacetyl), cidery, grassy (acetaldehyde), solventlike (alcohols other than ethanol); with some yeast strains an aroma of rotten eggs ($H_2S$, hydrogen sulfide) may occur. None of the above will harm you and may not even occur with the yeast strain that you use. Some may dissipate or reduce themselves with time, but when they don't it usually detracts from your beer.

   Just like people, yeasts don't like sudden changes in temperatures. When culturing or rehydrating yeast, slowly raise or lower the temperature of the yeast starter to that of the wort before pitching.

2. *pH and other physical conditions*—Distilled water is neutral; it is neither acid nor alkaline. The measure of neutrality on the pH scale is 7.0. A pH of less than 7.0 is acid, while a pH greater than 7.0 is alkaline (or called basic).

   Most beer yeasts enjoy an environment that is acidic at a pH of 5.0–5.5. This environment will naturally occur in all beer worts with which quality water has been used. The homebrewer need not make adjustments unless certain conditions and excess minerals exist in the water—namely calcium carbonate.

   During the course of fermentation, the by-products of yeast will decrease the pH of the beer to about 4.5.

   With regard to other conditions, yeasts can be very sensitive to what is called the "osmotic" pressure of their surroundings. For example, plain water will exert a much different pressure on the cell walls (the "skin") of yeast than a solution of malt sugars and water or beer. As a jet airliner must gradually adjust the pressure of the cabin in order to minimize the strain on its "skin," so would a yeast cell going from one liquid environment to another.

If sudden and drastic osmotic pressure changes are made in yeasts' environment, many will literally implode or explode (what an ugly sight on a microbial level) and those that do survive such changes reduce their activity while they adjust to the shock.

For optimal yeast health, think like a yeast (sure it does) and make gradual transitions.

3. *Nutrients and food*—These are the building blocks for all life and occur on the cellular level. In order for any living organism to function properly, life's metabolic activity and healthy cell walls must be maintained. Yeasts require sugars, proteins, fats, and trace minerals (elements).

Sugars are a source of food energy.

Proteins are nutrients that are in the form of (free) amino acids. They are developed in the malting process or during the mashing process. They are required for healthy cell structure.

Fats (oils) are derived from hops and malt. The small amount required is necessary, again, for healthy cell building.

Trace elements are necessary for the overall life processes of yeast cells, the two most important being zinc and calcium. Zinc is derived from malt. Calcium is derived from malt and water. In excess, both elements are toxic to yeast.

Without proper nutrition, many things will result. Generally, a few of these are: sluggish fermentation, mutation of yeasts and a subsequent change in their behavior, poor sedimentation, off-flavors, and poor beer stability.

Nutrition requirements will vary with yeast strains. As a malt extract homebrewer, the nutritional requirements are invariably included in the products that you use. Additional nutrients need not be considered.

4. *Oxygen*—Oxygen is an extremely important requirement in the initial stages of the life cycle of yeasts. Essentially, yeast undergoes a process called respiration through which it will store energy derived from sugar and oxygen for the remainder of its life cycle. This process is often described as being aerobic because it utilizes "free oxygen" that is dissolved in the beer wort. There is little disadvantage to having too much oxygen in your initial wort.

Oxygen can be dissolved into the wort by splashing or agitating the wort as it goes into the fermenter. Boiled water or wort does not have very much dissolved oxygen; the cooled wort must be agitated. Cold tap water that is added to hot concentrated malt extract wort may already have dissolved oxygen. Once the yeast has been added to the wort and fermentation commences, oxygen should never be introduced.

A lack of oxygen in the initial wort may result in stuck, sluggish, or incomplete fermentation.

NOTE: According to research done by the Brewing Industry Research Foundation in Surrey, England, it was found that the "method of yeast culture and propagation will alter response to oxygen" and significantly affect fermentation. The important thing to consider is that oxygen *is* required at some stage. Many of the very active dried beer yeasts that are available to homebrewers are cultured under (aerated) conditions that decrease the requirement of oxygen in a homebrewer's wort. If you choose to culture your own yeast from a liquid culture, the oxygen requirement is much more significant.

5. *Good initial health*—Some of the precursors to healthy yeast at the time that it is added to the wort have already been mentioned. In addition, storage or packaging conditions will also affect the health of the yeast. Liquid cultures can be stored in a refrigerated or, with special treatment, in a frozen state. The dried yeast that is used by homebrewers is often warm-air-dried and approximately 70 percent viable. It can be stored at room temperature but will have a longer "shelf life" if refrigerated.

## THE LIFE CYCLE OF BEER YEASTS

### Introduction

As a homebrewer, you will observe variability in your fermentation because of the comparatively small scale at which you brew, the variability of conditions and variety of yeast preparations that you use. This need not cause anxiety. (Relax. Don't worry. Have a homebrew.) Consider yourself privileged. You have the opportunity to observe variations that are not even allowed in many commercial breweries.

The life cycle of yeast is activated from dormancy when it is *pitched* (added) to the wort. During the respiration and fermentation cycle, the population of yeast will multiply three or four times. Yeast cells reproduce by a process called budding approximately every 24 hours until an optimum population of 50 million cells per milliliter of wort is reached. As it reproduces it is also metabolizing food and nutrients.

All yeast activities can be assigned to three main cycles: 1) respiration, 2) fermentation, and 3) sedimentation.

*Respiration* is the initial process that yeast undergoes when pitched into the wort. It is an aerobic process through which the yeast cells utilize oxygen. From the available oxygen, the yeast derives energy and other requirements for reproduction, cell construction, and fermentation. The energy derived during respiration is almost completely used during fermentation.

Respiration will last about 4 to 8 hours and varies quite a bit with conditions. During the respiration cycle, the yeast will reproduce and produce carbon dioxide, water, and flavor characteristics (there is no alcohol produced during respiration). The flavor characteristics are by-products of yeast metabolism, the most noticeable ones being esters and diacetyl.

The name "ester" is given to the chemicals that are responsible for certain aromas. The ones that are often noticeable in beer are described as strawberry, apple, banana, grapefruit, pear, blueberry, and raspberry. The type of ester produced will vary with yeast strain, temperature, and other conditions. Beer drinkers usually prefer some degree of estery quality in beer.

Diacetyl is the name given to describe a buttery or butterscotch flavor in beer. It can be produced sometimes by bacteria but is always produced to one degree or another by the metabolic activity of yeast. This flavor is later reduced during the fermentation stage while the yeast is in suspension. Sometimes, if the yeast does not stay in suspension long enough it is unable to reduce the butterscotch flavor of diacetyl, which comes out in the final flavor of the beer. Many beer drinkers appreciate this character in certain styles, many do not.

The Samuel Smith Brewery in County York, England, produces a
beer called Sam Smith's Pale Ale or Bitter. Historically, it has
a subtle but noticeably butterscotch palate. The original
fermentation process of this brewery's beer takes place in what is
called Yorkshire stones—square fermenters made of slate. This
method of fermentation and the particular strain of ale yeast
used do create some problems in keeping the yeast in suspension
long enough during fermentation. They occasionally have to
"rouse" (stir) the yeast back into suspension. Because of the
yeast's tendency to flocculate (sediment or rise to the surface), it
is unable to reduce the diacetyl responsible for the butterscotch
character. However, the special character of this beer has made
it unique, very enjoyable, and well known. Modern fermentation
systems may someday change this historic character.

*Fermentation*—The fermentation cycle quickly follows the respiration cycle.
Fermentation is called an anaerobic process and does not require any free oxygen
in solution. As a matter of fact, any remaining oxygen in the wort is "scrubbed"
(stripped) out of solution by the carbon dioxide bubbles produced by the yeast.

During the fermentation cycle, the yeast will continue to reproduce until
optimum population is reached. Once suspended throughout the wort, it converts sugars to alcohol, carbon dioxide, and beer flavors. It is the nature of strains
of beer yeast to remain in suspension long enough to quickly convert fermenta
bles. Most beer yeasts that you will use will remain in suspension for anywhere
from 3 to 7 days, after which time flocculation and sedimentation will commence.

Occasionally homebrewers will experience a rotten egg aroma in their fermentation. This is not an unusual occurrence of fermentation. It is caused by
certain strains of yeast that produce hydrogen sulfide that is, in turn, carried
away by carbon dioxide. Changing your yeast or fermentation temperature will
often minimize the aroma.

A number of things happen during flocculation. At mid-fermentation, the
yeast will begin to sense that its energy stores are near depletion. As fermentation moves closer to completion and food is no longer available, the yeast begins to prepare for dormancy by settling to the bottom and creating sediment.

*Sedimentation*—During sedimentation, the yeast produces a substance called
glycogen. Glycogen is necessary for cell maintenance during dormancy and is
used as an energy source for initial activity if the yeast is added to new beer
wort. The sediment of yeast produced during the first week of sedimentation is
the most viable form of yeast to use if you wish to propagate it.

Very little fermentation occurs after the yeast has sedimented; what little
does occur, occurs very slowly. If sedimentation occurs prematurely, it can result

## 5 Secrets to Fermentation

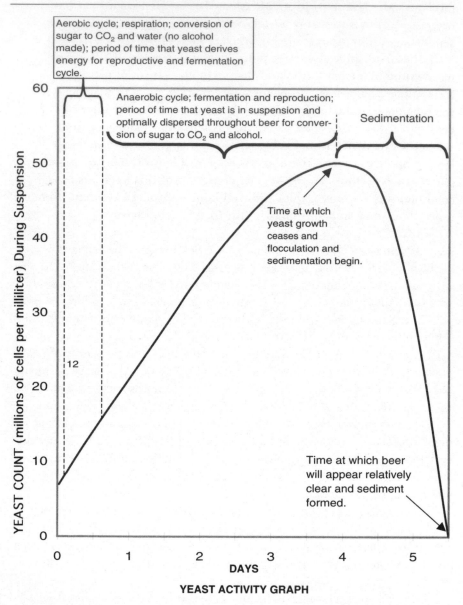

Aerobic cycle; respiration; conversion of sugar to $CO_2$ and water (no alcohol made); period of time that yeast derives energy for reproductive and fermentation cycle.

Anaerobic cycle; fermentation and reproduction; period of time that yeast is in suspension and optimally dispersed throughout beer for conversion of sugar to $CO_2$ and alcohol.

Sedimentation

Time at which yeast growth ceases and flocculation and sedimentation begin.

Time at which beer will appear relatively clear and sediment formed.

YEAST COUNT (millions of cells per milliliter) During Suspension

DAYS

**YEAST ACTIVITY GRAPH**

in long and slow fermentation. In this case a brewer may contemplate rousing the yeast, but extreme care must be taken not to introduce oxygen or bacterial contamination. As a homebrewer, you need not be concerned with premature sedimentation. If you feel that sedimentation occurred too quickly, you are better off relaxing and not worrying. With healthy and adequate amounts of yeast at pitching, 3-day complete fermentations are common for homebrewers, but due to conditions such as cool or fluctuating temperatures, underpitching, low initial wort oxygen, insufficient nutrients, high gravity (lots of sugar), and poor yeast health, some primary fermentations can take 7 to 14 days. Have a homebrew.  •

If the brewer chooses to mature the beer over a period of many weeks or even months, the beer should be removed from the sediment of yeast. After fermentation is completed, the presence of yeast in great amounts is not necessary. Even though your beer may appear clear, there are still millions of yeast cells present in the beer—an adequate amount for final fermentation and carbonation in the bottle.

Flavor changes during maturation are not predominantly yeast-related unless there is sediment present. Over a period of time, the yeast cells will begin a process of deterioration called autolysis. The by-products of autolysis can contribute a yeasty flavor to the beer. The degree of these yeast-derived flavors is also dependent on the strain of yeast.

Almost paradoxically, the small amount of yeast present in bottle-conditioned homebrew actually helps stabilize the flavor of beer, mostly by scavenging any oxygen that remains in the beer. A little live yeast in bottled beer is a significant advantage to flavor stability.

## LISTENING TO YOUR YEAST

A summary of tidbits for the homebrewer:

1. If using dried yeast, enhance your yeast's performance by rehydrating it in hot water (100 degrees F [38 degrees C]) for 15 minutes. Use boiled water that has been allowed to cool in a sanitized jar. Cover the jar with a clean unused piece of aluminum foil during the rehydration period.

2. Can liquid yeast cultures make a positive difference in the quality of your beer? The answer is clearly yes, assuming that you have a clean culture. The quality of most liquid yeast cultures currently available through homebrew supply stores is excellent. If they are handled properly, they can markedly improve the quality of your beer. Liquid cultures are more expensive to purchase and require some understanding of how they should be handled. Despite the added risk of anxiety (don't worry), your investment and patience will certainly be rewarded. For beginners, follow the instructions that are printed on the package of yeast. Keep in mind that when using liquid cultures, it is essential to thoroughly aerate your wort before introducing them. Not doing so will result in long, sluggish fermentations. Aerate your unfermented wort thoroughly by shaking or agitating your sealed fermenter.

3. Behavior will vary with batch size. For example, beer brewed in a 1-gallon (3.8 l) jug as opposed to a 5-gallon (19 l) jug will be more influenced by

temperature changes in the room due to the smaller volume and also because relatively there is more surface area (per volume) of the beer in contact with the glass. The yeast will clear more quickly because it has a shorter distance to travel to the bottom. The brew usually ferments to completion in a much shorter period.

4. Behavior will vary with ingredients. Different malts, malt extracts, and adjuncts will provide variety in the balance of fermentable sugars and nutrients.

5. Behavior will vary with temperature. Warmer fermentations increase the rate of activity while colder temperatures inhibit. Cooler temperatures will also aid in sedimentation of the yeast.

6. Behavior will vary with contamination. Bizarre behavior is usually the result of contamination by certain other microorganisms, rather than the yeast or ingredients that you are using. Give more attention to your sanitation procedures.

7. If you culture yeast, it is likely that it will change and adapt to your brewery environment. Yeast that has been cultured to be used in

a 1,000-barrel (1,120 hl) fermenter will not behave the same if used to brew the same ingredients in a 5-gallon (19 l) batch. Remember, yeasts are living organisms that will adapt.

8. Pitching rates will influence the behavior of yeast. If you do not add enough yeast to the wort, the yeast will not be able to achieve the optimum population to effect quick and complete fermentation. If too much yeast is added, the yeast will only reproduce until the population reaches the optimum 50 million cells per milliliter (approximate). There is a subtle flavor called "yeast-bite" associated with overpitching. Scientific explanations have not been found.

9. Your at-home brewery may develop what are called "house flavors." Because of the uniqueness of the conditions under which you brew—and your attitude—very real "house" character may subtly manifest itself in all your beers. It may be partly attributed to a nonspoiling bacteria or microorganism that lives at your address.

10. If you experience a fermentation that seems to take forever or there is a flavor in your beer that is reminiscent of bananas or plastic Band-Aid strips, then change your yeast, especially if you are using a nameless package of dried yeast. Choose a name-brand dried yeast that you or your homebrew supply shop owner trusts to have consistency and a dependable supply. If you are brewing from kit beers and haven't been quite satisfied, then avoid using the nameless and labelless yeast package provided with the kit. Yeast strains vary tremendously. Some will produce flavors you don't prefer because they are a particular strain, while others will produce strange plasticlike flavors or long, slow fermentations because of wild yeast contamination of the cultured yeast. When yeast is packaged in a simple white foiled or paper envelope, you can't depend on it. If your results have been inconsistent or consistently frustrating, progress from one name brand of yeast to another until you find one that suits your preference.

11. Do not add tap water to your beer once fermentation has begun. It contains oxygen, which, if added to fermenting or finished beer, will contribute to oxidation and bacterial spoilage. If you want to dilute your beer at bottling time or after it goes into the secondary fermenter, use boiled and cooled water.

12. Mixing strains of beer yeast can lead to some interesting results. Sometimes the blending of ale yeasts with lager yeasts can produce desired behavior. Sometimes when breweries do this, the yeasts are added separately and at distinctly different phases of fermentation activity. The point is that the yeasts will work and that you can mix them without worrying.

## CLEANING AND SANITATION
## IN THE HOMEBREWERY

*"Cleanliness is next to goodliness."* —Merlin

The single most important factor in being able to make delicious beer is cleanliness. The more that you can minimize the chances of unwanted bacteria and wild yeast contaminating your beer the better your beer will be. The contamination of your beer by uninvited microorganisms can result in cloudy beer, sour beer, overcarbonation, surface mold, off-flavors, and a host of other bizarre occurrences. There are some contaminants that won't drastically affect your beer. Obviously, some are worse than others. You can assure yourself that there are no known pathogens (toxic microorganisms) that can survive in beer. Your occasional mistake may look weird, taste awful, and momentarily depress you, but it won't kill you.

Now don't run away! Keeping your brewery clean is not that difficult. It is simply a question of giving the matter consideration and then doing it. You might still brew good beer even if you don't attend to keeping things clean, but your beer will improve significantly when you do decide to maintain sanitary procedures.

I use the words *clean* and *sanitary* (or *sanitized*) very deliberately. Discouraging unwanted microorganisms is a two-part process. The word *clean* is used to describe the physical appearance of your equipment. The word *sanitized* describes the equipment that has been disinfected. Sterilization is impractical and nearly impossible. The largest breweries in the world don't sterilize; they sanitize. Sanitization with disinfectants will reduce the population of bacteria and wild yeast to such a degree that the good beer yeast *you* introduce will be in the majority and do its thing before the bad guys have a chance.

Relax, for crying out loud. Don't get any silly notions that you're going to have to play doctor or pressure-cook your beer. Cleaning can be achieved with a little elbow grease and patience. Sanitization is as easy as rinsing or soaking your equipment. And keeping your beer wort free of contamination is as easy as not touching it.

There are a number of cleaners and disinfectants that can be used by homebrewers. One of the most effective is household bleach. Other very effective and easy-to-use cleaners and disinfectants are available at homebrew supply shops and are well worth using.

What follows is a summary of common cleaners and sanitizers used by homebrewers. But before you use any of them, a very serious word of WARNING: NEVER EVER COMBINE OR MIX ANY CLEANERS OR DISINFECTANTS! *The gases that may be released by chemical reactions are toxic and can kill you.*

## CLEANSERS AND SANITIZERS

*Household ammonia*—Household ammonia and water is most effectively used as a glass bottle label remover. One cup per 5 gallons (19 l) of cold water and an overnight soaking of bottles will remove all but metallic labels. Ammonia is unpleasant to work with. Use in a ventilated area and *never* mix with chlorinated cleaners. A good substitute for household ammonia is plain washing soda.


*Chlorine (household bleach)*—In certain forms, chlorine is a very powerful cleaner, sanitizer, and sterilant. Do not confuse chlorine with chloride. They are two very different chemicals, the latter (chloride) being dissociated from sodium when common salt is dissolved in water. Never mix acids, ammonia, or anything else, for that matter, with chlorinated cleaners.

Household bleach is inexpensive and possibly the most accessible and effective disinfectant that a homebrewer can use. Most forms of household bleach have only 5 percent available chlorine. The other ingredients are inert and have no disinfecting potential. But don't underestimate the power of household bleach. To give you an idea of just how strong it is, consider the fact that it takes only 0.25 ppm of pure chlorine in distilled water to sanitize it—that is ⅓ teaspoon of household bleach for every 100 gallons of water (1 ml per 1,000 l).

How does chlorine work? The chlorine in household bleach is available as sodium hypochlorite. The chlorine becomes an effective sanitizer only when it combines with water (of which there is some already in solution) to form hypochlorous acid. Hypochlorous acid is very unstable in that it breaks down or reacts to form other chemicals that are not useful as sanitizers but can contribute nasty characters to the water. Hypochlorous acid is reduced by sunlight, heat, or by its combination with nitrogen compounds (just about any organic matter, some of which are available from beer wort as protein and yeast nutrients). The combination of chlorine with nitrogen compounds presents a problem because the resulting compounds are very stable compounds such as chlorophenols, chloroform, and chloramines; not only can they contribute off-flavors to beer, but they are toxic when present in significant amounts. These nasty compounds are odorless. The odor of chlorine comes from what is referred to as "free available chlorine" (FAC). It is the FAC that has the ability to disinfect, but is unstable in sunlight or at high temperatures.

How does one safely use household bleach? Not only is chlorine bleach an effective disinfectant but it is also an effective cleaner. It is able to remove some of the most stubborn and inaccessible stains and residues in your glass fermenters and bottles.

Two fluid ounces (60 ml) of bleach in 5 gallons (19 l) of cold water and an overnight soak will remove the most hardened fermentation residues from the inside surface of your glass fermenter. This strong solution should be thoroughly rinsed with warm or hot water. Chlorine bleach sanitizing solutions are corrosive to stainless steel and if used on already cleaned stainless steel, the contact time should only be for a few minutes.

For homebrewers, an effective sanitizing solution can be prepared by mixing ⅓ to 1½ teaspoons (3 to 10 ml) of household bleach in 5 gallons (19 l) of cold water. This mixture will yield chlorine in solution at 5 to 25 ppm—an effective sanitizer, with a ½- to 1-hour soak, immersion, or contact with clean equipment. The necessity of rinsing off this sanitizing solution is debated among homebrewers. Some choose to let the utensils drip dry or don't dry or rinse at all, out of anxiety about the cleanliness of their water supply. If you drink your water from the tap, don't hesitate to rinse all chlorine solutions thoroughly with hot tap water. Hot water from your water heater is partly sanitized, especially if it has been residing in the tank reservoir for hours. Besides, by that point, you have already minimized the presence of bacteria in your wort to such a degree that any introduction of bacteria from the water would be negligible.

*Chlorine dioxide*—A very effective sanitizer. When chlorine dioxide breaks down it does not form nasty compounds like chlorine, nor does it have a chlorinelike flavor. It is more environmentally friendly than chlorine bleach, does not dry out your skin, and is a very effective sanitizer.

One brand-name product available to homebrewers is called Oxine, available through homebrew supply shops. This is a stable 2 percent solution to which water and either food-grade citric or phosphoric acid must be added to dilute and activate it to a working solution. When a properly activated working solution is made, rinsing is not necessary. The working solution breaks down with time, so it cannot be saved, except under carefully controlled conditions. READ THE INSTRUCTIONS that accompany any chlorine dioxide product and follow the directions. The following chart is a guide to make a 100 ppm working solution:

| *Oxine (2% chlorine dioxide)* | | | *Water* | | | *Citric Acid* |
|---|---|---|---|---|---|---|
| OUNCES (FL) | TEASPOONS | MILLILITERS | LITERS | QUARTS | GALLONS | GRAMS |
| 3 | 18 (6 Tbsp.) | 96 | 19 | 20 | 5 | 10 |
| 0.65 | 4 | 20 | 3.8 | 4 | 1 | 2 |
| 0.16 | 1 | 5 | 1 | 1 | .30 | 0.5 |

*Detergents*—Detergents can be an aid to cleaning your homebrew equipment. The nonperfumed varieties are preferable. Applied with a little elbow grease, detergents will remove dirt, grease, and oils, making your equipment physically clean. Rinse very well, as residues can alter the character of your beer. NOTE: Do not mix soap with detergents. They are not the same thing, and their combination will render both useless.

*Heat*—Boiling water or temperatures held above 170 degrees F (71 C) will sanitize equipment.

*Iodine*—Iodine disinfectant called Iodaphor is available at your local home-brew supply shop. Sold commercially as "iodine detergent germicide," these solutions are very concentrated and have acids such as phosphoric acid added for their cleansing ability. Read the instructions of these concentrates very carefully. A typical dilution ratio of 2 teaspoons (10 ml) of about a 1.5 percent iodine concentrate added to 5 gallons (19 l) of cold water will achieve an effective sanitizing solution.

If these disinfectants are available (they are often used in the dairy industry), they offer a practical alternative to the homebrewer. Iodine can be as toxic as chlorine, so care should be taken when handling it. It will permanently stain clothes and other things.

*Metabisulfite, sodium or potassium*—Sodium or potassium metabisulfite is a bacterial inhibitor. It does not necessarily have the ability to disinfect. It works by releasing sulfur dioxide ($SO_2$) gas when combined in solution with acids. Metabisulfites added to water alone are not at all effective for sanitizing home-brew equipment.

Metabisulfites should not be used in beermaking. Their use in mead and winemaking is justified, in that their addition to the acidic wine creates sulfur dioxide. Also, wine has a higher alcohol content, which further inhibits bacteria. Metabisulfite is not strong enough for use in beermaking, and its addition to beer should be avoided entirely.

*Oxine*—See "Chlorine dioxide."

*PBW*—This is a brand-name cleanser that is not caustic and is biodegradable. When used properly it can soak off the most amazing caked-on residues on your glass fermenters and even on your brewpots. It can even remarkably improve the appearance of an old baking sheet you've had in your kitchen since antiquity.

Before using this cleaner, use a little elbow grease and brush or soft sponge as much residue off of your equipment as possible. Follow the instructions for dosage, but generally 2 ounces (60 g) of PBW powder is mixed with 2 to 5 gallons of warm water. Soaking time depends on what strength you mix it and how stubborn the residual filth is. It could be a quick sponge-off, 30 minutes, or overnight for the most difficult cleaning jobs.

Rinse this cleaner off very well with warm water.

*Quaternary ammonia*—This very powerful and persistent disinfectant is occasionally mentioned by homebrewers and in homebrew literature. A very stable and toxic disinfectant, it is sometimes used in commercial breweries to clean floors and the outside of brewhouse equipment. It should never be used to clean anything that comes in contact with the beer. I do not recommend its use by homebrewers.

*Soap*—Soap and elbow grease can be used to clean homebrewery equipment. If soap is used, attention should be given to rinsing all residues with warm water.

*Star San*—This brand of sanitizer has grown in popularity with homebrewers as well as professional brewers because it is biodegradable, environmentally friendly, flavorless, odorless, and does not require rinsing. It may seem a bit on the pricey side, but is well worth it when you consider that you spread each application's cost over sixty 12-ounce (355 ml) bottles of beer. In fact it becomes downright cheap.

The active ingredients are dodecylbenzenesulfonic acid and phosphoric acid. When Star San is mixed at a strength of 1 ounce (30 ml) per 5 gallons (19 l), you have a solution that will sanitize cleaned surfaces. Five gallons (19 l) is a lot of sanitizer, but serves well to soak hoses and fermentation locks in a bucket. Smaller working solutions can be conveniently used in a spray bottle for spraying. Here are some convenient mixing ratios:

| *Star San* | | | *Water* | | |
|---|---|---|---|---|---|
| OUNCES (FL) | TEASPOONS | MILLILITERS | LITERS | QUARTS | GALLONS |
| 1 | 6 (2 Tbsp.) | 30 | 19 | 20 | 5 |
| 0.25 | 1.5 | 7.5 | 4.8 | 5 | 1.25 |
| Use pipette—measure in ml | 1.5 | | 1 | 1 | — |

Star San foams a lot. The foaming action helps get the sanitizer into the cracks and crevasses where microorganisms hide. So don't overagitate when using. But remember the working solution of Star San when properly drained requires no rinsing. It will not affect the taste of your beer.

*Washing soda (sodium carbonate)*—Washing soda is an alkaline cleanser. A solution of ¼ to ½ cup (60 to 120 ml) of washing soda and 5 gallons (19 l) of warm water will remove most labels from glass beer bottles. Washing soda solutions will corrode aluminum and release explosive hydrogen gas. Naturally, don't use an aluminum pot to hold your solution.

## CLEANING AND SANITIZING PLASTIC HOMEBREW EQUIPMENT

Siphon hoses and plastic fermenters should appear clean, scratchless, and stain-free. Scratches and stains will harbor bacteria and shield them from the most caustic sanitizing solutions. Any of the preceding cleaners and disinfectants can be used. If stains cannot be removed or there are scratches in your plastic and you've been brewing some funky beer, it is time to throw them away. (NOTE: Old siphon hoses are ideal for transferring emergency gasoline—put one in your car.)

All plastic equipment can be immersed or swabbed with disinfectants. Avoid boiling soft plastic such as fermentation locks unless you want some useless pieces of sculpture.

## CLEANING AND SANITIZING GLASS CARBOYS AND BOTTLES

Glass should appear stain-free when clean. Any disinfectant can be used to sanitize glass. Five-gallon (19 l) carboys are awkward to clean and will be slippery when wet—use great caution. A long-handled bottle brush is useful in order to remove the majority of fermentation stains. Carboys and beer bottles should be attended to as soon as they are empty. Dried beer-related residues are very difficult to remove. A quick rinsing along with agitation while contents are still wet will remove most residues. An overnight soak in a solution of 1 to 2 ounces (30 to 60 ml) of bleach per 5 gallons (19 l) of cold water will remove all residues from the sides of the carboy.

When cleaning beer bottles, make a quick inspection to see if they are stained or have a dried bacterial deposit ringing the inside neck of the bottle. *Inspect them carefully.* If they are stained inside, then immerse them for 1 hour in a bucket of bleach cleaning solution: 2 ounces (60 ml) of bleach per 5 gallons (19 l) of cold water. If beer bottles are physically clean, then an immersion and a 5-minute wet contact with a sanitizing solution—1 teaspoon (7 ml) of bleach per 5 gallons (19 l) of cold water—will suffice. Rinse with hot tap water. If bottles are still not cleaned after using these methods, then they are NWDW (not worth dealing with) anymore.

## CLEANING AND SANITIZING THE MISCELLANEOUS

Immersing your bottle caps in a cup of 80-proof neutral spirits (like vodka) is a way to help assure that your bottle caps are sanitized. Boiling your bottle caps is also an option; who knows where they've been? Wooden spoons are impossible to sanitize. That charismatic wooden spoon is fine and should be used when stirring your boiling wort, but do not immerse the wooden spoon into the wort when it has cooled below 160 degrees F (71 C). "What then do I stir the cooled wort with?" you may ask. Don't, other than to remove some of the wort when measuring its specific gravity or to siphon. There is really no reason to be mucking about in your beer once it is cooled and fermenting. Though if you must, use an all stainless steel, long-handled spoon that is easily sanitized.

Avoid putting your hands in the beer when siphoning; if you must, at least wash and rinse them thoroughly beforehand (no pun intended).

Avoid using your mouth to start your siphon. If you must, gargle with the best brandy you can find (you deserve it) or 150-proof rum (if you feel the need to suffer). Your mouth has lots of beer-harmful bacteria, bacteria that love to sour beer. An easy way to start a siphon is to fill it with water before you immerse it in the beer (see the "Treatise on Siphoning," Appendix 10, page 440).

## AND DON'T FORGET . . .

Don't be intimidated by those invisible critters that want to jump in your beer. You really can't blame them, can you? After you go through your first experience of cleaning and sanitizing, you will develop your own system and the whole procedure will become mindlessly automatic.

Relax. Don't worry. Have a homebrew. Believe me, the quality of the beer that you make will be worth it.

## GETTING YOUR WORT TOGETHER

You are about to embark on a journey from which there is no returning, no middle, no end, and no bottom. A journey into an area in which there is more meaning—an area called the Twilight Foam.

The Twilight Foam is one step beyond; a simple conjecture, an impulse that leads to the wonderful world of worts. With a little experience comes the realization that there is more choice, variety, and quality beer to be brewed by you, the homebrewer, than you had ever imagined.

By this time, you have made the choice and it is simple enough to follow recipes and brew great beer—it's that easy. But to understand your beer and why it is you are brewing—now that's what makes the best beer *every single time!* We all know how much satisfaction we get when we serve our beer to our friends and can say, "I made that beer," but being able to transmit the depth of feeling brewed into that beer is even more satisfying. You become a brewer who passes on the inspiration to others. Be careful about leaving this book lying around. Warning: As mentioned at the beginning, this book, if loaned, may never be returned.

The following sections will not only review procedures with which you should already be familiar, but will also detail the whys and what-fors to making better brew. Different combinations of plain malt extracts, hops, and grains will allow you an almost overwhelming variety of homebrewed beers. Knowing the reasons for combining ingredients and how these ingredients interact with one another will comfort you and allow you to fearlessly concoct better and better brews. REMEMBER: Relax . . . don't worry . . . have a homebrew!

## KEEPING RECORDS

The very first thing that you should do before embarking on brewing a batch of beer is to pop a few bottles of beer into the refrigerator. And get ready to brew.

The second thing that you'll want to consider is your ability to remember what you did to brew that best batch of beer. Because your beer will be memorable and you will be using such a variety of ingredients, it is worth your effort to keep a log of recipes and procedures. Keeping a record of your beermaking will enable you to duplicate favorite recipes and improve upon them (not to mention passing them on to friends).

You don't have to record an inordinate amount of detail. Keep it simple. Don't get so involved that keeping records becomes a bother. I assure you that you won't regret it. Here's a simple list of things that you'll want to record in your "Homebrew Recipe Log":

1. Date of brewing
2. Name of beer
3. Volume of beer being brewed (batch size)
4. List of all ingredients and amounts used
5. Time of boil
6. When and how grains and hops are added
7. Temperature of wort when yeast is added (pitched)
8. Beginning specific gravity
9. Dates of when beer is transferred (racked)
10. Date when bottled and amount of priming sugar
11. Ending specific gravity
12. Comments and blow-by-blow descriptions worth saving for posterity

EXAMPLE

*February 30, 2042*
*Grizzly Beer Ale*
*5 gallons (19 l)*

| | |
|---|---|
| 5 pounds | Americana plain light malt extract syrup |
| 1 pound | crystal malt |
| 2 teaspoons | gypsum |
| 1½ ounces | Fuggles hops (for boiling) |

½ ounce   Hallertau hops (finishing hop)
1 package   GotUCovered brand ale yeast

Boiled water, malts, gypsum, and Fuggles hops for 60 minutes. Added Hallertau hops during final 5 minutes for flavor.

| | |
|---|---|
| 2/30/42 | Pitched yeast. 75 degrees F (24 C). Specific gravity 1.044 (11). |
| 3/4/42 | Racked beer to secondary fermenter. Specific gravity 1.017 (4). Still fermenting. |
| 3/6/42 | Activity has almost stopped. |
| 3/14/42 | Bottled with ¾ cup sugar. Ending specific gravity 1.013. Tastes real good, but a little yeasty. |
| 3/20/42 | Tasted first bottle—GREAT—still needs another week for better carbonation. |
| 4/31/42 | WOW! Crystal clear. Tastes perfect. Best beer ever. Next time I'll try ½ ounce more Fuggles hops in boil for more bitterness. *Boy, oh boy, am I glad I kept good notes!* |

## A REVIEW OF THE BREWING PROCESS

1. Have a homebrew. Relax. Don't worry.
2. Preparation of ingredients
3. Boiling the wort
4. Straining and sparging
5. Fermentation
6. Bottling
7. Have a homebrew. Relax. Don't worry.

### 1. Have a Homebrew

Like sourdough bread, it is a good idea to begin your next batch of beer with a tribute to your last batch.

### 2. Preparation of Ingredients

Your hops and malt extract will not need any preparation other than weighing or proportioning the necessary amounts.

When you use specialty grains such as crystal, black, and chocolate malts or roasted barley, you will need to do some simple preparation. In order to most efficiently utilize these grains, it is recommended that they be gently cracked, which can very easily be accomplished by using a rolling pin or an unopened can of malt extract. Spread a small amount of grain on a flat, hard surface and apply a small amount of pressure as you roll over the grains. (HOT TIP: Put the grains in a resealable plastic bag and crush them in the bag. No muss, no

*A crystal gaze! Crystal malt, shown here, has been crushed into granules and is now ready for the brewpot. Crushing allows the gracious goodness of specialty malts to more easily dissolve into the wort.*

fuss.) The objective is to break the grains into pieces, not to pulverize them into dust, so that the goodness of these grains may be extracted in the hot water or wort to which they will be added. Do not use a blender or food processor, as the possibility of making specialty grain "flour" is more likely. If you are fortunate enough to have a grain or flour mill, adjust the grinding plates so that their surfaces are far enough apart to crack the grains into four or five pieces rather than grind them into flour.

Overgrinding specialty malts will create difficulty in straining them out of the wort. If an excessive amount of grain powder is allowed to pass on to the fermenter, off-flavors in the beer may result.

The grinding of all your grains should be done in an area away from your fermentation. There is always a small amount of grain dust created when cracking or grinding. This dust carries bacteria that can very easily contaminate your beer.

### 3. Boiling the Wort

During this process, you will boil water, malt extract, hops, minerals, other sugars, and adjuncts and finings. Most of these ingredients can be added indiscriminately at the beginning of the boil, but some yield better results when added discriminately.

The simplest and most effective way to introduce the goodness of specialty grains in malt extract brewing is to add the cracked grains to the cold water before you add any other ingredients and before bringing the mix to a boil. Just before the water comes to a boil, simply use a small kitchen strainer and remove as much as possible without undue fuss. You will find that you can easily remove 90 to 98 percent of the grains. It's that simple! Want something even simpler? Use a grain bag (available from your local homebrew supply shop); place your grains in it and use it like a giant tea bag.

After the specialty grains are removed from the water, add your malt extract, minerals, boiling hops, and all other sugars. Now, many of you will chuckle when I tell you that your wort will boil over and make a horrendous mess if you don't watch out and watch it. But don't tell me I didn't warn you. It happens to all of us at least once, and if you're human, twice. It's one of those things that we don't learn except by making the same mistake twice.

So, as you continue to heat and bring your wort back to a boil, use your wooden spoon (with charisma) to stir well and dissolve all of the ingredients so they won't stick and scorch on the bottom of the brewpot. You will want to time your boil from when it begins with all of the ingredients. One hour is an adequate time for boiling your wort.

Hops that are used as flavor or aromatic finishing hops are best added during the final 1 to 10 minutes of the boil. Generally, the most flavor will be extracted and preserved for no longer than 10 minutes of boiling. The aromatics of hops will dissipate more quickly so are best allowed to steep for only 1 to 2 minutes if hop aroma is desired in the finished beer.

*Why boil?* Boiling extracts with hops converts hop compounds to the bittering qualities desired in beer. It is necessary to boil hops for at least 30 minutes in order to facilitate the desired chemical reactions that allow the bittering resins to dissolve into your wort. The combination of the bittering qualities of the hops along with certain minerals and the physical process of boiling helps coagulate and precipitate undesirable proteins out of the wort. This reaction helps clarify the beer and improves the fermentation and flavor. Called the "hot-break," this reaction can be seen taking place in your brewpot. After a short period of boiling, your wort begins to exhibit a cloudiness and has flakes of coagulated protein floating in it. This coagulation and precipitation can be dramatically demonstrated by removing a small amount of boiling wort into a preheated glass. You will observe the pea-size flakes of protein settle to the bottom.

The addition of a small amount—¼ teaspoon (1 to 2 g) for 5 gallons (19 l)—of Irish moss during the final 10 minutes of the boil will aid in settling proteins. It is usually not necessary to boil wort for any longer than 1 hour, but you can if necessary (like when the phone rings and you need to answer it).

## 4. Straining and Sparging

Sparging is the process of rinsing the removed spent grains from a grain soak or "mash" prior to boiling and/or hops from the wort. Hot water is used to sparge (rinse) in order to get their goodness out.

When straining mashed or hot-water-soaked grains, the liquid is destined to your brewpot.

When straining hops out of your boiled wort and sparging, the wort is destined for your fermenter. When sparging into your fermenter, a few things must be attended to first in order to maintain sanitation. Your fermenter, strainer, and ladling device (usually a saucepan) should be sanitized. Procedures for sanitizing your fermenter have already been described in the "Cleaning and Sanitation" section on page 130. Once the fermenter has been sanitized, partially fill it with cold water. Sanitize your strainer by immersing it into your boiling wort (if it is a plastic strainer, use a sanitizing solution). Likewise, immerse your saucepan into the boiling wort or place it in a hot oven to sterilize (only if saucepan is ovenproof). Don't worry; these procedures are simpler than the space it takes to describe them to you—and they work.

If there are no whole or pellet hops used, and hop-flavored malt extract has been used, then there is no need to sparge. The hot concentrated wort may be ladled directly into the awaiting cold water.

If whole hops have been used, the hot wort should be passed through a strainer on its way to the fermenter. The spent hops that are caught in your strainer can be rinsed (called "sparging") with a small amount of hot water in order to remove all of the goodness to the fermenter.

There is an advantage to sparging out whole hops in that the hops will form a natural filter, filtering out much of the protein coagulated during the hot-break. If the sparging process is bypassed you may notice a significant amount of sediment on the bottom of your fermenter. This sediment is called "trub" (pronounced "troob"). Commercial brewers go to great lengths to remove this trub by sparging or whirlpooling the wort as it is drawn from the brewpot. (The whirlpool effect can be evoked by stirring a cup of tea—the tea leaves will go to the center of the cup; similarly so will beer trub—the wort is drawn off from the sides of the vessel rather than from the bottom.) The presence of trub in the fermenting wort does affect fermentation and flavor, but for a homebrewer its overall significance is slight compared to all of the other variables that more

*Another strained relationship! Have a homebrew, and remember: Separate the hops
or grains in your brewpot from the wort before you put it in the fermenter. Here,
boiling wort is strained into a fermenter containing cold water.*
NOTE: *If a plastic fermenter is used, it is essential that it be fitted with a lid.*

dynamically affect the outcome of your beer. Relax. Don't worry. Have a home-brew.

It is from this point on that strict attention must be given to sanitation. After sparging, the wort becomes cool and susceptible to contaminating microorgan-isms. So relax, don't worry, put your charismatic wooden spoon back in storage, and assure yourself that you have sanitized your equipment.

## 5. Fermentation

Once the cooled wort is in your fermenter, you should muck about in it as little as possible, preferably not at all. If necessary, the wort should be stirred or agi-tated with a sanitized long-handled plastic or metal spoon. A temperature should be taken, and a small amount of wort should be poured or carefully ladled into a hydrometer flask so that a specific gravity can be read. Take notes.

Once yeast has been added, put your fermenter in a relatively quiet, out-of-the-way place and away from direct light. Strong light will react with hops and create a skunky or rubbery aroma and flavor. In strong sunlight this reaction can take place in a matter of minutes.

"Primary" (the first stage) fermentation should be maintained at tempera-tures of 60 to 70 degrees F (16 to 21 C) for ale yeast, but is best started at 70 to 76 degrees F (21 to 24 C). True lager yeasts are best begun at wort temperatures between 50 and 60 degrees F (10 to 16 C) and maintained at stable tempera-tures of 45 to 55 degrees F (7.5 to 13 C) during primary fermentation.

Once the yeast has been added, signs of fermentation will be noticed within 24 hours, and usually within 36 hours there is a massive amount of activity as the yeast churns a rich foamy head (called "kraeusen"). The kraeusen is topped with a very bitter and brown resinous scum, some of which will adhere to the sides of the fermenter as the kraeusen soon disappears and falls back into the beer. The removal of this resin before it falls back into the fermentation will result in a less bitter "bite" to your beer. In the process of removing the bitter resins, "fusel" oils are also removed. Fusel oils are a by-product of fermentation and contribute to what are often referred to as "beer headaches." If the removal of hop resins during the kraeusen stage can be done under sanitary conditions, then it is your choice to do so. The closed fermentation system described in the Beginner's Section ("blow-out" hose and glass carboy) automatically facilitates the removal of the kraeusen during the initial stages of fermentation. If open fermentation is used and there is a risk of contamination, then avoid removing the kraeusen because contamination will affect the flavor of your beer much more than will the minimal effect of the mostly insoluble resins and oils. When in doubt, relax, and don't worry—your beer will taste just fine.

After the first 3 to 6 days of fermentation, the kraeusen will fall back into the beer and the yeast will begin to settle. If a one-stage open fermentation proce-dure is undertaken (only one fermenter is used), then the brewer should bottle the beer between the seventh and fourteenth day or when fermentation activity has stopped, whichever comes first.

When fermentation activity stops, the protective layer of foam and/or carbon dioxide is no longer present and the possibility of contamination increases. Fermentation activity can be measured by a hydrometer.

If you are planning to mature the beer in the fermenter over a period longer than 10 days, then it is advisable to transfer the beer into a closed fermenter. A closed fermenter can simply be a 5-gallon (19 l) carboy with a fermentation lock attached. The advantage to "racking" (transferring) the beer under these circumstances is that the beer is locked away from contaminants in the air and is removed from the sediment. After about 2 weeks the sediment will begin to break down and may contribute off-flavors to the beer.

*Racking your beer*—"Racking" is the name used by brewers to describe the transfer of beer from one container to another. The easiest and most effective way for the homebrewer to accomplish this is by siphoning with a clean, sanitized, clear plastic hose.

Your choice of fermenters will have a bearing on the amount of attention you have to give to your beer. A closed fermentation system requires the least amount of attention and has many other advantages. An open fermentation system (the plastic bucket) will produce excellent beer but more attention must be given to the timeliness of transferring and bottling.

*Open fermentation*—At first, this type of fermentation appears simpler and more economical. In certain ways it is, but it doesn't really allow you the freedom from concern that you deserve. For those of you who choose it, or perhaps have no choice, here are a few hints to ensure excellent beer:

1. Keep the fermenter covered at all times, except when taking hydrometer readings.
2. Do not skim the kraeusen foam. Risk of contamination is too great, especially when using a strainer.
3. The disappearance of the kraeusen is a perfect indication that the beer is ready to transfer to a secondary fermenter. You will usually find that by this time your specific gravity has fallen to two-thirds of the original specific gravity.
4. Maturing your beer over long periods of time is unnecessary. You should be drinking your beer within four weeks.

*Closed fermentation*—The closed fermentation system that is described in the Beginner's Section is the most relaxing way to brew beer. It is a system in which the primary stage of fermentation is done in a sanitized container, usually a 5-gallon (19 l) carboy with an overflow hose attached on top, or a 6½-gallon (19 l) carboy that has enough headroom above a 5-gallon (19 l) batch to make an overflow hose unnecessary. The advantages of these systems are many. Maximum sanitation is ensured and, with the "blow-off," the bitter resins and fusel oils that form on the kraeusen are very efficiently blown out through the overflow hose—without the brewer so much as worrying a tat. The disadvantage is that you may lose a quart or two of precious brew, but it is an insignificant price to pay for the best beer you've ever brewed.

Racking and siphoning your beer will be necessary if prolonged maturation before bottling is desired (for example, that vacation you wanted to take or those bottles that haven't materialized yet, or the free time you don't have until next week).

Longer and successful maturation of beer is possible with closed fermentation because contamination has been minimized. Thus your beer will be more stable.

### 6. Bottling

Once fermentation has stopped or you are satisfied that your beer is finished, you should bottle. Bottling procedures for the intermediate brewer are no different than those for the beginner. The ¾ cup—NOT POUNDS!—(180 ml) of corn sugar (or 1¼ cups [300 ml] dried malt extract) per 5 gallons (19 l) of beer is adequate priming sugar for carbonation. It is an amount that will allow you to serve your beer at cool room temperatures without gushing. One cup (240 ml) of corn sugar, or 1⅔ cups (400 ml) dried malt extract, per 5 gallons (19 l) of beer can safely increase the amount of carbonation, but gushing is likely to occur if the beer is opened when not cold.

The entire amount of priming sugar should be boiled with a pint (0.5 l) or so of water before adding it to the beer. DON'T AERATE OR SPLASH YOUR BEER WHEN BOTTLING. Stick your siphon hose clear down to the bottom of each of the bottles. *Siphon quietly.*

The amount of air space left in the bottle is an area of concern to many homebrewers. Generally speaking, the less air space the better. The oxygen in the air that you leave in the bottle will react, to some degree, with the beer in the bottle. A normal amount of air space to leave is about 1 to 1½ inches (2.5 to 3.5 cm). My own observations have indicated that a bottle that is filled right to the top, with no air space whatsoever, will not develop enough carbonation. An air space of ½ inch (1.2 cm) will develop the same carbonation as a bottle of beer with 2 inches (5 cm) of air space. A bottle that is half filled with beer may become excessively carbonated and very dangerous if it explodes. My educated explanation is that insufficient or excessive carbonation, due to over- or underfill is related to the fact that yeast activity is inhibited by pressure. A small air space (overfill) will quickly develop high pressure, while a large air space (underfill) will not develop enough pressure to inhibit yeast activity. I may not be quite right, but hey, relax, don't worry, have a homebrew—I tried.

*Kegging your beer*—Homebrew can be kegged and served on draft. It is an extremely convenient way to "put up" your brew. See "Kegging Your Beer," Appendix 2, on page 405 for complete details on ways to keg your brew. You'll need to reduce your priming sugar so your beer doesn't pour all foam.

### 7. Have a Homebrew.

## SOME WORLD CLASSIC STYLES OF BEER

How many different kinds of beer are there in the world? Based on the fact that there are about 7,000 commerical breweries in the world, I'll take an educated guess that there are between 50,000 and 60,000. And that's probably conservative. One brewery might make five to ten different styles of beer in the course of a year. So you see, 50,000 is quite a reasonable guess.

What makes one beer style distinct from another? How does one classify styles? The first distinction one might make is whether or not a beer is top-fermented (ale) or bottom-fermented (lager). From these two classes spring the immense variety of top- and bottom-fermented brews.

There are many, many styles of ale being brewed, many indigenous to the areas in which they are brewed.

Since 1979, on behalf of the Brewers Association (formerly the Association of Brewers), I developed and have revised beer style descriptions on an annual basis as a reference for brewers and beer competition organizers throughout the world. Much of the early work was based on the assistance and contributions of beer journalist Michael Jackson. The task of creating a realistic set of guidelines is complex. The beer style guidelines I have developed on behalf of the Brewers Association use sources from the commercial brewing industry, beer analysis, beer judges' critiques, and consultations with beer-industry experts and knowledgeable beer enthusiasts.

The style guidelines reflect, as much as possible, historical significance or a high profile in the current commercial beer market. Often, the historical significance is not clear, or a new beer in a current market may be only a passing fad, and thus quickly forgotten. For these reasons, the addition of a style or the modification of an existing one is not undertaken lightly. Revisions are the product of research, consultation, and

consideration of current market trends and may take place over a period of time. Another consideration is that current commercial examples of a style do not always fit well into the historical record, and instead represent a modern version of the style. The decision to include a particular historical beer style takes into consideration the style's brewing traditions and the need to preserve those traditions in today's world of beer. The more a beer style has withstood the test of time, marketplace, and beer drinkers' acceptance, the more likely it is to be included in the Brewers Association's style guidelines.

The availability of commercial examples plays a large role in whether or not a beer style "makes the list." It is important to consider that not every historical or commercial beer style can be included, nor is every commercial beer representative of the historical tradition (i.e., a brewery labeling a brand as a particular style does not always indicate a fair representation of that style).

In my research, almost all of the classic and traditional beer style guidelines have been cross-referenced with data from commercially available beers representative of the style. The data referenced for this purpose has been Professor Anton Piendl's comprehensive work published in the German *Brauindustrie* magazine through the years 1982 to 1994, from the series Biere Aus Aller Welt.

For the most up-to-date version of the Brewers Association's Beer Style Guidelines, visit www.brewersassociation.org.

Following are some of the more popular and classic styles of beer brewed by today's homebrewers.

Data for each style may be abbreviated as follows:

1. International Bitterness Units: BUs
2. Color in degrees SRM (EBC): Standard Reference Method (European Brewing Convention)
3. Alcohol expressed in percent alcohol by volume (abv) unless otherwise noted
4. The numerical value in parenthesis following the Original Gravity expressed in degrees Plato

## ALES OF BRITISH AND IRISH ORIGIN

British-style ales are top-fermented beer. When traditionally brewed, they are usually made of 100 percent malted barley, hops, water, and yeast, although these days in England adjuncts such as sugar, barley, corn, rice, or potato starch sometimes find their way into some British ales. They are fermented at temperatures between 60 and 70 degrees F (16 and 21 C) for 3 to 5 days, then racked to cellar fermenters to clarify at temperatures closer to 50 degrees F (10 C). From the cellar conditioning, the ale is racked into casks and bunged (with wooden "corks"). The ale is allowed to condition for 2 to 3 days before being served in the British pubs.

If British ale is not filtered, pasteurized, nor pushed out with compressed $CO_2$ gas, it is often referred to as "real ale." Served at cellar temperatures of 55 degrees F (13 C), it is slightly carbonated and expresses a variety of character depending on the style being brewed.

Some of the traditional varieties of hops used in British ales are Brewers Gold, Challenger, First Gold, Fuggles, Kent Goldings, Northdown, Northern Brewer, Progress, and Wye Target.

## Some Classic Styles of British Ale

BITTER—A light ale that may be generally available in three strengths. *Ordinary Bitter* is brewed from specific gravities between 1.033 and 1.038 (8 to 9.5). *Special Bitter* is brewed from specific gravities between 1.038 and 1.045 (9.5 to 11), and *Extra Special Bitter* may be brewed from specific gravities between 1.046 and 1.060 (11.5 to 15). While these are generalizations, most bitters fall in these ranges.

Bitter may be highly or lightly hopped. Bitterness: 20 to 55 BU. It may express hop aroma or none at all. Some styles will have a rich creamy head while others will be served in a less carbonated condition. There are many regional styles of bitter. Color: 5 to 14 SRM (10 to 28). Alcohol: 3 to 5.8 percent

There are a few bottled versions of English-made bitter imported to the United States, but most are not really indicative of a true draft or bottle-conditioned English Bitter. There are numerous commercial microbreweries and pub breweries in both the United States and Canada that authentically brew this style of ale, as do, fortunately, hundreds of thousands of homebrewers.

English Bitter is one of the easiest, quickest, and most satisfying styles of beer that a homebrewer can make.

MILD—Mild is a brown ale of low alcoholic strength. Its tradition evolved from the working-class areas of northern England where great thirsts developed in the steel mills. The consumption of much beer was tempered by the low alcoholic strength. Beer was and still is a very social institution, to be enjoyed and savored, rather than a vehicle for drunkenness.

Mild is not particularly robust or hoppy; rather it is thirst-quenching, low-alcohol, flavorful, and light- to medium-bodied. A small amount of brown, black, chocolate, or other roasted malt influences the color more than the flavor and aroma.

Other than homebrewed and a few American craft pub brewers, there are few draft versions of this style of British ale available in the United States. Homebrewed versions of English mild are quick to mature, very satisfying, and easy to duplicate authentically.

Original gravities: 1.030 to 1.036 (7.5 to 9). Alcohol: 3.2 to 4 percent. Bitterness: 10 to 20 BU. Color: 8 to 34 SRM (16 to 68).

PALE ALE—Pale ale is a special variety of British ale that tends to be more hoppy and higher in alcohol than its relative, English Bitter.

The *classic style* of English pale ale is brewed with water that is extraordinarily hard and contains a lot of minerals, particularly calcium sulfate and carbonates. The high mineral content lends itself to the use of more hops; the high sulfate content of the water contributes a dry character. Today, pale ales can be found in England on draft or in bottles. There are very few breweries that use traditional bottle-conditioning techniques (as homebrewers still do) containing a yeast sediment. If you want to taste traditional old-world flavor, homebrewing is often the only way to go.

Many small American breweries brew this style of beer. A nationally available classic example is Sierra Nevada Pale Ale, though this is brewed using American hops lending a distinctive American-style character to the beer. Widely available imports from England representative of this style are Bass Ale, Young's Special London Ale, Whitbread's Pale Ale, and Samuel Smith's Pale Ale. Pale ale is probably one of the more popular styles of homebrew in the United States, because of its clean taste and stability.

For pale ales of English origin—Original gravities: 1.040 to 1.056 (10 to 14). Alcohol: 4.5 to 5.5 percent. Bitterness: 20 to 40 BU (American pale ales range a bit higher in bitterness: 28 to 45 BU). Color: 5 to 14 SRM (10 to 28).

INDIA PALE ALE—"IPA," as it is fondly referred to by loving beer enthusiasts, is a special style of pale ale that has more hop flavor, aroma, and bitterness, and a higher alcohol content than "pale ale." This is a popular style among psychopathic enthusiasts. There are more than a thousand commercial American-made IPAs. Widely available and perhaps the first American-style IPA made is the Anchor Brewing Company's Liberty Ale. It could be considered the classic example of the IPA style, but there are now so many popular hop variations of IPA that it is hard to frame this style with generalities and sweeping proclamations. There are few true-to-style English-made IPAs, even though the British invented this style more than a hundred years ago.

In general, English-style IPA has less alcohol and is more mildly hopped than the American-style version.

Original gravities: 1.050 to 1.075 (12.5 to 18.2). Alcohol: 5 to 7.5 percent. Bitterness: 35 to 70 BU. Color: 6 to 14 SRM (12 to 28).

OLD ALE AND STRONG ALE—These two styles of ales are high-alcohol versions of pale ale. With greater strength comes a darker color, more body, and sweetness. Strong ales are often aged longer; consequently, the sharpness of hop bitterness softens with time. Higher original gravities also lend a more fruity character to these styles of ale. The original British traditional old and strong ales were originally brewed to a lower alcohol cap, peaking around 9 percent. With the growing popularity of strong ales as specialty beers for food accompaniment and special occasions, the alcohol percentage of some strong ales exceeds 11 percent.

Original gravities: 1.058 to 1.1125 (14.3 to 31.5). Alcohol: 6 to 11+ percent. Bitterness: 30 to 65 BU. Color: 8 to 30 SRM (16 to 60).

BROWN ALE—Several distinctive *English styles* of brown ale are brewed in Great Britain. Generally they are sweeter, fuller-bodied, and stronger than their relative, mild ales. Some brown ale, such as Newcastle Brown Ale, is very light brown in color and has a sweet nutty character, while others are less sweet and have a mild but evident roasted malt character, more robust and unusual.

Original gravities: 1.040 to 1.050 (10 to 12.5). Alcohol: 4.5 to 5.5 percent. Bitterness: 15 to 25 BU. Color: 13 to 25 SRM (26 to 50).

A more bitter style of brown ale with elevated hop character emerged among American homebrewers during the 1980s. The style was popularized even more by American microbrewers. For lack of a better name, the style was dubbed American-Style Brown Ale, somewhat akin to dark pale ale with lots of hops.

Original gravities: 1.040 to 1.060 (10 to 15). Alcohol: 4 to 6.4 percent. Bitterness: 25 to 45 BU. Color: 15 to 26 SRM (30 to 52).

Many homebrewers begin their homebrewing endeavors with quickly maturing full-bodied and satisfying brown ale. Its full yet nonaggressive flavor is most impressive, especially for the beginner or someone who has not tasted good homebrew before.

### Other Ales of British and Irish Origin

STOUT—Stouts are black ales that owe their character to roasted barley and a flavorful hop rate. There are several styles of stout: imperial, sweet, oatmeal, and the more commercially popular dry stout. There are also American twists to these traditional styles with the creative addition of new hop flavors and aromas.

***Dry Stout.*** Draft versions of Irish-style dry stout are usually surprisingly low in alcohol and often brewed from original specific gravities of 1.038 to 1.048 (9.5 to 12). The classic Guinness Stout, when it was traditionally brewed and served in Dublin, Ireland, was low in alcohol, dry, and had a clean bitterness but no hop flavor or aroma; part of the bitter character was contributed by roasted barley. Its rich foamy head is enhanced by using nitrogen gas when it is dispensed from the cask or a package containing a nitrogen-releasing "widget." The degree of sweetness and dryness will vary in different brands of dry stouts, yet they are all top-fermented and have the singularly unique and special character of roasted barley.

Original gravities: 1.038 to 1.048 (9 to 12). Alcohol: 3.5 to 5 percent. Bitterness: 30 to 40 BU. Color: 40+ SRM (80+).

*Foreign (Export) Stout.* The "Export" version of Guinness and other dry stouts have more roasted barley character, more alcohol, and a bit more malt sweetness. Several commercial brands will have a notable degree of acidity.

Original gravities: 1.052 to 1.072 (13 to 17.5). Alcohol: 5.7 to 9.3 percent. Bitterness: 30 to 60 BU. Color: 40+ SRM (80+).

*American-Style Stout.* Over the past few decades American brewers have developed another version of stout that is highlighted with American hop flavor and character. Usually coffeelike roasted barley and roasted-malt aromas and flavors are prominent.

Original gravities: 1.050 to 1.075 (12.4 to 18.2). Alcohol: 5.7 to 8.8 percent. Bitterness: 35 to 60 BU. Color: 40+ SRM (80+).

*Imperial Stout* is a robust and sincerely stronger version of dry stout. American versions are highly hopped for bitterness and often dosed with flavor and aroma hops as well. American homebrewers and small brewers revived this style during the latter part of the twentieth century. With its high alcohol and high hopping rate, this American-style of imperial stout can be aged with much grace, meandering through many wonderful changes in flavor complexity. Contrary to logic and truer to the original tradition, British-style imperial stout is not necessarily black in color. Deep and dark copper tones are traditional variations, and hop bitterness and character are much more subdued. American craft ale brewers often have imperial stout as a seasonal specialty, sometimes even aged in oak barrels.

Original gravities: 1.080 to 1.100 (20 to 23). Alcohol: 7 to 12 percent. Bitterness: 45 to 80 BU. Color: 20 to 80+ SRM (40+).

*Sweet Stout* is a rarity among commercially made beers both in the United States and in England. It lacks most of the hop bitterness and roasted barley character of its dry counterpart. In England the style is often bottled as "farm stout." To achieve the sweet character, sugar or other sweeteners may be added to carbonated beer, which is then pasteurized to stop fermentation activity, a difficult process for the homebrewer. Also, unfermentable lactose sugar may be added, not so much for the minimal sweetness it contributes but for the contribution of body.

The world-classic and unique Mackeson Sweet Stout was traditionally brewed, then sweetened with sucrose and given more body with lactose sugar just before bottling. It was pasteurized in order to stop all fermentation. Mackeson Sweet Stout can be described as very sweet black ale appropriately served as an after-dinner liqueur. There are several examples of American-made "milk" or sweet stout that are more balanced and suitable for enjoying anytime.

Original gravities: 1.045 to 1.056 (11 to 14). Alcohol: 3 to 6 percent. Bitterness: 15 to 25 BU. Color: 40+ SRM (80+).

*Oatmeal Stout* has made a comeback in America among commercial craft brewers and homebrewers. It is made with oatmeal as part of the grain ingredients.

It is moderately hoppy with full cocoalike malt sweetness and a pleasing, velvety, and thirst-quenching consistency.

If you like stout, you will no doubt pursue a recipe that will brew this robust and satisfying style of beer. The freshness of brewing it yourself and the satisfaction of making a stout that is every bit as good or better than what you are used to buying is quite an experience. Stout is truly the espresso of the beer world.

Original gravities: 1.038 to 1.056 (9.5 to 14). Alcohol: 3.8 to 6 percent. Bitterness: 20 to 40 BU. Color: 20+ SRM (40+).

BARLEY WINE—Because of their unusual strength, some ales are referred to as barley wines. They can reach an alcoholic strength of 12 percent by volume and are brewed from specific gravities as high as 1.120 (28)! They are indeed alcoholic and full-bodied. Their natural sweetness is usually balanced with a high rate of hop bitterness. The counterpoint is the beer drinker in between, slowly sipping and savoring the often estery, fruity, and well-aged character of this specialty, brewed most often to celebrate special occasions. Because of the high hop rate and alcohol content, skillfully made barley wines can be aged for more than twenty-five years! These cherished brews make you feel as if you were born to weep with joy.

Most barley wines are golden or copper colored, with some American-style barley wines almost a pale straw color. English-made barley wines tend to be much less hoppy (40 to 60 BU) than what one might refer to as the American style of barley wine, full of fruity hop flavor, aroma, and complex bitterness (60 to 100 BU).

Original gravities: 1.090 to 1.120 (21.5 to 28). Alcohol: 8.5 to 12 percent. Bitterness: 40 to 100 BU. Color: 11 to 22 SRM (22 to 44).

PORTER—A traditional description of this style would be hard to come by and likely to be controversial. It is dark ale; unlike stout its character does not come from roasted barley but more from dark malts. Generally, it is medium- to full-bodied with varying degrees of sweetness and hop character.

Historically, it was a style of ale that was the granddaddy of today's stout. Porter was the common drink and often homebrewed. Its character was expressed with a wild assortment of adjuncts, herbs, and miscellaneous ingredients. Arthur Guinness and Sons in Ireland originally brewed it commercially. When the alcoholic strength of porter was boosted, it was described as stout porter. The name "stout" was soon adopted for this style.

Today, porter is brewed by small craft brewers throughout the United States; it is no longer popular in England, where it is brewed by only a few small craft brewers, though with the recent resurgence of independent small brewers in England, porters may grow in popularity.

There are two variations of porter, often referred to as "robust porter" and "brown porter." Both are full-flavored, but as the names imply, the robust

version is darker, stronger, more full-bodied than its relatively milder cousin, brown porter. In the United States, Anchor Brewing Company of San Francisco, California, brews a robust black and sharply bittersweet representation of robust porter. It is one of the original modern-day brands of porter that has helped set the standards for this style. Hundreds of other American small breweries and microbreweries brew both robust and brown versions. England's Samuel Smith Brewery still brews a medium-brown, sweet version of brown porter.

This style of ale offers the homebrewer an opportunity to brew a rich black ale without the coffeelike character of roasted barley used in stouts.

Original gravities: 1.040 to 1.060 (10 to 15). Alcohol: 4.5 to 6.5 percent. Bitterness: 20 to 40 BU. Color: 20+ SRM (40+).

SCOTTISH ALE—These ales brewed in the northern climates of the United Kingdom are the counterparts of English ale. The significant differences are reflected in their maltier flavor, relatively darker colors, and occasional faint smoky character. Scottish Light 60/ ("/" means shillings), Heavy 70/, and Export 80/ are cousins of English Bitter. Strong "Scotch" Ale is actually a Belgian style of ale, maltier and darker than English Old/Strong Ale.

*Light 60*—Original gravities: 1.030 to 1.035 (7.5 to 9). Alcohol: 2.8 to 3.5 percent. Bitterness: 9 to 20 BU. Color: 8 to 17 SRM (16 to 34).

*Heavy 70*—Original gravities: 1.035 to 1.040 (9 to 10). Alcohol: 3.5 to 4 percent. Bitterness: 12 to 20 BU. Color: 10 to 19 SRM (20 to 38).

*Export 80*—Original gravities: 1.040 to 1.050 (10 to 12.5). Alcohol: 4 to 5.5 percent. Bitterness: 15 to 25 BU. Color: 10 to 19 SRM (20 to 38).

*Strong "Scotch" Ale*—Original gravities: 1.072 to 1.085 (17.5 to 20). Alcohol: 6.2 to 8 percent. Bitterness: 25 to 35 BU. Color: 15 to 30 SRM (30 to 60).

### Irish-Style Ale

Of course porters and Irish stout are world classic styles, so please refer to those descriptions.

IRISH RED ALE—These have been around for some time, but they weren't quite popular enough to make the homebrew radar screen until recently. They are light red amber/deep copper in color with a medium hop bitterness and flavor. One distinctive character is the subtle and evident candylike caramel sweetness—almost like freshly baked cookies. It's a refreshing and quite flavorful ale.

Original gravities: 1.040 to 1.048 (10 to 12). Alcohol: 4 to 4.5 percent. Bitterness: 22 to 28 BU. Color: 11 to 18 SRM (22 to 36).

## ALES OF GERMAN ORIGIN

### Wheat Beers

Until the mid-1980s beers made with wheat were available only in the countries of their origin: Belgium and Germany. With the popularization of homebrewing and new small breweries opening in America, some traditional styles of wheat beer are enjoying growing popularity and are brewed worldwide. Of the traditional styles of wheat beer from Germany and Belgium, there are four better-known and very distinct styles: Weizenbier or Weissbier from southern Germany, Berliner-style Weisse, Belgian White or Wit(bier), and Belgian Lambic.

GERMAN WEIZENBIER (OR WEISSBIER)—These are the very popular Bavarian wheat beers of southern Germany. Their character is refreshing, light-bodied, lightly hopped, yeasty, highly effervescent, slightly sour, and with flavor and aroma suggestive of cloves and banana. Well over 25 percent of all of the beer consumed in Germany is this style of beer. It has become very popular with homebrewers now that wheat extracts and special yeasts are available to brew this style.

Weizenbiers have at least 50 percent wheat malt. The yeast is a special top-fermenting type and produces a clovelike and banana flavor, and the balance of these flavors is very dependent on fermentation temperatures and type of fermenter (open or closed). The wheat contributes to the fruitiness of Weizenbier. Traditionally, the special top-fermenting yeast is filtered out before bottling or kegging, at which time a more flocculent (better settling) lager yeast is added for natural bottle conditioning. Southern Germans love their Weizenbier and they love it with the yeast (*mit Hefe*) as Hefeweizen. A perfectly balanced Weizenbier is poetry in a cloud of joy.

Original gravities: 1.047 to 1.056 (12 to 14). Alcohol: 5 to 5.5 percent. Bitterness: 10 to 15 BU. Color: 3 to 9 SRM (6 to 18).

DUNKELWEIZEN—This dark version of Weizenbier has a balanced chocolatelike maltiness, tones down the clove and banana character somewhat, but still maintains the tang and pizzazz of the style. Sometimes called Dunkel Weissbier.

Original gravities: 1.048 to 1.056 (12 to 14). Alcohol: 4.8 to 5.5 percent. Bitterness: 10 to 15 BU. Color: 10 to 19 SRM (20 to 38).

WEIZENBOCK—This beer is everything you'd expect it to be if you know the traditional bock style. Stronger and more robust than Dunkelweizen, but with the telltale traits of the traditional southern style, it can be either light or dark (*helle* or *dunkel*). Sometimes called Weissbock.

Original gravities: 1.066 to 1.080 (16.5 to 20). Alcohol: 7 to 9 percent. Bitterness: 10 to 15 BU. Color: 5 to 30 SRM (10 to 60).

BERLINER-STYLE WEISSE—Brewed with 60 to 75 percent malted wheat, this commercially made brand of beer is a most unusual German beer. It undergoes a combination of yeast and bacterial (including lactic) fermentation, resulting in a mouth-puckering sourness. This north German style is very pale and effervescent, has virtually no bitterness, and in Berlin it is often considered a summer drink. Disciples of Berliner Weisse mix in sweet syrups of raspberry, lemon, or woodruff (an herb).

Because of the uncontrollable nature and unpredictability of the lactobacillus bacteria and the unique strains of top-fermenting yeast employed in making this style, homebrewing northern Weisse beer is a very challenging exercise. Consult "Sour Beers and Belgian Lambic" (page 372) for more information on how to make a controlled sour beer.

Original gravities: 1.028 to 1.032 (7 to 8). Alcohol: 2.8 to 3.5 percent. Bitterness: 3 to 6 BU. Color: 2 to 4 SRM (4 to 8).

## Other German-Style Ales

A German ale tradition survives in the Düsseldorf and Köln (Cologne) areas of Germany. There are two very distinct varieties brewed with pure cultures of top-fermenting yeast.

DÜSSELDORF-STYLE ALTBIER—*Altbier*, literally translated, means "old beer"; the way it used to be made in the old days before the discovery of lager yeast. Altbier is an ale tradition that survives in the Düsseldorf area of Germany. It is deep amber to dark brown ale lacking hop flavor or aroma and sometimes having an assertive bitterness. Fruitiness from top fermentation can be a character, but is often minimized by the unique process of "lagering" or storing in a secondary fermenter at very cold temperatures, much colder than your typical English ale.

Original gravities: 1.044 to 1.052 (11 to 13). Alcohol: 4.3 to 5.5 percent. Bitterness: 25 to 52 BU. Color: 11 to 19 SRM (22 to 38).

KÖLSCH—A light, fruity, medium-hopped, dry, and subtly malt-sweet top-fermented ale brewed in the area of Köln (Cologne in English). Kölsch ale yeast strains are unique and necessary to duplicate the traditional character during the primary fermentation. Sometimes malted wheat is used as an ingredient. Lager yeast is sometimes used in the bottle or during cold conditioning. With the popularity of this beer on the rise in the United States, this ale yeast strain is quite available to homebrewers.

Original gravities: 1.042 to 1.048 (10.5 to 12). Alcohol: 4.8 to 5 percent. Bitterness: 18 to 25 BU. Color: 4 to 6 SRM (8 to 12).

## ALES OF BELGIAN ORIGIN

BELGIAN-STYLE WHITE OR WIT—From the Disneyland of beer emerges yet another delightfully fun, unzipped, and awesome brew. Belgian white ales are brewed using unmalted wheat and malted barley (and sometimes oats) and are spiced with coriander and orange peel. The wheat, herbs, and spices, along with a special yeast, harmonize to produce a light, zesty, and refreshing beer pleasing the palates of even those who say, "I don't like beer." These very pale beers are commercially bottle-conditioned and served cloudy and with yeast. Aroma and flavor-type hops such as Czech Saaz or German Hallertau (Santiam, Crystal, and Mt. Hood are great American hop choices) are best used for this style to help maintain the overall character. This is another style of wheat ale that has become very popular among homebrewers since special yeasts have become available.

Original gravities: 1.044 to 1.050 (11 to 12.5). Alcohol: 4.8 to 5.2 percent. Bitterness: 10 to 17 BU. Color: 2 to 4 SRM (4 to 8).

BELGIAN LAMBIC—Of all the beers in the world, I personally think this surely rates as one of the most intriguing, mysterious, and erotic styles of beer ever made. If you succumb to transfixion, these are beers that zig and then zag their way into your life.

Airborne wild yeasts and bacteria unique to a 15-square-mile area southwest of Brussels, Belgium, fall into freshly brewed wort to slowly transform the wort to a uniquely sour and complex wheat beer. Lambic breweries are

temples where dirt is evident everywhere and spiders are worshipped. Thirty to 40 percent unmalted wheat is cooked, then combined and mashed with malted barley. Hops that have been aged for years at room temperatures are used exclusively and sparingly. Traditionally fermentation takes place in age-old wooden vessels.

There are several stylistic variations of lambic, but generally all of them are, at the very least, pungently sour, very low in bitterness, very effervescent, peculiarly aromatic, aged for years, and wonderfully and strangely addictive.

Original gravities: 1.040 to 1.072 (10 to 17.5). Alcohol: 5.6 to 8.6 percent. Bitterness: 11 to 23 BU. Color: 6 to 13 SRM (12 to 26).

**Gueuze** is a combination of a young (approximately 3 months fermenting) lambic with an old lambic. New fermentation begins in the bottle and is ready after one more year. This beer is unflavored and may be very dry or mildly sweet.

**Faro** is a unique combination of high- and low-alcohol lambic to which sugar and sometimes caramel (for coloring) are added. The beer is enjoyed soon after blending or is pasteurized to arrest fermentation and maintain sweetness.

**Kriek lambic** continues in the tradition of engaging brews. Cherries are combined with young lambic, inducing a new fermentation lasting 4 to 8 months. The kriek is then filtered, bottled, and aged yet another year before it's ready.

*Framboise, peche, and cassis lambic* styles are similar to kriek lambic with a substitution of a particular fruit such as raspberry, peach, or black currant.

## Belgian Specialty Ales

Belgium is the hunkahunka burning love of the beer world. It is a land of hundreds of unique styles of beers. My time would be better spent (and so would yours) going to Belgium and sampling fifty varieties than listing them each here.

However, a few styles often available outside the homeland are definitely worth highlighting.

FLANDERS BROWN ALE (OUD BRUIN)—Not easy to find, this is a unique blend of mirthful and refreshing lactic and/or vinegarlike sourness and richness of brown malts with the fruitiness of a top- and warm-fermented ale. As far as hop flavor and aroma are concerned, this style is a cat without a meow and does not make an impression, but hops are quietly evident and help stage an exotic balance of flavors. Combination cultures of yeast and bacteria are available to homebrewers to replicate this old-world tradition. This is a beer right out of a Flemish Brueghel painting!

Original gravities: 1.044 to 1.056 (11 to 14). Alcohol: 4.8 to 6.5 percent. Bitterness: 15 to 25 BU. Color: 12 to 20 SRM (24 to 40).

SAISON—Brewed traditionally in the spring for the summer season, and as with many Belgian ales, saison has a unique Belgian fruitiness and sometimes acidity. It is often graced with spices, herbs, complex alcohols, and aroma hops. Clove and smokelike character are rare but not unusual for some formulations. Golden to deep amber in color, this ale's hop character is often moderate and not assertive. A caramel-like maltiness is sometimes evident. Strength can vary greatly, but most saisons are brewed in the middle range.

Original gravities: 1.055 to 1.080 (14 to 20). Alcohol: 4.5 to 8.5 percent. Bitterness: 20 to 40 BU. Color: 4 to 14 SRM (8 to 28).

BELGIAN TRAPPIST ALE—Not really a style by itself, but rather the hoptheosis of beer. "Trappist" is the tag given to beers brewed by the six remaining Trappist monasteries in Belgium, which are often (but certainly not always) strong, amber to copper colored, and fruity with a unique Belgian spiciness and sometimes slight acidity that sets them apart from most other ale traditions. In most of these monasteries three varieties are made: a house brew, a special (or double malt), and an extra special (or triple malt). In order to duplicate these brews, access to the original yeast from each brewery is almost essential. Lucky homebrewers: It's possible because most of the Trappist beers are not pasteurized. Many have been cultured by homebrewers with great success. And only recently have they become widely available at homebrew supply stores to homebrewers as commercial strains. It is indeed a wonderful world of beer, isn't it?

*House brew*—Original gravities: 1.060 to 1.065 (15 to 16). Alcohol: 6 to 6.5 percent. Bitterness: 25 to 40 BU. Color: 15 to 25 SRM (30 to 50).

*Double malt*—Original gravities: 1.075 to 1.085 (18 to 20.5). Alcohol: 7.5 to 8 percent. Bitterness: 30 to 40 BU. Color: 17 to 30 SRM (34 to 60).

*Triple malt*—Original gravities: 1.090 to 1.100 (21.5 to 23.5). Alcohol: 8 to 10 percent. Bitterness: 35 to 50 BU. Color: 20 to 30 SRM (40 to 60).

BELGIAN-STYLE DUBBEL—A wonderful dark amber to brown-colored ale, with malty sweetness and a nutty, cocoalike roast malt aroma. Hop aroma is subtle but lovely and combines gently, with an almost bananalike character. Belgian ale yeast strains are a must to honestly make this classic. This is a wonderful ale to introduce to people who think they don't like dark beer. Start a revolution!

Original gravities: 1.060 to 1.075 (14.7 to 18.2). Alcohol: 6.25 to 7.5 percent. Bitterness: 20 to 30 BU. Color: 16 to 36 SRM (32 to 72).

BELGIAN-STYLE TRIPEL—A pale, light-colored, devilishly deceiving brew with a deranged punch, full of complexity; spicy, fruity (banana), moderately malty-sweet, relatively low hop character. This beer appears light, but is full and big. It's a beer symphony if there ever was such a thing. So if you make this in America, call it American Triple or better yet an American home run!

Original gravities: 1.070 to 1.092 (17 to 22). Alcohol: 7 to 10 percent. Bitterness: 20 to 45 BU. Color: 4 to 9 SRM (8 to 18).

## ALES OF FRENCH ORIGIN

Particularly in the north and east of France you'll find a triumph of ales influenced by both German and Belgian brewing traditions, creating something uniquely French. There's more to France than wine, baguettes, and cheese.

FRENCH-STYLE BIÈRE DE GARDE—Golden to deep copper or even light brown in color, these beers offer a variety of character, though they are generally characterized by a toasted malt aroma, slight malt sweetness in flavor, and a medium level of hop bitterness, flavor, and aroma. Warm ale fermentation creates a balanced fruitiness and complexity of alcohol character that are often quite evident. Commercially this type of beer is almost always bottle-conditioned, creating a pleasing and soft yeast character.

Original gravities: 1.060 to 1.080 (15 to 19.5). Alcohol: 4.5 to 8 percent. Bitterness: 20 to 30 BU. Color: 8 to 16 SRM (16 to 32).

## ALES OF AMERICAN ORIGIN

Small craft brewers and homebrewers in America commonly emulate ale styles of British origin, almost always using 100 percent malted barley, with perhaps the occasional addition of specialty sugars. While they may sometimes replicate the original British flavor with British malts and hops, more often American brewers use American-made malt and a tremendous variety of American-grown hops such as Cascade, Willamette, Centennial, Chinook, Amarillo, Simcoe, Columbus, Vanguard, Citra, Glacier, and Crystal (and other Washington-, Idaho-, and Oregon-grown varieties), lending what has become a distinctive American character to these English styles of ale. These differently hopped ales are referred to as American-style ales, but for the most part the fundamentals originated in the United Kingdom. It's worth mentioning here that there are even more distinctive international characters available using hops from Australia and New Zealand.

AMERICAN AMBER ALE—The interest in amber lager as a style was inspired during the American microbrewery renaissance in the 1990s. Fat Tire, an amber ale brewed by the New Belgium Brewery in Fort Collins, Colorado, became the standard for this type of ale. In today's beer world of such choice and diversity it seems disturbingly strange that smooth, mellow, malty, mildly yet distinctly hopped amber color ales were absent from the beer landscape not that long ago. Happily, now there seems to be a choice of amber ales wherever you go. This style has a range of character that brewers worldwide continue to explore.

Original gravities: 1.048 to 1.058 (12 to 14.5). Alcohol: 4.5 to 6 percent. Bitterness: 30 to 40 BU. Color: 11 to 18 SRM (22 to 36).

AMERICAN IMPERIAL OR DOUBLE RED ALE—Another American invention resulting from goosing American amber ale with lots of malt and lots of hops. The pioneer of this style was San Diego's Stone Brewing Company with its then very original Arrogant Bastard Ale, a flamboyantly hopped red ale with a bombshell of alcohol. Since then the brand has been replicated by others, including homebrewers. Double red or imperial red ale was militantly born in America. Toasted malts and American hop bitterness, flavor, and aroma unmercifully define this style.

Original gravities: 1.080 to 1.100 (19.3 to 23.7). Alcohol: 7.9 to 10.5 percent. Bitterness: 55 to 85 BU. Color: 10 to 15 SRM (20 to 30).

AMERICAN CREAM ALE—This style of ale at one time employed the use of both ale and lager yeasts during fermentation. Essentially its character is reminiscent of a hoppier, slightly stronger, slightly fruitier cousin to a standard American light lager. Now, more often than not, it is brewed with adjuncts such as corn or rice. Well carbonated and refreshing on a hot day when you want a childish squeak of bitterness in that cold light American beer.

Original gravities: 1.044 to 1.056 (11 to 14). Alcohol: 4.2 to 5.6 percent. Bitterness: 10 to 22 BU. Color: 2 to 5 SRM (4 to 10).

AMERICAN WHEAT BEER—After all of the special characters attributable to European-origin wheat beers, the new avuncular American wheat beers may at first seem to lack luster. Furthermore, they defy definition. For the most part, what has been referred to as the American wheat style is no more than substituting wheat for a portion of malted barley. Malted or unmalted wheat is not substantially responsible for the unique characters of the European styles of wheat beer, so their impact on recipe formulation is low. Unique yeasts and bacterial fermentations used in German and Belgian styles of wheat beer are absent from the cradle for the American style. So what makes it for American wheat? Generally I'd have to say American wheat beers are low in bitterness with a somewhat fruity esteriness from the wheat and typical ale ferment. Wheat is used to lighten body and thus there are a lot of light and refreshing versions of this "style," though there are several types that are quite flavorful with an evident toasted malt character. Many are bottle-conditioned and cloudy. The yeast sediment is encouraged with the pour as a healthy dose of nourishment.

Original gravities: 1.036 to 1.050 (9 to 12.5). Alcohol: 3.8 to 5 percent. Bitterness: 10 to 35 BU. Color: 2 to 10 SRM (4 to 20).

## LAGERS OF GERMAN AND OTHER EUROPEAN ORIGIN

German lager brewing is a style of beer that has sustained its popularity throughout the world. German brewmasters have taken their art to the United States, China, Japan, Latin America, and most major brewing nations of the world.

Lager beers are brewed with bottom-fermenting types of yeast at temperatures generally below 50 degrees F (10 C). It was not until the late nineteenth century that lager yeasts were recognized, identified, and isolated. It was noted that beers brewed with cold fermentation techniques were cleaner tasting and more stable, perhaps initially due to the inability of many beer-spoiling bacteria to propagate in cold beer wort. Beers could be aged for longer periods of time, and with this new technique enjoyable flavor characteristics were discovered.

The German word *lager* means "to store." Initial or primary fermentation usually takes place for 4 to 6 days at temperatures of 40 to 55 degrees F (4 to 12.5 C). All true lager beers are lagered and matured for usually a minimum of 3 weeks in a secondary fermenter at temperatures below 40 degrees F (4 C). Some styles of lager beer are lagered for more than 3 months.

Lager beers may be available to the beer drinker pasteurized or not, filtered or unfiltered, on draft or bottled. There is a tremendous variety of German and other European styles of lager beer, but many are difficult to come by. They are all best served chilled at 45 to 55 degrees F (7 to 13 C), are well carbonated, and display a rich, dense head of foam.

Some of the traditional types of hops that are used are Hallertau, Northern Brewer, Perle, Spalt, Saaz, Tettnang, and Hersbruck, though there are some excellent American-grown substitutes that are not quite the same but certainly do the trick.

Some of the classic styles of German and other European lagers are:

PILSENER—The original pilsener beer was brewed in Plzen (which means "green meadow"), Czech Republic. Upon introduction in 1842, it created quite a stir in the brewing community because of its pale golden color. Prior to this all beers were dark. The golden beer from Plzen gained in popularity as its fame spread and was duplicated in all parts of Europe, America, and throughout the world. There are two classic styles recognized as pilsener today. Both are pale to golden colored, brewed with very soft water, and made with an assertive but varying amount of hops.

**Bohemian/Czech Pilsener.** What remains of the original style is pale, golden, and alluring. A creamy dense head tops a well-carbonated brew with an accent on the rich, sweet malt that the beer is made from. Medium-bodied Bohemian-style pilsener really makes its impression with the bitterness, flavor, and aromatic character of the indigenous Czech Saaz hop. Clean, crisp, hop-spicy, bitter with malty overtones, pale, and simply luscious.

Original gravities: 1.044 to 1.056 (11 to 14). Alcohol: 4 to 5 percent. Bitterness: 30 to 45 BU. Color: 3 to 7 SRM (6 to 14).

**German Pilsener.** Called "Pils" for short, this style is an offspring of the original from the neighboring Czech Republic, but with an inclination for more bitterness and a drier, less malty character. The most popular beer style in all of Germany, German Pils is brewed with exactness and an erudite and refreshing bitterness. To duplicate the definitive German Pils character, German "Noble Hops" such as Spalt, Hersbruck, Tettnang, Hallertau, or Saaz plus very soft water are absolute musts in the brewing process.

Original gravities: 1.044 to 1.050 (11 to 12.5). Alcohol: 4 to 5 percent. Bitterness: 25 to 40 BU. Color: 3 to 4 SRM (6 to 8).

OKTOBERFEST, MÄRZEN, AND VIENNA LAGERS—These similar styles of beer originated in southern Germany and Austria, where beers tend to express themselves with malty sweetness. These three lagers are easily brewed by homebrewers. Their homebrewed freshness often surpasses the imported varieties that have traveled thousands of miles from the brewery under uncertain conditions.

**Oktoberfest and Märzen** were once one and the same beer, but with the international popularity of Munich's annual Oktoberfest, beers offered in the big tents have evolved to light, mild beers, more reminiscent of a Dortmunder/Export-style lager (see below). German-style Märzens are rich, amber-orange, copper-colored lagers. Their aroma is assertively malty and appropriately balanced with quickly sharp but not lingering hop bitterness. A seasonal style, traditionally brewed in March (März).

Original gravities: 1.050 to 1.060 (12.5 to 15). Alcohol: 5.3 to 6 percent. Bitterness: 18 to 25 BU. Color: 4 to 15 SRM (8 to 30).

*Vienna-Style Lager.* A style of beer that's on the "endangered" beer style list. Its popularity in Austria has waned. Perhaps new small brewers are reviving this style in its motherland. Until the end of the twentieth century it used to be brewed true to form at a few breweries in Mexico, but not any longer. It was to Mexico that Austrian brewmasters emigrated during the political events that preceded World War II, but even in Mexico there were but a very, very few examples of this style. Negra Modelo is a similar example (though brewed with corn and barley malt) that is available in the United States on a limited basis. Traditionally this lager is an amber-red to copper color, with an overall character reminiscent of German Oktoberfest, but with a less robust, sweet malt character. You'll find it being nurtured by homebrewing enthusiasts and several brewpubs and small craft brewers throughout the world.

Original gravities: 1.046 to 1.056 (11.5 to 14). Alcohol: 4.8 to 5.5 percent. Bitterness: 22 to 38 BU. Color: 8 to 12 SRM (16 to 24).

BOCK AND DOPPELBOCK—No, bock beer is not made from the bottom of the barrel, and it is only in America that this rumor could have originated, probably during the periods of anti-German sentiment preceding both World War I and World War II. Bock beer is a highly respected all-malt dark lager of considerable alcoholic strength. German law even dictates requirements for what a bock beer is. It is traditionally a well-lagered beer that is sometimes associated with a goat (*bock* in German means "goat"). Christmas bocks often are brewed to be consumed under the astrological sign of Capricorn (the goat). This style of beer also is celebrated in the spring as a tribute to Saint Joseph (March 19) by monasteries in Munich. Bock beers can be easily brewed by any homebrewer. Most brands of malt extract and specialty malts will brew an unmercifully luscious strong batch of bock beer.

*German-Style Bock* beers can be either dark or light (*Heller Bock* or *Maibock*) in color. They are strong in alcohol with a very malty-sweet overall character. Hop bitterness is low and only suggests itself in order to offset the sweetness of malt. The character of the dark malts should not taste roasted or burnt in bock beer. Traditional German bocks do not have hop aroma or hop flavor of any consequence. This is a difficult beer for hophead homebrewers to make, for it requires a light touch of hops and an adroit malt emphasis.

Original gravities: 1.066 to 1.074 (16.5 to 18). Alcohol: 6 to 8 percent. Bitterness: 20 to 35 BU. Color: For Heller Bock: 4 to 10 SRM (8 to 20); for dark bock: 20 to 30 SRM (40 to 60).

*Doppelbocks* are a stronger version of bock beers with a minimum original gravity decreed by German law. They can be pale or dark, very sweet or balanced with bitterness. But they all pack a deranged punch and offer a lesson in the etiquette of malt. In Germany all doppelbocks can be identified by the suffix "-ator" on the name. Elevator, Alligator, Exterminator, Incubator, Fishbator—whatever you name it, it certainly is a beer to be respected and if you drink too much, well, see you -ator.

Original gravities: 1.074–1.080 (18–19.5). Alcohol: 6.5–8 percent. Bitterness: 17 to 27 BU. Color: 12 to 30 SRM (24 to 60).

MUNICH HELLES AND DUNKEL—The mainstay of Bavarian festive beer drinking, light (*helles*) Munich-style lager is served everywhere throughout Bavaria. The style offers the homebrewer easy access to the rich brewing tradition of southern Germany. Generally lower in alcohol than many of the other celebratory styles, this is a beer for everyday quaffing. Even I have downed two or three liters of the stuff with only a grin to show for it (a really big grin).

***Munich Helles.*** A mildly hopped, malty, pale-colored beer. A common tendency for homebrewers is to overhop this beer. Go easy on the hops. Yes, there is a pleasing bitterness, but it does not linger at all. Furthermore, hop aroma and flavor are either subtle or absent in this style.

Original gravities: 1.044 to 1.050 (11 to 13). Alcohol: 4.5 to 5.5 percent. Bitterness: 18 to 25 BU. Color: 4.5 to 5.5 SRM (9 to 11).

***Munich Dunkel.*** The dark counterpart to Munich Helles has a distinctly roasted (yet never burnt), chocolatelike character complemented with an overall malty sweetness and low hop bitterness. The perception of dunkel is that it is slightly more bitter than Helles because of the contribution of bitterness by the roasted malts used in the formulation.

Original gravities: 1.048 to 1.056 (12 to 14). Alcohol: 4.5 to 5 percent. Bitterness: 16 to 25 BU. Color: 15 to 20 SRM (30 to 40).

SCHWARZBIER—Literally translated, this is "black beer." A Bavarian tradition, this specialty black lager is colored as its name implies, but with judicious amounts of roasted malts so as to not impart a burnt flavor. Debitterized (huskless) German black malt is a perfect ingredient for this old-world style. Schwarzbier is a relatively low-alcohol brew with the smoothness of a lighter beer. Moderate bitterness and very little hop aroma or flavor round out the character.

Original gravities: 1.044 to 1.052 (11 to 13). Alcohol: 3.8 to 5 percent. Bitterness: 22 to 30 BU. Color: 25 to 30 SRM (50 to 60).

DORTMUNDER/EXPORT—Generally a strong pale lager that is characterized by more bitterness and less maltiness than Munich Helles but far less bitterness and more malt body than German pilseners. It was originally brewed for export from the city of Dortmund, hence its name.

Original gravities: 1.048 to 1.056 (12 to 14). Alcohol: 5 to 6 percent. Bitterness: 23 to 29 BU. Color: 3 to 5 SRM (6 to 10).

RAUCHBIER—Smoke-flavored beers! One of my personal favorites. I was

introduced to this style with a taste of Schlenkerla Rauchbier from the Franco-
nian brewing town of Bamberg, Germany. Holy smokes, was I ever impressed!
A velvety smooth Oktoberfest style of lager beer laced with a rich smoke flavor.
This brew goes exceptionally well with almost any kind of meat dish and is a
real treat if you like smoked food. Malts that have been dried over wood flames
and smoke impart the flavor. German beechwood is used, but the homebrewer
may smoke his or her malts with apple, peach, hickory, cherry, mesquite, or other
favorite barbecue smoking wood. Malt smoked with cherry wood is currently
made in the United States and available in homebrew shops. German-style
Helles, Marzen, Bock, and Weizen are popular lagers that occasionally become
engaged with smoked malt. In America, brewers have infused smoked malt into
pale ales, dark ales, porters, and stouts to name but a few.

Original gravities: varies with style. Alcohol: varies with style. Bitterness:
18 to 25 BU. Color: varies with style.

## OTHER STYLES OF LAGER BEERS

Most of the world is a lager-drinking world, influenced by a German brewing
tradition. Yet for the most part the lager beers brewed by these countries are
lighter; specifically one might refer to the style as a very light-flavored pilsener,
very often brewed with such adjuncts as corn, rice, or refined sugars.

## LAGERS OF AUSTRALIAN, CANADIAN, AND AMERICAN ORIGIN

AUSTRALIAN, LATIN AMERICAN, AND TROPICAL LAGERS—In
a country that experiences dry, hot summers, Australian lagers quench the thirst
of Australians with almost a macho gusto; Australia is one of the biggest beer-
drinking (per capita) countries in the world. Generally, the alcohol content of
their lagers is similar to those of other light lager beers that are brewed in the
United States and Canada. In Australia and many tropical areas of the world,
this style is often brewed with sugar as an adjunct in order to lighten the flavor
and body, sometimes contributing a slightly applelike fruitiness. The notion
that Australian beers are stronger is probably a false impression perpetuated by
the packaging of some of their beers in 1-liter cans! The recent emergence of
Australian small and craft brewers has kindled a growing interest in some very
distinctive ales and stouts, but these are exceptions and not at all categorized as
Australian lagers.

More than likely, you'll have to go to the Caribbean, the South Pacific,
Mexico, Belize, Australia, or New Zealand to enjoy a quality tropical-style light
lager. I find myself seeking special brews from small breweries but sometimes
have to settle for a cold light lager or a margarita. Or you can brew one yourself.

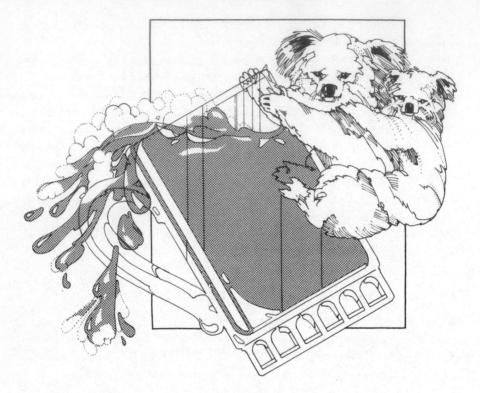

Although brands of light lagers from tropical countries are commonly available in the United States, their quality often suffers during the long, hot journey to your favorite beer store.

CANADIAN LAGERS—The most common style of beer produced in Canada and the United States can be referred to simply as American lager (the color "light" is ubiquitously implied). With all due respect to the Canadians, the mass-produced beer called Canadian lager or Canadian ale is too similar to an American lager to be called anything else. Canadian light lagers may suggest a bit more hop character, but in general the lighter style of American lager is what most North Americans are drinking.

AMERICAN LAGER—This style of beer is usually brewed with 60 to 75 percent barley malt, the remainder being exclusively or a combination of rice, corn, or sugar syrups. The beers are dry, lightly hopped, light-bodied, and highly carbonated.

Original gravities: 1.040 to 1.046 (10 to 11.5). Alcohol: 3.8 to 5 percent. Bitterness: 5 to 13 BU. Color: 2 to 4 SRM (4 to 8).

AMERICAN PREMIUM—Rarely an all-malt beer, but maybe made with fewer nonmalt adjuncts. It is an eensy weensy bit bigger beer all around, but still is a relative to American lager. It's hardly worth mentioning, but then, allow me my own prejudice.

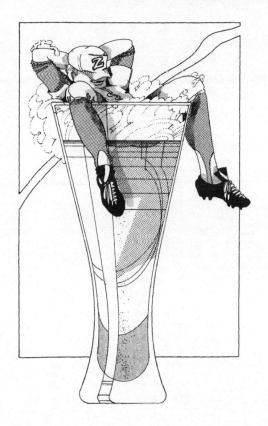

Original gravities: 1.044 to 1.048 (11 to 12). Alcohol: 4.3 to 5 percent. Bitterness: 6 to 15 BU. Color: 2 to 6 SRM (4 to 12).

DIET ("LOW-CAL" OR "LITE") BEER—Often referred to as a watered-down version of an American lager. This is close to the truth in flavor, but often low-cal beers will carry just as much alcohol as some of their American lager counterparts. Low-calorie beers are often processed with added enzymes to break down tasty nonfermentable carbohydrates, so the beer will be thinner and have less flavor and fewer calories. Homebrewers can come close to this style by brewing lower-gravity adjunct-infused beers that are very fermentable.

Original gravities: 1.024 to 1.040 (6 to 10). Alcohol: 3.5 to 4.4 percent. Bitterness: 5 to 10 BU. Color: 1.5 to 4 SRM (3 to 8).

CLASSIC AMERICAN-STYLE PRE-PROHIBITION PILSENER—Now this is worth brewing, for you'll rarely find a commercially made example. It's an American classic, uniquely brewed with up to 25 percent corn in the time before Prohibition and by hundreds of small brewers who eventually went out of business after World War II. It's straw to deep gold in color. Hop bitterness, flavor, and aroma are medium to high. Bullion and Cluster hops were the traditional favorite for decades. These hops are not grown in any significant

# Beer Styles Chart

| | ORIGINAL GRAVITY (BALLING/PLATO) | FINAL GRAVITY | PERCENT ALCOHOL BY VOLUME | INTERNATIONAL BITTERING UNITS | MALT/SWEET CHARACTER |
|---|---|---|---|---|---|
| **Ales** | | | | | |
| **Pale Ale** | | | | | |
| American Blonde or Golden Ale | 1.045–1.056 (11–13.8) | 1.008–1.016 (2–4) | 4–5 % | 15–25 | Light |
| Classic English Pale Ale | 1.040–1.056 (10–13.8) | 1.008–1.016 (2–4) | 4.5–5.5% | 20–40 | Low to medium |
| American-Style Pale Ale | 1.044–1.050 (11–12.5 ) | 1.008–1.014 (2–3.5) | 4.5–5.6% | 30–42 | Low to medium |
| American Wheat | 1.036–1.056 (9–13.8) | 1.006–1.018 (1.5–4.5) | 3.5–5.5% | 10–35 | Low to medium |
| English-Style Summer Ale | 1.036–1.050 (9–12.5) | 1.006–1.012 (1.5–3) | 3.6–5% | 20–30 | Low to medium |
| English-Style India Pale Ale | 1.050–1.064 (12.5–15.7) | 1.012–1.018 (3–4.5) | 5–7% | 35–63 | Medium |
| American-Style India Pale Ale | 1.060–1.075 (14.7–18.2) | 1.012–1.018 (3–4.5) | 6.3–7.5% | 50–70 | Medium |
| **Bitter** | | | | | |
| Ordinary Bitter | 1.033–1.038 (8–9.5) | 1.006–1.012 (1.5–3) | 3–4.1% | 20–35 | Low to medium |
| Special or Best Bitter | 1.038–1.045 (9.5–11) | 1.006–1.012 (1.5–3) | 4.1–4.8% | 28–40 | Medium |
| Extra Special Bitter | 1.046–1.060 (11.5–15) | 1.010–1.016 (2.5–4) | 4.8–5.8 % | 30–45 | Medium to medium-high |
| **Scottish Ales** | | | | | |
| Scottish Light | 1.030–1.035 (7.5–9) | 1.006–1.012 (1.5–3) | 2.8–3.5% | 9–20 | Low to medium-low |
| Scottish Heavy | 1.035–1.040 (9–10) | 1.010–1.014 (2.5–3.5) | 3.5–4% | 12–20 | Medium |
| Scottish Export | 1.040–1.050 (10–12.5) | 1.010–1.018 (2.5–4.5) | 4–5.3% | 15–25 | Medium to medium-high |
| Scotch Ale (see Belgian) | — | — | — | — | — |
| **German Ales** | | | | | |
| Berliner Weisse | 1.028–1.032 (7–8) | 1.004–1.006 (1–1.5) | 2.8–3.4% | 3–6 | None |
| Kölsch | 1.042–1.048 (10.5–12) | 1.006–1.010 (1.5–2.5) | 4.8–5.3% | 18–25 | Low |
| Düsseldorf-Style Altbier | 1.044–1.052 (11–13) | 1.008–1.014 (2–3.5) | 4.3–5.5% | 25–52 | Medium-low to medium |
| Bavarian Hefeweizen/ Weissbier (wheat beer) | 1.047–1.056 (12–13.8) | 1.008–1.016 (2–4) | 4.9–5.5% | 10–15 | Low to medium-low |
| Bavarian Dunkel Hefeweizen/ Weissbier (dark wheat) | 1.048–1.056 (12–13.8) | 1.008–1.016 (2–4) | 4.8–5.5% | 10–15 | Medium |
| Weizenbock/Weissbock | 1.066–1.080 (16–19.5) | 1.016–1.028 (4–7) | 6.9–9.3% | 15–35 | Medium to medium-high |
| **Amber Ales** | | | | | |
| Irish Red Ale | 1.040–1.048 (10–12) | 1.010–1.014 (2.5–3.5) | 4–4.5% | 20–28 | Low to medium |
| American Amber Ale | 1.048–1.058 (12–14.5) | 1.012–1.018 (3–4.5) | 4.5–6% | 30–40 | Medium-high to high |
| Imperial or Double Red Ale | 1.080–1.100 (19.3–23.7) | 1.020–1.028 (5–7) | 7.9–10.5% | 55–85 | Medium to high |
| Imperial or Double India Pale Ale | 1.075–1.100 (18.2–23.7) | 1.012–1.020 (3–5) | 7.5–10.5% | 65–100 | Medium to high |
| English Old Ale | 1.058–1.088 (14.3–21) | 1.014–1.030 (3.5–7.5) | 6–9% | 30–65 | Medium to medium-high |
| English Strong Ale | 1.060–1.125 (15–31.5) | 1.014–1.040 (3.5–10) | 7–11% | 30–65 | Medium to medium-high |
| **Brown Ales** | | | | | |
| English Brown | 1.040–1.050 (10–12.5) | 1.008–1.014 (2–3.5) | 4–5.5% | 15–25 | Low to medium |
| English Dark Mild | 1.030–1.036 (7.5–9) | 1.004–1.008 (1–2) | 3.2–4% | 10–24 | Low to medium-low |
| American Brown | 1.040–1.060 (10–15) | 1.010–1.018 (2.5–4.5) | 4–6.4% | 25–45 | Medium-low to medium |

| AVG SENSITIVITY HOP BITTERNESS PERCEPTION | AVG SENSITIVITY HOP FLAVOR | AVG SENSITIVITY HOP AROMA | COLOR SRM (EBC) COLOR DESCRIPTION |
|---|---|---|---|
| Low to medium | Low to medium | Low to medium | 3–7 (6–14) pale to light amber |
| | | | |
| Medium to medium-high | Medium to medium-high | Medium to medium-high | 5 - 14 (10–28) gold-copper |
| Medium to medium-high | Medium to medium-high | Medium to medium-high | 6–14 (12–28) gold-copper |
| Low to medium | Low to medium | Low to medium | 4–10 (8–20) pale to medium amber |
| Medium-low to medium | Low to medium-low | Low to medium-low | 4–7 (8–14) pale to light amber |
| Medium to medium-high | Medium to high | Medium to high | 6–14 (12–28) gold-copper |
| Medium-high to very high | Medium-high to very high | Medium-high to very high | 6–14 (12–28) gold-copper |
| | | | |
| Medium | Low to medium | Low to medium | 5–12 (10–24) gold-copper |
| Medium | Low to medium | Low to medium | 6–14 (12–28) gold-copper |
| Medium to medium-high | Medium to medium-high | Medium to medium-high | 8–14 (16–28) amber-copper |
| | | | |
| Very low | None | None | 8–17 (16–34) amber-brown |
| Low to medium-low | None | None | 10–19 (20–38) dark amber-dark brown |
| Low to medium | None | None | 10–19 (20–38) dark amber-dark brown |
| | | | |
| Extremely low | None | None | 2–4 (4–8) pale straw |
| Low to medium | Low | Low | 4–6 (8–12) pale gold |
| Medium to very high | Low to medium | Low to medium | 11–19 (22–38) copper-dark brown |
| Very low | None | None | 3–9 (6–18) straw to medium amber |
| Very low | None | None | 10–19 (20–38) medium amber-dark brown |
| Low | None | None | 4.5–30 (9–60) very dark gold |
| | | | |
| Medium | Very low to none | Very low to none | 11–18 (22–36) medium amber-copper dark red |
| Medium | Medium | Medium | 11–18 (22–36) medium amber-dark red brown |
| Very high | Very high | Very high | 10–15 (20–30) copper red-red brown |
| Very high | Very high | Very high | 5–13 (10–26) gold-copper |
| Very low | None to medium | Very low | 12–30 (24–60) very dark copper |
| Very low | Very low to medium | Very low | 8–21 (16–42) amber-dark brown |
| | | | |
| Low to medium-low | None to very low | None to very low | 13–25 (26–50) light brown to dark brown |
| Low to medium | None to very low | None to very low | 17–34 (34–68) light amber-dark brown |
| Medium to high | Low to medium | Low to medium | 15–26 (30–52) light brown to very dark brown |

(continued)

# Beer Styles Chart

| | ORIGINAL GRAVITY (BALLING/PLATO) | FINAL GRAVITY | PERCENT ALCOHOL BY VOLUME | INTERNATIONAL BITTERING UNITS | MALT/SWEET CHARACTER |
|---|---|---|---|---|---|
| **Porter** | | | | | |
| Robust Porter | 1.045–1.060 (11–15) | 1.008–1.016 (2–4) | 5–6.5% | 25–40 | Medium |
| Brown Porter | 1.040–1.050 (10–12.5) | 1.006–1.014 (1.5–3.5) | 4.5–6% | 20–30 | Low to medium |
| **Stouts** | | | | | |
| Classic Irish Dry Stout | 1.038–1.048 (9.5–12) | 1.008–1.012 (2–3) | 3.8–5% | 30–40 | Low to medium-low |
| Foreign Export Stout | 1.052–1.072 (13–17.5) | 1.008–1.020 (2–5) | 5.7–9.3% | 30–60 | Medium to medium-high |
| Sweet Stout | 1.045–1.056 (11–13.8) | 1.012–1.020 (3–5) | 3–6% | 15–25 | Medium-high to high |
| Oatmeal Stout | 1.038–1.056 (9.5–13.8) | 1.008–1.020 (2–5) | 3.8–6% | 20–40 | Medium to medium-high |
| American-Style Stout | 1.050–1.075 (12.4–18.2) | 1.010–1.022 (2.5–5.5) | 5.7–8.8% | 35–60 | Low to medium |
| British-Style Imperial Stout | 1.080–1.100 (19.5–23.5) | 1.020–1.030 (4–7.5) | 7–12% | 45–65 | High to very high |
| American-Style Imperial Stout | 1.080–1.100 (19.5–23.5) | 1.020–1.030 (4–7.5) | 7–12% | 50–80 | High to very high |
| **Black Ales** | | | | | |
| American-Style Black Ale | 1.056–1.075 (14–18.2) | 1.012–1.018 (3–4.5) | 6–7.5% | 50–70 | Medium |
| **Barley/Wheat Wine** | | | | | |
| British-Style Barley Wine | 1.085–1.120 (20.4–28) | 1.024–1.028 (6–7) | 8.4–12% | 40–60 | High |
| American-Style Barley Wine | 1.090–1.120 (21.6–28) | 1.024–1.028 (6–7) | 8.4–12% | 60–100 | High |
| Wheat Wine | 1.088–1.120 (21–28) | 1.024–1.032 (6–8) | 8.4–12% | 45–85 | High |
| **Specialty Ales** | | | | | |
| Smoked Ales | Varies | Varies | Varies | 20–40 | Medium to medium-high |
| **Belgian & French Styles** | | | | | |
| Belgian Blonde | 1.054–1.068 (13.5–16.8) | 1.008–1.014 (2–3.5) | 6–7.8% | 15–30 | Low |
| Belgian Pale Ale | 1.044–1.054 (11–13.5) | 1.008–1.014 (2–3.5) | 4–6% | 20–30 | Low |
| Belgian Pale or Dark Strong Ale | 1.064–1.096 (16–23) | 1.012–1.024 (3–6) | 7–11% | 20–50 | Low to medium |
| Dubbel | 1.060–1.075 (14.7–18.2) | 1.012–1.016 (3–4) | 6.3–7.5% | 20–30 | Medium |
| Tripel | 1.070–1.092 (17–22) | 1.010–1.018 (2.5–4.5) | 7–10% | 20–45 | Low to medium-low |
| Flanders Brown/Red | 1.044–1.056 (11–13.8) | 1.008–1.016 (2–4) | 4.8–6.5% | 15–25 | Very low/acidic |
| Scotch Ale | 1.072–1.085 (17.5–20.5) | 1.016–1.028 (4–7) | 6.2–8% | 25–35 | Medium-high to high |
| Lambic | 1.047–1.056 (11.8–13.8) | 1.000–1.010 (0–2.5) | 6.2–8.1% | 11–23 | None |
| Gueuze | 1.044–1.056 (11–13.8) | 1.000–1.010 (0–2.5) | 6.8–8.6% | 11–23 | None |
| Fruit Lambic (Framboise, Kriek, Pêche, Cassis) | 1.047–1.056 (11.8–13.8) | 1.000–1.010 (0–2.5) | 6.2–8.1% | 11–23 | None |
| Wit/White | 1.044–1.050 (11–12.5) | 1.006–1.010 (1.5–2.5) | 4.8–5.2% | 10–17 | Very low to low |
| French & Belgian-Style Saison | 1.055–1.080 (14–19.5) | 1.004–1.016 (1–4) | 4.5–8.5% | 20–40 | Low |
| French Biére de Garde | 1.060–1.080 (15–19.5) | 1.012–1.024 (3–6) | 4.5–8% | 20–30 | Low to medium-low |

| | AVG SENSITIVITY HOP BITTERNESS PERCEPTION | AVG SENSITIVITY HOP FLAVOR | AVG SENSITIVITY HOP AROMA | COLOR SRM (EBC) COLOR DESCRIPTION |
|---|---|---|---|---|
| | Medium to high | None to medium | None to medium | 30+ (60+) black |
| | Low to medium-low | None to medium | None to medium | 20–35 (40–70) very dark brown |
| | Medium | None to very low | None to very low | 40+ (80+) black |
| | Medium to medium-high | None to very low | None to very low | 40+ (80+) black |
| | Low to medium-low | None to very low | None to very low | 40+ (80+) black |
| | Low to medium-low | None to low | None to low | 20+ (40+) very dark+ |
| | Medium to high | Medium to high | Medium to high | 40+ (80+) black |
| | Medium | Very low to medium | Very low to medium | 20–35+ (40–70+) dark brown-black |
| | Medium-high to very High | Medium-high to very High | Medium-high to very high | 40+ (80+) black |
| | Medium-high to high | Medium-high to high | Medium-high to high | 35+ (70+) black |
| | Low to medium | Very low to medium | Very low to medium | 14–22 (28–44) deep copper-dark brown |
| | High to very high | Medium to very high | Medium to very high | 11–22 (22–44) copper-dark brown |
| | Medium to medium-high | Low to medium | Low to medium | 6–9 (12–18) gold-amber |
| | Low to medium-low | Low | Low | Varies |
| | Low to medium-low | Low to medium-low | None to medium-low | 4–7 (8–14) pale to light amber |
| | Low to medium-low | Low to medium-low | Low to medium-low | 6–12 (12–24) gold-copper |
| | Medium-low to medium-high | Medium-low to medium-high | Medium-low to medium-high | Pale: 3.5–10 (7–20); Dark: 9–35 (18–70) |
| | Medium-low to medium | Very low to low | Very low to low | 16–36 (32–72) brown to very dark brown |
| | Medium to medium-high | Very low to low | Very low to low | 4–9 (8–18) pale to medium amber |
| | Low to medium | None | None | 12–20 (24–40) copper-dark brown |
| | Very low | None to very low | None to very low | 15–30 (30–60) light brown to very dark brown |
| | Very low | None | None | 6–13 (12–26) gold-copper |
| | Very low | None | None | 6–13 (12–26) gold-copper |
| | Very low | None | None | Color of fruit |
| | Low | None to very low | None to very low | 2–4 (4–8) pale straw |
| | Medium to medium-high | Low to medium | Low to medium | 4–14 (8–28) pale to medium amber |
| | Low to medium | Low to medium | Low to medium | 6–16 (12–32) gold-chestnut brown |

(continued)

# Beer Styles Chart

| | ORIGINAL GRAVITY (BALLING/PLATO) | FINAL GRAVITY | PERCENT ALCOHOL BY VOLUME | INTERNATIONAL BITTERING UNITS | MALT/SWEET CHARACTER |
|---|---|---|---|---|---|
| **Lagers** | | | | | |
| **Light Lagers** | | | | | |
| **Pilseners** | | | | | |
| German Pilsener | 1.044–1.050 (11–12.5) | 1.006–1.012 (1.5–3) | 4–5% | 25–40 | Low to medium-low |
| Bohemian/Czech Pilsener | 1.044–1.056 (11–13.8) | 1.014–1.020 (3.5–5) | 4–5% | 30–45 | Medium-low |
| American Pilsener | 1.045–1.060 (11.5–15) | 1.012–1.018 (3–4.5) | 5–6% | 25–40 | Medium |
| **Other Pale Lagers** | | | | | |
| Dortmunder/Export/ Oktoberfest | 1.048–1.056 (12–13.8) | 1.010–1.014 (2.5–3.5) | 5–6% | 23–29 | Very low to low |
| Munich Helles | 1.044–1.050 (11–13) | 1.008–1.012 (2–3) | 4.5–5.5% | 18–25 | Medium-low |
| **American Light Lagers** | | | | | |
| Low Carb/Low Calorie/Lite | 1.024–1.040 (6–10) | 0.992–1.008 (-2–2) | 3.5–4.4% | 3–10 | None |
| American Lager | 1.040–1.046 (10–11.5) | 1.006–1.010 (1.5–2.5) | 3.8–5% | 5–13 | Low |
| Australian, Latin American & Tropical Light Lagers | 1.038–1.046 (9.5–11.5) | 1.006–1.010 (1.5–2.5) | 3.8–5% | 9–18 | Very low |
| **Amber Lagers** | | | | | |
| American Amber | 1.042–1.056 (10.5–13.8) | 1.010–1.018 (2.5–4.5) | 4.8–5.4% | 18–30 | Low to medium |
| German Märzen | 1.050–1.060 (12.5–15) | 1.012–1.020 (3–5) | 5.3–6% | 18–25 | Medium-low to medium |
| Vienna (Austrian) | 1.046–1.056 (11.5–13.8) | 1.012–1.018 (3–4.5) | 4.8–5.4% | 22–28 | Low to medium-low |
| German (smoked) Märzen Rauchbier | 1.050–1.060 (12.5–14.5) | 1.012–1.020 (3–5) | 5.3–5.9% | 18–25 | Medium-low to medium |
| **Bock Beers (Strong, Dark, or Light)** | | | | | |
| Dark Bock | 1.066–1.074 (16–18) | 1.018–1.024 (4.5–6) | 6.3–7.5% | 20–30 | Low to medium-low |
| Heller (light) Maibock | 1.066–1.074 (16–18) | 1.012–1.020 (3–5) | 6–8% | 20–38 | Low to medium |
| Doppelbock | 1.074–1.080 (18–19.3) | 1.014–1.020 (3.5–5) | 6.5–8% | 17–27 | Medium-high to high |
| **Dark Lagers** | | | | | |
| American Dark | 1.040–1.050 (10–12.5) | 1.008–1.012 (2–3) | 4–5.5% | 14–20 | Low |
| Munich Dunkel | 1.048–1.056 (12–13.8) | 1.014–1.018 (3.5–4.5) | 4.5–5% | 16–25 | Medium-low |
| Schwarzbier | 1.044–1.052 (11–13) | 1.010–1.016 (2.5–4) | 3.8–5% | 22–30 | Low to medium-low |
| Baltic-Style Porter | 1.072–1.085 (17.5–20.5) | 1.016–1.022 (4–5.5) | 7.5–9% | 35–40 | Medium-low to medium |
| **Hybrid Beers/Lagers, Ales** | | | | | |
| California Common | 1.045–1.056 (11.2–13.8) | 1.010–1.018 (2.5–4.5) | 4.5–5.6% | 35–45 | Low to medium-low |
| Cream Ale | 1.044–1.052 (11–13) | 1.004–1.010 (1–2.5) | 4.2–5.6% | 10–22 | Very low |

| AVG SENSITIVITY HOP BITTERNESS PERCEPTION | AVG SENSITIVITY HOP FLAVOR | AVG SENSITIVITY HOP AROMA | COLOR SRM (EBC) COLOR DESCRIPTION |
|---|---|---|---|
| Medium to high | Low to medium-low | Low to medium-low | 3–4 (6–8) pale straw |
| Medium | Low to medium-low | Low to medium-low | 3–7 (6–14) straw-light amber |
| Medium to high | Medium to high | Medium to high | 3–6 (6–12) straw-gold |
| Medium | Very low to low | Very low to low | 3–6 (6–12) straw-gold |
| Low | Very low to low | Very low to low | 4–5.5 (8–11) pale gold |
| None to very low | None | None | 1.5–4 (3–8) very light to pale |
| None to very low | None | None | 2–4 (4–8) pale straw |
| Very low to low | None | None | 2–5 (4–10) pale straw |
| Low to medium | Low to medium | Low to medium | 6–14 (12–28) amber-deep copper |
| Medium-low to medium | Low | Low | 5–15 (10–30) gold-deep copper |
| Medium-low to medium | Low | Low | 12–16 (24–32) copper-red brown |
| Low to medium-low | None to low | None to very low | 5–15 (10–30) gold-light brown |
| Medium-low to medium | Low | Very low | 20–30 (40–60) very dark deep copper |
| Low | Low to medium-low | Low to medium-low | 4–10 (8–20) pale-copper |
| Low | Low | None | 12–30 (24–60) very dark copper |
| Low | Low | Low | 14–25 (28–50) light brown to very dark brown |
| Medium-low | Low | Low | 15–20 (30–40) light brown to dark brown |
| Low to medium | Low | Low | 25–30 (50–60) very dark |
| Low to medium-low | Very low | Very low | 40+ (80+) black |
| Medium to medium-high | Low to medium-low | Low to medium-low | 8–15 (16–30) amber-light brown |
| Very low to low | None to very low | None to very low | 2–5 (4–10) straw-gold |

# Basic Guidelines for Brewing 5-Gallon (19 l)
## Other hop varieties may be used. See hop variety

### For Malt Extract

| | LIGHT MALT EXTRACT SYRUP POUNDS (KG) | AMBER MALT EXTRACT SYRUP POUNDS (KG) | DARK MALT EXTRACT SYRUP POUNDS (KG) | CRYSTAL MALT POUNDS (G) | BLACK ROASTED MALT POUNDS (G) | CHOCOLATE MALT POUNDS (G) | ROASTED BARLEY POUNDS (G) |
|---|---|---|---|---|---|---|---|
| **Ales** | | | | | | | |
| **Barley Wine** | 12–14 (5.4–6.4) | | | | | | |
| **Belgian & French Styles** a) Dubbel | | 9 (4.1) | | ½ (225) | | ¼ (110) | |
| b) Tripel | 10–12 (4.5–5.5) | | | | | | |
| c) Flanders Brown | | 6.5 (3) | | 1 (450) | | ¼ (110) | |
| d) Scotch Ale | 10–11 (4.5–5) | | | 1 (450) | | ¼ (110) | |
| e) Wit/ White | 6.5 (3) with wheat malt extract | | | | | | |
| f) Biére de Garde | 7.5 (3.4) | | | ¾ (340) | | | |
| **Bitter** a) Ordinary | 5 (225) | or 5 (225) | | | | | |
| b) Special | 6 (2.7) | or 6 (2.7) | | | | | ¼ (110) for red bitter (optional) |

# Interpretations of Traditional Beer
## chart for reference and hop similarities.

### Brewing Using Whole Hops

| TOASTED MALT POUNDS (G) | OTHER INGREDIENTS POUNDS (G) | BOILING WHOLE HOPS OUNCES (G) HOMEBREW BITTERNESS UNITS (METRIC) (SEE PAGE 67. IF HOP PELLETS ARE USED, USE 15% LESS HOPS.) | FINISHING HOPS OUNCES (G) | YEAST TYPE | ORIGINAL GRAVITY (BALLING) | PERCENT ALCOHOL (BY VOLUME) |
|---|---|---|---|---|---|---|
| | | 4–4.5 (113–128) American: Chinook, Galena, Horizon, Magnum English: Admiral, Target, Challenger, Northdown. 48–54 HBU (1340–1500) | 1–2 (28–56) American: Cascade Centennial; English: Fuggles, Goldings, First Gold | English or American Ale | 1.086–1.100 (21–24) | 8.4–11 |
| ½ (225) | ½ (225) candi sugar | 2¼ (64) Goldings. 11 HBU (310) | ½ (14) Santiam or Mt. Hood | Belgian Ale | 1.060–1.075 (14.7–18.2) | 6.25–7.5 |
| ½ (225) | ½ (225) candi sugar | 1¾ (50) Styrian Goldings. 9 HBU (250) | ½ (14) Santiam or Strisselspalt | Belgian Ale | 1.076–1.089 (18.4–21.3) | 7–9 |
| | | 1 (28) total Goldings & Hallertau. 5 HBU (140) | | Ale & special bacteria | 1.044–1.056 (11–14) | 4.8–6.5 |
| | | 2 (56) Willamette, Styrian Golding or 1.25 (35) Brewers, Gold, Northern Brewer. 10 HBU (280) | | Ale | 1.075–1.080 (18–19) | 6–7.5 |
| | 1 oz (28) coriander, ¼ oz (7) orange peel | 1 (28) Sterling or 1.5 (42) Mt. Hood, Vanguard, Liberty, Hallertau. 6.5 HBU (180) | ½ (14) Saaz | Belgian Witbier | 1.044–1.050 (11–12.5) | 4.8–5.2 |
| | 1 (450) white candi sugar | 2 (56) French Strisselspalt, Hallertau, Saaz. 8 HBU (225) | ½ (14) Strisselspalt, Santiam, Crystal | Ale | 1.065–1.070 (16–17) | 6.5–7 |
| | | 1.5–2 (42–56) Goldings, Fuggles, Willamette, Cascade or 1–1.5 (28–42) Glacier, First Gold, Challenger. 7.5–10 HBU (210–280) | ½–1 (14–28) Goldings, Fuggles, Willamette, Cascade, Glacier | Ale | 1.033–1.038 (8–9.52) | 3–3.7 |
| | | 2–2.5 (56–70) Goldings, Fuggles, Willamette, Cascade or 1.5–1.75 (42–50) Glacier, First Gold, Challenger. 10–12 HBU (280–335) | ½–1 (14–28) Goldings, Fuggles, Willamette, Cascade, Glacier | Ale | 1.038–1.045 (9.5–11) | 4–4.8 |

(continued)

# Basic Guidelines for Brewing 5-Gallon (19 l)
## Other hop varieties may be used. See hop variety

### For Malt Extract

| | LIGHT MALT EXTRACT SYRUP POUNDS (KG) | AMBER MALT EXTRACT SYRUP POUNDS (KG) | DARK MALT EXTRACT SYRUP POUNDS (KG) | CRYSTAL MALT POUNDS (G) | BLACK ROASTED MALT POUNDS (G) | CHOCOLATE MALT POUNDS (G) | ROASTED BARLEY POUNDS (G) |
|---|---|---|---|---|---|---|---|
| c) Extra Special | 7 (3.2) | | | ¾ (340) | | | |
| **Brown Ales**<br>a) English Brown | 5–6 (2.3–2.7) | or 5–6 (2.3–2.7) | | ½ (225) | ¼ (110) | ¼ (110) | |
| b) English Mild | 4–5 (1.8–2.3) | | | | ¼–½ (110–225) | or ¼–½ (110–225) | |
| c) American Brown | | 6.5–7 (2.9–3.2) | | | ¼ (110) | ¼ (110) | |
| Irish Red Ale | | 5 (2.3) | | 1½ (680) | | ¼ (110) | |
| **Pale Ale**<br>a) Classic English Pale Ale | 6.5 (3) | | | ½ (225) | | | |
| b) Classic American Pale Ale | 6.5 (3) | or 6.5 (3) | | ½ (225) | | | |
| c) India Pale Ale | 7.5 (3.4) | | | 1 (450) | | | |
| d) Old/Strong Ale | 9–10 (4.1–4.5) | or 9–10 (4.1–4.5) | | 1 (450) | | ¼ (110) | |

# Interpretations of Traditional Beer

chart for reference and hop similarities.

## Brewing Using Whole Hops

| TOASTED MALT POUNDS (G) | OTHER INGREDIENTS POUNDS (G) | BOILING WHOLE HOPS OUNCES (G) HOMEBREW BITTERNESS UNITS (METRIC) (SEE PAGE 59. IF HOP PELLETS ARE USED, USE 15% LESS HOPS.) | FINISHING HOPS OUNCES (G) | YEAST TYPE | ORIGINAL GRAVITY (BALLING) | PERCENT ALCOHOL (BY VOLUME) |
|---|---|---|---|---|---|---|
| | | 2.5–3 (70–84) Goldings, Fuggles, Willamette, Cascade or 1.75–2 (50–56) Glacier, First Gold, Challenger. 13–14 HBU (365–390) | ½–1 (14–28) Goldings, Fuggles, Willamette, Cascade, Glacier | Ale | 1.052–1.056 (13–14) | 5–5.5 |
| | | 2 (56) Goldings, Fuggles, Willamette or 1.5 (42) Glacier, First Gold, Challenger. 10 HBU (280) | ½ (14) Goldings, Fuggles, Willamette, Glacier | Ale | 1.040–1.045 (10–11) | 4.5–5 |
| | | 1–1.5 (28–42) Goldings, Fuggles, Willamette, Cascade or ¾–1 (21–28) Glacier, First Gold, Challenger. 5–7.5 HBU (140–210) | | Ale | 1.032–1.038 (8–9.5) | 3.2–3.6 |
| | | 2.5–3.0 (70–98) Willamette, Cascade or 1.5 (42) Amarillo, Centennial, Horizon, Magnum, Simcoe, Galena. 13–20 HBU (364–560) | ½–1 (14–28) Cascade, Centennial, Amarillo | Ale | 1.046–1.050 (11.5–12.5) | 5–5.5 |
| ¼ (110) | | 1 (28) Northern Brewer, Challenger, Brewers Gold. 8 HBU (225) | ½ (14) Santiam, American Tettnang | Irish Ale | 1.042–1.046 (10.5–11.5) | 4.4–4.6 |
| | | 1–1.25 (28–35) First Gold, Target, Challenger or 2 (56) Kent Goldings, Fuggles. 10 HBU (280) | 1 (28) Kent Goldings, Willamette | English Ale | 1.044–1.056 (10.5–14) | 4.5–5 |
| | | 1–1.25 (28–35) Centennial, Chinook, Horizon or 2.5 (70) Cascade, Willamette. 12–13 HBU (335–360) | 1 (28) Cascade, Centenial, Amarillo, Horizon | American Ale | 1.044–1.056 (10.5–14) | 4.5–5 |
| ½ (225) | | 1.5–2 (42–56) Centennial, Chinook, Citra, Horizon, Magnum, Amarillo or 4 (112) Cascade, Goldring. 15–20 HBU (420–560) | 1–2 (28–56) any of the boiling hops | Ale | 1.056–1.060 (14–15) | 5.8–6.2 |
| | | 1.5 (42) Northern Brewer, Perle, Brewers Gold or 3 (84) Cascade, Vanguard, Willamette 15 HBU (420) | ½ (14) Cascade, Willamette, Crystal, Goldings, Fuggles | Ale | 1.070–1.075 (17–18) | 7–8 |

(continued)

# Basic Guidelines for Brewing 5-Gallon (19 l)
## Other hop varieties may be used. See hop variety

### For Malt Extract

| | LIGHT MALT EXTRACT SYRUP POUNDS (KG) | AMBER MALT EXTRACT SYRUP POUNDS (KG) | DARK MALT EXTRACT SYRUP POUNDS (KG) | CRYSTAL MALT POUNDS (G) | BLACK ROASTED MALT POUNDS (G) | CHOCOLATE MALT POUNDS (G) | ROASTED BARLEY POUNDS (G) |
|---|---|---|---|---|---|---|---|
| **Porter** | | | | | | | |
| a) Robust Porter | | 7–8 (3.2–3.6) | | | 1 (450) | | |
| b) Brown Porter | | 7–8 (3.2–3.6) | | | | ½ (225) | |
| **Scottish Ales** | | | | | | | |
| a) Light | 4 (1.8) | 4 (1.8) | | 1 (450) | | | |
| b) Heavy | 4.5 (2) | 4.5 (2) | | 1 (450) | | | |
| c) Export | 5.5 (2.5) | | | 1 (450) | | | |
| d) Scotch Ale (see Belgian) | | | | | | | |
| **Stouts** | | | | | | | |
| a) Dry Stout | | | 5.5 (2.5) | ¾ (340) | ⅓ (150) | | ⅓ (150) |
| b) Foreign Export Stout | | | 8 (3.6) | ¾ (340) | ⅓ (150) | | ⅓ (150) |
| c) Sweet Stout | | | 6–6.5 (2.7–3) | 1 (450) | ¼ (110) | | ¼ (110) |
| d) Imperial Stout | | 11.5 (5.2) | | | | ½ (225) | ½ (225) |

## Brewing Using Whole Hops

| TOASTED MALT POUNDS (G) | OTHER INGREDIENTS POUNDS (G) | BOILING WHOLE HOPS OUNCES (G) HOMEBREW BITTERNESS UNITS (METRIC) (SEE PAGE 59. IF HOP PELLETS ARE USED, USE 15% LESS HOPS.) | FINISHING HOPS OUNCES (G) | YEAST TYPE | ORIGINAL GRAVITY (BALLING) | PERCENT ALCOHOL (BY VOLUME) |
|---|---|---|---|---|---|---|
| | | 2.5 (70) Cascade, Fuggles, Willamette, Vanguard, Glacier or 1.25 (35) Perle, Northern Brewer. 12–14 HBU (335–390) | ½ (14) Tettnang, Santiam, Mt. Hood, Liberty, Cascade | Ale | 1.045–1.060 (11–15) | 5–6.5 |
| | | 2 (56) Cascade, Fuggles, Willamette, Vanguard, Glacier or 1 (28) Perle, Northern Brewer. 10–12 HBU (280–335) | ½ (14) Tettnang, Santiam, Mt. Hood, Liberty, Cascade | Ale | 1.040–1.050 (10–12.5) | 4.5–6 |
| | | ¾–1 (21–28) Goldings, Fuggles, Willamette, Cascade. 4–5 HBU (110–140) | | Scottish or English Ale | 1.033–1.038 (8–9.5) | 2.8–3.5 |
| | | 1–1.25 (28–35) Goldings, Fuggles, Willamette, Cascade. 5–6 HBU (140–170) | | Scottish or English Ale | 1.038–1.045 (9.5–11) | 3.5–4 |
| | | 1.25–1.5 (35–42) Goldings, Fuggles, Willamette, Cascade. 6–8 HBU (170–225) | | Scottish or English Ale | 1.040–1.050 (10–12.5) | 3.2–4.2 |
| | | | | | | |
| | | 2 (56) Goldings, Fuggles, Willamette, Cascade or 1 (28) Northern Brewer, Perle. 8–10 HBU (225–280) | ½ (14) hops, optional for American-Style Stout | Irish Ale | 1.038–1.048 (9–14) | 4–4.5 |
| | | 3 (84) Goldings, Fuggles, Willamette, Cascade or 1.5 (42) Northern Brewer, Perle. 12–15 HBU (336–420) | ½ (14) hops, optional for American-Style Stout | Irish Ale | 1.060–1.065 (15–16) | 6.5–7 |
| | | 1 (28) Goldings, Fuggles, Willamette, Cascade or ½ (14) Northern Brewer, Perle. 4–6 HBU (10–170) | | Ale | 1.048–1.052 (12–13) | 4.5–5 |
| | | 5 (140) Cascade, Mt. Hood, Liberty, Vanguard or 2–2.5 (56–70) Centennial, First Gold, Glacier, Horizon, Magnum. 25–28 HBU (700–785) | 1–1.5 (28–42) any of the boiling hops | Ale | 1.080–1.090 (20–22.5) | 8–9 |

(continued)

# Basic Guidelines for Brewing 5-Gallon (19 l)
## Other hop varieties may be used. See hop variety

### For Malt Extract

| | LIGHT MALT EXTRACT SYRUP POUNDS (KG) | AMBER MALT EXTRACT SYRUP POUNDS (KG) | DARK MALT EXTRACT SYRUP POUNDS (KG) | CRYSTAL MALT POUNDS (G) | BLACK ROASTED MALT POUNDS (G) | CHOCOLATE MALT POUNDS (G) | ROASTED BARLEY POUNDS (G) |
|---|---|---|---|---|---|---|---|
| **Lagers** | | | | | | | |
| **American Dark** | | 5.5–6 (2.5–2.7) | | ½ (225) | ¼ (110) | | |
| **American Light Lagers** a) Diet/Lite | 4.5–5 (1.8–2) | | | | | | |
| b) American Lager | 6 (2.7) | | | | | | |
| Australian, Latin American & Tropical Light Lagers | 6 (2.7) | | | | | | |
| **Bavarian Dark** a) Munich Dunkel | 6.5–7 (3–3.2) | or 6.5–7 (3–3.2) | | ½ (225) | | ½ (225) | |
| b) Schwarzbier | | 6.5 (3) | | ½ (225) | | | |
| **Bock** a) Dark Bock | | 9 (4.1) | | ½ (225) | | ½ (225) | |
| b) Heller/ Maibock | 9.5 (4.3) | | | | | | |
| c) Doppelbock | | 10.5 (4.8) | | ½ (225) | | ½ (225) | |

# Interpretations of Traditional Beer
## chart for reference and hop similarities.

### Brewing Using Whole Hops

| TOASTED MALT POUNDS (G) | OTHER INGREDIENTS POUNDS (G) | BOILING WHOLE HOPS OUNCES (G) HOMEBREW BITTERNESS UNITS (METRIC) (SEE PAGE 59. IF HOP PELLETS ARE USED, USE 15% LESS HOPS.) | FINISHING HOPS OUNCES (G) | YEAST TYPE | ORIGINAL GRAVITY (BALLING) | PERCENT ALCOHOL (BY VOLUME) |
|---|---|---|---|---|---|---|
| | | 1 (28) Mt. Hood, Santiam, Hallertau, Liberty, Spalt, Sterling. 5 HBU (140) | ½ (14) Crystal, Hallertau, Saintiam, Tettnang | Lager | 1.042–1.046 (10.5–11.5) | 4.5–5 |
| | | ½ (14) Cascade, Mt. Hood, Liberty, Saaz, Lublin. 2.5 HBU (70) | ¼ (7) Santiam, Tettnang, Crystal | Lager | 1.028–1.032 (7–8) | 3.2–3.6 |
| | | ½–¾ (14–21) Cascade, Mt. Hood, Sterling, Hallertau, Liberty, Saaz, Lublin. 2.5–4 HBU (70–110) | ¼ (7) Santiam, Tettnang, Crystal | Lager | 1.042–1.044 (10.5–11) | 4.2–4.6 |
| | 1 (450) corn sugar | ½ (14) Northern Brewer, Perle, Pride of Ringwood 5 HBU (140) | | Lager | 1.040–1.044 (10–11) | 3.9–4.4 |
| ½ (225) | | 1¼ (35) Hallertau, Hersbruck, Spalt, Mittelfrueh, Mt. Hood, Liberty. 6 HBU (170) | ¼ (7) Crystal, Santiam, Hallertau, Tettnang | German Lager | 1.052–1.056 (13–14) | 5–5.5 |
| | ½ (225) debitterized black malt | 1½ (42) Hallertau, Hersbruck, Spalt, Mittelfrueh, Mt. Hood, Liberty. 7–8 HBU (200–225) | ¼ (7) Crystal, Santiam, Hallertau, Tettnang | German Lager | 1.048–1.052 (12–13) | 4.4–5 |
| | ¼ (110) debitterized black malt | 2 (56) Spalt, Hallertau, Mittelfrueh, Hersbruck, Liberty, Crystal or 1 (28) Perle, Northern Brewer. 10 HBU (280) | | German Lager | 1.066–1.070 (16–17) | 6.5–7 |
| ½ (225) | | 2 (56) Spalt, Hallertau, Mittelfrueh, Hersbruck, Liberty, Crystal or 1 (28) Perle, Northern Brewer. 10 HBU (280) | ¼ (7) Hallertau, Crystal, Santiam | German Lager | 1.066–1.070 (16–17) | 6.5–7 |
| | ¼ (110) debitterized black malt | 2–2.5 (56–70) Spalt, Hallertau, Mittelfrueh, Hersbruck, Liberty, Crystal or 1–1.25 (28–35) Perle, Northern Brewer. 10–13 HBU (364) | | German Lager | 1.076–1.080 (18.4–19.3) | 7.5–8.5 |

(continued)

# Basic Guidelines for Brewing 5-Gallon (19 l)
## Other hop varieties may be used. See hop variety

### For Malt Extract

| | LIGHT MALT EXTRACT SYRUP POUNDS (KG) | AMBER MALT EXTRACT SYRUP POUNDS (KG) | DARK MALT EXTRACT SYRUP POUNDS (KG) | CRYSTAL MALT POUNDS (G) | BLACK ROASTED MALT POUNDS (G) | CHOCOLATE MALT POUNDS (G) | ROASTED BARLEY POUNDS (G) |
|---|---|---|---|---|---|---|---|
| **Classic Pilsener** a) German | 6–7 (2.7–3.2) | | | | | | |
| b) Bohemian/ Gzech | 6–7.5 (2.7–7.9) | | | | | | |
| **Other German– Austrian Styles** Dortmunder/ Export/ Oktoberfest | 7–7.5 (3.2–3.4) | | | | | | |
| Munich Helles | 6.5 (3) | | | | | | |
| Märzen | | 7 (3.2) | | ½ (225) | | ⅛ (4) | |
| Vienna | | 7 (3.2) | | ½ (225) | | ¼ (7) | |

# Interpretations of Traditional Beer
chart for reference and hop similarities.

## Brewing Using Whole Hops

| TOASTED MALT POUNDS (G) | OTHER INGREDIENTS POUNDS (G) | BOILING WHOLE HOPS OUNCES (G) HOMEBREW BITTERNESS UNITS (METRIC) (SEE PAGE 59. IF HOP PELLETS ARE USED, USE 15% LESS HOPS.) | FINISHING HOPS OUNCES (G) | YEAST TYPE | ORIGINAL GRAVITY (BALLING) | PERCENT ALCOHOL (BY VOLUME) |
|---|---|---|---|---|---|---|
|  |  | 1.5 (42) Spalt, German Tradition, Hallertau, Mt. Hood or 2 (56) Crystal, Hersbruck, Strisselspalt. 8–9 HBU (225–250) | ½ (14) Hallertau, Crystal, Saaz, Spalt, Tettnang | German Lager | 1.044–1.050 (11–12.5) | 4–5 |
| ½ (225) | 0–¼ (0–110) aromatic malt | 2.75 (80) Saaz, Lublin or 1.5 (42) Sterling. 10–11 HBU (280–310) | ½ (14) Saaz, Lublin, Sterling | German or Czech Lager | 1.048–1.056 (12–14) | 4.5–5.5 |
|  |  | 1.5 (42) Spalt, German Tradition, Hallertau or 1 (28) Perle, Northern Brewer. 7–8 HBU (200–225) | ¼ (7) Spalt, German Tradition, Hallertau | German Lager | 1.050–1.056 (12.5–14) | 5–6 |
|  |  | 1–1¼ (28–35) Spalt, German Tradition, Hallertau, Mt. Hood Liberty, Strisselspalt. 6–7 HBU (170–200) | ¼ (7) Santiam, Tettnang, Mt. Hood, Hallertau | German Lager | 1.046–1.048 (11.5–12) | 4.5–5 |
| ½ (225) |  | 1–1¼ 4 (28–35) Spalt, German Tradition, Hallertau, Mt. Hood, Liberty, Strisselspalt. 6–8 HBU (170–230) | ½ (7) Santiam, Tettnang, Mt. Hood, Hallertau | German Lager | 1.054–1.058 (13.5–14.5) | 5.3–5.8 |
|  |  | 1.5–2 (42–56) Spalt, German Tradition, Hallertau, Mt. Hood, Liberty, Strisselspalt. 7–10 HBU (200–280) | ½ (14) Santiam, Tettnang, Mt. Hood, Hallertau | German Lager | 1.050–1.054 (12.5–13.5) | 5.2–5.4 |

(continued)

# Basic Guidelines for Brewing 5-Gallon (19 l)
## Other hop varieties may be used. See hop variety

### For Malt Extract

| | LIGHT MALT EXTRACT SYRUP POUNDS (KG) | AMBER MALT EXTRACT SYRUP POUNDS (KG) | DARK MALT EXTRACT SYRUP POUNDS (KG) | CRYSTAL MALT POUNDS (G) | BLACK ROASTED MALT POUNDS (G) | CHOCOLATE MALT POUNDS (G) | ROASTED BARLEY POUNDS (G) |
|---|---|---|---|---|---|---|---|
| **Hybrid Beers/Lagers, Ales** | | | | | | | |
| **Altbiers** a) Düsseldorfer Altbier | | 6 (2.7) | | ¾ (340) | | | |
| b) Kölsch | 6 (2.7) | | | | | | |
| California Common | | 6.5 (3) | | ½ (225) | | | |
| Cream Ale | 6.5 (3) | | | | | | |
| **Wheat Beer** a) Bavarian Weizen | 7 (3.2) with wheat malt extract | | | | | | |
| b) Bavarian Dunkel Weizen | 7 (3.2) with wheat malt extract | | | | | ½ (225) | |
| c) Weizen-bock | | 10 (4.5) with wheat malt extract | | | | | |
| d) American Wheat | 6 (2.7) | | | | | | |

# Interpretations of Traditional Beer
chart for reference and hop similarities.

## Brewing Using Whole Hops

| TOASTED MALT POUNDS (G) | OTHER INGREDIENTS POUNDS (G) | BOILING WHOLE HOPS OUNCES (G) HOMEBREW BITTERNESS UNITS (METRIC) (SEE PAGE 59. IF HOP PELLETS ARE USED, USE 15% LESS HOPS.) | FINISHING HOPS OUNCES (G) | YEAST TYPE | ORIGINAL GRAVITY (BALLING) | PERCENT ALCOHOL (BY VOLUME) |
|---|---|---|---|---|---|---|
| | ⅓ (150) debitterized black malt | 1–1.5 (28–42) Northern Brewer, Perle, German Tradition or 2 (56) Spalt, Hallertau, Mt. Hood. 10–13 HBU (280–360) | | German Ale | 1.046–1.048 (11.5–12) | 4.4–4.6 |
| | | 1.5 (42) Hallertau, Santiam, Tettnang, Liberty, Crystal, Saaz, Lublin. 7–8 HBU (200–225) | ¼ (7) Santiam, Liberty, Crystal, Tettnang | German Ale | 1.042–1.044 (10.5–11) | 4–4.3 |
| | | 1.5 (42) Northern Brewer, Perle or 2.5 (70) Cascade, Willamette. 12–13 HBU (340–365) | ½ (14) Willamette, Glacier, Brewers Gold | Lager | 1.048–1.052 (12–13) | 4.5–5 |
| | | 1 (28) Santiam, Sterling, Mt. Hood, Liberty, Vanguard. 5 HBU (140) | ¼–½ (7–14) Santiam, Sterling, Mt. Hood, Liberty, Vanguard, Cascade | Lager | 1.046 1.050 (11.5–12.5) | 4.4–4.8 |
| | | ¾ (21) Hallertau, Crystal, Liberty, Mt. Hood. 3–4 HBU (85–110) | 0–¼ (0–7) Saaz, Tettnang, Hallertau | German Wheat Ale | 1.048–1.052 (12–13). | 4.8–5.2 |
| ¼ (110) | | ¾ (21) Hallertau, Crystal, Liberty, Mt. Hood. 3–4 HBU (85–110) | ¼ (7) Saaz, Tettnang, Hallertau | German Wheat Ale | 1048–1.052 (12–13). | 4.8–5.2 |
| | ½ (225) debitterized black malt | 1 (28) Hallertau, Mt. Hood, Liberty, Santiam, Tettnang, Spalt, Strisselspalt. 5 HBU (140) | ¼ (7) Santiam, Tettnang, Sterling, Crystal | German Wheat Ale | 1.070–1.074 (17–18) | 7–8 |
| | | 1 (28) Willamette, Cascade, Amarillo. 5–8 HBU (140–225) | ½ (14) Cascade, Willamette, Amarillo | Ale | 1.040–1.046 (10–11.5) | 3.8–4 |

quantities and are difficult to find. Low-bitterness flavor and aroma hops can be substituted. Avoid highly bitter (high alpha acid) hops if you strive for traditional authenticity.

Original gravities: 1.045 to 1.060 (11.5 to 15). Alcohol: 5 to 6 percent. Bitterness: 25 to 40 BU. Color: 3 to 6 SRM (6 to 12).

CALIFORNIA COMMON BEER—This could also be referred to as American Steam Beer, but the remnant of this style commercially available today is Anchor Steam brewed by the Anchor Brewing Company in San Francisco. The name "Steam Beer" is trademarked by this company. Its fine product Anchor Steam Beer is perhaps representative of a style that originated in the mid-1800s in California before ice was available for cooling lager fermentation. In general, California Common beer is a style of beer brewed with lager yeasts but at ale fermentation temperatures. Aggressively hopped and having a residual sweetness of caramel or crystal malt, Anchor Steam Beer is but one brand of this type, but is considered a standard because there are no known brewing records that can define the flavor character of this almost forgotten beer style. Commercial brewers who brew this style refer to it as California Common beer.

Original gravities: 1.045 to 1.056 (11.2 to 13.8). Alcohol: 4.5 to 5.6 percent. Bitterness: 35 to 45 BU. Color: 8 to 15 SRM (16 to 30).

AMERICAN DARK LAGER—Essentially colored versions of American lager and premium lagers with minimal, or sometimes no, roasted or chocolate-like characters contributed by the darker malts. They are usually a bit heavier than the lightest of the American standard lagers. American-style bock beers sometimes come under this category because of their low original gravity and alcohol, compared to their German counterparts.

Original gravities: 1.040 to 1.050 (10 to 12.5). Alcohol: 4 to 5.5 percent. Bitterness: 14 to 20 BU. Color: 14 to 25 SRM (28 to 50).

# WORTS ILLUSTRATED

### A COMPENDIUM OF 45 MALT EXTRACT RECIPES

The joy of brewing lies partly in concocting your own recipes, and the preceding sections of this book have provided the foundation for your doing so.

Whatever concoction you put together, the responsibility for success is yours alone. A recipe is only the result of somebody's trial and error and hopefully their ultimate success. Use your own imagination, flair, courage, and common sense. Above all, whatever you do, relax. Don't worry. Have a homebrew.

The recipes presented in this section are for those who would like a bit more direction in their first batches and are looking for something in particular but don't know which malts and hops result in which brews. The recipes are favorites and have enjoyed notoriety for their superlative qualities. Many will result in award-winning brews—not for me, but for you!

Before you get yourself involved with these recipes, be sure to read the following section, "Notes, Substitutions, and Adjustments."

## NOTES, SUBSTITUTIONS, AND ADJUSTMENTS

1. Don't be too cheap. Spending an extra $10 on the *best ingredients* for a 5-gallon (19 l) batch is like spending 16 cents more on a 12-ounce (355 ml) bottle of beer. Remember that when you fork over $5 or $6 for your next beer at your favorite bar or restaurant and you wish you had a homebrew.

2. Don't be afraid to substitute other *varieties of hops*. All hop additions are with whole hops unless otherwise indicated. You may substitute hop pellets for whole hops at any time. For more accuracy in bitterness levels, substitute 15 percent less when using hop pellets rather than whole hops. And don't worry about it.

3. Several recipes call for *toasted malt*. While you can buy aromatic malts from your local homebrew supply store, home-toasting provides an extra special dimension to the flavor and aroma qualities of your brews. Toasting malted barley is a simple process. Preheat your oven to 350 degrees F (177 C) and spread the whole malted barley grain on a screen or cookie sheet. Within 10 minutes a wonderful aroma will emanate from your oven and the malted barley will have turned a slight reddish color. Remove the grain at this time. Prolonged toasting will turn the inside of the malted barley a deeper nut brown and will contribute a roasted flavor. The nutty malt aromatics of a 10-minute toasting are desired for many recipes.

4. Don't be afraid to *substitute ale yeast for lager yeast* and vice versa. Of course if using ale yeast, don't let the fermentation get below 65 degrees F (18.5 C).

5. All specific gravity readings are made with a *hydrometer* accurate at 60 degrees F (16 C). Degrees Balling (or Plato) are given in parentheses.

6. Always use 3/4 *cup* (175 ml) of *corn sugar* or 1 1/4 *cups* (300 ml) dried malt extract for each 5 gallons (19 l) brewed when bottling (except where noted). Do not make the error of misinterpreting this—i.e., do not use 3/4 *pound* of corn sugar. If honey is substituted for sugar, use 1/2 cup (120 ml).

7. If *kegging* your beer, use only 1/3 cup (80 ml) corn sugar or 1/2 cup (120 ml) dried malt extract for each 5 gallons (19 l) brewed. Because of the physics of kegging and dispensing your beer in a larger container, less carbonation is needed. Adding 3/4 cup of sugar would result in excessive foaming when dispensed.

8. When brewing you may always *substitute malt extract for corn sugar* for a brew with more body and character. Substitute approximately pound for pound.

9. All recipes may be *lightened in body* and flavor (while not diminishing alcohol) by substituting corn sugar (approximately pound for pound) for malt extract. For best results, corn sugar should never be substituted for more than 20 percent of the malt extract.

10. To *lighten body, flavor, and alcohol*, the amount of malt extract may be decreased. The amount of hops should be decreased proportionately.

11. You may always *substitute malt extract syrup for dried malt extract* and vice versa. If substituting syrup for dry malt extract use 18 percent more syrup than the amount of syrup called for. Likewise if substituting dry malt extract for syrup use 15 percent less dry malt than the amount of syrup called for in the recipe. Here are a few convenient formulas:

**Converting dried extract to malt extract syrup**

Weight of dried extract × 1.18 = Amount of syrup equivalent

or

Weight of dried extract ÷ 0.85 = Amount of syrup equivalent

**Converting malt extract syrup to dried extract**

Weight of malt syrup × 0.85 = Amount of dried extract equivalent

or

Weight of malt syrup ÷ 1.18 = Amount of dried extract equivalent

12. The *addition of crushed specialty grains* in the malt extract recipes can be simplified by adding the crushed grains in water during the 15 to 30 minutes it takes to bring the water to a boil. The spent grains can then simply be removed with a kitchen strainer just before boiling. A better method is also featured in recipes where the crushed grains are held at 150 to 160 degrees F (65 to 71 C) for 30 minutes, then removed with a strainer.

13. You may end up with a *beginning specific gravity* other than noted. Relax, don't worry. There may be some variation due to varieties or batches of

However, there is still a great deal of satisfaction in knowing that although the moon is smaller than the earth, it is much further away!

—Jackson Wolfe

malt extract, temperature, or inadequate mixing of the wort in the fermenter. The important thing is not to worry.

14. Manufacturers of *malt extract* sometimes change their *packaging*. What may be available in a 2-pound (0.9 kg) can at the time of this publication may later only be available in 3½-pound (1.6 kg) cans. Use your common sense when making adjustments.

15. Don't be afraid to use *a pound more or a pound less* in any given recipe. It will alter the character of the beer, but it certainly will not ruin it. And it may even be better. Of course—because you made it.

16. *Abbreviations:* lb(s). = pound(s), Tbsp. = tablespoon(s), tsp. = teaspoon(s), c. = cup(s), pkg(s). = package(s), oz. = ounce(s), g = gram(s), kg = kilogram(s), ml = milliter(s), O.G. = Original Specific Gravity, F.G. = Final Specific Gravity, SRM = Standard Reference Method (color), EBC = European Brewing Convention (color), BU = International Bittering Units, L = Lovibond (a measure of malt or beer color), *(asterisk) = no amount is needed.

17. When grains and whole or pellet hops are added to the wort, always use a sanitized strainer to *separate particulates* from the wort as it passes into the fermenter. Hops or grains may clog the "blow-out" hose and cause hazardous pressure buildup in the fermenter.

18. There are some brands of *dried ale and lager yeasts* that are excellent. At the same time, motivate yourself to learn how to use liquid cultured ale and lager yeasts. With the great new products available at most homebrew supply shops, all it takes is spending the extra few dollars, opening a cap, and pouring fresh yeast into your fermenter. *Liquid yeast cultures* available to homebrewers can dramatically improve the quality of your homebrew. Liquid yeasts may be substituted for dried yeast in *all* recipes.

19. The yeast I used to develop nearly all of these recipes in this book was a strain of lager yeast used for both ale and lager fermentations. It is a yeast I've kept cultured since 1983. It is now available from White Labs and is called Cry Havoc yeast strain.

20. *Equivalents:*

- Five U.S. gallons equal 19 liters.
- One ounce equals 28.3 grams.
- One kilogram equals 2.2 pounds, 3.3 pounds equals 1.5 kilograms.
- One U.S. gallon equals 0.8 Imperial British or Canadian gallon.
- One Imperial British or Canadian gallon equals 1.2 U.S. gallons.

These are conversions you may find useful when using British, Australian, or Canadian products. Conversions throughout this book are conveniently rounded off and are not necessarily exact.

21. *HBUs, or Homebrew Bitterness Units,* are a measure of the total amount of bitterness potential in a given volume of beer. They are very easy and

useful units to use for beginning and intermediate homebrewers when formulating or converting recipes. Bitterness units are calculated by multiplying the percent of alpha acid in the hops by the number of ounces. For example, if 2 ounces of Northern Brewer hops (9 percent alpha acid) and 3 ounces of Cascade hops (5 percent alpha acid) were used in a 10-gallon batch, the total amount of bitterness units would be 33: $(2 \times 9) + (3 \times 5) = 18 + 15 = 33$. Bitterness units per gallon would be 3.3 in a 10-gallon batch or 6.6 in a 5-gallon batch, so it is important to note volumes whenever expressing Homebrew Bitterness Units. HBUs are *not* related to BUs except that they both are related to bitterness in beer.

22. *MBUs or Metric (homebrew) Bittering Units* are the metric equivalent of HBUs, where grams are used as the measure rather than ounces. 1 HBU = 28 MBUs.

23. All boiling hops in recipes quote *HBUs (and MBUs), as a guide* for the homebrewer should he or she desire to substitute other varieties of hops. For example, 2 ounces of 4.5 percent Saaz hops equals 9 HBUs, which is equivalent to 1 ounce of 9 percent Northern Brewer in the boil.

So let's cut the shuck and jive and get on with the recipes.

## 45 MALT EXTRACT RECIPES

Pale and Amber American Ales

Pale and Amber English and Irish Ales

Lighter Beers from Around the World

Weizenbier/Weissbier

Specialty Beers

## ALL RECIPES ARE FORMULATED USING WHOLE HOPS UNLESS OTHERWISE NOTED.

## PALE AND AMBER AMERICAN ALES

### *Righteous American Real Ale*

The taste of Righteous American Real Ale is excellent and authentic within 14 days of brewing. It is brewed in a style of the "ordinary bitter" served in parts of London and in hop country to the south. It is created with American hops, making exquisitely flavorful ale with a beautiful American hop aroma. Bear in mind that authentic bitter may not be as carbonated as you are used to. If more carbonation is desired, add ¼ cup (60 ml) additional corn sugar at bottling time.

Ingredients for 5 gallons (19 l):

| | |
|---|---|
| 4½ lbs. (2 kg) | amber dried malt extract |
| 1½ oz. (42 g) | Cascade hop pellets (boiling): 7–8 HBU (200–225 MBU) |
| ½ oz. (14 g) | Yakima Goldings, Centennial, or Willamette hop pellets (finishing) |
| 2 tsp. (8 g) | gypsum |
| ¼ tsp. (1 g) | Irish moss powder |
| * | English-type ale yeast |

½ c. (120 ml)    corn sugar or ¾ c. (175 ml) corn sugar (for bottling) or ¼
                 cup (60 ml) corn sugar (for kegging)
1 c. (240 ml)    dried malt extract (for bottling)


O.G.: 1.040 (10)
F.G.: 1.007–1.010 (2–2.5)
Bitterness: 30 BU; Color: 10 SRM (20 EBC); Alcohol: 4.1% by volume


Boil for 60 minutes with 2 gallons (7.5 l) of water the malt extract, Cascade hops, and gypsum. Add the Irish moss for the final 10 minutes of the boil. Add the finishing hops for the final 1 minute of the boil. Strain, sparge, and transfer immediately to 2½ gallons (9.5 l) of cold water in the fermenter. Top off with additional water to make 5 gallons (19 l). Aerate the wort very well. Pitch the yeast when the temperature of the wort is about 70 degrees F (21 C). Ferment at about 70 degrees F (21 C) for about 1 week or when fermentation shows signs of calming and stopping.

After the tenth day you should be able to bottle with the addition of ½ cup corn sugar. Store for 4 days and try it. It will be terrific within 7 days of bottling.

### Whitey's Gone Fishin' Pale Ale

If it's simplicity you're looking for and time to go fishing—and better yet, a pale ale with great drinkability and an ultimate sense of satisfaction—well then, read no further. You have arrived and are about to land a whopper! This pale ale proves the point that great beers don't have to be born of complex recipes. If you have any hesitation, don't—just brew it.

Ingredients for 5 gallons (19 l):

6.6 lbs. (3 kg)    light malt extract syrup
1 oz. (28 g)       Amarillo hops (boiling): 8 HBU (225 MBU)
¾ oz. (21 g)       Mt. Hood hops (10 minutes, flavor)
½ oz. (14 g)       Sterling hops (aroma)
¼ tsp. (1 g)       Irish moss powder
*                  English-type ale yeast or White Labs Cry Havoc yeast
¾ c. (175 ml)      corn sugar (for bottling) or ⅓ c. (80 ml) corn sugar
                   (for kegging)


O.G.: 1.050 (11.5–12.5)
F.G.: 1.010–1.014 (2.5–3.5)
Bitterness: 27 BU; Color: 10 SRM (20 EBC); Alcohol: 4.7% by volume

Add the malt extract and Amarillo hops to 2 gallons (7.5 l) of water and boil for 60 minutes. Add the Irish moss and Mt. Hood hops for the final 10 minutes of the boil. Next, turn off the heat and add the Sterling hops (for aroma). Strain, sparge, and transfer immediately to 2 gallons (7.5 l) of cold water in the fermenter. Top off with additional water to make 5 gallons (19 l). Aerate the wort very well. Pitch the yeast when the temperature of the wort is about 70 degrees F (21 C). Ferment at about 70 degrees F (21 C) for about 1 week or when fermentation shows signs of calming and stopping.

Prime with sugar and bottle or keg when fermentation is complete. You should be fishing and enjoying this pale ale in 3 weeks—and that ain't no fish tale.

## Wild Women India Pale Ale

American-style India Pale Ale (IPA) is loaded with citrusy, fruity, and bold American hop character. A well-balanced American IPA will make both women and men wild about homebrewed beer. This beer's namesake is inspired by a few wild women in my life who came up with an IPA recipe that shook the planet. You'll fool the homebrew experts with this beer. They'll think you're an advanced all-grain brew-it-from-scratch homebrewer. Simply put, this beer will knock your socks off if you like hop character. For decades I've been saying that you can make excellent quality malt-extract beers that are absolutely indistinguishable from all-grain batches. This brew will send you off your axis.

Ingredients for 5 gallons (19 l):

| | |
|---|---|
| 5½ lbs. (2.5 kg) | light dried malt extract |
| 1 lb. (454 g) | crystal malt (10 L) |
| ½ oz. (14 g) | Simcoe or Columbus hops (boiling): 7 HBU (196 MBU) |
| 1 oz. (28 g) | Amarillo or Citra hops (boiling): 7 HBU (196 MBU) |
| 3 oz. (84 g) | Cascade whole hops (30 minutes, flavor): 15 HBU (420 MBU) |
| 2 oz. (56 g) | Cascade whole hops (10 minutes, flavor and aroma) |
| 3 oz. (84 g) | Cascade whole hops (2 minutes, aroma) |
| ⅓ oz. (10 g) | Simcoe or Columbus hop pellets (dry hopping in secondary) |
| ¼ tsp. (1 g) | Irish moss powder |
| * | English- or American-type ale yeast |
| ¾ c. (175 ml) | corn sugar (for bottling) or ⅓ c. (80 ml) corn sugar (for kegging) |

O.G.: 1.053 (13.5)
F.G.: 1.014 (5 )
Bitterness: 80–90 BU; Color: 7 SRM (14 EBC); Alcohol: 5.2% by volume

Place the crushed malt in 2 gallons (7.5 l) of 150-degree F (68 C) water and let steep for 30 minutes. Strain out, rinse with 3 quarts (3 l) hot water, and discard the crushed grains reserving the approximately 2½ gallons (9.5 l) of liquid to which you will now add malt extract and the boiling hops. Bring to a boil and boil for a total of 60 minutes. After 30 minutes, add the 30-minute hops. When 10 minutes remain, add the 10-minute hops and Irish moss. When 2 minutes remain, add the 2-minute hops. After a total wort boil of 60 minutes, turn off the heat.

Immerse the covered pot of wort in a cold water bath and let sit for 15 to 30 minutes, or the time it takes to have a couple of homebrews.

Strain out and sparge the hops and direct the hot wort into a sanitized fermenter to which 2 gallons (7.5 l) of cold water have been added. If necessary, add additional cold water to achieve a 5-gallon (19 l) batch size.

Aerate the wort very well. Pitch the yeast when the temperature of the wort is about 70 degrees F (21 C). Ferment at about 70 degrees F (21 C) for about 1 week or when fermentation shows signs of calming and stopping.

Rack from your primary to a secondary and add the hop pellets for dry hopping. If you have the capability, "cellar" the beer at about 55 degrees F (12.5 C) for about 1 week.

Prime with sugar and bottle or keg when complete.

### *"The Sun Has Left Us on Time"* Steam Beer

Thomas Edison once wrote in his diary, "The sun has left us on time, am going to read from the *Encyclopaedia Britannica* to steady my nerves and go to bed early. I will shut my eyes and imagine a terraced abyss, each terrace occupied by a beautiful maiden. To the first I will deliver my mind and they will pass it down, down to the uttermost depths of silence and oblivion." One can only imagine that he might have been holding a homebrew as he continued his conjectures with vivid details of a hundred maidens offering him solace.

"The Sun Has Left Us on Time" Steam Beer is a dry, yet paradoxically full-bodied, hoppy beer traditionally brewed with lager yeast at ale-fermenting temperatures. The adding of distinctive Perle hops and finishing with Cascade hops lend a wonderful hop character to this refreshing quencher. A bit of crystal malt is added to sweeten and round out some of the hop character. "Steam Beer" is the trademark of Anchor Brewing Company and that name cannot be used for commercial purposes.

When you reach the bottom of the glass, indeed, you too will see that the sun has left us on time.

Ingredients for 5 gallons (19 l):

7½ lbs. (3.4 kg)   light malt extract syrup
½ lb. (225 g)      crystal malt (10 L)

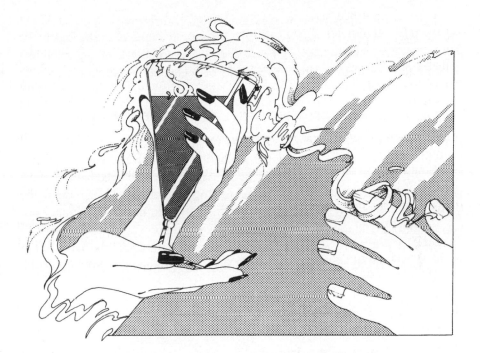

1½ oz. (42 g)   Perle or Vanguard hops (boiling): 12 HBU (24 MBU)
½ oz. (14 g)    Crystal or Liberty hops (2 minutes, finishing, aroma)
¼ tsp. (1 g)    Irish moss powder
*               White Labs Cry Havoc yeast
¾ c. (175 ml)   corn sugar (for bottling) or ⅓ c. (80 ml) corn sugar
                (for kegging)

O.G.: 1.044–1.048 (11–12)
F.G.: 1.009–1.013 (2–3)
Bitterness: 36 BU; Color: 10–12 SRM (20–24 EBC); Alcohol: 4.6% by
volume

Combine the crushed crystal malt with 1½ gallons (5.7 l) of water and let steep
at 150 to 160 degrees F (65–71 C) for 30 minutes, then remove the grains with a
strainer. Add the malt extract and boiling hops and boil for 60 minutes. When 10
minutes remain, add the Irish moss powder. Add the Crystal or Liberty finishing
hops for the final 2 minutes of the boil. Strain, sparge, and transfer immediately to
2 gallons (7.5 l) of cold water in the fermenter. Top off with additional water to
make 5 gallons (19 l). Aerate the wort very well. Pitch the yeast when the temperature of the wort is about 70 degrees F (21 C). Ferment at about 70 degrees F (21 C)
for about 1 week or when fermentation shows signs of calming and stopping.

If two-stage fermentation is used, rack from your primary to a secondary. The beer will improve if matured for 2 to 3 weeks at a temperature of about 50 degrees F (10 C) before bottling. Prime with sugar and bottle or keg when fermentation is complete or after 2 to 3 weeks of secondary maturation.

## PALE AND AMBER ENGLISH AND IRISH ALES

### Palace Bitter (English-Style)

Everyone's house can be a castle, but if I had my druthers, I'd go for a palace. And if I had a palace, then naturally my house bitter would become my Palace Bitter. Brewing your own gives a special feeling to your home, whatever shape it's in. Brewing Palace Bitter and having it on tap or in bottles will make your home that much more special. I guarantee it.

Brewed in a very traditional style of "special bitter," this light amber English ale has the earthy character of English hops and extraordinary drinkability.

Ingredients for 5 gallons (19 l):

| | |
|---|---|
| 4½ lbs. (2 kg) | English light dried malt extract |
| 12 oz. (340 g) | crystal malt (10 L) |
| ½ oz. (14 g) | English Fuggles hops (boiling): 2.5 HBU (70 MBU) |
| ¾ oz. (21 g) | Kent Goldings hops (boiling): 3.5 HBU (98 MBU) |
| ¼ oz. (7 g) | English Fuggles hops (30 minutes, flavor) |
| ¼ oz. (7 g) | Kent Goldings hops (30 minutes, flavor) |
| ½ oz. (14 g) | Kent Goldings hops (10 minutes, flavor/aroma) |
| ½ oz. (14 g) | Kent Goldings hops (2 minutes, aroma) |
| ¼ tsp. (1 g) | Irish moss powder |
| * | English-type ale yeast |
| ¾ c. (175 ml) | sugar (for bottling) or ⅓ c. (80 ml) corn sugar (for kegging) |

O.G.: 1.040–1.044 (10–11)
F.G.: 1.008–1.012 (2–3)
Bitterness: 26 BU; Color 13 SRM (26 EBC); Alcohol: 4.2% by volume

Add crushed crystal malt to 1½ gallons (5.7 l) of water and let steep at 150 to 160 degrees F (65–71 C) for 30 minutes, then remove the grains with a strainer. Add the malt extract and bring to a boil. Add both charges of boiling hops and boil for 60 minutes. Add ¼ ounce (7 g) each of Fuggles and Goldings hops for flavor for the last 30 minutes of the boil. Add the Irish moss and another ½ ounce (14 g) of Goldings hops (for flavor and aroma) for the last 10 minutes of the boil. Add a final ½ ounce (14 g) Goldings for the last 2 minutes of the boil for aroma. Strain, sparge, and transfer immediately to 2 gallons (7.5 l) of cold water in the fermenter. Top off with additional water to make 5 gallons (19 l). Aerate the wort very well. Pitch the yeast when the temperature of the wort is about 70 degrees F (21 C). Ferment at about 70 degrees F (21 C) for about 1 week or when fermentation shows signs of calming and stopping. Prime with sugar and bottle or keg when fermentation is complete. Excellent within 2 weeks, sometimes sooner.

## Palilalia India Pale Ale

English-style India pale ale is a style of ale noted for its moderate yet notable alcoholic strength and bitterness. Palilalia India Pale Ale is not quite as dry as a traditional English IPA, having a distinctively pleasant malty character, contributed to by a generous amount of crystal malt and your own toasted malt. The hop character is moderate yet evidently bitter with a smooth hop flavor/aroma finish. The toasted malted barley lends a copper color and malty aroma to the brew. Palilalia tends to become drier with age. For additional authenticity you may want to add a generous handful of steamed (sanitized) oak chips during primary or secondary fermentation, for IPA is sometimes aged in oak.

Ingredients for 5 gallons (19 l):

| | |
|---|---|
| 5½ lbs. (2.5 kg) | light or amber dried malt extract |
| 1 lb. (450 g) | crystal malt (10 L) |
| ½ lb. (225 g) | toasted malted barley |
| 2 tsp. (8 g) | gypsum |
| 2 oz. (56 g) | Northdown or Challenger English hops (boiling): 16 HBU (450 MBU) |
| ¾ oz. (21 g) | Glacier or Willamette hops (1 minute, aroma, finishing) |
| ¼ tsp. (1 g) | Irish moss powder |
| * | American-type ale yeast or White Labs Cry Havoc yeast |
| ¾ c. (175 ml) | sugar (for bottling) or ⅓ c. (80 ml) corn sugar (for kegging) |

O.G.: 1.052–1.056 (13–14)
F.G.: 1.014–1.018 (3.5–4.5)
Bitterness: 50 BU; Color: 10–15 SRM (20–30 EBC); Alcohol: 5% by volume

Toasting malted barley is a simple process. Preheat the oven to 350 degrees F (177 C). Spread the whole malted barley grain on a cookie sheet and place in the oven. Within 10 minutes a wonderful aroma will emanate from your oven and the malted barley will have turned a slight reddish color. Remove the toasted grain and let cool. (Toasting for longer than 10 minutes will turn the inside of the malted barley a deeper nut brown and will contribute a roasted flavor. The nutty malt aromatics of a 10-minute toast are desired for this recipe.)

Add the crushed crystal malt and crushed toasted malted barley to 1½ gallons (5.7 l) of cold water and let steep at 150 to 160 degrees F (65–71 C) for 30 minutes, then remove the grains with a strainer.

Add the malt extract, Northdown or Challenger hops, and gypsum and boil for 60 minutes. Add the Irish moss for the last 10 minutes of the boil. Add the Glacier or Willamette hops for the final 1 minute of boiling. Strain, sparge, and transfer immediately to 2 gallons (7.5 l) of cold water in the fermenter. Top off with additional water to make 5 gallons (19 l). Aerate the wort very well. Pitch the yeast when the temperature of the wort is about 70 degrees F (21 C). Ferment at about 70 degrees F (21 C) for about 1 week or when fermentation shows signs of calming and stopping. Prime with sugar and bottle or keg when fermentation is complete.

Because of Palilalia's complex flavor and hop character, this ale is best aged 3 to 4 weeks in the bottle before drinking, but that's not saying it won't be good within 2 weeks.

### *No Sham Shamrock Irish Red Ale*

Sunsets over the Emerald Isle were never as good as the sunset you'll be watching over your homebrewed Irish Red Ale, full of toasted malt flavor and aroma, yet truly awesome and drinkable. You may choose to have more than one pint of this brew at one sitting. While you're at it, you may as well make that an imperial (20 oz.) pint! You'll please your friends and soon-to-be friends as well as derive your own satisfaction.

Ingredients for 5 gallons (19 l):

| | |
|---|---|
| 5 lbs. (2.3 kg) | amber malt extract syrup |
| 1 lb. (450 g) | crystal malt (10 L) |
| ½ lb. (225 g) | toasted malted barley |
| 1 oz. (28 g) | Northern Brewer or Perle hops (boiling): 8 HBU (225 MBU) |
| 1 oz. (28 g) | Santiam, Crystal, or American Tettnang hops (1 minute, aroma) |

| ¼ tsp. (1 g) | Irish moss powder |
| * | American-type ale yeast or White Labs Cry Havoc yeast |
| ¾ c. (175 ml) | corn sugar (for bottling) or ⅓ c. (80 ml) corn sugar (for kegging) |

O.G.: 1.042–1.046 (10.5–11.5)
F.G.: 1.010–1.014 (2.5–3.5)
Bitterness: 30 BU; Color: 15 SRM (30 EBC); Alcohol: 4.2% by volume

Preheat the oven to 350 degrees F (177 C). Spread the whole malted barley grain on a baking sheet and place in the oven. Toast for 10 minutes. Let the toasted grain cool.

Add the cracked crystal malt and cracked toasted malted barley to 1½ gallons (5.7 l) of cold water and let steep at 150 to 160 degrees F (65–71 C) for 30 minutes, then remove the grains with a strainer.

Add the malt extract and Northern Brewer or Perle hops and boil for 60 minutes. Add the Irish moss for the last 10 minutes of the boil. Add the aroma hops for the final 1 minute of boiling. Strain, sparge, and transfer immediately to 2 gallons (7.5 l) of cold water in the fermenter. Top off with additional water to make 5 gallons (19 l).

Aerate the wort very well. Pitch the yeast when the temperature of the wort is about 70 degrees F (21 C). Ferment at about 70 degrees F (21 C) for about 1 week or when fermentation shows signs of calming and stopping.

Prime with sugar and bottle or keg when fermentation is complete, and watch the sunset over an Irish Red.

## LIGHTER BEERS FROM AROUND THE WORLD

### *Propensity Czech Pilsener*
Although the honey may seem unusual for this traditional style of beer, it adds a character reminiscent of authentic Czech pilsener. It is one malt-extract beer that has come close to the lusciousness of twentieth-century brewed Pilsner Urquell or the original full-flavored and wonderful malt- and hop-graced Czech Budweiser. The use of light honey in this recipe helps introduce the character of a light-bodied pilsener while celebrating the roundness of malt and the crispness of hops. Simply brewed, Propensity Czech Pilsener is a treat for the connoisseur of true, traditional, and original Czech-style pilseners.

Ingredients for 5 gallons (19 l):

| 7 lbs. (3.2 kg) | light malt extract syrup |
| ½ lb. (225 g) | crystal malt (10 L) |

| 1½ lbs. (0.7 kg) | light clover honey |
| 2½ oz. (70 g) | Czech Saaz hop pellets (boiling): 10 HBU (280 MBU) |
| ½ oz. (14 g) | Crystal or Czech Saaz hop pellets (5 minutes, flavor/aroma) |
| ¼ oz. (7 g) | Crystal or Czech Saaz hop pellets (dry hopping, aroma) |
| ¼ tsp. (1 g) | Irish moss powder |
| * | Pilsener-type lager yeast or White Labs Cry Havoc yeast |
| ¾ c. (175 ml) | sugar (for bottling) or ⅓ c. (80 ml) corn sugar (for kegging) |

O.G.: 1.050–1.054 (12.5–13.5)
F.G.: 1.010–1.014 (2.5–3.5)
Bitterness: 37 BU; Color: 6 SRM (12 EBC); Alcohol: 5.3% by volume

Add the crushed crystal malt to 1½ gallons (5.7 l) of water and let steep at 150 to 160 degrees F (65–71 C) for 30 minutes, then remove the grains with a strainer. Add the malt extract, honey, and boiling hops and boil for 60 minutes. Add the Irish moss for the last 10 minutes of the boil. Add ½ ounce (14 g) Crystal or Czech Saaz hop pellets (flavor and aroma) for the final 5 minutes of boiling. Do not add the final ¼ ounce of aroma hops to the wort. Strain, sparge, and transfer immediately to 2 gallons (7.5 l) of cold water in the fermenter. Top off with additional water to make 5 gallons (19 l). Aerate the wort very well. Pitch the yeast when the temperature of the wort is about 70 degrees F (21 C). Ferment at about 70 degrees F (21 C) for about 1 week or when fermentation shows signs of calming and stopping.

Using a two-stage fermentation method: Transfer the beer to a secondary fermenter after primary fermentation appears to be complete. Add the ¼ ounce (7 g) Crystal or Czech Saaz hop pellets (aroma) to the secondary and lager at a cool—below 60 degrees F (15.5 C)—temperature for about 2 weeks. Lager for 3 to 4 weeks if you can keep the temperature at about 40 degrees F (4 C); otherwise maintain the coolest temperature possible. When lagering is complete, siphon the beer off the hop pellets and yeast, which will have settled to the bottom of your secondary fermenter. Prime with sugar and bottle or keg when fermentation is complete.

Propensity Pilsener can be matured for about 7 days in the bottle at room temperature. After it has conditioned (carbonated), move the beer to the coolest (cold) place you have for keeping until you're ready to chill for serving. Drink and appreciate when you're ready!

### *Crabalocker German Pils*

Who remembers the crabalocker fishwife or the elementary penguins singing Hare Krishna? It was a bus ride indeed magical and mysterious, but there's nothing mysterious about this serious-tasting German-style pilsener beer. It is a bit drier and much more hoppy than its older Bohemian (Czech) cousin. With a rich white head of foam, this is a brew you could die and go to heaven for or with. Serve chilled and dream of Deutschland and the fresh taste of Pils.

Don't let the simplicity fool you. The secret is in the choice of the freshest hops of German origin and how their wondrous character is infused into the wort. The infusion of the flavor hops continues to add bitterness to the wort in various degrees and character.

Ingredients for 5 gallons (19 l):

| | |
|---|---|
| 5½ lbs. (2.5 kg) | extra-light dried malt extract |
| 1¾ oz. (52 g) | Hersbrucker-Hallertau hops (boiling): 6 HBU (170 MBU) |
| 1½ oz. (42 g) | Hersbrucker-Hallertau hops (20 minutes, flavor): 5 HBU (140 MBU) |
| ½ oz. (14 g) | Hersbrucker- or Hallertauer-Mittelfrüh or Crystal hop pellets (dry hopping, aroma) |
| ¼ tsp. (1 g) | Irish moss powder |
| * | Pilsener-type lager yeast or White Labs Cry Havoc yeast |
| ¾ c. (175 ml) | sugar (for bottling) or ⅓ c. (80 ml) corn sugar (for kegging) |

O.G.: 1.048–1.052 (12–13)
F.G.: 1.010–1.012 (2.5–3)
Bitterness: 27 BU; Color: 3 SRM (6 EBC); Alcohol: 5% by volume

Add the malt extract and boiling hops to 1½ gallons (5.7 l) of water, bring to a rolling boil, and boil for 60 minutes. Add the 1½ oz. (42 g) of the flavor hops for the last 20 minutes of the boil. Add the Irish moss for the final 10 minutes of the boil. Do not add the aroma hops to the wort. Strain, sparge, and transfer immediately to 2 gallons (7.5 l) of cold water in the fermenter. Top off with additional water to make 5 gallons (19 l). Aerate the wort very well. Pitch the yeast when the temperature of the wort is about 70 degrees F (21 C). Ferment at about 70 degrees F (21 C) for about 1 week or when fermentation shows signs of calming and stopping.

Use a two-stage fermentation method: Transfer the beer to a secondary fermenter after primary fermentation appears to be complete. Add ½ ounce (14 g) Hersbrucker- or Hallertauer-Mittelfrüh or Crystal hop pellets (aroma) to

the secondary fermenter and lager at a cool—below 60 degrees F (15.5 C)—temperature for about 2 weeks. Lager for 3 to 4 weeks if you can keep the temperature at about 40 degrees F (4 C). Regardless of what temperature you ferment, when lagering is complete, siphon the beer off the hop pellets and yeast, which will have settled to the bottom of your secondary fermenter. Prime with sugar and bottle or keg when fermentation is complete.

### *Jeepers Creepers American Light Lager*
A super-light-tasting beer, with a thirst-quenching balance. We're trying to brew one of the most popular styles of beer in the world, so it's designed for low-flavor impact and refreshing drinkability. The rice extract adds alcohol

and lightness. Be careful not to overdo the hop bitterness, unless you want a kapowww version of BudMillerCoors. But let's not forget that you're a home-brewer, so we'll add a wisp of malt character with an infusion of toasted malted barley and a subtle tingle of hop aroma with the addition of finishing hops. It's the balanced and flavorful lightness of this brew that makes it attractive. One typical response you may get from a friend is, "Hey, I like this beer and I don't normally like 'lite' beers."

Ingredients for 5 gallons (19 l):

| | |
|---|---|
| 4 lbs. (1.8 kg) | very light dried malt extract |
| 1 lb. (450 g) | rice extract |
| 4 oz. (114 g) | honey malt |
| ½ oz. (14 g) | Cascade hops (boiling): 3 HBU (85 MBU) |
| ¼ oz. (7 g) | American Tettnang, Santiam, or Hallertau hops (2 minutes, finishing) |
| ¼ tsp. (1 g) | Irish moss powder |
| * | American-type lager yeast or White Labs Cry Havoc yeast |
| ¾ c. (175 ml) | sugar (for bottling) or ⅓ c. (80 ml) corn sugar (for kegging) |

O.G.: 1.040–1.044 (10–11)
F.G.: 1.004–1.006 (1–1.5)
Bitterness: 9 BU; Color: 3 SRM (6 EBC); Alcohol: 4.7% by volume

Crush the honey malt and combine with 1½ gallons (5.7 l) of water and let steep at 150 to 160 degrees F (65–71 C) for 30 minutes, then remove the grains with a strainer. Add the malt extract, rice extract, and boiling hops and boil for 60 minutes. Add the Irish moss for the last 10 minutes of the boil. Add the finishing hops for the final 2 minutes of the boil. Strain, sparge, and transfer immediately to 2 gallons (7.5 l) of cold water in the fermenter. Top off with ad-ditional water to make 5 gallons (19 l). Aerate the wort very well. Pitch the yeast when the temperature of the wort is about 70 degrees F (21 C). Ferment at about 70 degrees F (21 C) for about 1 week or when fermentation shows signs of calming and stopping.

This beer should be ready to drink in a very short period of time unless very cold lagering temperatures are used; if two-stage fermentation is used, the beer will improve if matured for 2 to 3 weeks at a temperature of about 50 degrees F (10 C) before bottling. Prime with sugar and bottle when fermentation stops or after 2 to 3 weeks of secondary maturation.

## It's OK Kölsch

The Germans love their beer. Homebrewers love their beer. I love my beer. You will love this very pale German ale. It's OK, too. You might just cut out the shuck and jive and say, "It's OK." "It's OK" is the answer to wanting to brew a German pils, but not having the ability to lager for extended periods at cold temperatures. It's made with a combination of wheat malt to lighten the character and create a mild, malt-flavored, refreshing German-style ale. The Germans ferment this ale on the cool side and then lager it at cool temperatures, but if you can't, you're still going to get a good-tasting beer.

Ingredients for 5 gallons (19 l):

| | |
|---|---|
| 2 lbs. (0.9 kg) | extra-light dried malt extract |
| 3.7 lbs. (1.7 kg) | wheat malt extract syrup |
| ¼ oz. (7 g) | Liberty or Vanguard hops (boiling): 2 HBU (56 MBU) |
| ¾ oz. (21 g) | Saaz hops (boiling): 3 HBU (70 MBU) |
| ½ oz. (14 g) | Tettnang hops (30 minutes, flavor): 2 HBU (56 MBU) |
| ¼ tsp. (1 g) | Irish moss powder |
| * | Kölsch, German ale–type yeast, or White Labs Cry Havoc yeast |
| ¾ c. (175 ml) | sugar (for bottling) or ⅓ c. (80 ml) corn sugar (for kegging) |

O.G.: 1.044–1.046 (11–11.5)
F.G.: 1.010–1.012 (2.5–3)
Bitterness: 22 BU; Color: 4 SRM (8 EBC); Alcohol: 4.5% by volume

Add syrup and dried malt extract and boiling hops to 1½ gallons (5.7 l) of water, bring to a rolling boil, and boil for 60 minutes. During this time add the Tettnang hops for the last 30 minutes of the boil. Add the Irish moss for the final 10 minutes of the boil. Strain, sparge, and transfer immediately to 2 gallons (7.5 l) of cold water in the fermenter. Top off with additional water to make 5 gallons (19 l). Aerate the wort very well. Pitch the yeast when the temperature of the wort is about 70 degrees F (21 C). Ferment at about 70 degrees F (21 C) for about 1 week or when fermentation shows signs of calming and stopping.

If you can move it to a cooler area—between 55 and 60 degrees F (13–16 C)—do so and let it lager for 1 to 2 weeks. If you cannot move to a cooler temperature, relax, don't worry. Either way, when ready prime with sugar and bottle or keg when fermentation is complete. Let age for a couple of weeks or when clear and carbonated. Chill, serve, and have a homebrew.

## Elementary Penguin Maibock

If there's one beer type that outshines all other German-style lagers, it may be Maibock—rich, full-flavored, malty, strong, and high in alcohol, but quite drinkable. In fact, drinkable by the liter—but be sure you have a seat. Its smooth malty richness, brilliant golden color, soft palate, and sensuous body all combine for a homebrew that's sure to be one of your most refulgent brews. In Germany they traditionally enjoy this in May—springtime. But don't be fooled. You can enjoy this one anytime: summerbock, autumnal bock, winterbock, birthday bock.

Ingredients for 5 gallons (19 l):

| | |
|---|---|
| 9.9 lbs. (4.5 kg) | light malt extract syrup |
| 4 oz. (114 g) | honey malt |
| 4 oz. (114 g) | Belgian aromatic malt |
| 1½ oz. (42 g) | Vanguard or Santiam hops (boiling): 7 HBU (200 MBU) |
| ½ oz. (14 g) | Mt. Hood or German Saphir hops (30 minutes, flavor) |
| 1 oz. (28 g) | French Strisselspalt or New Zealand Hallertau hops (15 minutes, flavor) |
| ¼ tsp. (1 g) | Irish moss powder |
| * | German-type lager yeast or White Labs Cry Havoc yeast |
| ¾ c. (175 ml) | sugar (for bottling) or ⅓ c. (80 ml) corn sugar (for kegging) |

O.G.: 1.072–1.076 (17.5–18.5)
F.G.: 1.016–1.020 (4–5)
Bitterness: 29 BU; Color: 9 SRM (18 EBC); Alcohol: 7.4% by volume

Crush the aromatic and honey malts and combine with 2 gallons (7.5 l) of water and let steep at 150 to 160 degrees F (65–71 C) for 30 minutes, then remove the grains with a strainer. (Whether you realize it or not, you just did a "mini-mash," which you'll learn more about in the next section, "Introduction to Grain Brewing for the Malt Extract Homebrewer," page 254). To the wort you just created, add the malt extract syrup and boiling hops, bring to a rolling boil, and boil for 60 minutes. During this period, add the Mt. Hood or German Saphir flavor hops for the last 30 minutes of the boil. Add the French Strisselspalt or New Zealand Hallertau flavor hops for the last 15 minutes of the boil. Add the Irish moss for the final 10 minutes of the boil. Strain, sparge, and transfer immediately to 2 gallons (7.5 l) of cold water in the fermenter. Top off with additional water to make 5 gallons (19 l). Aerate the wort very well. Pitch the yeast when the temperature of the wort is about 70 degrees F (21 C). Ferment at about 70 degrees F (21 C) for about 1 week or when fermentation shows signs of calming and stopping.

If two-stage fermentation is used, the beer will improve if matured for 2 to 3 weeks at a temperature between 40 and 50 degrees F (4.5–10 C) before bottling. Prime with sugar and bottle when fermentation (or optional lagering) is complete. And don't worry about lagering at cold temperatures if you can't do it.

Find yourself a maypole and plant yourself down with friends. Enjoy the sunshine and contemplate the world going round and round as you enjoy your very own Elementary Penguin Maibock.

## EUROPEAN AMBER LAGERS

### *Winky Dink Märzen*

I've always wanted to name a beer after one of my favorite childhood cartoon heroes. Winky's ability to magically transcend spaces by way of crayoned lines drawn on the television screen always seemed to invite him into the house . . . but he never came. Now that there's homebrew, maybe he'll appear, star hat and all.

Winky Dink Märzen is a wonderfully golden German-style lager. Its rich, full-bodied, and aromatic character happens even when brewed at room temperature. The rich maltiness that is married to the crisp and flavorful hop bitterness enlivens this beer as a real treat for those inclined toward simplicity and German lagers.

It's most flavorful and best served at temperatures between 50 and 55 degrees F (10–13 C).

Ingredients for 5 gallons (19 l):

| | |
|---|---|
| 7 lbs. (3.2 kg) | German-made or other light malt extract syrup |
| ¾ lb. (340 g) | dark amber crystal malt (50–80 L) or caramel Munich-type malt (50–80 L) |
| 1¼ oz. (35 g) | Tettnang or Hallertau hops (boiling): 6 HBU (170 MBU) |
| ½ oz. (14 g) | German Saphir, Mt. Hood, or Santiam hops (2 minutes, aroma) |
| ¼ tsp. (1 g) | Irish moss powder |
| * | German-type lager yeast or White Labs Cry Havoc yeast |
| ¾ c. (175 ml) | sugar (for bottling) or ⅓ c. (80 ml) corn sugar (for kegging) |

O.G.: 1.050–1.054 (12.5–13.5)
F.G.: 1.014–1.018 (3.5–4.5)
Bitterness: 21 BU; Color: 14 SRM (28 EBC); Alcohol: 4.7% by volume

Add the crushed crystal or Munich malt to 1½ gallons (5.7 l) of water and let steep at 150 to 160 degrees F (65–71 C) for 30 minutes, then remove the grains with a strainer. Add the malt extract and the Tettnang or Hallertau boiling hops and boil for 60 minutes. During this period add the Irish moss for the last 10 minutes of the boil. Add the aroma hops for the final 2 minutes of the boil. Strain, sparge, and transfer immediately to 2 gallons (7.5 l) of cold water in the fermenter. Top off with additional water to make 5 gallons (19 l). Aerate the wort very well. Pitch the yeast when the temperature of the wort is about 70 degrees F (21 C). Ferment at about 70 degrees F (21 C) for about 1 week or when fermentation shows signs of calming and stopping.

If two-stage fermentation is used, the beer will improve if matured for 2 to 3 weeks at a temperature of about 50 degrees F (10 C) before bottling. Prime with sugar and bottle when fermentation is complete. "Beer" in mind that Winky Dink Märzen is wonderful stuff brewed at kitchen temperature; don't fret about cold-temperature lagering if you can't do it.

### Whoop Moffitt Vienna Lager

Whoop, a late-nineteenth-century Scandinavian architect and the father of the game of marbles, died from a steelie striking him between the eyes during a tournament for all of the marbles in the Vienna Classic. What a guy! What a thumb! What a beer!

It doesn't get much easier than this to experience a style of beer that is nearly extinct in the commercial world. Its smooth, malty flavor that isn't quite as rich in flavor as Oktoberfest is thirst quenching and the type of brew that would complement many a meal. It is deep amber with a touch of hop finesse, perhaps a bit more than was used traditionally a half century ago (but who's around to point the finger anymore?). Not too bitter, it is pleasing to almost any palate.

This recipe is brewed to a volume of 4½ gallons (17 l) in a 5-gallon (19 l) fermenter with ease to spare.

Ingredients for 4½ gallons (17 l):

| | |
|---|---|
| 6.6 lbs. (3 kg) | Briess amber malt extract syrup |
| 4 oz. (114 g) | chocolate or debittered black malt |
| 1½ oz. (42 g) | Hallertau hops (boiling): 7 HBU (200 MBU) |
| ½ oz. (14 g) | Santiam or Mt. Hood hops (15 minutes, flavor): 3 HBU (84 MBU) |
| ½ oz. (14 g) | Santiam or Crystal hops (1 to 2 minutes, aroma) |
| ¼ tsp. (1 g) | Irish moss powder |
| * | German-type lager yeast or White Labs Cry Havoc yeast |
| ¾ c. (175 ml) | sugar (for bottling) or ⅓ c. (80 ml) corn sugar (for kegging) |

O.G.: 1.052–1.056 (13–14)
F.G.: 1.012–1.016 (3–4)
Bitterness: 32 BU; Color: 18 SRM (36 EBC); Alcohol: 5.3% by volume

Add the crushed chocolate or debittered black malt to 1½ gallons (5.7 l) of water and let steep at 150 to 160 degrees F (65–71 C) for 30 minutes, then remove the grains with a strainer. Add the malt extract and Hallertau boiling hops and boil for 60 minutes. During this period add the flavor hops for the last 15 minutes of the boil. Add the Irish moss for the last 10 minutes of the boil. Add the aroma hops for the final 1 to 2 minutes of the boil. Strain, sparge, and transfer immediately to 2 gallons (7.5 l) of cold water in the fermenter. Top off with additional water to make 4½ gallons (17 l). Aerate the wort very well. Pitch the yeast when the temperature of the wort is about 70 degrees F (21 C). Ferment at about 70 degrees F (21 C) for about 1 week or when fermentation shows signs of calming and stopping.

If two-stage fermentation is used, the beer will improve if matured for 2 to 3 weeks at a temperature of about 50 degrees F (10 C) before bottling. Prime with sugar and bottle when fermentation is complete. And don't worry about lagering at cold temperatures if you can't do it.

## DARK ALES

### Elbro Nerkte Brown Ale
### (English-Style Brown Ale)

A world-renowned and award-winning recipe, heralded for its quick maturity, this favorite brown ale has long been a first-time brew for many impatient homebrewers, for it can be deliciously enjoyed within 10 to 14 days!

The addition of crystal and dark grain malts to an already luscious brown malt extract beautifully enhances the flavorful and mildly sweet richness of this brown ale. Elbro Nerkte might have been a famous late-nineteenth-century Scandinavian marbles player and cousin of Whoop Moffitt—but maybe not.

Ingredients for 5 gallons (19 l):

| | |
|---|---|
| 6.6 lbs. (3 kg) | dark malt extract syrup |
| ½ lb. (225 g) | crystal malt (10 L) |
| ¼ lb. (110 g) | black malt |
| 2 oz. (56 g) | Fuggles or Willamette hops (boiling): 10 HBU (280 MBU) |
| ½ oz. (14 g) | Fuggles or Cascade hops (10 minutes, flavor/aroma) |
| 4 tsp. (16 g) | gypsum (optional) |
| ¼ tsp. (1 g) | Irish moss powder |
| * | English or American ale–type yeast |

¾ c. (175 ml)   sugar (for bottling) or ⅓ c. (80 ml) corn sugar
              (for kegging)


O.G.: 1.046–1.050 (11.5–12.5)
F.G.: 1.010–1.014 (2.5–3.5)
Bitterness: 35 BU; Color: 25 SRM (50 EBC); Alcohol: 4.7% by volume

Add the crushed crystal and black malts to 1½ gallons (5.7 l) of water and let steep at 150 to 160 degrees F (65–71 C) for 30 minutes, then remove the grains with a strainer. Add the malt extract, gypsum (if using), and boiling hops and boil for 60 minutes. Add the Irish moss and flavor/aroma hops for the final 10 minutes of the boil. Strain, sparge, and transfer immediately to 2 gallons (7.5 l) of cold water in the fermenter. Top off with additional water to make 5 gallons (19 l). Aerate the wort very well. Pitch the yeast when the temperature of the wort is about 70 degrees F (21 C). Ferment at about 70 degrees F (21 C) for about 1 week or when fermentation shows signs of calming and stopping. Prime with sugar and bottle or keg when fermentation is complete. Because of the quickly maturing character of this recipe, Elbro Nerkte lends itself to single-stage fermentation, bottling within 5 to 6 days and drinkability within another 7 days. Quick? That's why they call it Elbro Nerkte.

### Avogadro's Expeditious Old Ale

Avogadro's Expeditious Old Ale is a modern variation of a traditional English-style recipe. This beer reflects a deep alliance with loads of malt character—from wheat malt extract, crystal and caramel Munich malts—and a touch of hop aroma contributed by the late hopping of English Golding or Crystal hops. "This is my kind of beer," an English lass once said of the original brew. I smiled and conceded another pour as this quenching ale proceeded in its dance with malt and hops.

The use of hop pellets contributes to the ease of brewing this recipe.

Ingredients for 5 gallons (19 l):

5 lbs. (2.3 kg)    wheat malt extract syrup
3 lbs. (1.36 kg)   light malt extract syrup
¾ lb. (340 g)      crystal malt (40 L)
½ lb. (225 g)      caramel Munich-type malt
¼ lb. (113 g)      crystal malt (80 L)
1 oz. (28 g)       English First Gold, Progress, or American Glacier
                   hop pellets (boiling): 7 HBU (196 MBU)
½ oz. (14 g)       Cascade or Crystal hop pellets (1 to 2 minutes,
                   finishing: flavor/aroma)

¼ tsp. (1 g)    Irish moss powder
*              English ale–type yeast or White Labs Cry Havoc yeast
¾ c. (175 ml)  sugar (for bottling) or ⅓ c. (80 ml) corn sugar
               (for kegging)


O.G.: 1.064–1.068 (15.7–16.6)
F.G.: 1.014–1.018 (3.5–4.5)
Bitterness: 28 BU; Color 17 SRM (34 EBC); Alcohol: 6.6% by volume

Add the crushed crystal and Munich-type malts to 2 gallons (7.5 l) of cold water and let steep at 150 to 160 degrees F (65–71 C) for 30 minutes, then remove the grains with a strainer.

Add the malt extracts and boiling hops and boil for 60 minutes. Add the Irish moss for the last 10 minutes of the boil. Add the finishing flavor/aroma hops for the final 1 to 2 minutes of the boil. Strain, sparge, and transfer immediately to 2 gallons (7.5 l) of cold water in the fermenter. Top off with additional water to make 5 gallons (19 l). Aerate the wort very well. Pitch the yeast when the temperature of the wort is about 70 degrees F (21 C). Ferment at about 70 degrees F (21 C) for about 1 week or when fermentation shows signs of calming and stopping. Prime with sugar and bottle or keg when fermentation is complete.

Avogadro will be ready to drink in 2 to 4 weeks, depending on how expeditious you feel.

## Naked Sunday Brown Ale

No comment on the name of this ale—just go for it.

You might like to try your hand at brewing malty, rich, brown ale similar in character to traditional brown ales from England now brewed only by the smallest of breweries. The simple combination of dark malt syrup with light engages to create a voluptuous balance of malt character. In fact it's so simple it leaves times for other extracurricular activities. In return you get a flavorful, nut-brown, mildly bittered brown ale with an almost floral-honey-like aroma.

Ingredients for 5 gallons (19 l):

2½ lbs. (1.2 kg)    light malt extract syrup
5 lbs. (2.3 kg)     very dark malt extract syrup
1¼ oz. (35 g)       Vanguard or Crystal hops (boiling): 7 HBU (192 MBU)
1 oz. (28 g)        Mt. Hood hops (1 to 2 minutes, flavor/aroma)
¼ tsp. (1 g)        Irish moss powder
*                   English-type ale yeast or White Labs Cry Havoc yeast
¾ c. (175 ml)       sugar (for bottling) or ⅓ c. (80 ml) corn sugar
                    (for kegging)

O.G.: 1.052–1.056 (13–14)
F.G.: 1.010–1.014 (1.5–2.5)
Bitterness: 24 BU; Color: 17 SRM (34 EBC); Alcohol: 5.5% by volume

Boil the malt extracts and hops with 1½ gallons (5.7 l) of water for 60 minutes. Add the Irish moss for the final 10 minutes of boiling. Add the flavor/aroma hops for the final 1 to 2 minutes of boiling. Pour the hot wort into 2 gallons (7.5 l) of cold water in the fermenter. Aerate the wort very well. Pitch the yeast when the temperature of the wort is about 70 degrees F (21 C). Ferment at about 70 degrees F (21 C) for about 1 week or when fermentation shows signs of calming and stopping. Prime with sugar and bottle or keg when fermentation is complete.

### Dithyrambic Roast Brown Ale

This unusual brown ale cannot be compared with any commercially available beers that I have ever encountered, domestic or otherwise. Medium in color, it is riotously flavored with the distinctively nutty, coffeelike character of roasted barley, an ingredient that is usually reserved for classically delicious stouts. And added as a shineblast undertone and hint of raisin/dried currant–like grace, a bit of Belgian Special-B malt is sprinkled in the malt mix.

This beer is simple to brew and offers a dry, roasted character with a complex zig-and-zag balance of malt sweetness. It is a refreshing alternative to the other, sweeter varieties of brown ale, perhaps comparable to a primo cup of coffee—hold the cream and sugar.

Ingredients for 5 gallons (19 l):

| | |
|---|---|
| 7½ lbs. (3.4 kg) | amber malt extract syrup |
| ½ lb. (225 g) | roasted barley |
| ¼ lb. (110 g) | black malt |
| ¼ lb. (110 g) | Belgian Special-B malt |
| 1½ oz. (42 g) | Northern Brewer hops (boiling): 13 HBU (360 MBU) |
| ¼ oz. (7 g) | Willamette or Cascade hops (5 to 10 minutes, finishing aroma/flavor) |
| ¼ tsp. (1 g) | Irish moss powder |
| * | English-type ale yeast or White Labs Cry Havoc yeast |
| ¾ c. (175 ml) | sugar (for bottling) or ⅓ c. (80 ml) corn sugar (for kegging) |

O.G.: 1.052–1.056 (13–14)
F.G.: 1.014–1.018 (3.5–4.5)
Bitterness: 40 BU; Color: 43 SRM (86 EBC); Alcohol: 5% by volume

Add the crushed roasted barley, Special-B, and black malts to 2 gallons (7.5 l) of water and let steep at 150 to 160 degrees F (65–71 C) for 30 minutes, then remove the grains with a strainer. Add the malt extract and Northern Brewer hops and boil for 60 minutes. Add the Irish moss for the last 10 minutes of boiling. Add the finishing hops for the final 5 to 10 minutes of the boil. Strain, sparge, and transfer immediately to 2 gallons (7.5 l) of cold water in the fermenter. Top off with additional water to make 5 gallons (19 l).

Aerate the wort very well. Pitch the yeast when the temperature of the wort is about 70 degrees F (21 C). Ferment at about 70 degrees F (21 C) for about 1 week or when fermentation shows signs of calming and stopping. Prime with sugar and bottle or keg when fermentation is complete.

### Cheeks to the Wind Mild Ale

For those who have a fondness for a traditional and very sessionable English mild, here's a light-bodied, delicately alelike fruitiness as a dark brown English classic with an untraditional "ta-da" finish of hop aroma and flavor. You'll be able to drink lots of Cheeks and continue to enjoy without getting cross-eyed.

Best of the low-cal and low-carb brews—ever, if you really care. If you don't, then have another.

Ingredients for 5 gallons (19 l):

6 lbs. (2.7 kg)   light malt extract syrup
½ lb. (225 g)    chocolate malt
1 oz. (28 g)     Fuggles or Willamette hops (boiling): 5 HBU (140 MBU)
½ oz. (14 g)     English Goldings or American Crystal hops (1 minute, finishing aroma/flavor)
¼ tsp. (1 g)     Irish moss powder
*                English-type ale yeast or White Labs Cry Havoc yeast
¾ c. (175 ml)    sugar (for bottling) or ⅓ c. (80 ml) corn sugar (for kegging)

O.G.: 1.032–1.035 (8–9)
F.G.: 1.006–1.010 (1.5–2.5)
Bitterness: 19 BU; Color: 32 SRM (64 EBC); Alcohol: 3.4% by volume

Add the crushed chocolate malt to 2 gallons (7.5 l) of water and let steep at 150–160 degrees F (65–71 C) for 30 minutes, then remove the grains with a strainer. Add the malt extract and boiling hops and boil for 60 minutes. Add the Irish moss for the final 10 minutes of the boil. Add the finishing hops for the final 1 minute of the boil. Strain, sparge, and transfer immediately to 2 gallons (7.5 l) of cold water in the fermenter. Top off with additional water to make 5 gallons (19 l).

Aerate the wort very well. Pitch the yeast when the temperature of the wort is about 70 degrees F (21 C). Ferment at about 70 degrees F (21 C) for about 1 week or when fermentation shows signs of calming and stopping.

Prime with sugar and bottle or keg when fermentation is complete.

### Osmosis Amoebas German Alt

A trip to Düsseldorf, Germany, is a trip to Alt heaven. My advice: Go to the Altstadt (the "old city") and spend your euros on more than a dozen different Altbiers, half of which are brewed on the premises of the pubs, which are all within walking distance of one another.

Osmosis Amoebas is what you might feel like after sucking up all that great Altbier. This recipe replicates the more bitter versions of this dark-brown style of German ale quite accurately with a subtle yet satisfying maltiness, simply complemented by assertive bitterness from hops. As is traditional in the Altstadt, there are no distinctive hop flavors or aromas in this homebrewed rendition, just good, clean German ale that satisfies until osmosis amoebas.

Ingredients for 5 gallons (19 l):

| | |
|---|---|
| 6.5 lbs. (3 kg) | amber malt extract syrup |
| 2 oz. (55 g) | chocolate malt |
| ¼ lb. (110 g) | debittered black malt |
| 1¾ oz. (49 g) | Northern Brewers or Perle hops (boiling): 16 HBU (450 MBU) |
| ¼ tsp. (1 g) | Irish moss powder |
| * | German ale–type yeast or White Labs Cry Havoc yeast |
| ¾ c. (175 ml) | sugar (for bottling) or ⅓ c. (80 ml) corn sugar for (for kegging) |

O.G.: 1.046–1.050 (10–11)
F.G.: 1.008–1.012 (2–3)
Bitterness: 49 BU; Color: 25 SRM (50 EBC); Alcohol: 5% by volume

Add the crushed roasted chocolate and black malts to 2 gallons (7.5 l) of water and let steep at 150 to 160 degrees F (65–71 C) for 30 minutes, then remove the grains with a strainer. Add the malt extract and hops and boil for 60 minutes. Add the Irish moss for the last 10 minutes of the boil. Strain, sparge, and transfer immediately to 2 gallons (7.5 l) of cold water in the fermenter. Top off with additional water to make 5 gallons (19 l). Aerate the wort very well. Pitch the yeast when the temperature of the wort is about 70 degrees F (21 C). Ferment at about 70 degrees F (21 C) for about 1 week or when fermentation shows signs of calming and stopping. If possible, after primary fermentation is complete, transfer into a secondary fermenter and age 2 more weeks at about 55 degrees F (13 C). Prime with sugar and bottle or keg when fermentation is complete.

### *Maverick India Black Ale*

I get requests regularly to talk about beer styles. I can see why. Beer culture in America is vibrant. People love to talk about beer. Brewers and beer enthusiasts hang their beer hopes on every competition. Great beers are being made and better beers being brewed with every cycle. Old styles are returning and new styles are providing a dose of nourishment. Flavor and diversity reign. The source of creativity and new ideas is in my opinion rooted in the past. Maintaining an understanding of beer history is essential to making great beer. Yet sometimes when you're about to pursue innovation, you need to digress and do something completely different. Don't be afraid to be a maverick. Why not? You can get unzipped and still admire and respect tradition. So how about considering the idea of an "India" Black Wheat Ale brewed by hacking into the metrics of American IPA and wheat styles, perhaps even dry-hopped with exotic hops. That's exactly what I did when I brewed my first India Black Ale in May of

1999 with friend Steve Perry. We schemed to be mavericks and brew maverickly. So we did. Here's a modern-day gem of a recipe for a beer type that might go by many names, but is all GREAT!

Ingredients for 5 gallons (19 l):

| | |
|---|---|
| 7 lbs. (3.2 kg) | Wheat malt extract syrup (50% wheat, 50% barley) |
| 1 lb. (450 g) | Belgian or German aromatic or American biscuit malt |
| 1 lb. (454 g) | crystal malt (75 L) |
| ½ lb. (225 g) | debittered black malt |
| 1¾ oz. (49 g) | German Tradition hops (boiling): 11.5 HBU (322 MBU) |
| 1 oz. (28 g) | Liberty hops (30 minutes, flavor/bitter): 5.2 HBU (146 MBU) |
| ½ oz. (14 g) | New Zealand Saaz hop pellets (5 minutes, flavor/aroma) |
| ½ oz. (14 g) | New Zealand Nelson Sauvin hop pellets (dry hopping, aroma) |
| ¼ tsp. (1 g) | Irish moss powder |
| * | German ale–type yeast or White Labs Cry Havoc yeast |
| ¾ c. (175 ml) | sugar (for bottling) or ⅓ c. (80 ml) corn sugar (for kegging) |

O.G.: 1.060–1.064 (14.7–15.7)
F.G.: 1.014–1.018 (3.5–4.5)
Bitterness: 61 BU; Color: 30 SRM (60 EBC); Alcohol: 6.2% by volume

Place crushed grains in 2 gallons (7.5 l) of 150 degrees F (68 C) water and let steep for 30 minutes. Then strain them out and rinse with 3 quarts (3 l) hot water); discard the crushed grains reserving the approximately 2½ gallons (9.5 l) of liquid to which you will now add the malt extract and boiling hops. Bring to a boil and boil for 60 minutes. Add the Liberty hops for the last 30 minutes of the boil. Add the add Irish moss for the last 10 minutes of the boil. Add the New Zealand Saaz hops for the last 5 minutes of the boil. Turn off the heat. Immerse the covered pot of wort in a cold water bath and let sit for 30 minutes, or the time it takes to have a couple of homebrews. Strain, sparge, and transfer immediately to 2½ gallons (9.5 l) of cold water in the fermenter. Top off with additional water to make 5 gallons (19 l).Aerate the wort very well. Pitch the yeast when the temperature of the wort is about 70 degrees F (21 C). Ferment at about 70 degrees F (21 C) for about 1 week or when fermentation shows signs of calming and stopping.

Rack from your primary to a secondary and add the hop pellets for dry hopping. If you can, either lager the beer at temperatures between 35–45 degrees F (1.5–7 C) or "cellar" the beer between 55 and 65 degrees F (13–18.5 C) for about 2 weeks. Regardless of at what temperature you ferment, prime with sugar and bottle or keg when fermentation is complete.

## STOUTS

### Toad Spit Stout

This is one of the top three favorite recipes in this book.

Guinness Stout? I enjoy Guinness as much as any stout lover can imagine. It's easy to brew from malt extract. The only character that this recipe is lacking is the unique "tang" that the real stuff has. The Guinness Brewery achieves its tang by actually adding a small amount (3 percent) of pasteurized soured beer to all of its stouts around the world. I enjoy my Toad Spit Stout as much as the original Guinness I've enjoyed in years past when Guinness was brewed with its original character. This recipe is a throwback to what the Irish tradition was born of. It is bittersweet, full-bodied, and dry, and typifies the roasted barley character of all stouts.

Use only the best roasted barley. Roasted barley that is jet black in appearance has been overdone; instead look for a deep, dark brown color. Black or chocolate malt is no substitute when you are making stout, especially when you typify classic "heirloom" Guinness.

Ingredients for 5 gallons (19 l):

| | |
|---|---|
| 3.3 lbs. (1.5 kg) | John Bull hopped dark malt extract syrup |
| 4 lbs. (1.8 kg) | plain dark dried malt extract |
| ¾ lb. (340 g) | crystal malt (10 L) |
| ⅓ lb. (150 g) | roasted barley |
| ⅓ lb. (150 g) | black malt |
| 1½ oz. (42 g) | Northern Brewer hops (boiling): 12 HBU (335 MBU) |
| ½ oz. (14 g) | Fuggles or Willamette hops (10 minutes, finishing) |
| 8 tsp. (32 g) | gypsum |
| ¼ tsp. (1 g) | Irish moss powder |
| * | Irish ale–type yeast |
| ¾ c. (175 ml) | sugar (for bottling) or ⅓ c. (80 ml) corn sugar (for kegging) |

O.G.: 1.060–1.064 (15–16)
F.G.: 1.016–1.020 (4–5)
Bitterness: 40 BU; Color: 40 SRM (80 EBC); Alcohol: 5.8% by volume

Add the crushed roasted barley, crystal and black malts to 1½ gallons (5.7 l) of water and let steep at 150 to 160 degrees F (65–71 C) for 30 minutes,

then remove the grains with a strainer. Add the malt extracts, gypsum, and Northern Brewer hops and boil for 60 minutes. Add the Irish moss and finishing hops for the final 10 minutes of the boil. Strain, sparge, and transfer immediately to 2 gallons (7.5 l) of cold water in the fermenter. Top off with additional water to make 5 gallons (19 l).

Aerate the wort very well. Pitch the yeast when the temperature of the wort is about 70 degrees F (21 C). Ferment at about 70 degrees F (21 C) for about 1 week or when fermentation shows signs of calming and stopping. Prime with sugar and bottle or keg when fermentation is complete.

You should be enjoying Toad Spit Stout within 3 to 4 weeks from the day you brewed it.

## Armenian Imperial Stout

One look at this recipe and you may think I've gone bonkers. Well, I haven't, but *you* may after putting your ever-loving lips to this most royal of stouts. At nearly 8 percent alcohol, this very bittersweet and hoppy stout with a full-bodied, creamy-headed sensation is a definite treasure among stout lovers. This brew will age nicely for years, but believe it: This brew is as smooth as velvet within 4 to 6 weeks of bottling.

Lots of hops are called for in this recipe in addition to the hop-flavored malt extract kit used. High-alpha hops are used in the boil to minimize the amount of sparging that's done at the end of the boil.

Ingredients for 5 gallons (19 l):

| | |
|---|---|
| 6.6 lbs. (3 kg) | Muntons Old Ale Kit (hopped malt extract syrup) |
| 3.3 lbs. (1.5 kg) | plain light malt extract syrup |
| ½ lb. (225 g) | black malt |
| ½ lb. (225 g) | roasted barley |
| 2 oz. (56 g) | Magnum, Galena, Simcoe, Horizon, or Chinook hops (boiling): 22–28 HBU (616–784 MBU) |
| 1 oz. (28 g) | Cascade hops (1 minute, finishing/aroma) |
| 3 tsp. (12 g) | gypsum |
| ¼ tsp. (1 g) | Irish moss powder |
| * | American ale–type yeast |
| ¾ c. (175 ml) | sugar (for bottling) or ⅓ c. (80 ml) corn sugar (for kegging) |

O.G.: 1.070–1.075 (17–18)
F.G.: 1.018–1.025 (4.5–6)
Bitterness: Like wow! Color: Like really dark; Alcohol: 6.8% by volume

Add the crushed roasted barley and black malt to 1½ gallons (5.7 l) of water and let steep at 150 to 160 degrees F (65–71 C) for 30 minutes, then remove the grains with a strainer. Add the malt extracts, gypsum, and boiling hops and boil for 60 minutes. Add the Irish moss for the last 10 minutes of the boil. Add the finishing hops for the final 1 minute of the boil. Strain, sparge, and transfer immediately to 2 gallons (7.5 l) of cold water in the fermenter. Top off with additional water to make 5 gallons (19 l). Aerate the wort very well. Pitch the yeast when the temperature of the wort is about 70 degrees F (21 C). Ferment at about 70 degrees F (21 C) for about 1 week or when fermentation shows signs of calming and stopping. Prime with sugar and bottle or keg when fermentation is complete.

Though this beer should be ready to drink about 2 weeks after bottling, wow, does it ever mellow out and get better with age. It's nice to have a batch of this in your house, because whenever you are away you are certain to know that things are improving at home. Can life get any better than that?

## PORTERS

### *Goat Scrotum Ale*

This recipe is famous throughout the world and a fun beer to brew. It offers you the opportunity to use everything but the kitchen sink as ingredients. Despite its free style it brews a deliciously well-balanced, slightly sweet style of porter with interesting nuances. Believe it or not, all of the ingredients were traditionally used in the brewing of porter hundreds of years ago and, thanks to you, continue to be to this day.

Enjoy yourself and do not be fearful; the wonderfulness of this porter is a tribute to creativity and the adventurousness that many homebrewers develop. Relax. Don't worry. And this is certainly a session of brewing with friends that calls for having a homebrew. (Commercial breweries, eat your heart out!) This Goat Scrotum's for you!

Ingredients for 5 gallons (19 l):

| | |
|---|---|
| 5 lbs. (2.3 kg) | dark malt extract syrup |
| 1 lb. (450 g) | crystal malt (10 L) |
| ¼ lb. (110 g) | black malt |
| ¼ lb. (110 g) | roasted barley |
| 1 c. (240 ml) | brown sugar |
| 1 c. (240 ml) | blackstrap molasses |
| 1 lb. (450 g) | corn sugar |
| 1½ oz. (42 g) | boiling hops (your choice) |
| ¼ oz. (7 g) | finishing hops (your choice) |
| 2 tsp. (8 g) | gypsum |
| ¼ tsp. (1 g) | Irish moss powder |
| * | ale yeast of your choice or White Labs Cry Havoc yeast |

*One or all of the following ingredients:*

| | |
|---|---|
| 2–4 oz. (56–110 g) | grated fresh ginger |
| 1–2 in. (2.5–5 cm) | brewing licorice or bruised licorice root |
| 2 Tbsp. (30 ml) | spruce essence or 4 oz. (110 g) of the new growth from a spruce tree |
| 1–10 | small fresh or dried chili peppers (be prepared for the Scoville effect) |
| ¼ c. (60 ml) | juniper berries (slightly crushed) |
| 6 oz. (170 g) | unsweetened chocolate or cocoa powder |

Enough homebrew for you and your friends to enjoy while brewing!

¾ c. (175 ml)    sugar (for bottling) or ⅓ c. (80 ml) corn sugar
                 (for kegging)

O.G.: 1.050–1.060 (12.5–15)
F.G.: 1.010–1.016 (2.5–4)
Bitterness: beats me; Color: SRM dark (EBC dark); Alcohol: 5.5–6% by volume

First of all, pop a homebrew and dissolve your anxieties.

Next, add the crushed grains to 2 gallons (7.5 l) of water and let steep at 150 to 160 degrees F (65–71 C) for 30 minutes, then remove the grains with a strainer. Add the malt extract, boiling hops, and all of the ingredients up to (but not including) the Irish moss. Boil for 60 minutes. Add the Irish moss for the last 10 minutes of the boil. Add the finishing hops for the last 2 minutes of the boil. Strain, sparge, and transfer immediately to 2 gallons (7.5 l) of cold water in the fermenter. Top off with additional water to make 5 gallons (19 l).

Aerate the wort very well. Pitch the yeast when the temperature of the wort is about 70 degrees F (21 C). Ferment at about 70 degrees F (21 C) for about 1 week or when fermentation shows signs of calming and stopping. Prime with sugar and bottle or keg when fermentation is complete.

Have another homebrew.

When ready, chill, serve, close your eyes, and slip back into the eighteenth century. It is a good porter! And you have a good life.

### Sparrow Hawk Porter

If you'd like to treat yourself to a gloriously bittersweet black porter, your heart will "soar like a hawk" when you part your lips for this treat.

Sparrow Hawk Porter is brewed in the tastefully done tradition of the Anchor Brewing Company's world classic Anchor Porter. Its character is complex: wonderfully black and bitter, yet sweet, medium-bodied, rich, and quenching. Served cold, the bitterness will be enhanced; served at temperatures above 50 degrees F (10 C), its sweet character will take the forefront. Its distinctly bitter bite does not linger long enough to be cloying. Its sweetness is like an impatiently singing songbird, hidden in the darkness of midnight.

As Sparrow Hawk lingers it becomes wisely more enjoyable.

Ingredients for 5 gallons (19 l):

4½ lbs. (2 kg)    German or other light or amber malt extract syrup
3.3 lbs. (1.5 kg)  John Bull plain dark malt extract syrup

| 1 lb. (450 g) | black malt |
| 1½ oz. (42 g) | Northern Brewer hops (boiling): 13 HBU (360 MBU) |
| 1 oz. (28 g) | Tettnang or Santiam hops (aroma) |
| ¼ tsp. (1 g) | Irish moss powder |
| * | American ale yeast or White Labs Cry Havoc yeast |
| ¾ c. (175 ml) | corn sugar or 1¼ c. (300 ml) dried malt extract (for bottling) |

O.G.: 1.058–1.062 (14.5–15.5)
F.G.: 1.014–1.020 (3.5–5)
Bitterness: 38 BU; Color: 50 SRM (100 EBC); Alcohol: 5.8% by volume

Add the crushed black malt to 2 gallons (7.5 l) of water and let steep at 150 to 160 degrees F (65–71 C) for 30 minutes, then remove the grains with a strainer. Add the malt extracts and Northern Brewer hops and boil for 60 minutes. Add the Irish moss for the last 10 minutes of the boil. Add the aroma hops for the final few minutes of the boil. Strain, sparge, and transfer immediately to 2 gallons (7.5 l) of cold water in the fermenter. Top off with additional water to make 5 gallons (19 l).

Aerate the wort very well. Pitch the yeast when the temperature of the wort is about 70 degrees F (21 C). Ferment at about 70 degrees F (21 C) for about 1 week or when fermentation shows signs of calming and stopping. Prime with sugar and bottle or keg when fermentation is complete.

## DARK LAGERS: BOCK BEER, DUNKEL (GERMAN DARK), AND SCHWARZBIER

### *Doctor Bock*

Whether you are on a starship or relaxing on your or someone else's couch, Doctor Bock will be sure to beam a smile of pleasure on your face. Doctor Bock is similar to a traditional German bock beer because it is brewed from a high original gravity. It consequently possesses the richness and alcoholic strength that German bock beers are meant to have. This brew is smooth and malty, but not overpowering. German varieties of malt extract and hops of German descent make this brew all the more authentic.

Ingredients for 5 gallons (19 l):

    9 lbs. (4.1 kg)   German light or amber malt extract syrup
    ½ lb. (225 g)   chocolate malt

1¾ oz. (49 g)   Hallertau, Spalt, or Vanguard hops (boiling): 8 HBU
                (225 MBU)
½ oz. (14 g)    Hallertau or Crystal hops (15 minutes, flavor)
¼ tsp. (1 g)    Irish moss powder
*               German lager–type yeast
¾ c. (175 ml)   sugar (for bottling) or ⅓ c. (80 ml) corn sugar
                (for kegging)


O.G.: 1.066–1.070 (16–17)
F.G.: 1.014–1.020 (3.5–5)
Bitterness: 26 BU; Color: 28 SRM (56 EBC); Alcohol: 6.8% by volume


Add the crushed chocolate malt to 2 gallons (7.5 l) of water and let steep at 150 to 160 degrees F (65–71 C) for 30 minutes, then remove the grains with a strainer. Add the malt extract and boiling hops and boil for 60 minutes. Add the flavor hops for the last 15 minutes of boiling. Add the Irish moss for the last 10 minutes of the boil. Strain, sparge, and transfer immediately to 2 gallons (7.5 l) of cold water in the fermenter. Top off with additional water to make 5 gallons (19 l). Aerate the wort very well. Pitch the yeast when the temperature of the wort is about 70 degrees F (21 C). Ferment at about 70 degrees F (21 C) for about 1 week or when fermentation shows signs of calming and stopping.

If you have temperature-controlled environments, use a two-stage fermentation method: Transfer the beer to a secondary fermenter after primary fermentation appears to be complete and lager at cool temperatures—between 35 and 55 degrees F (1.7–13 C)—for 2 to 4 weeks. Regardless of at what temperature you ferment, prime with sugar and bottle when lagering is complete.

Condition (another word for naturally carbonating beer) the beer for about 7 days in the bottle at room temperature. After it has conditioned (carbonated), move the beer to the coolest (cold) place you have for keeping until you are ready to chill for serving. Dr. Bock is seeing patients!

### Danger Knows No Favorites Dunkel

With a beer like this—hey, danger is my business. What a fantastic true original dark-style German Dunkel flavor. In German the word *dunkel* means "dark"— not amber. This is not your modern "amber" beer called dunkel brewed by many German and American breweries. This is a throwback to the original intent of this classic brew. Spiking the wort with flavor hops at 30 minutes and 15 minutes before the end of the boil adds bliss and eloquence that is hard, hard, hard to beat. The character is a rich, dark smoothness and soft bitterness that typify a well-brewed German Dunkel (dark) beer. It has medium to full body, wonderful hop flavor, and a rich creamy head that make it both immensely and freshly superior to St. Pauli Girl Dark, Beck's Dark, or Heineken's Dark—all by a long shot.

Ingredients for 5 gallons (19 l):

| | |
|---|---|
| 3.3 lbs. (1.5 kg) | amber malt extract syrup |
| 3 lbs. (1.4 kg) | dark dried malt extract |
| ¾ lb. (340 g) | crystal malt (10 L) |
| ¼ lb. (110 g) | chocolate malt |
| ¼ lb. (110 g) | debittered black malt |
| 1½ oz. (42 g) | French Strisselspalt or Tettnang hops (boiling): 6 HBU (170 MBU) |
| ½ oz. (14 g) | Crystal or Mt. Hood hops (30 minutes, flavor) |
| ½ oz. (14 g) | Crystal or Mt. Hood hops (15 minutes, flavor/aroma) |
| ¼ tsp. (1 g) | Irish moss powder |
| * | German lager–type yeast or White Labs Cry Havoc yeast |
| ¾ c. (175 ml) | sugar (for bottling) or ⅓ c. (80 ml) corn sugar (for kegging) |

O.G.: 1.050–1.055 (12.5–14)
F.G.: 1.010–1.014 (2.5–3.5)
Bitterness: 20 BU; Color: 37 SRM (74 EBC); Alcohol: 5.3% by volume

Add the crushed crystal, chocolate, and black malts to 2 gallons (7.5 l) of water and let steep at 150–160 degrees F (65–71 C) for 30 minutes, then remove the grains with a strainer. Add the malt extract and boiling hops and boil for 60 minutes. Add the ½ ounce (14 g) of flavor hops for the last 30 minutes of the boil. Add the ½ ounce (14 g) of flavor/aroma hops for the last 15 minutes of the boil. Add the Irish moss for the last 10 minutes of the boil. Strain, sparge, and transfer immediately to 2 gallons (7.5 l) of cold water in the fermenter. Top off with additional water to make 5 gallons (19 l).

Aerate the wort very well. Pitch the yeast when the temperature of the wort is about 70 degrees F (21 C). Ferment at about 70 degrees F (21 C) for about 1 week or when fermentation shows signs of calming and stopping.

If you have temperature-controlled environments, like a spare refrigerator, use a two-stage fermentation method: Transfer the beer to a secondary fermenter after primary fermentation appears to be complete and lager at cool temperatures—between 35 and 55 degrees F (1.7–13 C)—for 2 to 4 weeks. Regardless of at what temperature you ferment, prime with sugar and bottle when lagering is complete.

Condition and naturally carbonate the beer for about 7 days in the bottle at room temperature. After it has conditioned (carbonated), move the beer to the coolest (cold) place you have for keeping until you are ready to chill for serving. And remember—danger knows no favorites.

### Limp Richard's Schwarzbier

As gentle as a calm night in the Black Forest, Limp Richard's Schwarzbier is a deep, dark, smooth, mild German lager with just a hint of dark malt solemnly expressing its namesake. *Schwarz* in German means "black." It's a traditional German style of beer that few Germans have the opportunity to enjoy. That is the fantastic thing about homebrewing: You can have it for yourself anytime and any season. Schwarzbier is a brew for all seasons. It can make a dark beer drinker out of anyone.

Ingredients for 5 gallons (19 l):

| | |
|---|---|
| 6.6 lbs. (3 kg) | dark malt extract syrup |
| 1/3 lb. (150 g) | debittered black malt |
| 1 oz. (28 g) | Mt. Hood or German Spalt hops (boiling): 6 HBU (170 MBU) |
| 1/2 oz. (14 g) | Mt. Hood hops (45 minutes, flavor) |
| 1/2 oz. (14 g) | Tettnang hops (30 minutes, flavor) |
| 1/2 oz. (14 g) | Tettnang or Cascade hops (15 minutes, aroma/flavor) |
| 1/4 tsp. (1 g) | Irish moss powder |
| * | German lager–type yeast or White Labs Cry Havoc yeast |
| 3/4 c. (175 ml) | sugar (for bottling) or 1/3 c. (80 ml) corn sugar (for kegging) |

O.G.: 1.046–1.050 (11.5–12.5)
F.G.: 1.010–1.014 (2.5–3.5)
Bitterness: 23 BU; Color: 33 SRM (66 EBC) Alcohol: 4.7% by volume

Add the crushed black malt to 2 gallons (7.5 l) of water and let steep at 150 to 160 degrees F (65–71 C) for 30 minutes, then remove the grains with a strainer. Add the malt extract and the boiling hops and boil for 60 minutes. Add the Mt. Hood flavor hops for the last 45 minutes of the boil. Add the Tettnang flavor hops for the last 30 minutes of the boil. Add the Tettnang or Cascade aroma/flavor hops for the last 15 minutes of the boil. Add the Irish moss for the last 10 minutes of the boil. Strain, sparge, and transfer immediately to 2 gallons (7.5 l) of cold water in the fermenter. Top off with additional water to make 5 gallons (19 l). Aerate the wort very well. Pitch the yeast when the temperature of the wort is about 70 degrees F (21 C). Ferment at about 70 degrees F (21 C) for about 1 week or when fermentation shows signs of calming and stopping.

If you have temperature-controlled environments, use a two-stage fermentation method: Transfer the beer to a secondary fermenter after primary fermentation appears to be complete and lager at cool temperatures—between 35 and 55 degrees F (1.7–13 C)—for 2 to 4 weeks. Regardless of at what temperature you ferment, prime with sugar and bottle when lagering is complete.

Condition and naturally carbonate the beer for about 7 days in the bottle at room temperature. After it has conditioned (carbonated), move the beer to the coolest (cold) place you have for keeping until you are ready to chill for serving.

Serve this one slightly chilled to bring out the gentle richness of malt and soothing bitterness of the black malt and hops.

## Good Night in Mexico

Back in the late 1970s and early 1980s there was a wonderful dark (Dunkel) German-style lager brewed only for the Christmas season by the folks that bring you Dos Equis. It was called Noche Buena. Ohhhh, my! What a wonderful beer that was, especially if you could get it fresh in Mexico. The brand is still around, but it has long since been reformulated so as not to offend the palates of all their light-lager-only drinkers. But before I give you the lowdown on how to make it, let me digress.

If you want to brew one of those popular light lagers, often available in clear glass bottles, your best bet is to buy one of the excellent malt extract–based beer kits. Muntons makes a Mexican Beer kit you can't go wrong with. Follow the directions that come with the kit, but for extra finesse you might consider a liquid lager yeast and lagering for 3 weeks at 40 to 50 degrees F (4.5 to 10 C) before bottling. And if you really want to duplicate the authentic character you've enjoyed on a sunny beach in Mexico or simply in your own backyard, take your bottled beer and place the bottles in full bright sunlight for 10 to 15 minutes. I'm serious! The sunlight will cause a photochemical reaction resulting in that clear-bottle-beer taste that is immensely popular. If you still think I'm totally loco, I have it in very good trust that the brewery actually exposes its beer to ultraviolet light on its way to being packaged in cans (cans don't allow the light reaction) in order to duplicate the flavor and aroma millions have grown to appreciate. Meanwhile, all you brewmasters can cry in your beer or brew a batch of Good Night in Mexico.

Noche Buena was a delicious, full-flavored, relatively light-bodied, highly drinkable, German-style dark beer. It probably used some corn in the recipe, but the malt and hop character was so wonderfully evident, the corn only served to make this legendary brew more drinkable.

Ingredients for 5 gallons (19 l):

6.6 lbs. (3 kg)   dark malt extract syrup
1 lb. (450 g)     rice extract syrup or rice extract powder

| 1 lb. (450 g) | crystal malt (10 L) |
| ¼ lb. (113 g) | malted barley or honey malt |
| 1¼ oz. (35 g) | German Spalt or American Liberty hops (boiling): 6 HBU (170 MBU) |
| 1 oz. (28 g) | Czech Saaz hops (20 minutes, flavor): 4 HBU (110 MBU) |
| 1 oz. (28 g) | Hersbrucker-Hallertau or American Sterling hops (5 minutes, finishing/aroma) |
| ¼ tsp. (1 g) | Irish moss powder |
| * | German lager–type yeast or White Labs Cry Havoc yeast |
| ¾ c. (175 ml) | sugar (for bottling) or ⅓ c. (80 ml) corn sugar (for kegging) |

O.G.: 1.058–1.062 (14.3–15.2)
F.G.: 1.014–1.018 (3.5–4.5)
Bitterness: 20 BU; Color: 25 SRM (54 EBC); Alcohol: 5.8% by volume

If using malted barley, toast it in the oven; if using honey malt, use as is. Preheat the oven to 350 degrees F (177 C). Spread the whole malted barley grain on a baking sheet and place in the oven. Toast for 5 to 10 minutes.

Crush the crystal malt along with the toasted or honey malt. Combine with 1½ gallons (5.7 l) of water and let steep at 150–160 degrees F (65–71 C) for 30 minutes, then remove the grains with a strainer. Add the malt extract, rice extract, and boiling hops and boil for 60 minutes. Add the flavor hops for the final 20 minutes. Add the Irish moss for the final 10 minutes. Add the aroma hops for the final 5 minutes. Strain, sparge, and transfer immediately to 2 gallons (7.5 l) of cold water in the fermenter. Top off with additional water to make 5 gallons (19 l). Aerate the wort very well. Pitch the yeast when the temperature of the wort is about 70 degrees F (21 C). Ferment at about 70 degrees F (21 C) for about 1 week or when fermentation shows signs of calming and stopping.

Prime with sugar and bottle or keg when fermentation is complete; bottle within 2 weeks. This beer should be ready to drink in a very short period of time unless very cold lagering temperatures are used; if two-stage fermentation is used, the beer will improve if matured for 2 to 3 weeks at a temperature between 40 and 50 degrees F (4.5–10 C) before bottling. Bottle when fermentation stops or after 2 to 3 weeks of secondary maturation.

*Cerveza,* anyone? *Hecho en casa.*

## BELGIAN ALES

### *Dubbel Your Pleasure*

Dubbel Your Pleasure. Double your fun. If you like subtly dark fruity ales with lots of complexity and a velvety smoothness that goes down doubly fine, you'll love this Belgian style of brown ale that offers cocoalike and bananalike flavor and aroma notes while being soft on bitterness and strong on drinkability. Brewed at room temperatures, this ale is perfect for summer and warm-weather brewing: Big but not too big. Dark but not too dark. Malty but not too malty. Hoppy and herbal, but not too hoppy. Fruity but not too fruity. This is all too much pleasure.

Ingredients for 5 gallons (19 l):

| | |
|---|---|
| 3 lbs. (1.4 kg) | dark malt extract syrup |
| 3 lbs. (1.4 kg) | light malt extract syrup |
| 1½ lbs. (0.7 kg) | extra-light dried malt extract |
| 1 lb. (454 g) | Belgian-style candi sugar or pure cane sugar |
| 1½ oz. (42 g) | Styrian Goldings, Fuggles, or Willamette hops (boiling): 7.5 HBU (210 MBU) |
| ¼ tsp. (1 g) | Irish moss powder |
| * | Strong Belgian-type ale yeast |
| ¾ c. (175 ml) | sugar (for bottling) or ⅓ c. (80 ml) corn sugar (for kegging) |

O.G.: 1.064–1.068 (15–16)
F.G.: 1.014–1.018 (3.5–4.5)
Bitterness: 23 BU; Color: 16 SRM (32 EBC); Alcohol: 6.6% by volume

Boil the malt extract and boiling hops with 2 gallons (7.5 l) of water for 60 minutes. Add the Irish moss for the final 10 minutes of the boil. Strain, sparge, and transfer immediately to 2 gallons (7.5 l) of cold water in the fermenter. Top off with additional water to make 5 gallons (19 l).

Aerate the wort very well. Pitch the yeast when the temperature of the wort is about 70 degrees F (21 C). Ferment at about 70 degrees F (21 C) for about 1 week or when fermentation shows signs of calming and stopping.

Prime with sugar and bottle or keg when fermentation is complete.

Although this brew will be ready for your enjoyable indulgence 2 to 4 weeks after bottling, it ages well at cellar temperatures; you may want to brew a double batch of Dubbel Pleasure.

## Grand Slam American Tripel

If you live in the United States and brew a Belgian style of ale called Tripel it really isn't a "Belgian Tripel." It is an American Triple. If you're in Australia, call it an Australian Triple. If in Tripoli, well then how about a Tripolitan Triple? Anyway, you get what I mean, and once you've made this and fallen in love with the complexity of character you might just imagine "rounding the bases"

for a home run with your friends and family—that is, if you decide to share it. This brew doesn't get much easier. The malt extract does it all. Purchase a Brewferm Trappist-style beer kit, but don't follow directions. Instead use *The Complete Joy of Homebrewing* method for added quality.

Ingredients for 5 gallons (19 l):

| | |
|---|---|
| 6.6 lbs. (3 kg) | Brewferm Trappist-style Belgian Beer kit (hopped) extract |
| 2 lbs. (1.4 kg) | light dried malt extract |
| 1 lb. (450 g) | light honey |
| 1 oz. (28 g) | Styrian Goldings, Fuggles, or Willamette hops (boiling): 5 HBU (140 MBU) |
| ¼ tsp. (1 g) | Irish moss powder |
| * | Strong Belgian-type ale yeast |
| ¾ c. (175 ml) | sugar (for bottling) or ⅓ c. (80 ml) corn sugar (for kegging) |

O.G.: 1.080–1.084 (19.5–20)
F.G.: 1.016–1.022 (4–5.5)
Bitterness: about 25 BU; Color: 9 SRM (18 EBC); Alcohol: 8.4%
by volume

Boil the malt extracts, honey, and boiling hops with 2 gallons (7.5 l) of water for 60 minutes. Add the Irish moss for the last 10 minutes of the boil. Strain, sparge, and transfer immediately to 2 gallons (7.5 l) of cold water in the fermenter. Top off with additional water to make 5 gallons (19 l). Aerate the wort very well. Pitch the yeast when the temperature of the wort is about 70 degrees F (21 C). Ferment at about 70 degrees F (21 C) for about 1 week or when fermentation shows signs of calming and stopping.

Prime with sugar and bottle or keg when fermentation is complete. Although this brew will be ready for your enjoyable indulgence 3 weeks after bottling, this is one brew that ages well. With 2 to 12 months aging you will find the complexity of this brew evolves. If you find that you like this beer with age, better get to brewing a second batch right away—don't say I didn't warn you.

### Who's in the Garden Grand Cru

A most unusual brew that I love to love. Formulated and brewed in the spirit of a Belgian White beer (Witbier) flavored with coriander, orange peel, and the spiciness of German hops, Who's in the Garden is a copy of Belgium's legendary, award-winning Hoegaarden Grand Cru Ale. It is a bit more intense in its character and fresher in flavor—because it's homemade and you're your brewery! Honey is a part of this recipe and helps achieve a drier, less sweet, and more refreshing brew.

For those who have never experienced the floral spiciness of freshly ground coriander seed, next time you're at the grocery store pick up a few ounces of this inexpensive spice in its whole form and grind some yourself. It'll make your special beer even that more special. I encourage you to give it a try.

Ingredients for 5 gallons (19 l):

| | |
|---|---|
| 5 lbs. (2.3 kg) | light or extra-light dried malt extract |
| 2 lbs. (0.9 kg) | light honey |
| 1 oz. (28 g) | Hallertau hops (boiling): 5 HBU (140 MBU) |
| ½ oz. (14 g) | Hallertau hops (10 minutes, flavor) |
| ½ oz. (14 g) | Hallertau hops (1 or 2 minutes, aroma) |
| 1½ oz. (35 g) | freshly crushed coriander seeds |

½ oz. (14 g)    dried ground orange peel (available at your homebrew
               supply shop)
¼ tsp. (1 g)   Irish moss powder
*              Belgian Wit (wheat) beer–type yeast
¾ c. (175 ml)  sugar (for bottling) or ⅓ c. (80 ml) corn sugar
               (for kegging)

O.G.: 1.056–1.060 (14–15)
F.G.: 1.008–1.010 (4–4.5)
Bitterness: 18 BU; Color. 4 SRM (8 EBC); Alcohol: 6.3% by volume

Add malt extract, honey, and boiling hops to 2 gallons (7.5 l) of water and boil for 60 minutes. Add the flavor hops, ¾ ounce (21 g) of the coriander, and the Irish moss for the last 10 minutes of the boil. Add the remaining ¾ ounce (21 g) coriander and the orange peel for the final 5 minutes. Add the aroma hops for the final 1 to 2 minutes of boiling. Strain, sparge, and transfer immediately to 2 gallons (7.5 l) of cold water in the fermenter. Top off with additional

water to make 5 gallons (19 l).Aerate the wort very well. Pitch the yeast when the temperature of the wort is about 70 degrees F (21 C). Ferment at about 70 degrees F (21 C) for about 1 week or when fermentation shows signs of calming and stopping.

Prime with sugar and bottle or keg when fermentation is complete. Drink a homebrew. For an added attraction add one whole coriander seed to each bottle when bottling. Worried (heaven forbid) about bacteria on the seeds? Microwave them and sleep better.

## Purposefully Saison

The Belgians and French did not invent seasonal beers, but they sure have tickled the fancy of beer enthusiasts who love to say *seasonal* in French, *"saison."* Where the corners of France, Belgium, and Germany merge, any brew could happen. From this area emerges and spreads a special way of brewing that defies definition. Imported French and Belgian "saison-style" brews are matched in quality by both homebrewers and small craft brewers around the world. But what is a saison? I mentally shrug my shoulders and know one if I taste it and someone tells me that it's so. Saisons are yummy and they come in all ways, shapes, and tastes. Generally I might say they are kinky and delicious. Some I enjoy more than others. What seems part of the blessings is that they shimmer. Mirthful saisons are fruity, yeasty, and earthy and compel one to dance. Here's a recipe that highlights the fermentation character of the suggested strains of yeast in this recipe. This is a recipe to which you can add herbs, spices, fruits, and wishful thinking—all in moderation so as not to overpower the earthy, herbal, fruity characters derived from fermentation.

Ingredients for 5 gallons (19 l):

| | |
|---|---|
| 3 lbs. (1.4 kg) | light malt extract syrup |
| 2 lbs. (0.9 kg) | wheat malt extract syrup |
| ½ lb. (225 g) | crystal malt (10 L) |
| 1½ lbs. (0.7 kg) | light honey or cane sugar |
| 1¼ oz. (35 g) | Styrian Goldings, Fuggles, or English Kent Goldings hops (boiling): 5 HBU (140 MBU) |
| ½ oz. (14 g) | American Crystal or German Saphir hops (1 minute, flavor/aroma) |
| * | herbs, spices, fruits, and wishful thinking all in moderation (optional); be creative |
| ¼ tsp. (1 g) | Irish moss powder |
| * | Saison-type ale yeast such as White Labs WLP566 Belgian Saison II Yeast or Wyeast Labs 3711 French Saison |

¾ c. (175 ml) sugar (for bottling) or ⅓ c. (80 ml) corn sugar
(for kegging)

O.G.: 1.050–1.054 (12.5–13.5)
F.G.: 1.008–1.012 (2.5–3.5)
Bitterness: 21 BU; Color: 7 SRM (14 EBC); Alcohol: 5.5% by volume

Add the crushed malt to 2 gallons (7.5 l) of water and let steep at 150 to 160 degrees F (65–71 C) for 30 minutes, then remove the grains with a strainer. Add the malt extracts, honey or sugar, and boiling hops and boil for 60 minutes. Add Irish moss for the last 10 minutes of the boil. Add the aroma hops (and optional spices/herbs if used) for the final 1 minute of the boil. Strain, sparge, and transfer immediately to 2 gallons (7.5 l) of cold water in the fermenter. Top off with additional water to make 5 gallons (19 l). Aerate the wort very well. Pitch the yeast when the temperature of the wort is about 70 degrees F (21 C). Ferment at about 70 degrees F (21 C) for about 1 week or when fermentation shows signs of calming and stopping.

Prime with sugar and bottle or keg when fermentation is complete. This beer will age gracefully when kept in a cool environment, developing complex fruity and yeast flavors that intrigue and expand your brew horizons.

### Belgian Lambics

Belgian lambic beers are unmistakably unique, sour to the bone with a special pungency that wild yeast and bacterial fermentation naturally bring on in Belgium. Trying to duplicate these brews is a lot easier than it used to be for the American homebrewer. For those who love that special pungent tartness in their brew, detailed explanation about how you can come close to this style can be found in "Sour Beers and Belgian Lambic," page 372.

## WEIZENBIER/WEISSBIER

### Lovebite Weissbier

Mit hefe ("with yeast"), this is the real thing, and now homebrewers can make a superdeluxe version of this brew with barley and *wheat* malt extract. Not only does the ease of wheat malt extract make this superpopular beer style part of your beer cellar, but even the unique Bavarian wheat beer yeast is now available to homebrewers. Ask your local homebrew supply shop to special-order it for you if they don't carry it regularly.

Have you ever been to Bavaria and sipped a tall, cloudy Weissbier or at home had imports such as Ayinger, Paulaner, or Schneider Weizen or Weissbiers? If you enjoyed their spicy, clovelike and bananalike aroma and flavor along with the special and healthful yeastiness, then bud, this beer's for you.

Ingredients for 5 gallons (19 l):

| | |
|---|---|
| 6.6 lbs. (3 kg) | wheat malt extract syrup (50% wheat, 50% barley) |
| ¾ oz. (21 g) | Hallertau hops (boiling): 4 HBU (110 MBU) |
| ½ oz. (14 g) | German Saphir hops (1 minute, aroma/flavor) |
| * | German wheat beer–type yeast |
| ¾ c. (175 ml) | sugar (for bottling) or ⅓ c. (80 ml) corn sugar (for kegging) |

O.G.: 1.048–1.050 (12–12.5)
F.G.: 1.008–1.010 (4–4.5)
Bitterness: 13 BU; Color: 5 SRM (10 EBC); Alcohol: 5.4% by volume

Add the wheat and barley malt extract and boiling hops to 2 gallons (7.5 l) of water and boil for 60 minutes. Add the flavor/aroma hops for the final 1 minute of the boil. Strain, sparge, and transfer immediately to 2 gallons (7.5 l) of cold water in the fermenter. Top off with additional water to make 5 gallons (19 l). Aerate the wort very well. Pitch the yeast when the temperature of the wort is about 70 degrees F (21 C). Ferment at about 70 degrees F (21 C) for about 1 week or when fermentation shows signs of calming and stopping.

Prime with sugar and bottle or keg when fermentation is complete. After about 2 weeks, serve slightly chilled.

Many Germans roll the bottle on the table before opening it to get the yeast sediment well mixed with the beer. This is an option you might want to try for authenticity. And for real authenticity, set yourself in a sunshine sort of mood. Really relax and if it isn't summertime, pretend it is and you're taking a break to enjoy your very own homemade effervescent and refreshing Lovebite Weissbier. It'll be the next best thing to being at a Bavarian *Bierstube*. *Prost*, my friends.

### Phat Fired Weizenbock

As you'd say in certain company: "Wow, this beer is phat!" Cool. Just relax. Have a homebrew. Any way you want to say it, this beer is way all right and deserves to be noted as one of the best German-style dark beers you'll ever brew—a unique German-style wheat beer that will even impress your friends. You may need to hide a few for yourself. Remember, German Weizens and Weissbiers are not hoppy, so you hopheads either rein in your urge to use liberal amounts of hops or know that you are on a new frontier.

Ingredients for 5 gallons (19 l):

| | |
|---|---|
| 6.6 lbs. (3 kg) | wheat malt extract syrup (50% wheat, 50% barley) |
| 1½ lbs. (0.7 kg) | amber or light dried malt extract |

1 lb. (454 g)    crystal malt (10 to 20 L)
¼ lb. (110 g)    chocolate malt
¼ lb. (110 g)    debittered black malt
1½ oz. (42 g)    German Spalt or German Tradition hops (boiling):
                 7 HBU (200 MBU)
1 oz. (28 g)     Santiam, Mt. Hood, or American Tettnang hop pellets
                 (5 minutes, flavor/aroma)
1 oz. (28 g)     Santiam, Mt. Hood, or American Tettnang hop pellets
                 (2 minutes, aroma)
*                German wheat beer–type yeast
¾ c. (175 ml)    sugar (for bottling) or ⅓ c. (80 ml) corn sugar
                 (for kegging)


O.G.: 1.064–1.068 (15.5–16.5)
F.G.: 1.016–1.018 (4–5)
Bitterness: 30 BU; Color: 17 SRM (34 EBC); Alcohol: 6.3% by volume

Add the crushed crystal, chocolate, and black malts to 2 gallons (7.5 l) of water and let steep at 150 to 160 degrees F (65–71 C) for 30 minutes, then remove the grains with a strainer. Sparge with hot water and collect the liquid extract in your brewpot. Add the malt extracts and boiling hops and boil for 60 minutes. Add the flavor/aroma hops for the last 5 minutes of the boil. Add the aroma hops for the last 2 minutes of the boil. Turn off the heat. Strain, sparge, and transfer immediately to 2 gallons (7.5 l) of cold water in the fermenter. Top off with additional water to make 5 gallons (19 l). Aerate the wort very well. Pitch the yeast when the temperature of the wort is about 70 degrees F (21 C). Ferment at about 70 degrees F (21 C) for about 1 week or when fermentation shows signs of calming and stopping.

Prime with sugar and bottle or keg when fermentation is complete. Let age a couple of weeks and begin your odyssey.


## SPECIALTY BEERS

### Rocky Raccoon's Crystal Honey Lager (Original)

This is the original and internationally acclaimed Rocky Raccoon's Honey Lager with improved modifications. Use the lightest malt extract available, the freshest hops, and light honey. It is a clean, crisp, exceptionally great-tasting light beer with a mellow, aromatic hop flavor. The use of honey encourages a very complete fermentation and a bit higher alcohol content. The lightness of flavor really can do justice to your finest hops. This recipe should be your foundation for a wide variety of experimenting with toasted malts, hops, other grains,

and unusual ingredients. It is a real delight and hundreds of homebrewers have won first-place awards at homebrew competitions around the United States with this recipe or a variation of it.

This beer will change its character with age; most who have appreciated Rocky's consider age with respect and happily raised eyebrows of disbelief.

Rocky's has a slight resemblance to the character of some stronger types of very light Belgian Ales.

Ingredients for 5 gallons (19 l):

| | |
|---|---|
| 3½ lbs. (1.6 kg) | extra-light dried malt extract |
| 2½ lbs. (1.1 kg) | light clover honey |
| 1½ oz. (42 g) | Cascade hops (boiling): 7.5 HBU (210 MBU); or try 2 oz. (56 g) Saaz hops for a pilsenerlike character |
| ½ oz. (14 g) | Cascade hops (2 to 4 minutes, finishing) |
| ¼ tsp. (1 g) | Irish moss powder |
| * | American lager, pilsener-type, or American ale yeast, or White Labs Cry Havoc yeast |

¾ c. (175 ml)     sugar (for bottling) or ⅓ c. (80 ml) corn sugar
                  (for kegging)

O.G.: 1.048–1.052 (12–13)
F.G.: 1.004–1.008 (1–2)
Bitterness: 23 BU; Color: 4 SRM (8 EBC); Alcohol: 5.8% by volume

Add the malt extract, honey, and boiling hops to 1½ gallons (5.7 l) of water
and boil for 60 minutes. Add the Irish moss for the last 10 minutes of the boil.
Add the finishing hops during the final 2 to 4 minutes of boiling. Strain,
sparge, and transfer immediately to 2 gallons (7.5 l) of cold water in the fermenter. Top off with additional water to make 5 gallons (19 l).

Aerate the wort very well. Pitch the yeast when the temperature of the
wort is about 70 degrees F (21 C). Ferment at about 70 degrees F (21 C) for about
1 week or when fermentation shows signs of calming and stopping.

Prime with sugar and bottle or keg when fermentation is complete.

*Linda's Lovely Light Honey Ginger Lager*
Linda's Lovely is a variation of Rocky Raccoon's that offers the sparkle of fresh
ginger to an already delicate and exquisite, finely balanced honey lager. The variation can easily be accomplished by adding 2 to 4 ounces of grated fresh ginger
to the last 10 minutes of boiling the wort.

It is easily brewed and offers great refreshing summertime or holiday satisfaction.

## Bruce and Kay's Black Honey Spruce Lager

A heavenly delight for those who enjoy the rich taste of dark beers and the
lighter body of light beers. A well-brewed Bruce and Kay's will impress even
those friends who say they don't really like beer. Try this recipe if you see yourself as a homebrew missionary.

Bruce and Kay's Black Honey Spruce Lager does indeed have spruce essence
as one of its ingredients, as well as honey, malt, and hops. For a black beer it has
a light body because of the use of honey. Its rich, dark appearance and creamy
head lead deceivingly to a surprisingly refreshing and flavorful beer.

The recipe is for 5 gallons (19 l), but this is one time that you might consider
doubling or tripling the recipe. You'll run out all too soon.

Ingredients for 5 gallons (19 l):

3.3 lbs. (1.5 kg)   John Bull or other brand dark malt extract syrup
1 lb. (450 g)       amber dried malt extract
2 lbs. (0.9 kg)     light honey

¾ lb. (340 g)    crystal malt (10 L)
⅓ lb. (150 g)    black malt
¾ oz. (21 g)    Centennial hops (boiling): 7.5 HBU (210 MBU)
1 oz. (28 g)    Amarillo or Citra hops (1 minute, aroma/finishing)
1 oz. (30 ml)    spruce essence (available at homebrew supply stores)
¼ tsp. (1 g)    Irish moss powder
*    American ale–type yeast or White Labs Cry Havoc yeast
¾ c. (175 ml)    sugar (for bottling) or ⅓ c. (80 ml) corn sugar
    (for kegging)

O.G.: 1.050–1.054 (12.5–13.5)
F.G.: 1.013–1.017 (3–4)
Bitterness: 23 BU; Color 30 SRM (60 EBC); Alcohol: 5% by volume

Add the crushed crystal and black malt to 1½ gallons (5.7 l) of water and let steep at 150 to 160 degrees F (65–71 C) for 30 minutes, then remove the grains with a strainer. Add the malt extracts, honey, and boiling hops and boil for 60 minutes. Add the Irish moss for the last 10 minutes of the boil. Add the finishing hops and spruce essence during the final 1 minute of the boil. Strain, sparge, and transfer immediately to 2 gallons (7.5 l) of cold water in the fermenter. Top off with additional water to make 5 gallons (19 l). Aerate the wort very well. Pitch the yeast when the temperature of the wort is about 70 degrees F (21 C). Ferment at about 70 degrees F (21 C) for about 1 week or when fermentation shows signs of calming and stopping.

Prime with sugar and bottle or keg when fermentation is complete.

**". . . it was about spruce beer. Mr. Knightly had been telling him something about brewing spruce beer. . . . Talking about spruce beer—Oh! Yes—Mr. Knightly and I both saying we liked it and Mr. Elton's seeming resolved to learn to like it too. . . ."**
—*Emma*, Jane Austen

### Kumdis Island Spruce Beer

A spruce beer brewed in the tradition of authenticity, Kumdis Island Spruce was originally brewed with the fresh spring growth of tall Sitka spruce trees in the Queen Charlotte Islands of British Columbia, Canada. The aroma that filled the "brewhouse" cabin was as wonderful as gingerbread hot out of the oven. And the character of the beer when it was ready to drink? Well, let me tell you that it was a real surprise. It was a very light-bodied brown ale that tasted very, very similar to Pepsi-Cola. Now, that may or may not sound appropriate for beer, but the fact is, it tasted fantastic, like an unsweetened Pepsi-Cola with a real beer character. It is a wonderfully refreshing and quenching beer.

Ingredients for 5 gallons (19 l):

6.6 lbs. (3 kg)     dark malt extract syrup
4–6 oz. (165 g)   new green growth of spruce trees (spruce tips)
2 oz. (56 g)        Vanguard or Hallertau hops (boiling): 10 HBU
                            (280 MBU)
¼ tsp. (1 g)        Irish moss powder
*                           American ale-type yeast or White Labs Cry Havoc yeast
¾ c. (175 ml)      sugar (for bottling) or ⅓ c. (80 ml) corn sugar
                            (for kegging)

O.G.: 1.046–1.050 (11.5–12.5)
F.G.: 1.010–1.014 (2.5–3.5)
Bitterness: 32 BU; Color 20 SRM (40 EBC); Alcohol: 4.8% by volume

Add the malt extracts, spruce tips, and boiling hops to 1½ gallons (5.7 l) of water and boil for 60 minutes. Add the Irish moss for the last 10 minutes of the boil. Strain, sparge, and transfer immediately to 2 gallons (7.5 l) of cold water in the fermenter. Top off with additional water to make 5 gallons (19 l). Aerate the wort very well. Pitch the yeast when the temperature of the wort is about 70 degrees F (21 C). Ferment at about 70 degrees F (21 C) for about 1 week or when fermentation shows signs of calming and stopping.

Prime with sugar and bottle or keg when fermentation is complete.

### Vagabond Gingered Ale

Vagabond Gingered Ale is a deliciously dark, full-bodied ale, with the gentle essence of fresh ginger. The freshly grated ginger in this recipe offers a joyously refreshing balance to the sweetness of malt, counterbalanced by a shrewdly measured choice of hops. The blend of the main ingredients offers a complex triad of flavors—uniquely satisfying for the vagabond brewers who journey to places that have no boundaries.

A favorite of many who have tasted from mugs of those who have dared.

You will not regret this experience. And you'll never know until you check it out.

Ingredients for 5 gallons (19 l):

| | |
|---|---|
| 6.6 lbs. (3 kg) | plain dark malt extract syrup |
| ¾ lb. (340 g) | crystal malt (10 L) |
| ½ lb. (225 g) | chocolate malt |
| 2 oz. (56 g) | Cascade hops (boiling): 10 HBU (280 MBU) |
| 1 oz. (28 g) | Willamette, Australian Galaxy, or New Zealand Nelson Sauvin hops (1 minute, aroma/finishing) |
| 2–4 oz. (56–110 g) | grated fresh ginger |
| ¼ tsp. (1 g) | Irish moss powder |

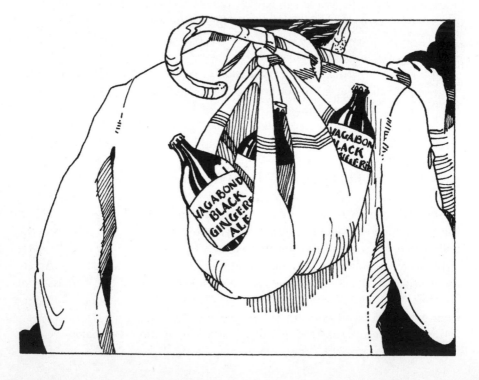

|  | American ale–type yeast or White Labs Cry Havoc yeast |
|---|---|
| ¾ c. (175 ml) | sugar (for bottling) or ⅓ c. (80 ml) corn sugar (for kegging) |

*

O.G.: 1.050–1.054 (12.5–13.5)
F.G.: 1.014–1.018 (3.5–4.5)
Bitterness: 31 BU; Color: 35 SRM (70 EBC); Alcohol: 4.8% by volume

Add the crushed crystal and chocolate malt to 1½ gallons (5.7 l) of water and let steep at 150 to 160 degrees F (65–71 C) for 30 minutes, then remove the grains with a strainer. Add the malt extract, ginger, and boiling hops and boil for 60 minutes. Add the Irish moss for the last 10 minutes of the boil. Add the finishing hops during the final 1 minute of the boil. Strain, sparge, and transfer immediately to 2 gallons (7.5 l) of cold water in the fermenter. Top off with additional water to make 5 gallons (19 l). Aerate the wort very well. Pitch the yeast when the temperature of the wort is about 70 degrees F (21 C). Ferment at about 70 degrees F (21 C) for about 1 week or when fermentation shows signs of calming and stopping.

Prime with sugar and bottle or keg when fermentation is complete.

### Coriandered Mild Brown Ale

Let's not forget thirst and refreshment and the pride of brewing a wonderfully complex 4 percent ale full of hop and malt personality. These are the kind of beers you remember because you'll spend more time enjoying more pints and quarts (minding your p's and q's, as they used to say) of them. These are beers brewed to enjoy while sharing conversation.

For sure I recognize that existing customers love big, bold, wonderful beers and there's a need for brewing them. I love them too, on occasion. This beer is brewed for the beer drinker who would rather have two or three beers than one strong beer.

You don't have to drift away from the triumph of flavor and diversity. Here's a brew that is a refreshing, moderately floral-spicy brown ale that'll go down easy quart after pint.

Ingredients for 5 gallons (19 l):

|  |  |
|---|---|
| 3½ lbs.(1.6 kg) | very light malt extract syrup or 2.8 lbs. (1.3 kg) very light dried malt extract |
| 1½ lbs. (680 g) | wheat malt extract syrup |
| ¾ lb. (340 g) | crystal malt (40 L) |
| ¼ lb. (113 g) | chocolate malt |

| ¾ oz. (21 g) | Vanguard or Brewers Gold hops (boiling): 3.75 HBU (105 MBU) |
| ¾ oz. (21 g) | Glacier or UK Goldings hops (30 minutes, flavor/aroma): 4.5 HBU (26 MBU) |
| 1 oz. (28 g) | Mt. Hood or Crystal hops (10 minutes, finishing/aroma) |
| 1¼ oz. (35 g) | freshly crushed coriander seeds |
| ¼ tsp. (1 g) | Irish moss powder |
| * | your favorite ale yeast or White Labs Cry Havoc yeast |
| ¾ cup (175 ml) | corn sugar (for bottling) or ⅓ c. (80 ml) corn sugar (for kegging) |

O.G.: 1.038–1.042 (9–10)
F.G.: 1.008–1.012 (2–3)
Bitterness: 25 BU; Color 15 SRM (30 EBC); Alcohol: 4% by volume

Add the crushed crystal and chocolate malts to 2 gallons (7.5 l) of water and let steep at 150 to 160 degrees F (65–71 C) for 30 minutes, then remove the grains with a strainer. Sparge with hot water and collect the liquid extract in your brewpot. Add the malt extracts and boiling hops and boil for 60 minutes. Add the flavor/aroma hops for the last 30 minutes of the boil. Add the finishing/aroma hops, Irish moss, and coriander seed for the last 10 minutes of the boil. Turn off the heat. Strain, sparge, and transfer immediately to 2 gallons (7.5 l) of cold water in the fermenter. Top off with additional water to make 5 gallons (19 l). Aerate the wort very well. Pitch the yeast when the temperature of the wort is about 70 degrees F (21 C). Ferment at about 70 degrees F (21 C) for about 1 week or when fermentation shows signs of calming and stopping.

Prime with sugar and bottle or keg when fermentation is complete. You only have to meander for a short time. This one can be ready to drink 10 to 12 days from brewday.

### Cherries in the Snow

A sinfully unique combination of sour cherries, malt extract, a mild blend of hops, and patient aging conspires to celebrate the rites of spring with the luscious memories of summers past.

The acidity of sour cherries slices through the subtle malt sweetness to awaken the palate's winter remorse. Cherries in the Snow nonchalantly hints at a Belgium Kriek, a style of beer brewed with sweet cherries, malt, and a lactobacillus bacteria for tartness. However, the tartness of Cherries in the Snow is not as explosive as a Belgium Kriek, lambic, or Gueuze (all sour-fermented beers); rather, it hints gently of a crisp tartness, inspiring a call for more. The hops are subtle, not bitter, yet flavorful in the style of an awakening spring.

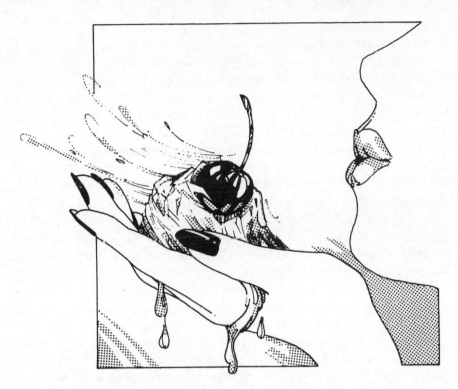

As does a good wine, Cherries in the Snow offers a wonderful potential to mature beautifully with age (years), to be called forth for unscripted special occasions. The last bottle of the original batch of this beer was 20 years old when we tried it! Wow! Did this beer ever turn some heads! It was fantastic, and the magnum bottle of the stuff was enjoyed by all. Now I don't figure you'll keep your beer around for 20 years, but I simply lost track of the bottle for a while. In this case, that was a good thing.

Ingredients for 5 gallons (19 l):

| | |
|---|---|
| 8½ lbs. (3.9 kg) | light malt extract syrup |
| 1½ oz. (42 g) | Santiam or Tettnang hop pellets (boiling): 9 HBU (250 MBU) |
| ½ oz. (14 g) | Santiam, Mt. Hood, or Tettnang hops (aroma/finishing) |
| 10 lbs. (4.5 kg) | sour cherries, crushed to break the skins and open the fruit (do not crush pits) |
| ¼ tsp. (1 g) | Irish moss powder |
| * | American ale–type yeast or White Labs Cry Havoc yeast |
| ¾ c. (175 ml) | sugar (for bottling) or ⅓ c. (80 ml) corn sugar (for kegging) |

O.G.: 1.060–1.064 (14.7–15.7)
F.G.: 1.012–1.016 (3–4)
Bitterness: 28 BU; Color: rose; Alcohol: 6.3% by volume

Add the malt extract and boiling hops to 1½ gallons (5.7 l) of water and boil for 60 minutes. Add the Irish moss for the last 10 minutes of the boil. Then use a strainer to remove as much of the boiling hops as you are able to do without worrying. Rinse/sparge those hops with some hot water to get all the good stuff out and back into the brewpot. Remove the brewpot from the heat, then add the crushed sour cherries and aroma/finishing hops to the boiled wort. The cherries should cool the wort to a temperature of about 160 degrees F (71 C). Let the cherries steep for a good 15 minutes at a temperature between 160 and 180 degrees F (71–88 C). These temperatures will pasteurize the cherried wort. Do not boil, as boiling will set the pectin in the fruit and create a (harmless) haze in the finished beer.

After the cherried wort has steeped for 15 minutes, pour the entire contents of the wort (without sparging) into a sanitized plastic 7- to 10-gallon (26.5–38 l) fermenter with cold water to make 5 gallons (19 l).

Aerate the wort very well. Pitch the yeast when the temperature of the wort is about 70 degrees F (21 C). Ferment at about 70 degrees F (21 C) for about 1 week or when fermentation shows signs of calming and stopping.

After 5 days of primary fermentation, carefully remove as much of the floating hops and cherries from the fermenter as humanly possible. REMEMBER: *Be sure that the strainer you use is sanitized* by boiling it and then immersing it briefly in a sanitizing solution. Rinse any sanitizing solution off with hot tap water.

After you have removed much of the floating debris, rack (siphon) the beer into a secondary fermenter. You will notice sediment of spent cherries and hops. Avoid siphoning this sediment. Don't worry, but be careful—the pits can create one hell of a nuisance once they get into your siphon hose. Attach an air lock to the secondary fermenter and continue with fermentation until the beer begins to show signs of clarity. Prime with sugar and bottle or keg when fermentation is complete.

Age and serve chilled. It is even appropriate to add ice cubes to Cherries in the Snow.

You deserve an embrace and a kiss for brewing this one!

## Cherry Fever Stout

*"The best beer you've ever made."* —A.W.

The combination of cherries and stout is an experience too wonderful for any homebrewer to miss. If you like stout, this brew will cheer your very soul.

Its velvety roasted malt character, already perfectly balanced with a pungent bitterness offered by Northern Brewer hops, is wholly blessed with the soft kiss of ripe cherries. The complex blend of sweetness, bitterness, and cherry tang is euphorically pursued with a fragrance of hops and cherry fever. Personally, it is my favorite stout to brew and enjoy—chilled in the heat of summer or at room temperature in the coldest of winter.

I have a difficult time describing the essence of this brew; so for now, at least until you've brewed it yourself, let it suffice to say Cherry Fever Stout is delightfully fine!

P.S. You can substitute red ripe raspberries and make an equally cosmic brew!

Ingredients for 5 gallons (19 l):

| | |
|---|---|
| 6.6 lbs. (3 kg) | John Bull or other brand of plain dark malt extract syrup |
| 1 lb. (450 g) | dark dried malt extract |
| 1 lb. (450 g) | crystal malt (10 L) |
| ½ lb. (225 g) | roasted barley |
| ½ lb. (225 g) | black malt |
| 1½ oz. (42 g) | Northern Brewer or Perle hops (boiling): 13 HBU (365 MBU) |
| ½ oz. (14 g) | Citra, Amarillo, New Zealand Nelson Sauvin, or Pacific Gem hops (aroma/finishing) |
| 4 tsp. (16 g) | gypsum |
| 3 lbs. (1.4 kg) | sour cherries, crushed to break the skins and open the fruit (do not crush pits) |
| 2 lbs. (900 g) | choke cherries, crushed to break the skins and open the fruit (do not crush pits) OR, if not available, substitute with 2 more lbs. of sour cherries |
| ¼ tsp. (1 g) | Irish moss powder |
| * | American ale–type yeast or White Labs Cry Havoc yeast |
| ¾ c. (175 ml) | sugar (for bottling) or ⅓ c. (80 ml) corn sugar (for kegging) |
| 5 gallons (19 l) | uncontrollable anticipation |

O.G.: 1.064–1.068 (16–16.5)
F.G.: 1.016–1.020 (4.5–6.5)
Bitterness: 35 BU; Color: 50 SRM (100 EBC); Alcohol: 6.3% by volume

Add the crushed crystal malt, black malt, and roasted barley to 1½ gallons (5.7 l) of water and let steep at 150 to 160 degrees F (65–71 C) for 30 minutes, then remove the grains with a strainer. Add the malt extracts, gypsum, and boiling hops and boil for 60 minutes. Add the Irish moss for the last 10 minutes of the boil. Then use a strainer to remove as much of the boiling hops as you are able to do without worrying. Rinse/sparge those hops with some hot water to get all the good stuff out and back into the brewpot. Then add the 5 pounds (2.3 kg) of crushed cherries to the boiling wort. The cherries should cool the wort to a temperature of about 160 degrees F (71 C). Let the cherries steep for a good 15 minutes at a temperature between 160 and 180 degrees F (71–88 C). These temperatures will pasteurize the cherried wort. Do not boil, as boiling will set the pectin in the fruit and will create a (harmless) haze in the finished beer.

After the cherried wort has steeped for 15 minutes, add the aroma/finishing hops and then pour the entire contents of the wort (without sparging) into a sanitized 7- to 10-gallon (26.5–38 l) plastic fermenter with cold water to make 5 gallons (19 l).

Aerate the wort very well. Pitch the yeast when the temperature of the wort is about 70 degrees F (21 C). Ferment at about 70 degrees F (21 C) for about 1 week or when fermentation shows signs of calming and stopping.

After 5 days of primary fermentation, carefully remove as much of the floating hops and cherries from the fermenter as humanly possible. REMEMBER: *Be sure that the strainer you use is sanitized* by boiling it and then immersing it briefly in a sanitizing solution. Rinse any sanitizing solution off with hot tap water.

After you have removed much of the floating debris, rack (siphon) the beer into a secondary fermenter. You will notice sediment of spent cherries and hops. Avoid siphoning this sediment. Don't worry, but be careful—the pits can create one hell of a nuisance once they get into your siphon hose. Attach an air lock to the secondary fermenter and continue with fermentation until the beer begins to show signs of clarity. Prime with sugar and bottle or keg when fermentation is complete.

### Holiday Cheer

This creation for the spirit of the holiday season is much better for you than a fruitcake.

Unusual as this recipe may be, if you think that you will enjoy it—brew it. This basic recipe has won the hearts of many, and prizes, too. Another one of the top five most popular recipes in this book.

Ingredients for 5 gallons (19 l):

| | |
|---|---|
| 7 lbs. (3.2 kg) | plain light malt extract |
| 1 lb. (450 g) | light honey (clover or alfalfa) |
| ½ lb. (225 g) | crystal malt (10 L) |
| 2 oz. (56 g) | Cascade hops (boiling): 10 HBU (280 MBU) |
| ½ oz. (14 g) | Saaz, Sterling, or Santiam hops (aroma/finishing) |
| 1 oz. (28 g) | grated fresh ginger |

| 6 in. (15 cm) | stick of cinnamon or 3 tsp. (10 g) ground cinnamon grated orange zest from 4 organic oranges |
| ¼ tsp. (1 g) | Irish moss powder |
| * | American ale–type yeast or White Labs Cry Havoc yeast |
| ¾ c. (175 ml) | sugar (for bottling) or ⅓ c. (80 ml) corn sugar (for kegging) |

O.G.: 1.054–1.060 (13.5–15)
F.G.: 1.016–1.20 (4.5–6.5)
Bitterness: 27 BU; Color: 14 SRM (28 EBC); Alcohol: 5.3% by volume

Add the crushed crystal and black malts to 1½ gallons (5.7 l) of water and let steep at 150 to 160 degrees F (65–71 C) for 30 minutes, then remove the grains with a strainer. Add the malt extract, honey, and boiling hops and boil for 60 minutes. Add the Irish moss, ginger, cinnamon, and orange zest and continue to boil for the last 10 minutes. Add the aroma/finishing hops during the final 1 minute of the boil. Strain, sparge, and transfer immediately to 2 gallons (7.5 l) of cold water in the fermenter. Top off with additional water to make 5 gallons (19 l).

Aerate the wort very well. Pitch the yeast when the temperature of the wort is about 70 degrees F (21 C). Ferment at about 70 degrees F (21 C) for about 1 week or when fermentation shows signs of calming and stopping.

Prime with sugar and bottle or keg when fermentation is complete.

## O Golpe Yarrow Ale

And now for something completely different, but uncompromisingly good. O Golpe Yarrow Ale is a traditional ale recipe brewed by brewers throughout Europe before hops were popularized. Grab yourself a good herbal book (*Sacred Herbal and Healing Beers,* Stephen Buhner, Brewers Publications) and learn about the health-giving properties of yarrow. Use mostly fresh flowers and some greens for best results. And no, there isn't a mistake in this recipe—there are no hops. Not quite sure about this kinky concept? Well then, brew a small batch and prepare yourself to wait for the next season of flowering yarrow to brew a full batch.

Ingredients for 3 gallons (11.5 l):

| | |
|---|---|
| 3 lbs. (1.4 kg) | extra-light dried malt extract |
| ¼ lb. (113 g) | fresh yarrow flowers |
| 1 oz. (28 g) | fresh yarrow leaves |
| 0.8 g | sweet gale (myrica) (available at homebrew shops) |
| * | American ale–type yeast or White Labs Cry Havoc yeast |
| ½ c. (140 ml) | corn sugar (for bottling) |

Add the malt extract, sweet gale, and 2 oz. (56 g) of yarrow to 1½ gallons (5.7 l) of water and boil for 60 minutes. Add the remaining 2 oz. (56 g) yarrow flowers during the final 5 minutes of the boil. Strain, sparge, and transfer immediately to 1 gallon (4 l) of cold water in the fermenter. Top off with additional water to make 3 gallons (11.5 l).

Aerate the wort very well. Pitch the yeast when the temperature of the wort is about 70 degrees F (21 C). Ferment at about 70 degrees F (21 C) for about 1 week or when fermentation shows signs of calming and stopping.

Prime with sugar and bottle or keg when fermentation is complete. Chill when carbonated, pour a glass, and be prepared to be speechless.

## RESOURCES FOR 63 MALT EXTRACT RECIPES

Other malt extract recipes can be found in *Microbrewed Adventures, The Homebrewer's Companion, Second Edition,* and *Home Brewer's Gold.*

### MALT EXTRACT RECIPES IN *MICROBREWED ADVENTURES*:

Samuel Adams 1880
George Killian's Irish Red Ale from Pellforth
1447 Belgium Zwarte Rose Ale
Irish Cocoa Wood Porter
Andech's Weekday Bock
Original Dogbolter Ale—Goose & Firkin

Puritanical Nut Brown Ale
Beyond the Ordinary Ordinary Bitter
"Original" Ballard Bitter
Belgian-Style Cherry–Black Currant (Kriek-Cassis) Lambic
Magic Bolo #9.1
Crazy Old Man Altbier
65-65-65-65 India Pale Ale
Telluride India Pale Ale
MickViRay Papazian Pilsener
Swakapmund Cowboy Lager
1982 Original Sierra Nevada Pale Ale
Piozzo Italian Pale Ale
1981 Boulder Christmas Stout
Bert Grant's Planet Imperial Stout
Brooklyn's Original Chocolate Stout
Felicitous Stout
Jeff Bagby's Hop Whompus 2004
John 1981—a homebrewed version of Charlie 1981
Monastic Bleue Strong Belgian-Style Ale
Old Lighthouse in the Fog Barleywine Ale
Stone 03 Vertical Epic
19th-Century Leipziger Gose
Alaskan Winter Spruce Old Ale
Frog & Rosbif's Brown Wheat Coriander
Mile-High Green Chile Ale
Hans Weissbier
Original Pyramid Wheaten Ale

## MALT EXTRACT RECIPES IN *THE HOMEBREWER'S COMPANION, SECOND EDITION*:

Tits Up in the Mud Best Bitter
BaBaBa Bo Amber Ale
Belgian Tickle (Honey Ale)
Colorado Cowgirl's American Brown Ale
Unspoken Passion Raspberry Imperial Stout
Topple-Over Anise-thetic Brown Ale
Frumentacious Framboise
Get Rio All-Malt Light Lager

## MALT EXTRACT RECIPES IN *HOME BREWER'S GOLD*:

Aventinus, Private Weissbierbrauerei G. Schneider & Son K.G.,
    Munich, Germany

Capstone ESB, Oasis Brewery, Boulder, Colorado USA

Cascade Pale Ale, Cascade Brewery, Hobart, Tasmania, Australia

Delaney's Ale, South China Brewing Co. Ltd, Aberdeen, Hong Kong

Dos Equis Special Lager, Cerveceria Cuauhtémoc, Monterrey, Mexico

Edelweiss Dunkel, Österreichische Bräu-Aktiengesellschaft, Linz, Austria

Founders Stout, Mishawaka Brewing Co., Mishawaka, Indiana USA

Griffon Extra Pale Ale, McAuslan Brewing Inc., Montreal, Quebec Canada

Hoegaarden, Brouwerij de Kluis, Hoegaarden, Belgium

Mackeson XXX Stout, Whitbread Beer Co., London, England

Miller Lite, Miller Brewing Co., Milwaukee, Wisconsin USA

Ozone Ale, Hubcap Brewery/Brewing Co. of Vail, Vail, Colorado USA

Pauwel Kwak, Brewery Bosteels, Buggenhout, Belgium

Point Amber Lager, Barton Beers Ltd., Chicago, Illinois USA

Redwood Coast Brown, Redwood Coast Brewing Co., Alameda, California USA

Ruddles Best Bitter, Ruddles Brewery, Rutland, England

Slow Down Brown Ale, Il Vicino Inc., Albuquerque, New Mexico USA

Snake River Pale Ale, Snake River Brewing Co., Inc., Jackson, Wyoming USA

Star Brew 1000 (Wheat Wine), Marin Brewing Co., Larkspur, California USA

Stoddards ESB, Stoddard's Brewhouse and Eatery, Sunnyvale, California USA

Sundance Hefe-Weizen, Palmer Lake Brewing Co., Palmer Lake, Colorado USA

Wet Mountain India Pale Ale, Il Vicino, Salida, Colorado USA

## INTRODUCTION TO GRAIN BREWING FOR THE MALT EXTRACT HOMEBREWER

Don't let anyone ever fool you into thinking that homebrew made from malt extract is inferior to homebrew made from all grain. With the quality of ingredients, yeast, and techniques available today, premium quality can be made either way. I started brewing in 1970 and still homebrew using both techniques. Time is the factor I consider when choosing which way to brew. I love to spend more time brewing and that's often why I prefer making all-grain homebrew. But when I don't have enough time or a favorite beer just so happens to be a malt extract recipe, I brew extract beer. And to tell you the truth, after it's all in the bottle or kegs and I'm enjoying my efforts, I can't recall which beer was made which way.

Keep this in mind and don't be intimated into thinking extract is inferior. Yes, it is simple. Yes, you still are a homebrewer. And yes, your beer will shine-blast excellent quality.

But perhaps you find your homebrew passion is out of control. You have a fermenting desire to learn more. You have been bitten. You are intrigued. Well, then, the world of beer has just opened up for you. Welcome. Let's dispel some of the mysticism.

Indeed, the alchemy of converting starch molecules to fermentable sugars with the aid of little "critters" called enzymes ultimately romances every home-brewer. With missionary zeal you may experience conversion! All-grain fanatics will tell you how much better their beer is, . . . . . . and then you watch, you read, you try to discover what all the brew-haha is all about. With so much information and so many opinions, it's easy to become overwhelmed at the unlimited possibilities, the limitless opportunity to improvise, to manipulate, to fashion your own specialized equipment.

But hey, wait a minute. Not so fast. Hold your donkeys. What if you're a malt extract brewer who is basically content but simply wants to begin your grain journey by dabbling in mash-mysticism in order to understand a little bit more? Experiencing the mysteries of enzyme conversion and knowing that there are other horizons in the world of brewing is enlightenment. Let's ease into this with gentle passion and go from there.

Relax. Don't worry. Have a homebrew.

## MASH-EXTRACT TRANSITION BREWS

Introduction to the world of grain brewing can be very simple, painless, and rewarding. The recipes that follow are a combination of malt extract and grain mash. They serve to increase your flexibility and offer you more diversity, while maintaining the quality of your homebrew. It's a phenom that will introduce you to the unlimited brewing versatility achievable with the use of grains.

Essentially, your introduction to all-grain brewing will be by mashing a small and very manageable amount of malted barley and other grains. The sweet liquid wort that you produce by converting starches to sugars is added to malt extract syrups or dry powders; from then on, the brewing process used in malt extract brewing continues without change.

This method offers some very significant advantages:

1. Mash-extract brewing retains the simplicity of malt extract brewing while developing your confidence and offering a sane introduction to new ingredients and the process of all-grain brewing.

2. Mash-extract brewing introduces you to enhanced flavors that can be achieved with care and understanding that all-grain brewing can and should inspire.
3. You can learn how to mash your own grains without additional equipment or boiling huge and perhaps unwieldy volumes of wort.

A detailed theory of mashing and using grains is covered later in "Advanced Homebrewing for the Practical Homebrewer," page 285. This section will briefly introduce the theory of mashing and basic homebrewing-mashing procedures. Be aware that there are many methods used to convert and mash grains to fermentable sugars. The method used in this introduction is purposefully presented because of its simplicity, instructional potential, and the absence of special equipment.

## A SHORT COURSE ON THEORY

Mashing converts the soluble starch in grain to fermentable sugars and unfermentable "dextrins," each of which present in most styles of beer wort. There are starch-to-sugar-converting "diastatic" enzymes in malted barley. These enzymes will become active under proper conditions. When the temperature of a water-and-malted-barley "soup" reaches a certain range, the enzymes become active and literally break starch molecules into sugar molecules. Malted barley usually has more than enough enzymes to convert its own starches to sugars and convert measured amounts of additional soluble starches (adjuncts such as cooked rice, wheat, corn, barley, oats, etc.) to fermentable sugars.

For the mash-extract brewer, the seemingly magical sweet liquor that is produced from the following procedures is combined with malt extract and boiled with other beer ingredients.

## MASH-EXTRACT EQUIPMENT AND PROCEDURE

### Equipment
For a 5-gallon (19 l) batch you will need:

1. A 4- to 5-gallon brewpot.
2. A means of crushing the grain. If preground malted barley is unavailable you may find it necessary to purchase a grain or flour mill in order to grind your grains. Many homebrew supply shops have a grain mill for their customers. The grinding plates of your mill should be set so that the grains are crushed or, rather, cracked into small pieces. They should retain their integrity as pieces rather than be pulverized

to flour. The grinding should suffice to break the husks away from the grain.

3. A lauter-tun. This can be no more than a strainer that will have the capacity to hold the amount of grains that you mash and sparge. There are many varieties available in homebrew shops. If unavailable in your area, a clean 4–5-gallon (15–19 l) food-grade plastic bucket can be easily converted into a lauter-tun by drilling hundreds of 1/8-inch holes in the bottom; there you have a homemade strainer, sparger, lauter-tun.

4. Tincture of iodine. This will be used to test for starch conversion.

## Procedure

1. The grains are crushed.
2. Water and minerals (if called for) are added to the crushed grains.
3. The temperature may be raised to between 113–133 degrees F (45–56 C) and held for 30 minutes. This is called a protein rest and develops nutrients for the yeast and better beer head retention.
4. The temperature is raised and held at temperatures between 150 and 158 degrees F (65–70 C) and held for 30 minutes. This develops fermentable sugars and some unfermentable dextrins (dextrins contribute body to beer).
5. An iodine test is made to confirm that starch has been converted to sugars and dextrins: A drop of tincture of iodine in a starch solution will turn purple/black. If starch is not present, the iodine will not turn black. This test is simply done by removing a tablespoon of converted mash and pouring it onto a clean, cool, or room-temperature white plate. A drop of iodine into the solution will indicate whether conversion has been achieved.
6. Strain and sparge grains to retrieve sweet wort and separate from spent grains. The sweet wort is destined for your brewpot. You will need an extra bucket or pot. A plastic fermenter can also be used for this purpose.
7. Add malt extracts, hops, and other ingredients and continue to brew.
8. Relax. Don't worry. Have a homebrew.

## 12 MASH-EXTRACT RECIPES

Light Amber Lagers and Ales

Dark Beers

Strong Ales and Lagers

Specialty Beers

## LIGHT AMBER LAGERS AND ALES

### Top Drop German Pilsener

This brew offers a hopotheosislike resemblance to German light-lagered pilseners, but there is a big difference. Your homebrew will have a wonderful and mellow hop floral character because you are using the complete essence of the hops and not just its bitterness. I guarantee you will like this beer better than anything you're paying good money for. With a touch of sweetness, thirst-quenching medium-light body, and a gorgeous hop floral aroma this beer will let you continue to marvel at yourself even after you admire the attractively creamy head.

Ingredients for 5 gallons (19 l):

| | |
|---|---|
| 3 lbs. (1.4 kg) | extra-light dried malt extract |
| 3½ lbs. (1.6 kg) | pilsener-type malted barley |
| ½ lb. (225 g) | aromatic malt |
| 2 oz. (56 g) | German Saphir, Hallertauer Mittelfrüh, or Hallertau hops (boiling): 10 HBU (280 MBU) |
| ½ oz. (14 g) | American Liberty hops (boiling): 2.6 HBU (73 MBU) |
| ½ oz. (14 g) | Santiam hops (2 minutes, aroma/finishing) |
| ½ oz. (14 g) | Crystal hop pellets (dry hopping) |
| ¼ tsp. (1 g) | Irish moss powder |
| * | Czech- or German-type pilsener lager yeast or White Labs Cry Havoc yeast |

¾ c. (175 ml)   sugar (for bottling) or ⅓ c. (80 ml) corn sugar
         (for kegging)


O.G.: 1.048–1.052 (12–13)
F.G.: 1.010–1.014 (2.5–3.5)
Bitterness: 43 BU; Color: 6 SRM (12 EBC); Alcohol: 5% by volume


Add the crushed malted barley and aromatic malt to 4 quarts (4 l) of 140-degree F (60 C) water and mix well. The temperature will stabilize between 130 and 135 degrees F (54.5–57 C). Add heat if necessary and hold the temperature at about 133 degrees F (56 C) for 30 minutes. Don't worry about a 3- to 5-degree F (2–3 C) temperature drop during this time.

Then add 2 quarts (2 l) of boiling water to this mash. This will raise the temperature to about or just below 155 degrees F (68 C). Hold at 149 to 155 degrees F (65–68 C) for 30 minutes, stirring occasionally. Complete conversion by raising the temperature to 158 degrees F (70 C) and holding for 10 to 20 minutes or until an iodine test indicates complete conversion. Then add more heat to raise the temperature to 167 degrees F (75 C). Then pour your mash into your lauter-tun and sparge with 2 gallons (7.5 l) of hot water at 170 degrees F (76 C). The sweet wort ends in your brewpot.

Bring the sweet wort to a boil and add the malt extract and boiling hops and continue to boil for 60 minutes. Add the Irish moss for the final 10 minutes of the boil. Add the finishing/flavor hops for the final 2 minutes of the boil. Strain, sparge, and transfer immediately to 2 gallons (7.5 l) of cold water in the fermenter. Top off with additional water to make 5 gallons (19 l). Aerate the wort very well. Pitch the yeast when the temperature of the wort is about 70 degrees F (21 C). Ferment at about 70 degrees F (21 C) for about 1 week or when fermentation shows signs of calming and stopping.

If you have the capacity to primary ferment at about 55 degrees F (13 C), then add the yeast at about 70 degrees F (21 C) and once you see visible signs of fermentation, drop the temperature to 55 degrees F (13 C). Regardless of what temperature you ferment at, after primary fermentation is complete and there is little sign of fermentation activity, transfer the beer to a closed secondary fermenter, add ½ ounce (14 g) Crystal hop pellets and lager at temperatures between 35 and 55 degrees F (2–13 C) for 3 to 5 weeks. Prime with sugar and bottle or keg the beer after lagering. Let condition at room temperature for about a week before storing at colder temperatures.

And remember: If you don't have the capacity to cold ferment, Top Drop German Pilsener will still be an excellent beer bottled right after fermentation is complete.

## Daisy Mae Czech Lager

Daisy Mae and Daisy may not. To get to Daisy, it takes a lot!

An exceptionally fine light Czech-style lager alludes to the traditional and authentic Bohemian character. A rich golden luster is imparted to the brew by the toasted aromatic malt, while the bitterness and sweetness melt into Daisy Mae's full body and rich creamy head. This deliciously satisfying beer is worth brewing in any season. *Na zdraví.*

Ingredients for 5 gallons (19 l):

| | |
|---|---|
| 3 lbs. (1.4 kg) | pilsener-type malted barley |
| 4½ lbs. (2 kg) | extra light malt extract syrup |
| ½ lb. (225 g) | aromatic malt |
| 1¼ oz. (35 g) | Czech Saaz hops (boiling): 5 HBU (140 MBU) |
| ½ oz. (14 g) | Czech Saaz hops (5 minutes, flavor/aroma/finishing) |
| ¾ oz. (21 g) | Czech Saaz or Crystal hop pellets (dry hopping) |
| ¼ tsp. (1 g) | Irish moss powder |
| * | Bohemian/Czech lager–type yeast or White Labs Cry Havoc yeast |
| ¾ c. (175 ml) | sugar (for bottling) or ⅓ c. (80 ml) corn sugar (for kegging) |

O.G.: 1.048–1.052 (12–13)
F.G.: 1.010–1.014 (2.5–3.5)
Bitterness: 43 BU; Color: 6 SRM (12 EBC); Alcohol: 4.7% by volume

Add the crushed malted barley and aromatic malt to 3½ quarts (3.5 l) of 140-degree F (60 C) water and mix well. The temperature will stabilize between 130 and 135 degrees F (54.5–57 C). Add heat if necessary and hold the temperature at about 133 degrees F (56 C) for 30 minutes. Don't worry about a 3- to 5-degree F (2–3 C) temperature drop during this time.

Then add 1½ quarts (1.5 l) of boiling water to this mash. This will raise the temperature to about or just below 155 degrees F (68 C). Hold at 149 to 155 degrees F (65–68 C) for 30 minutes, stirring occasionally. Complete conversion by raising the temperature to 158 degrees F (70 C) and holding for 10 to 20 minutes or until an iodine test indicates complete conversion. Then add more heat to raise the temperature to 167 degrees F (75 C). Then pour your mash into your lauter-tun and sparge with 7 quarts (6.5 l) of hot water at 170 degrees F (76 C). The sweet wort ends in your brewpot.

Bring the sweet wort to a boil and add malt extract and boiling hops and boil for 60 minutes. Add the Irish moss during the final 10 minutes of the boil. Add the finishing hops during the final 5 minutes of the boil. Strain, sparge, and transfer immediately to 2 gallons (7.5 l) of cold water in the fermenter. Top off with additional water to make 5 gallons (19 l). Aerate the wort very well. Pitch the yeast when the temperature of the wort is about 70 degrees F (21 C). Ferment at about 70 degrees F (21 C) for about 1 week or when fermentation shows signs of calming and stopping.

If you have the capacity to primary ferment at about 55 degrees F (13 C), then add the yeast at about 70 degrees F (21 C) and once you see visible signs of fermentation drop the temperature to 55 degrees F (13 C). Regardless of what temperature you ferment at, after primary fermentation is complete and there is little sign of fermentation activity, transfer the beer to a closed secondary fermenter, add the hop pellets and lager at temperatures between 35 and 55 degrees F (2–13 C) for 3 to 5 weeks. Prime with sugar and bottle the beer after lagering. Let condition at room temperature for about a week before storing at colder temperatures.

And remember: If you don't have the capacity to cold ferment, Daisy will still be an excellent beer bottled right after fermentation is complete.

## What the Helles Münchner

What the Helles Münchner lager is the stuff of liters. For all of you who have been and all of you who will go and all of you who wish you could go, under a village big tent at a midsummer's fest or indoors at the Höfbrauhaus in Munich, liters and liters of this golden nectar are consumed all over southern Germany.

A mildly hoppy and extremely drinkable lager, Helles is best served on draft at chilled temperatures to express smooth carbonation and maltiness. The secret is in using fresh hops of German origin or hybrids thereof and infusing them at various points during the boil. And not overdoing the bitterness. Cold fermentation will further enhance the exceptionally true tradition of this jovial German lager.

Ingredients for 5 gallons (19 l):

| | |
|---|---|
| 3 lbs. (1.4 kg) | 2-row American or German pale malted barley |
| 4 lbs. (1.8 kg) | extra-light dried malt extract |
| ¾ oz. (21 g) | Hallertauer Hersbruck, Hersbrucker Mittelfrüh, Hallertauer Hallertau hops, or any combination of these (boiling): 4.5 HBU (126 MBU) |
| ½ oz. (14 g) | Hallertauer Hersbruck, Hallertau, or Saphir hops (30 minutes, flavor): 2.5 HBU (70 MBU) |
| 1 oz. (28 g) | American Tettnang or Mt. Hood hops, or a combination of these (5 minutes, aroma) |
| ½ oz. (14 g) | American Crystal hop pellets (dry hopping) |
| ¼ tsp. (1 g) | Irish moss powder |
| * | German lager–type yeast or White Labs Cry Havoc yeast |
| ¾ c. (175 ml) | sugar (for bottling) or ⅓ c. (80 ml) corn sugar (for kegging) |

O.G.: 1.048–1.052 (12–13)
F.G.: 1.010–1.014 (2.5–3.5)
Bitterness: 24 BU; Color: 4 SRM (8 EBC); Alcohol: 4.7%

Add the crushed malted barley to 3 quarts (3 l) of 140-degree F (60 C) water and mix well. The temperature will stabilize between 130 and 135 degrees F (54.5–57 C). Add heat if necessary and hold the temperature at about 133 degrees F (56 C) for 30 minutes. Don't worry about a 3- to 5-degree F (2–3 C) temperature drop during this time.

Then add 1½ quarts (1.5 l) of boiling water to this mash. This will raise the temperature to about or just below 155 degrees F (68 C). Hold at 149 to 155 degrees F (65–68 C) for 45 minutes, stirring occasionally. Then add more heat to raise the temperature to 167 degrees F (75 C). Then pour your mash into your lauter-tun and sparge with 6 quarts (6 l) of hot water at 170 degrees F (76 C). The sweet wort ends in your brewpot.

Bring the sweet wort to a boil and add the malt extract and boiling hops and continue to boil for 60 minutes. Add the flavor hops for the last 30 minutes of the boil. Add the Irish moss for the last 10 minutes of the boil. Add the aroma hops for the last 5 minutes of the boil. Strain, sparge, and transfer immediately to 2 gallons (7.5 l) of cold water in the fermenter. Top off with additional water to make 5 gallons (19 l). Aerate the wort very well. Pitch the yeast when the temperature of the wort is about 70 degrees F (21 C). Ferment at about 70 degrees F (21 C) for about 1 week or when fermentation shows signs of calming and stopping.

If you have the capacity to primary ferment at about 55 degrees F (13 C), then add the yeast at about 70 degrees F (21 C) and once you see visible signs of fermentation drop the temperature to 55 degrees F (13 C). Regardless of what temperature you ferment at, after primary fermentation is complete, and there is little sign of fermentation activity, transfer the beer to a closed secondary fermenter, add ½ ounce (14 g) Crystal hop pellets and lager at temperatures between 35 and 55 degrees F (2–13 C) for 3 to 4 weeks. Prime with sugar and bottle the beer after lagering. Let condition at room temperature for about a week before storing at colder temperatures.

And remember: If you don't have the capacity to cold ferment, Helles will still be paradise bottled right after fermentation is complete.

## Laughing Heart India Pale Ale

A rich, white, creamy head contrasts eloquently with the very deep copper-gold transparency of this well-hopped but softly balanced ale. The generous amount of hops adds an assertive bitterness, yet the equally generous amount of crystal malt brings the crescendo of bitterness to a soft alluring finale with full body and sweetness. A rich brew for the beer drinkers who enjoy having a hunka-hunka burning love affair with their beer.

Ingredients for 5 gallons (19 l):

| | |
|---|---|
| 4 lbs. (1.8 kg) | plain light dried malt extract |
| 3½ lbs. (1.6 kg) | pale malted barley |
| ½ lb. (225 g) | dark crystal malt (40 L) |
| ½ lb. (225 g) | aromatic malt |
| 2 tsp. (8 g) | gypsum |
| 1½ oz. (42 g) | Centennial or Chinook hops (boiling): 15 HBU (420 MBU) |
| ½ oz. (28 g) | Amarillo hops (5 minutes, flavor/aroma/finishing) |
| ½ oz. (28 g) | Columbus or Simcoe hops (5 minutes, flavor/aroma/finishing) |
| ½ oz. (14 g) | Australian Galaxy or New Zealand Mouteka hop pellets (dry hopping) |
| ¼ tsp. (1 g) | Irish moss powder |
| * | American ale–type yeast or White Labs Cry Havoc yeast |
| ¾ c. (175 ml) | sugar (for bottling) or ⅓ c. (80 ml) corn sugar (for kegging) |

O.G.: 1.058–1.062 (14.3–15)
F.G.: 1.014–1.020 (4.5–6.5)
Bitterness: about 42 BU; Color: 12 SRM (24 EBC); Alcohol: 5% by volume

Add the crushed malted barley, crystal and aromatic malts to 4½ quarts (4.5 l) of 140-degree F (60 C) water and mix well. The temperature will stabilize between 130 and 135 degrees F (54.5–57 C). Add heat if necessary and hold the temperature at about 133 degrees F (56 C) for 30 minutes. Don't worry about a 3- to 5-degree F (2–3 C) temperature drop during this time.

Then add 2½ quarts (2.5 l) of boiling water to this mash. This will raise the temperature to about or just below 155 degrees F (68 C). Hold at 149 to 155 degrees F (65–68 C) for 30 minutes, stirring occasionally. Then add more heat to raise the temperature to 167 degrees F (75 C). Then pour your mash into your lauter-tun and sparge with 2½ gallons (9.5 l) of hot water at 170 degrees F (76 C). The sweet wort ends in your brewpot.

Bring the sweet wort to a boil and add malt extract and boiling hops and continue to boil for 60 minutes. Add the Irish moss for the final 10 minutes of the boil. Add the finishing hops for the final 5 minutes of the boil. Strain, sparge, and transfer immediately to 2 gallons (7.5 l) of cold water in the fermenter. Top off with additional water to make 5 gallons (19 l).

Add the yeast when the temperature of the wort is about 70 degrees F (21 C). Ferment at about 70 degrees F (21 C) for about 1 week or when fermentation shows signs of calming and stopping.

If you have the capacity to primary ferment at about 55 degrees F (13 C), then add the yeast at about 70 degrees F (21 C) and once you see visible signs of fermentation, drop the temperature down to 55 degrees F (13 C). Regardless of what temperature you ferment at, after primary fermentation is complete, and there is little sign of fermentation activity, transfer the beer to a closed secondary fermenter, and add the hop pellets for dry hopping and lager at temperatures between 35 and 55 degrees F (2–13 C) for 3 to 5 weeks. Prime with sugar and bottle the beer after lagering.

## DARK BEERS

### Uckleduckfay Oatmeal Stout

Oatmeal stout was a legendary and almost forgotten stout before its revival by homebrewers and small breweries in America. Uckleduckfay is a lusciously smooth stout with a medium bitterness, an intimate chocolaty finish, and a hint of coffeelike roasted barley. Quaffing pints of oatmeal stout gives one the feeling of nourishment. And why not? It's good for your soul.

Ingredients for 5 gallons (19 l):

| | |
|---|---|
| 3.3 lbs. (1.5 kg) | John Bull or Muntons English-made dark malt extract syrup |
| 4 lbs. (1.8 kg) | 6-row pale malted barley |
| 1 lb. (450 g) | quick (cut and rolled) oats |
| ½ lb. (225 g) | crystal malt (10 L) |
| ½ lb. (225 g) | chocolate malt |

¼ lb. (110 g)  roasted barley
2 oz. (56 g)  Willamette, Glacier, Fuggles, or Goldings hops (boiling):
          10–12 HBU (280–336 MBU)
½ oz. (14 g)  Crystal or Goldings hop pellets (dry hopping)
4 tsp. (16 g)  gypsum
¼ tsp. (1 g)  Irish moss powder
*          American or Irish ale–type yeast
¾ c. (175 ml)  sugar (for bottling) or ⅓ c. (80 ml) corn sugar
          (for kegging)


O.G.: 1.052–1.056 (13–14)
F.G.: 1.012–1.016 (3–4)
Bitterness: 32 BU; Color 31 SRM (62 EBC); Alcohol: 5.3% by volume

Add the crushed malted barley, oats, crystal malt, chocolate malt, and roasted barley to 6 quarts (6 l) of 140-degree F (60 C) water and mix well. The temperature will stabilize between 130 and 135 degrees F (54.5–57 C). Add heat if necessary and hold the temperature at about 133 degrees F (56 C) for 30 minutes. Don't worry about a 3- to 5-degree F (2–3 C) temperature drop during this time.

Then add 3 quarts (3 l) of boiling water to this mash. This will raise the temperature to about or just below 155 degrees F (68 C). Hold at 149–155 degrees F (65–68 C) for 45 minutes, stirring occasionally. Then add more heat to raise the temperature to 167 degrees F (75 C). Then pour your mash into your lauter-tun and sparge with 2 gallons (7.5 l) of hot water at 170 degrees F (76 C). The sweet wort ends in your brewpot.

Bring the sweet wort to a boil and add malt extract and boiling hops and continue to boil for 60 minutes. Add the Irish moss during the final 10 minutes of the boil. When boiling is complete, leave the lid on the pot and immerse the entire pot in a cold water bath/sink to help cool the wort for about 20 minutes. Then strain, sparge, and transfer to 1 gallon (4 l) of cold water in the fermenter. Top off with additional water to make 5 gallons (19 l).

Aerate the wort very well. Pitch the yeast when the temperature of the wort is about 70 degrees F (21 C). Ferment at about 70 degrees F (21 C) for about 1 week or when fermentation shows signs of calming and stopping. Rack from your primary to a secondary and add the hop pellets for dry hopping. If you have the capability, "cellar" the beer at about 55 degrees F (12.5 C) for about 1 week. Prime with sugar and bottle or keg when complete.

### Heaven's Orbit German Dunkel

Well, now, how about a recipe for one of those German-style Dunkels blended with the casual comfort of a Bavarian evening? A soft caress of amber and choc-olate malts coupled with a mild hop flavor helps define the simple yet relaxing quality of this premium-style German Dunkel, called Heaven's Orbit because that is where it will send you.

Ingredients for 5 gallons (19 l):

| | |
|---|---|
| 4½ lbs. (2 kg) | amber malt extract syrup |
| 2 lbs. (0.9 kg) | German Pilsener malted barley |
| 2 lbs. (0.9 kg) | Munich malt |
| 6 oz. (170 g) | debittered black malt |
| 1 oz. (28 g) | German Spalt, Mittelfrüh, or American Liberty hops (boiling): 5 HBU (140 MBU) |
| ¼ oz. (14 g) | German Tradition hops (boiling): 1.5 HBU (42 MBU) |
| ¼ oz. (7 g) | Santiam or Mt. Hood hop pellets (5 minutes, finishing/aroma) |
| ½ oz. (14 g) | Crystal or Saphir hop pellets (dry hopping) |
| ¼ tsp. (1 g) | Irish moss powder |
| * | German/Bavarian lager–type yeast or White Labs Cry Havoc yeast |

¾ c. (175 ml)   sugar (for bottling) or ⅓ c. (80 ml) corn sugar
(for kegging)

O.G.: 1.050–1.054 (12.5–13.5)
F.G.: 1.012–1.018 (3–4.5)
Bitterness: 1–4 BU; Color: 9 SRM (18 EBC): Alcohol: 5% by volume

Add the crushed malted barley, Munich and black malts to 4 quarts (4 l) of
140-degree F (60 C) water and mix well. The temperature will stabilize between
130 and 135 degrees F (54.5–57 C). Add heat if necessary and hold the temperature at about 133 degrees F (56 C) for 30 minutes. Don't worry about a 3- to
5-degree F (2–3 C) temperature drop during this time.

Then add 2 quarts (2 l) of boiling water to this mash. This will raise the
temperature to about or just below 155 degrees F (68 C). Hold at 149 to 155
degrees F (65–68 C) for 45 minutes, stirring occasionally. Then add more heat
to raise the temperature to 167 degrees F (75 C). Then pour your mash into
your lauter-tun and sparge with 2 gallons (7.5 l) of hot water at 170 degrees F
(76 C). The sweet wort ends in your brewpot.

Bring the sweet wort to a boil and add the malt extract and both boiling
hops and boil for 60 minutes. Add the Irish moss for the final 10 minutes of the
boil. Add the finishing/aroma hops during the final 5 minutes of the boil. Strain,
sparge, and transfer immediately to 2 gallons (7.5 l) of cold water in the fermenter.
Top off with additional water to make 5 gallons (19 l). If you have the capacity
to primary ferment at about 55 degrees F (13 C), then add the yeast at about 70
degrees F (21 C) and once you see visible signs of fermentation drop the temperature to 55 degrees F (13 C). Regardless of what temperature you ferment at,
after primary fermentation is complete, and there is little sign of fermentation
activity, transfer the beer to a closed secondary fermenter, add ½ ounce (14 g)
of the dry hopping hop pellets and lager at temperatures between 35 and 55
degrees F (2–13 C) for 3 to 4 weeks. Prime with sugar and bottle or keg when
lagering is complete. Let condition at room temperature for about 1 week before
storing at colder temperatures.

And remember: If you don't have the capacity to cold ferment you will still
be in Heaven's Orbit—a most excellent beer bottled right after fermentation is
complete.

## STRONG ALES AND LAGERS

### Potlatch Doppelbock

The menagerie of malts blends together to balance into one expressive bombshell.
A richly dark doppelbock (a stronger version of bock) in the true and fashionable

German style, this brew possesses the sweetness, medium bitterness, and unhinged alcohol content to make any homebrewer as proud as a German bockmaster.

Close your eyes, swallow, and imagine that velvety darkness sliding down your throat, its warm glow inspiring a smile and a sense of satisfaction. It's yours and only you, the brewmaster, can experience this lugubrious affair and offer to share it with your most special friends.

Ingredients for 5 gallons (19 l):

| | |
|---|---|
| 7 lbs. (3.2 kg) | plain amber dried malt extract |
| 2 lbs. (0.9 kg) | pale malted barley |
| 6 oz. (170 g) | toasted malted barley |
| 6 oz. (170 g) | Munich malt (for malt sweetness) |
| ¼ lb. (110 g) | crystal malt (for caramel sweetness) |
| ¼ lb. (110 g) | chocolate malt (for a hint of cocoa) |
| ¼ lb. (101 g) | debittered black malt |
| 1½ oz. (42 g) | Northern Brewer or Perle hops (boiling): 12 HBU (340 MBU) |
| ½ oz. (14 g) | Hallertau or Mt. Hood hops (5 minutes, finishing/flavor) |
| ¼ tsp. (1 g) | Irish moss powder |
| * | German lager–type yeast, White Labs Cry Havoc yeast, or rehydrated Saflager dried lager yeast |
| ¾ c. (175 ml) | sugar (for bottling) or ⅓ c. (80 ml) corn sugar (for kegging) |

O.G.: 1.076–1.080 (18.5–19.5)
F.G.: 1.018–1.026 (4.5–6.5)
Bitterness: 33 BU; Color 33 SRM (66 EBC); Alcohol: 7.6% by volume

Add the crushed malts to 3 quarts (3 l) of 140-degree F (60 C) water and mix well. The temperature will stabilize between 130 and 135 degrees F (54.5–57 C). Add heat if necessary and hold the temperature at about 133 degrees F (56 C) for 30 minutes. Don't worry about a 3- to 5-degree F (2–3 C) temperature drop during this time.

Then add 1½ quarts (1.5 l) of boiling water to this mash. This will raise the temperature to about or just below 155 degrees F (68 C). Hold at 149 to 155 degrees F (65–68 C) for 45 minutes, stirring occasionally. Then add more heat to raise the temperature to 167 degrees F (75 C). Then pour your mash into your lauter-tun and sparge with 1½ gallons (5.7 l) of hot water at 170 degrees F (76 C). The sweet wort ends in your brewpot.

Bring the sweet wort to a boil and add the malt extract and boiling hops and boil for 60 minutes. Add the Irish moss for the final 10 minutes of the boil. Add the finishing hops during the final 5 minutes of the boil. Strain, sparge, and transfer immediately to 2 gallons (7.5 l) of cold water in the fermenter. Top off with additional water to make 5 gallons (19 l).

Aerate the wort very well. Pitch the yeast when the temperature of the wort is about 70 degrees F (21 C). Ferment at about 70 degrees F (21 C) for about 1 week or when fermentation shows signs of calming and stopping.

If you have the capacity to primary ferment at about 55 degrees F (13 C), then add the yeast at about 70 degrees F (21 C) and once you see visible signs of fermentation drop the temperature to 55 degrees F (13 C). Regardless of what temperature you ferment at, after primary fermentation is complete, and there is little sign of fermentation activity, transfer the beer to a closed secondary fermenter and lager at temperatures between 35 and 55 degrees F (2–13 C) for 3 to

4 weeks. Prime with sugar and bottle or keg when lagering is complete. Let condition at room temperature for about 1 week before storing at colder temperatures.

And remember: If you don't have the capacity to cold ferment, your gift of beer to yourself and friends will still be most excellent.

### *Limnian Wheat Doppelbock*

It often takes all the skill a brewer can muster to brew a high-alcohol, well-balanced doppelbock—a doppelbock that will be recollected as a malty brew with just enough bitterness to briefly retain a linger of sweetness. Doppelbock is not a bitter beer even when the strength gets up to 9 to 10 percent alcohol, as Limnian Wheat Doppelbock does.

The recipe for Limnian Wheat Doppelbock makes choosing the right ingredients for this aberration of a legendary style of German lager a sure thing. I've never heard of a wheat doppelbock being brewed in Germany. Have you? But sure as shootin', malted wheat lends a wonderful toastiness to the character of this brew. Call it a Weizendoppelbock.

What you need to attend to is getting hold of a good-quality lager yeast that will ferment to 9 to 10 percent alcohol and create a cool fermentation environment to inhibit the formation of warm-temperature, alelike fruity esters. Worried? Don't be. Give it your best shot and you'll be gallons ahead of everyone else who never tried.

High-alcohol Limnian Wheat Doppelbock is best reserved for special occasions or perhaps a quiet, peaceful afternoon on the shore of your favorite lake, gazing up at the heavens and contemplating your accomplishments and the 5 gallons (19 l) of Limnian Wheat Doppelbock you've got back home. I've had the astonishing pleasure of opening one of my original Limnian Weizendoppelbocks when it was twenty-five years old. That's right, I managed to stash it away that long. Not only was it still enjoyable, but it had good carbonation and believe it or not the Cry Havoc yeast sediment came back from its dormancy to brew more beer—after twenty-five years!

Ingredients for 5 gallons (19 l):

    10 lbs.  (4.5 kg)   dried light malt extract
    2 lbs.   (0.9 kg)   malted wheat
    2 lbs.   (0.9 kg)   pale malted barley
    ¾ lb.    (340 g)    Munich malt
    ¼ lb.    (110 g)    chocolate malt
    ½ lb.    (225 g)    crystal malt (10 L)

*(NOTE: 3.3 lbs. [1.5 kg] of wheat malt extract syrup and 1 lb. [450 g] of dried amber malt extract may be substituted for the above malts if you want to go all malt extract for this special brew.)*

| | |
|---|---|
| 2 oz. (56 g) | Galena, Horizon, or Magnum hops (boiling): 20–25 HBU (560–700 MBU) |
| 1 oz. (28 g) | Tettnang or Santiam hops (10 minutes, flavor) |
| 1 oz. (28 g) | Hallertau or Mt. Hood hops (1–2 minutes, aroma) |
| ¼ tsp. (1 g) | Irish moss powder |
| double dose | Alcohol-resistant healthy lager yeast, White Labs Cry Havoc yeast, or a package or two of rehydrated Saflager dried lager yeast |
| ¾ c. (175 ml) | sugar (for bottling) or ⅓ c. (80 ml) corn sugar (for kegging) |

O.G.: 1.100 (23.5)
F.G.: 1.022–1.030 (5.5–7.5)
Bitterness: about 50 BU; Color: 16 SRM (32 EBC); Alcohol: 10.2% by volume

Add the crushed malts to 5½ quarts (5 l) of 140-degree F (60 C) water and mix well. The temperature will stabilize between 130 and 135 degrees F (54.5–57 C). Add heat if necessary and hold the temperature at about 133 degrees F (56 C) for 30 minutes. Don't worry about a 3- to 5-degree F (2–3 C) temperature drop during this time.

Then add 2½ quarts (2.5 l) of boiling water to this mash. This will raise the temperature to about or just below 155 degrees F (68 C). Hold at 149 to 155 degrees F (65–68 C) for 45 minutes, stirring occasionally. Complete conversion by raising the temperature to 158 degrees F (70 C) and holding for 10 to 20 minutes or until an iodine test indicates complete conversion. Then add more heat to raise the temperature to 167 degrees F (75 C). Then pour your mash into your lauter-tun and sparge with 2½ gallons (9.5 l) of hot water at 170 degrees F (76 C). The sweet wort ends in your brewpot.

Bring the sweet wort to a boil and add the malt extract and boiling hops and boil for a full 60 minutes. Then add the Irish moss and flavor hops and continue to boil for an additional 10 minutes. Add the aroma hops for the final 1 to 2 minutes of this phase of boiling. You've boiled this wort for a total of 70 minutes. Because of all the malt ingredients in this recipe, you will have about 4 gallons (15 l) of hot wort. Before you strain and sparge, secure the lid on your brewpot and then immerse the hot wort in a cold-water "bath" and let cool for 30 to 40 minutes. Change the bath water a few times to accelerate cooling. Then strain, sparge, and transfer to 1 gallon (3.8 l) of cold water in the fermenter.

Temporarily seal the fermenter and agitate the wort in order to aerate. Remove the seal (rubber stopper) and then top off with additional water to make 5 gallons (19 l). Aerate the wort very well. Add a double amount of healthy active yeast when the temperature of the wort is about 70 degrees F (21 C). Ferment at about 70 degrees F (21 C) for about 1 week or when fermentation shows signs of calming and stopping.

If you have the capacity to primary ferment at about 55 degrees F (13 C), then add the yeast at about 70 degrees F (21 C) and once you see visible signs of fermentation drop the temperature to 55 degrees F (13 C). Regardless of what temperature you ferment at, after primary fermentation is complete, and there is little sign of fermentation activity, transfer the beer to a closed secondary fermenter and lager at temperatures between 35 and 55 degrees F (2–13 C) for 3 to 4 weeks. Prime with sugar and bottle or keg when lagering is complete. Let condition at room temperature for about 1 week before storing at colder temperatures.

A good time to celebrate is during the rituals of springtime. *Prost.*

### *Heart of the Tide Imperial Porter*

In 1996 while tasting one of the winners of the World Beer Cup® I was awestruck by an Imperial "Porter-Stout" beer. One of the most exquisite beers I've ever tasted, it was a silver medal winner from the Wiibroes Brewery in Helsingor, Denmark. The labels on the bottle proclaimed both "Imperial Stout" and "Porter."

Is there such a thing as Imperial Porter? Of course there is—we're now in your world of homebrewing. The assertiveness of roasted barley is almost altogether lacking, while the overall rich, velvety character enjoys a smoothness that I'd attribute to cool lagering. Yes, we're using a lager yeast for this Imperial Porter. Furthermore, unlike most other styles prefixed with "Imperial," this is one exquisite brew that goes light and easy on the hops. This is altogether unique: smooth and balanced with a rich, light brown head securing a beautifully aromatic mild roast coffee/chocolate malt character. Also woven into this tapestry is a fleeting suggestion of floral hops.

Ingredients for 5 gallons (19 l):

| | |
|---|---|
| 6 lbs. (2.7 kg) | extra-light dried malt extract |
| 1 lb. (0.5 kg) | 2-row pale malt |
| 2½ lbs. (1.1 kg) | Munich malt |
| 1 lb. (0.9 kg) | dark crystal malt (40–80 L) |
| ½ lb. (225 g) | aromatic malt |
| ½ lb. (225 g) | wheat malt |
| ¾ lb. (340 g) | debittered black malt |
| ½ lb. (340 g) | roasted barley |

| ¼ lb. (150 g) | chocolate malt |
|---|---|
| 1¼ oz. (50 g) | German Spalt or German Traditional hops (boiling): 7 HBU (200 MBU) |
| ½ oz. (14 g) | Perle or Northern Brewer hops (boiling): 5 HBU (140 MBU) |
| ½ oz. (14 g) | Czech Saaz hops (30 minutes, flavor) |
| 2 oz. (56 g) | French Strisselspalt or American Santiam hops (1 to 2 minutes, aroma) |
| ¼ tsp. (1 g) | Irish moss powder |
| double dose | German lager–type yeast, White Labs Cry Havoc yeast, or rehydrated Saflager dried lager yeast. |
| ¾ c. (175 ml) | sugar (for bottling) or ⅓ c. (80 ml) corn sugar (for kegging) |

OG: 1.080–1.084 (20–21)
FG: 1.018–1.024 (4.5–6)
Bitterness: 40 BU; Color: 58 SRM (116 EBC); Alcohol: 8.1% by volume

This is a hefty recipe, using a lot of grains and malt extract. Be sure your brewpot is at least 6 gallons (23 l) in size, though it's best boiled in a 10-gallon (38 l) brewpot.

Add the crushed malts and roasted barley to 7 quarts (6.5 l) of 140-degree F (60 C) water and mix well. The temperature will stabilize between 130 and 135 degrees F (54.5–57 C). Add heat if necessary and hold the temperature at about 133 degrees F (56 C) for 30 minutes. Don't worry about a 3- to 5-degree F (2–3 C) temperature drop during this time.

Then add 3½ quarts (3 l) of boiling water to this mash. This will raise the temperature to about or just below 155 degrees F (68 C). Hold at 149 to 155 degrees F (65–68 C) for 45 minutes, stirring occasionally. Complete conversion by raising the temperature to 158 degrees F (70 C) and holding for 10 to 20 minutes or until an iodine test indicates complete conversion. Then add more heat to raise the temperature to 167 degrees F (75 C). Then pour your mash into your lauter-tun and sparge with 3 gallons (11.5 l) of hot water at 170 degrees F (76 C). The sweet wort ends in your brewpot.

A long boil will reduce the volume of wort, making later handling more manageable. Bring the sweet wort to a boil. Add the malt extract and both of the boiling hops and boil for a full 60 minutes. Then add the flavor hops and boil for 30 more minutes. Add the Irish moss and continue to boil for an additional 10 minutes. Add the aroma hops during the final 1 to 2 minutes of this phase of boiling. You've boiled this wort a total of 100 minutes—that's time for a few brews, but pay attention to what you're doing. Because of all the malt ingredients in this recipe you will have about 4 gallons (15 l) of hot wort. Before you strain and sparge, secure the lid on your brewpot and then immerse the hot wort in a cold-water "bath" and let cool for about 30 to 40 minutes. Change the bath water a few times to accelerate cooling. Then strain, sparge, and transfer to 1 gallon (3.8 l) of cold water in the fermenter. Temporarily seal the fermenter and agitate the wort in order to aerate. Remove the seal (rubber stopper) and then top off with additional water to make 5 gallons (19 l). Aerate the wort very well. Add a double amount of healthy active yeast when the temperature of the wort is about 70 degrees F (21 C). Ferment at about 70 degrees F (21 C) for about 1 week or when fermentation shows signs of calming and stopping.

If you have the capacity to primary ferment at about 55 degrees F (13 C), then add the yeast at about 70 degrees F (21 C) and once you see visible signs of fermentation drop the temperature to 55 degrees F (13 C). Regardless of what temperature you ferment at, after primary fermentation is complete and there is little sign of fermentation activity, transfer the beer to a closed secondary fermenter and lager at temperatures between 35 and 55 degrees F (2–13 C) for 3 to 4 weeks. Prime with sugar and bottle or keg when lagering is complete. Let condition at room temperature for about 1 week before storing at colder temperatures.

## Colonel Coffin Barley Wine Ale

> "A barley wine before its time is like a mountain without a peak."
> —Charlie "Barley" Papazian

If ever there were a style of beer to brew and then glow with pride over, then it must be barley wine ale. If ever there were ale truly distinct and complex, a flavor and aroma worth savoring slowly, then it would be barley wine ale. If you ever had dreams of brewing ale so memorable it would linger for a lifetime, then try Colonel Coffin Barley Wine Ale, a perfect beer brewed to alcoholic strength up to 11 percent by volume.

Colonel Coffin is powerfully alcoholic, stunningly hopped, with fruity esters reminiscent of strawberry, raspberry, pear, black currant, and other tantalizing characters. The abundance of hops proliferates first in the aroma. The alcohol vapors warm the nostrils and titillate the lungs. First sweetness turns to a wonderfully complex and compensating bitterness.

It's expensive and demands patience and aging. But what a reward! Life's other rewards should be so grand. And it's easy to make.

Ingredients for 5 gallons (19 l):

9 lbs. (4.1 kg)  light dried malt extract
3 lbs. (1.4 kg)  pale malted barley

| | |
|---|---|
| 1 lb. (450 g) | crystal malt (10 L) |
| 6–7 oz. (168–196 g) | Magnum, Horizon, Simcoe, Chinook, or Galena hops (boiling): 70–80 HBU (1960–2240 MBU) |
| 1½ oz. (42 g) | Centennial, Australian Galaxy, New Zealand Pacific Gem, or Cascade hops (10 minutes, flavor) |
| 1½ oz. (42 g) | Cascade or Centennial hops (1 to 2 minutes, aroma) |
| 1 oz. (28 g) | New Zealand Nelson Sauvin or Amarillo hop pellets (dry hopping) |
| ¼ tsp. (1 g) | Irish moss powder |
| double dose | Strong ale-type yeast, White Labs Cry Havoc yeast |
| ¾ c. (175 ml) | sugar (for bottling) or ⅓ c. (80 ml) corn sugar (for kegging) |

O.G.: 1.100 (23.5)
F.G.: 1.022–1.035 (5.5–9)
Bitterness: 80+ BU; Color 14 SRM (28 EBC); Alcohol: 10.2% by volume

(NOTE: *The total volume of the boil will be close to 4 gallons (15 l), requiring a very large brew kettle.*)

Add the crushed malted barley and crystal malt to 4 quarts (4 l) of 140-degree F (60 C) water and mix well. The temperature will stabilize between 130 and 135 degrees F (54.5–57 C). Add heat if necessary and hold the temperature at about 133 degrees F (56 C) for 30 minutes. Don't worry about a 3- to 5-degree F (2–3 C) temperature drop during this time.

Then add 2 quarts (2 l) of boiling water to this mash. This will raise the temperature to about or just below 155 degrees F (68 C). Hold at 149 to 155 degrees F (65–68 C) for 45 minutes, stirring occasionally. Complete conversion by raising the temperature to 158 degrees F (70 C) and holding for 10 to 20 minutes or until an iodine test indicates complete conversion. Then add more heat to raise the temperature to 167 degrees F (75 C). Then pour your mash into your lautertun and sparge with 2 gallons (7.5 l) of hot water at 170 degrees F (76 C). The sweet wort ends in your brewpot.

Bring the sweet wort to a boil and add the malt extract and boiling hops and boil for 90 minutes. After the 1½ hours of boiling, remove most of the boiling hops with a strainer (rinse off the good stuff back into the brewpot with boiling water). Then add the Irish moss and flavor hops and bring back to a boil and continue to boil for 10 more minutes. Add the aroma hops during the last 1 to 2 minutes of the boil. Immerse your hot brewpot in cold water (with the lid securely on) for 30 minutes or longer to help cool the wort before you transfer it into your fermenter. Then strain, sparge, and transfer to 1½ gallons (5.7 l) of cold water in the fermenter. Top off with additional water to make 5 gallons (19 l).

Aerate the wort very well. Pitch the yeast when the temperature of the wort is about 70 degrees F (21 C). Ferment at about 70 degrees F (21 C) for about 1 week or when fermentation shows signs of calming and stopping. Rack from your primary to a secondary and add the hop pellets for dry hopping. If you have the capability, "cellar" the beer at about 55 degrees F (12.5 C) for about 1 month. Prime with sugar and bottle or keg when fermentation is complete.

Age will transform this ale dramatically. The initial sharp bitterness of Colonel Coffin Barley Wine Ale will mellow with age. Just remember: "A barley wine before its time is like a mountain without a peak." I said that.

## SPECIALTY BEERS

In 1994 the American Homebrewers Association's *Zymurgy* magazine published a special edition called "Special Ingredients & Indigenous Beers." It's been a timeless treasure and resource for tens of thousands of homebrewers. Now there is interest in indigenous beers from all over the world. Old traditional and unusual beers are being rediscovered at the same time new innovative indigenous brews are being created.

Here's a story and recipe that illustrate the depth to which beer culture pervades society. This extraordinary article was originally researched and written by longtime friend Jim Walton (now a resident of Longmont, Colorado), titled "400 Rabbits, or Aztec Social Beverages at the Time of Conquest." Jim and I collaborated at the time and came up with a recipe that included

corn, cocoa, chili pepper, honey, and other beer ingredients—and appeared in *Zymurgy*.

At the end of Jim's article there is a final tribute to whom this recipe was originally dedicated. The original beverage was named after the Aztec lords and ladies of precious intoxication—the 400 Rabbits—and Mayahuel, the first Mexican brewer to transform the sap of a giant agave into a divine elixir.

What caught my eye was: "the sap of the giant agave." In 1994, when the story was written, agave extract was all but unknown in the United States. Now it is a common sweetener and available in many local natural food and grocery stores. Agave used for making tequila is not the same agave used as a sweetener. Agave used as a sweetener has a long and rich agricultural heritage in Mexico. Aztecs used this agave extract in the brewing of their beers.

Here is the original article in its entirety, reprinted with permission from Jim, along with my original recipe for 400 Rabbits Aztec-Style Ale. Also added is my reformulation I call Mayahuel—Lady of the Tortoise Throne Ale.

### 400 Rabbits, or Aztec Social Beverages at the Time of Conquest

by James Walton

Hernando Cortés arrived in the Aztec city of Tenochtitlan around 1520 and was amazed to find a civilization as complex and magnificent as his own. When invited to banquet with the ruler, Moctezuma II, the Spaniards were treated to a spectacle of music and dance and feasted on chocolate, partridge and turkey. Tobacco smoking already was known to Cortés from the Caribbean, but the Aztecs had many other foods and herbs to surprise their guests. The Spanish were especially intrigued by beverages of chocolate, or cacao. Their very preparation was dependent on class status and the rulers had a special etiquette prescribing their use. Some recipes may have included psychoactive agents such as *teonanacati*, the divine mushroom, but the majority of chocolate drinks were laced with chili peppers and the petals of fragrant flowers.

Ritual intoxication was an important feature of Aztec social life on all levels, and the preparation of maguey, a fermented beverage from the sap of the giant agave, was the alcoholic beverage of the masses. *Ocotli*, or pulque, was regulated by a pantheon of gods known collectively as the Centzon Totochtin—the 400 (or innumerable) Rabbits. This stemmed from the Mesoamerican image of a rabbit on the face of the moon fostering the notion that this sign ruled the night sky and ecstatic behavior. As in all other cultures, there was a thin line between ecstasy and licentiousness, and the 400 Rabbits had an alternative meaning best translated by the English expression "three sheets to the wind."

In pre-Columbian Mexico, fermentation was believed to be a mystical process and, in addition to ocotli there were two types of fermented alcoholic beverages that are still ceremonially prepared today. In the north the Tarahumara [see *Zymurgy*, fall 1980, "Native Brewing in America" by Bill Litzinger] tribe drinks huge quantities of *tesguino*, a fermented corn beer brewed in huge earthen pots. In the southern lowlands a ritual beverage is made by the Lacandone Maya called *balche*, which is honey fermented in a hollow log and flavored by the bitter bark of the balche tree. Because the taste is so bitter and emetic, the beverage is only prepared for special occasions, such as invoking the rain gods during a time of drought.

Following long tradition, Mexico City still has its pulquerias where pulque-ocotli is consumed by Nahuatl and Otomi Indians for refreshment. The original ceremonial function of this beverage has not been forgotten. Even today pulque brewing is accompanied by singing and incantations, reflecting the days when the fermentation of ocotli was ruled by the goddess Mayahuel, Lady of the Tortoise Throne and patroness of precious drink and childbirth. As the deity most involved with the creation of ritual libations, she was the chief of the 400 Rabbits. Even beverages prepared for domestic consumption were attended by considerable ritual and sacred songs. Ocotli is good for only about 24 hours before it degenerates into unpalatable slime. No drinking could occur in Aztec times without the collusion of Mayahuel's ladies who brewed this social beverage, often by beginning the fermentation process with their own saliva. Spanish chronicles report such frequent drinking for the innumerable Aztec festivals that ocotli-making must have burdened many women with full-time specialization.

Although drinking ocotli in the service of the gods was not considered to be a bad thing, licentious behavior was a clear and present danger to the Aztec social order. There are many reports of secular drinking and if this was taken to excess the Aztec state reacted with swift and decisive punishment. Public drunkenness was considered to be such an indecency that harsh penalties, increasing in severity according to rank, were meted out to offenders. A noble who couldn't hold his ocotli in public was put to death, while a tipsy *macehualli*, or common peasant, had his head shaved and his property confiscated. Repeat offenders were only given two strikes and then they were out—usually by the method of strangulation.

However, there was a prominent exception to these laws. A special dispensation to drink in public was given to those who had reached the age of an Aztec century, or a full calendar cycle (52 modern-day years). Perhaps the conditions of life were such that the elderly were honored for their sheer survival, but the Aztecs certainly recognized that lewd and violent behavior passes with youth while the aged usually conduct themselves with more dignity and containment.

Because I have recently completed one Aztec cycle I wanted to honor the occasion with a pre-Columbian beer. By chance I ran into Charlie Papazian at a local pub and we discussed my project over a couple of beers. Not knowing of any bottled beer that is based on foods of purely pre-Columbian origin, Charlie proposed fusing the European process of brewing beer with the Mesoamerican ingredients known to be the basis of their ritual beverages. We chose corn and honey plus chocolate and chili—the unlikely ingredients of mole, Mexico's national dish—to add to the standard hops, barley malt and sugar of a conventional beer. The resulting beverage was named after the Aztec lords and ladies of precious intoxication—the 400 Rabbits—and Mayahuel, the first Mexican brewer to transform the sap of a giant agave into a divine elixir.

[Original] Recipe for 400 Rabbits, a Mesoamerican "Aztecan" style ale:
Inspired by a conversation of what it might have been like drinking the beer of the Aztecs. Our conclusion was that surely they made beer. And it was likely that corn, honey, chocolate, chili peppers and hallucinogens would probably have been the primary ingredients. Not quite the same as the German Beer purity law.

We left out the hallucinogens, and added a relatively low dose of hops for bitterness, knowing full well that quite a bit of bitterness would come from the cocoa. We also used malted barley, because this is the twentieth century and wanted to start out with something that resembled modern day beer, while still paying tribute to the Aztec culture.

The beer is soothingly warm without burning. Szechuan chilies have the effect of warming the back of your throat. 400 Rabbits has a distinct, but mild chocolate bitterness. Hops also contributed to the bitterness, but the overall character was rounded by the addition of the Special-B malt. The effects of the corn and honey lightened the flavor, body and overall character of what could have been a much heavier bodied beer without.

400 Rabbits is just the beginning.

## *400 Rabbits Aztec-Style Ale*

Mash-extract recipe for 5 gallons (19 l):

| | |
|---|---|
| 1¾ lbs. (.8 kg) | light dried malt extract |
| 2¼ lbs. (1 kg) | 2-row American lager malt |
| 1¼ lbs. (.57 kg) | pregelatinized flaked corn |
| ¼ lb. (114 g) | Belgian Special-B malt |
| ¼ lb. (114 g) | chocolate malt |
| 1 lb. (.45 kg) | honey |

| | |
|---|---|
| 6 oz. (170 g) | cocoa powder |
| ½ oz. (14 g) | crushed dried hot red chili peppers |
| 1 oz. (28 g) | Mt. Hood, Crystal, or Liberty hops (boiling): 5 HBU (140 MBU) |
| ½ oz. (14 g) | Crystal or French Strisselspalt hop pellets (finishing/aroma) |
| ¼ tsp. (1 g) | Irish moss powder |
| * | ale-type yeast or White Labs Cry Havoc yeast |
| ¾ c. (175 ml) | sugar (for bottling) or ⅓ c. (80 ml) corn sugar (for kegging) |

O.G.: 1.044–1.048 (11–12)
F.G.: 1.012–1.016 (3–4)
Bitterness: 23 BU; Color: 16 SRM (32 EBC); Alcohol: 4.2% by volume

Add 4 quarts (3.8 l) of 130-degree F (54.5 C) water to the crushed grain and flaked corn, stir, stabilize, and hold the temperature at 122 degrees F (50 C) for 30 minutes. Add 2 quarts (1.9 l) of boiling water and stabilize temperature (add heat if needed) at about 150 to 152 degrees F (65.5–67 C) and hold for about 45 minutes. Temperature may be allowed to drop from 152 to 148 degrees F (67–64.5 C) with no worrying. Then raise temperature to 160 degrees F (71 C) and hold for 10 to 15 minutes to complete conversion.

After conversion, raise temperature to 167 degrees F (75 C), lauter, and sparge with 2 gallons (7.5 l) of 170-degree F (77 C) water. Collect about 2½ to 3 gallons (9.5–11.4 l) of runoff into your brewpot and add the malt extract, honey, cocoa, chili pepper, and boiling hops and bring to a full boil.

The total boil time will be about 60 minutes. When 10 minutes remain add Irish moss. After a total wort boil of 60 minutes turn off the heat, add the finishing/aroma hops, then strain and sparge into a sanitized fermenter to which you've added 2 gallons (7.5 l) of water. It helps to prechill (33 degrees F [1 C]) the water added to the fermenter rather than simply adding warmer tap water.

Aerate the wort very well. Pitch the yeast when the temperature of the wort is about 70 degrees F (21 C). Ferment at about 70 degrees F (21 C) for about 1 week or when fermentation shows signs of calming and stopping. Rack from your primary to a secondary and let "cellar" or rest to clarify

Prime with sugar and bottle or keg when fermentation is complete.

## Mayahuel—Lady of the Tortoise Throne Ale

Ingredients for 5 gallons (19 l):

| | |
|---|---|
| 2½ lbs. (1.15 kg) | pale malt |
| 1¼ lbs. (568 g) | flaked corn |
| ¼ lb. (113 g) | Belgian Special-B malt |
| 2½ lbs. (1.15 kg) | agave extract |
| 1 lb. (454 g) | light honey |
| ½ lb. (225 g) | unsweetened cocoa powder |
| ½ oz. (14 g) | dried hot chili or cayenne pepper |
| ½ oz. (14 g) | Mt. Hood, Liberty, or Vanguard hops (boiling): 2.5 HBU (70 MBU) |
| 1¼ oz. (35 g) | Mt. Hood or Santiam hops (30 minutes, flavor): 6.25 HBU (175 MBU) |
| ¼ tsp. (1 g) | Irish moss powder |
| * | Ale yeast—type your choice |
| ¾ c. (175 ml) | sugar (for bottling) or ⅓ c. (80 ml) corn sugar (for kegging) |

O.G.: 1.044–1.048 (11–12)
F.G.: 1.010–1.012 (2.5–3)
Bitterness: 22 BU; Color: 12 SRM (24 EBC); Alcohol: 4.6% by volume

Add 4 quarts (3.8 l) of 130-degree F (54.5 C) water to the crushed grain and flaked corn, stir, stabilize, and hold the temperature at 122 degrees F (50 C) for 30 minutes. Add 2 quarts (1.9 l) of boiling water and stabilize temperature (add heat if needed) at about 150 to 152 degrees F (65.5–67 C) and hold for about 45 minutes. Temperature may be allowed to drop from 152 to 148 degrees F with no worrying. Then raise temperature to 160 degrees F (71 C) and hold for 10 to 15 minutes to complete conversion.

After conversion, raise temperature to 167 degrees F (75 C), lauter, and sparge with 2 gallons (7.5 l) of 170-degree F (77 C) water. Collect 2½ to 3 gallons (9.5–11.4 l) of runoff into your brewpot and add the honey, agave extract, cocoa, chili pepper, and boiling hops. Bring to a full boil and boil for 60 minutes. Add the flavor hops for the final 30 minutes of the boil. Add the Irish moss for the final 10 minutes of the boil. After a total wort boil of 60 minutes turn off the heat, strain and sparge into a sanitized fermenter to which you've added 2 gallons (7.5 l) of water. It helps to prechill (33 degrees F [1 C]) the water added to the fermenter rather than simply adding warmer tap water.

Aerate the wort very well. Pitch the yeast when the temperature of the wort is about 70 degrees F (21 C). Ferment at about 70 degrees F (21 C) for about 1 week or when fermentation shows signs of calming and stopping. Rack from your primary to a secondary and let "cellar" or rest to clarify, and prime with sugar and bottle or keg when fermentation is complete.

## RESOURCES FOR 59 MASH EXTRACT RECIPES

Other mash-extract recipes in *The Homebrewer's Companion, Second Edition, Microbrewed Adventures,* and *Home Brewer's Gold*

### MASH-EXTRACT RECIPES IN *THE HOMEBREWER'S COMPANION, SECOND EDITION*:

"You'll See" Coriander Amber Ale
Nomadic Kölsch
Tennessee Waltzer Dunkelweizenbock
Saunder's Nut Brown Ale
Slanting Annie's Chocolate Porter
Pelhourino Stout—The Other Irish Stout
Gnarly Roots Lambic-Fringed Barley Wine Ale
Here to Heaven Snow Angel Oktoberfest Wine Ale
Carla Vitoria's Barley Wheat Wine Ale
For Peat's Sake "Scotch" Ale
Quarterbock Low Alcohol
Autumnal Equinox Special Reserve
Jah Mon Irie Dopplebock

### MASH-EXTRACT RECIPES IN *MICROBREWED ADVENTURES*:

Vienna-Style *Ouro de Habanera* (Havana Gold)
Quingdao Dark Lager
Switch and Toggles Preposterous Porter
Zaltitis Baltic Porter

Masterbrewer's Doppelbock
New Wisconsin Apple/Raspberry/Cherry Beer
Czech-Mex Tijuana Urquell (light lager)
Klibbety Jibbit (light lager)
Masterbrewer's Celebration Light Lager
Pumpernickel Rye Stout
Wolaver's Organic Oatmeal Stout
Flying Fish Baby Saison Farmhouse Ale
Poetic Brighella Italian-Belgian-German-English-American Ale
Quito Abbey Ale—1534 (dark ale)
Vello's Gotlandsdricke (specialty ale)
Zeezuiper Spiced Nederlander Strong Ale

## MASH-EXTRACT RECIPES IN *HOME BREWER'S GOLD*:

Aecht Schlenkerla Rauchbier, Brauerei Heller-Trum, Bamberg, Germany
B&H Breakfast Toasted Ale, Barley & Hopp's, San Mateo, California USA
Bow Valley Premium Lager, Bow Valley Brewing Co., Canmore, Alberta
     Canada
Brick Red Baron, Brick Brewing Co. Ltd., Waterloo, Ontario Canada
California Blonde Ale, Coast Range Brewing Co., Gilroy, California USA
Coriander Rye Ale, Bison Brewing Co., Berkeley, California USA
Derailer Doppelbock, Tabernash Brewing Co., Denver, Colorado USA
Grain D'Orge, Brasserie Jeanne D'Arc, Ronchin-Lille, France
Icehouse, Plank Road Brewery, Milwaukee, Wisconsin USA
Leinenkugel's Red Lager, Jacob Leinenkugel Brewing Co., Chippewa
     Falls, Wisconsin USA
Liefmans Frambozen, Brouwerij Liefmans, Oudenaarde, Belgium
Liefmans Goudenband, Brouwerij Liefmans, Oudenaarde, Belgium
Lindemans' Cuvée René, Lindeman's Farm Brew, Blezenbeek, Belgium
OB Lager, Oriental Brewery Co. Ltd., Seoul, Korea
Old Rasputin Russian Imperial Stout, North Coast Brewing Co. Inc.,
     Fort Bragg, California USA
Olde English 800 Malt Liquor, Pabst Brewing Co., Milwaukee, Wisconsin
     USA
Radegast Birell, Radegast Brewery J.S.C., Nosovice, Czech Republic
Redwood Coast Alpine Gold Pilsner, Redwood Coast Brewing Co.,
     Alameda, California USA
Ruffian Mai-Bock, Mountain Valley Brew Pub, Suffern, New York USA
Ruffian Pilsner, Mountain Valley Brew Pub, Suffern, New York USA
Saint Brigid's Porter, Great Divide Brewing Co., Denver, Colorado USA

San Quentin's Breakout Stout, Marin Brewing Co, Larkspur, California USA

Scotch Ale, Samuel Adams Brewhouse, Philadelphia, Pennsylvania USA

Seabright Session Ale, Seabright Brewery, Santa Cruz, California USA

St. Charles Porter, Blackstone Restaurant & Brewery, Nashville, Tennessee USA

Stoddards Kölsch, Stoddard's Brewhouse and Eatery, Sunnyvale, California USA

Stoudt's Export Gold, Stoudt Brewing Co., Adamstown, Pennsylvania USA

Tabernash Munich Dark Lager, Tabernash Brewing Co., Denver, Colorado USA

Thomas Kemper Hefeweizen, Thomas Kemper Lagers, Seattle, Washington USA

Zoser Oatmeal Stout, Oasis Brewery, Boulder, Colorado USA

# ADVANCED HOMEBREWING FOR THE PRACTICAL HOMEBREWER

*"Beer does not make itself properly by itself. It takes an element of mystery and of things that no one can understand. As a brewer you concern yourself with all the stuff you can understand, everywhere."*

—Fritz Maytag, past president,
Anchor Brewing Company

## INTRODUCTION

How sophisticated and elaborate does the brewing process need to get for a homebrewer to be considered advanced? Is it brewing beer solely from grains? Is it cultivating your own yeast? Is it treating your water with the perfect combination of minerals? Or, is it just being able to make perfectly delicious beer every single time, with malt extract or all grain? For each homebrewer "advanced" takes on its own special meaning. But one symptom is clearly recognizable when you are ready to take the next step, and that is an "advanced state of passion."

You find yourself talking to just about anyone who will listen about your beer, about the beer you buy, about the beer on television, about the beer in your neighbor's refrigerator. People tell you that when you are having a beer, you look at it with a long loving gaze. You find yourself smelling the beer before you drink it. You're looking in the classified advertising section for used refrigerators. You daydream at work that your next beer will even be more perfect. You wake up refreshed in the morning after having a series of beer dreams. You are indeed in an advanced state of beermaking.

Advanced homebrewing means appreciating and being involved on an intimate level with the entire brewing process, considering each phase singularly and as part of a whole. Advanced homebrewing is your passion to cultivate an

understanding of the limitless variability of the brewing process and the versatility of ingredients.

With experience and labor come rewards and a special satisfaction. The reward is the glass of beer you created and know something more about; the satisfaction is of creating something special for yourself and your friends.

This book provides fundamentals from which to grow. No one completely understands what goes on in the brewing process. As brewers, we observe, take note, and base our next batch of beer on our own experience and that of others. It is sheer folly to be taken by the hand and led down the path of better brewing by someone who says that they know it all. No, it is your experience that counts most. It is your experience that will always lead you to more questions.

> *"Always the beautiful answer who asks a more beautiful question."*
> —e. e. cummings

## ADVANCED HOMEBREWING AND THE ALL-GRAIN HOMEBREWER

### WHAT HAVE YOU GOTTEN YOURSELF INTO?

For the homebrewer who is inclined to brewing beer from all grains, rather than malt extract syrups and powders, the most significant area of brewing that you will become involved in is enzymes—how they behave and influence the taste of beer.

Enzymes are like organic catalysts that are influenced by environmental conditions of time, temperature, raw ingredients, and minerals, among other things. They significantly alter the raw ingredients of beer to a more desirable and useful form for processing and fermenting into quality beer.

Numerous enzymes are present in the ingredients of beer; some are more significant than others. The two types of enzymes that are most important to the practical homebrewer are those that break down proteins into yeast nutrients and those that break down soluble starches to fermentable (sugars) and unfermentable (dextrins) carbohydrates. The all-grain homebrewer becomes aware of variables and makes choices by understanding both the desirable and the undesirable.

The all-grain homebrewer, in contrast to the malt extract homebrewer, deals with the entire wort (rather than a concentrated wort of syrup and water) throughout the brewing process, boiling and quickly cooling the beer wort, while simultaneously maintaining sanitary brewing conditions. The brewer becomes a symphonic maestro.

## WHAT SPECIAL EQUIPMENT WILL YOU NEED?

Because of the volumes of liquid that are used in brewing 5 gallons (19 l) of all-grain beer you will find it necessary to purchase or make a mash-tun, a vessel that holds the grains during controlled-temperature mashing. You'll also need to purchase or make a lauter-tun (a sparging system) for separating your spent grains from the sweet liquid. You will certainly find the need to have a brewpot that has at least an 8- to 10-gallon capacity and a system for cooling your boiled wort as quickly as possible.

Relax. Don't worry. Have a homebrew!

Of course, all-grain brewing is much more involved but believe me, once you've thought out the process and gathered the extra equipment you will develop a system that gets easier with every batch of beer. My very first batch of all-grain beer left my kitchen looking like the aftermath of a Civil War battle: every strainer, pot, pan, spoon, and measuring device had been impulsively used.

Needless to say, I had not thought out my system. I learned about many things that I should not do. But that first batch of all-grain beer, my very first, well, it won me a Best of Show in an International Homebrew Competition in 1980. You can be a winner, too.

Remember that you are a homebrewer! Don't look upon variability negatively. Quality beer can vary in flavor. If your brewing sanitation is attended to and your starch conversion is complete, you are much more likely to brew great beer every time—beer you can be proud of, no matter what the variables are. Your persistence and experience will pay off.

# THE MASH!

Mashing is the process of physically combining water with crushed malted barley, specialty malts, and prepared starchy adjuncts. The process is continued over a period of time with controlled temperature adjustments that activate different enzymes in order to break down soluble starches and proteins.

But before we get into the nitty-gritty of mashing, it helps to understand what malted barley is. By now you should know that malting is a natural process. Briefly, whole unmalted barley is germinated to a certain degree and then dried to make malted barley. The process of malting not only develops enzymes but also develops a small amount of fermentable sugar (mostly maltose) and unfermentable dextrins and very significantly converts rock-hard insoluble starch to a very crushable, convertible, and soluble starch. About 80 percent of malted barley is soluble starch that awaits conversion by enzymes.

The enzymes that are developed in the malting process act directly to degrade nitrogen-based proteins (amino acids) and soluble starches.

## ENZYMES AND MYSTICISM

Perhaps the most mystifying part of brewing is the behavior of enzymes. They aren't living organisms, yet like creatures they are triggered to react under appropriate conditions. They can also be "deactivated" or, more properly put, "denatured" by conditions that cannot be tolerated. Invisible to the eye and influenced by dozens of factors, enzymes magically convert a soup of starchy liquid to a delicious sweetness in a relatively short period of time.

There are many variables that can influence the behavior and efficiency of enzymatic activity; these variables, in turn, directly influence the flavor of the beer.

There are two types of enzymes whose behavior a homebrewer can significantly control. They are: 1) proteases or proteolytic enzymes (protein degrading), and 2) diastase or diastatic enzymes (starch degrading).

## Protein Degradation by Proteolytic Enzymes

Proteolytic enzymes break down long, complex chains of protein molecules into forms of protein that improve the quality and fermentation characteristics of beer. There are two temperature ranges that activate proteolytic enzymes, whereby they do their things.

At temperatures ideally 113 to 122 degrees F (45 to 50 C), certain proteolytic enzymes break down nitrogen-based proteins into amino acid proteins, which in turn can be used by yeast as a valuable nutrient. The degree to which yeast can ferment and convert fermentable sugars to alcohol and carbon dioxide is referred to as the attenuation of the wort. Nutrients that are developed by proteolytic enzymes are very significant in determining how well attenuated the beer wort will be. The process of developing these nutrients in the mash is not necessary in fully modified (usually English-grown 2-row) malts, as the nutrients are developed in a specialized malting process (more on modified malts later). Nor is this process essential with all malt beer, because other starchy adjuncts such as corn or rice are not used.

At temperatures ideally 122 to 140 degrees F (50 to 60 C), other proteolytic enzymes break down proteins into forms that improve the quality and appearance of beer foam and aid in clarity. This is a nice "stage" to rest at and go through in order to develop that creamy, dense head.

The process and stage at which a brewer activates these proteolytic enzymes is called the *protein rest*.

## Starch Degradation by Diastatic Enzymes

Diastatic enzymes convert starch molecules into fermentable sugars and unfermentable dextrins (responsible for giving beer fuller body and a creamier mouthfeel).

There are two diastatic enzymes that become active during the mashing process. They are alpha-amylase and beta-amylase. The combination of their action literally breaks down very long chains of soluble or gelatinized (cooked to a necessary degree) starch molecules into shorter chains of molecules we call sugars and dextrins. During the mashing process the brewer wants to convert all starches to dextrins or sugars. The yield of this process is called *extract*.

In order to clarify what these diastatic enzymes do, it will be helpful to explain the molecular structure of starches, sugars, and dextrins:

1. Starch molecules are basically a very long chain of very fermentable glucose molecules (the simplest of sugars), but because they are all attached they are not fermentable.
2. Maltose is a chain of two glucose molecules linked together and is very fermentable.

3. Dextrins are chains of four or more glucose molecules that result from a breakdown of starch. They are not fermentable. They are tasteless, yet add body and "mouthfeel" to beer.

Keep these molecular points in mind as you begin to understand how enzymes work.

### Alpha-amylase

Alpha-amylase breaks down very long chains of glucose molecules (starch) by literally "chopping" them at the middle and reducing them into shorter and shorter chains. Until these secondary chains are reduced to chains of one, two or three molecules of glucose, they are unfermentable and called dextrins. The process of reducing the very large chains of starch molecules is called *liquefication* or *dextrinization*.

### Beta-amylase

Beta-amylase breaks down both long and very long chains of glucose molecules (starch or dextrins) by literally "nibbling" at the ends, rather than chopping at them from the middle. When the beta-amylase has achieved the reduction of long chains of glucose molecules to chains of one (glucose), two (maltose), or three (maltotriose) glucose molecules, the starch has been finally converted to fermentable sugar. This process is called *saccharification*.

### Nibbling and Chopping

Keeping the preceding points in mind, one can imagine that the conversion to fermentable sugars by the beta-amylase will be quicker if the chains that get nibbled at from the ends are more numerous. If alpha-amylase were not present, it would take too long for the beta-amylase to nibble its way through the very long chain of glucose (starch) molecules. Thus, with alpha-amylase chopping up the starch molecules, these two enzymes—alpha- and beta-amylase—work together in the mashing process to produce a yield of both unfermentable and fermentable malt extract. Proportionally, diastase is made up of approximately 25 percent alpha-amylase and 75 percent beta-amylase.

### Variables, Variables . . . Nothing's Perfect

Unfortunately, many variables interfere with the perfect enzymatic progression. Let's take a look at some of them.

## TEMPERATURE

Alpha-amylase works best (but not exclusively!) at temperatures between 149 and 153 degrees F (65 to 67 C). It will become deactivated within 2 hours at a temperature of 153 degrees F (67 C).

Beta amylase works best (but not exclusively!) at temperatures between 126 and 144 degrees F (52 to 62 C). It will become deactivated within 40 to 60 minutes at a temperature of 149 degrees F (65 C).

**It is important that the all-grain homebrewer realize that both enzymes generally work well together at temperatures between 145 and 158 degrees F (63 to 70 C).** In general, the higher mash temperatures will produce dextrinous (heavy-bodied beer) worts in a very short, active period, while lower temperatures produce more fermentable (lighter-bodied, more alcoholic beer) worts over a longer period.

When mashing, the brewer, especially the homebrewer, must compromise with regard to the equipment at hand and the degree of sophistication that is practical.

## TIME ($E = mc^2$: TIME IS RELATIVE)

The time it takes to fully convert starch to dextrins and fermentable sugars varies with temperature, amount of enzymes, and amount of starch to be converted.

Generally, higher temperatures will trigger quicker conversions but will produce more dextrins.

In practice, most homebrewers will experience conversion within 15 to 25 minutes at temperatures of about 158 degrees F (70 C) and conversion within 45 to 90 minutes at temperatures of about 150 degrees F (65 C). These times are based on mashes consisting of malt with a proportion of adjuncts no greater than 25 percent.

## PH

pH is a numerical measure of either acidity, neutrality, or alkalinity. Neutral is 7.0, less than 7.0 is acid, and greater than 7.0 is alkaline. The optimum pH for diastatic enzymes is 5.2 to 5.8. The optimum pH for proteolytic enzymes is 4.2 to 5.3. Usually a compromise is made at 5.2. Fortunately, a pH of about 5.2 is naturally achieved when water is mixed with the grains, because there are enzymes (not discussed in this book) and chemical reactions that occur almost immediately upon mixing. These reactions lower the pH of the mash even when the water is neutral.

A small amount of calcium sulfate ($CaSO_4$, gypsum) present or added to the brewing water helps the enzymes achieve a mashable pH.

In practice, monitoring the pH of the mash is not a high priority for a homebrewer, unless extremely soft or distilled water or water high in bicarbonates is used for brewing (see "Advanced Homebrewing and Water," page 304).

## THICKNESS OF THE MASH

The ratio of water to malt will have an effect on the activity of enzymes. Generally, thicker mashes favor proteolytic activity and thinner mashes favor diastatic activity.

## MINERAL CONTENT OF BREWING WATER

The most significant mineral that should be considered by the homebrewer is the calcium ion. The most natural and common source is calcium sulfate (gypsum). Its presence in the mash aids in acidifying the mash and helps inhibit alpha-amylase from deactivation caused by high temperatures.

Excessive amounts of bicarbonates or carbonates in the water can adversely affect mash yield.

## INGREDIENTS: VARIETIES OF BARLEY AND HOW MALTED

The type of malted barley a brewmaster chooses is a significant factor in the mashing procedures. Generally, there are three factors that the brewer needs to consider:

1. The variety of 2-row or 6-row barley used for malt.
2. The degree to which barley has been malted: fully modified or undermodified.
3. Enzymatic power: high or low.

## *Varieties of Barley*

Until about 1970, most American brewers used a 6-row variety of barley for the brewing of beer. One of the major factors for this choice was that the farmer could produce more yield per acre (approximately 160 bushels per acre) than from a 2-row variety (approximately 80 bushels per acre). Due to the many agricultural changes, agriculturists have been able to develop strains of 2-row barley that approach quality and yields comparable to 6-row varieties.

*2-row*—Physically, 2-row barley appears to be a plumper kernel, having less husk than 6-row varieties. Because of its plumpness, the kernel has more starch and potential yield (extract) per weight. Some brewers believe that the thinner husk associated with 2-row varieties of malted barley makes for mellower beers due to the reduction in the amount of tannins and "phenolic" flavors derived from husk material. However, the lesser amount of husk creates some problematic considerations in that the husk material is utilized by the brewer as a filter bed during the sparging process (separation of the sweet liquid from the spent grains). Extra care is often required by professional brewers to ensure adequate filtering by the husks.

The enzyme potential of 2-row malted barley varies with the strain being used. Generally, 2-row malt has less enzyme potential than 6-row varieties, but the gap continues to narrow as new strains are bred. American 2-row has more enzyme potential than English varieties. New strains are always being developed to try to match 6-row enzyme potential.

In summary, the brewer can achieve greater extract per weight of 2-row malted barley. The brewer should realize that the types of sugars and dextrins produced during mashing are not influenced by the type of malted barley used as long as the mashing procedures are identical.

*6-row*—A higher percentage of the entire weight of 6-row varieties of malted barley is attributable to the husk and embryo. Generally, 6-row varieties have a greater enzyme potential and are able to convert as much as 30 to 40 percent extra starch (adjuncts) to sugars and dextrins. The greater amount of husk material enables easier filtering during the sparging and lautering process. Brewers often are concerned with the amount of husk tannins that may be leached out during excessive or improper sparging techniques.

In summary, 6-row varieties of malted barley will yield less extract per weight of kernel but are desirable for mashing with adjuncts due to their generally higher enzyme content.

## MALTING AND MODIFICATION

To the maltster, *modification* is defined as the degree to which the "meaty part" or starchy "endosperm" is converted to soluble malt starch (and usable amino acids). Modification begins near the sprouting embryo and progresses through the kernel.

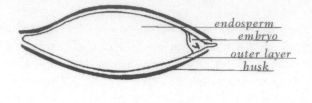

endosperm
embryo
outer layer
husk

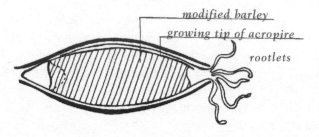

modified barley
growing tip of acropire
rootlets

Full modification is at the expense of malt yield because as time progresses toward full modification a lot of waste (weight of kernel, potential yield) goes into the growth of the acrospire (the growing shoot). The maltster has the choice of producing fully modified or undermodified malt depending on the needs of the brewer.

Full modification also results in the conversion of very long chains of proteins to usable yeast nutrients (amino acids). If fully modified malt is used in the brewing process, a protein rest (see the proteolytic enzymes section on page 289) during the initial phases of mashing is not necessary.

Undermodification will result in the potential for more yield per weight of barley but necessitates a protein rest during the mash in order to develop amino acids to be utilized by the yeasts as nutrients.

NOTE: Modification does not have anything to do with high or low enzyme content. There are strains of 2-row and 6-row barley possessing either high or low enzyme content.

After barley has been malted its composition will be approximately:

soluble starches.......... 82 to 88 percent
fermentable sugars..... 12 to 18 percent
glucose....................... 1 to 2 percent
maltose ...................... 8 to 11 percent
maltotriose................. 3 to 5 percent
sucrose....................... less than 1 percent

## In Summary

*Highly modified malt* has fewer complex proteins and more free amino acids available to the yeast as nutrients. The brewer who uses highly modified malt has less concern about haze problems created by the raw proteins that are in undermodified malt. The degree of attenuation is largely dependent on mash temperatures.

*Undermodified malt* has more complex proteins and fewer free amino acids. If this type of malt does not go through proteolytic conversions during the protein rest, then yeast nutrients may be lacking and attenuation will not be optimal. This is a more critical consideration when brewing with starch adjuncts such as rice and corn. Slower or stuck fermentations may result. Protein haze problems in the finished beer may also occur. It is not a critical consideration with all malt beer. The degree of attenuation is dependent on mash temperatures and development of yeast nutrients during the mashing process.

*Enzymatic power*—As already discussed, the variety of barley will not necessarily indicate the amount of enzymatic power the malt will have. But in general, it can be considered that 6-row varieties have more enzymes; some varieties can convert as much as 30 to 40 percent additional adjuncts. The 2-row varieties can convert 10 to 20 percent additional adjuncts.

The homebrewer with the limitations and variability of ingredients and techniques should consider the lower percentage range of adjuncts. There should be very little problem in converting 20 percent adjuncts with high enzyme varieties of malted barley and 5 to 10 percent adjuncts with lower enzyme varieties.

## THE USE OF ADJUNCTS (STARCH)

Fermentable sugars other than those derived from malt can be used in the brewing process. Although the traditional ingredients in German-style beers are malt, hops, yeast, and water, brewers have found that economic considerations will often require that locally grown starchy foods be utilized in the beer process.

> Until the late 1980s, Germany was the only country in the world that had a strict law against using anything but the four basic ingredients. They still consider beer to be their national drink, but the law, called the *Reinheitsgebot*, is an option now that Germany has become a member of the EEC (European Economic Community). The option enables German brewers to brew non-*Reinheitsgebot* beer for export and non-*Reinheitsgebot* "beer" for its own national consumption—but they are not permitted to call it beer. The world is changing and these rules are constantly under pressure for reconsideration.

All forms of starch can be converted to fermentable sugars. Often the abundance of certain cereal grains or vegetable starches in a particular region will provide a cheaper source of a beer ingredient than malted barley. Some of the unmalted cereal grains and vegetables that can be used in the brewing process are: barley, corn (maize), oats, wheat, rye, triticale, potato, rice, sorghum, millet, milo maize, and tapioca (cassava, manioc). Adjuncts are often used to achieve in the finished beer certain characteristics such as flavor, visual appearance, and stability (flavor and foam). The use of properly prepared adjuncts will often contribute a neutral flavor to the beer and promote a lighter body. Some adjuncts and variability in processing adjuncts can produce unique flavors, both desirable and undesirable.

Commercial brewers using sophisticated brewing techniques may use up to 40 percent adjuncts in their mashes. Homebrewers, with proper processing, attention to mashing techniques, and quality ingredients, can effectively utilize 10 to 20 percent adjuncts in their homebrews.

Although economy and distinctiveness can be achieved with adjuncts, there are some problems that can be encountered by both professional brewers and homebrewers. With attention to proper processing, many problems can be overcome. For the homebrewer some of the problems are not as easily overcome. However, these problems should never deter you from using adjuncts if you are inclined to use them. It is easy to homebrew quality beer with the use of adjuncts. Your endeavors will lead you to some very classic, enjoyable, and unique styles of beer.

With some adjuncts, the most common problem that you will likely encounter is a stuck runoff during the lautering and sparging process. Stuck runoffs are due to the presence of vegetable gums that serve to clog the filter bed created by spent grains. Another problem often caused by the use of adjuncts is haze in the finished beer. Haze problems are caused by insoluble proteins that were not or could not be fully degraded by proteolytic enzymes during the mashing process. Still another problem that may be encountered is poor foam stability due to vegetable oils that may be present in whole unprocessed grains.

Most problems can be alleviated or avoided by using properly prepared adjuncts.

## Preparation of Adjuncts

All starch adjuncts must go through a process called gelatinization before they can be utilized and converted by enzymes to fermentable sugars and nonfermentable dextrins. Gelatinization describes the process of cooking insoluble starch to a degree that allows it to "swell" and become soluble and vulnerable to enzyme degradation. Some starches will gelatinize at temperatures below 140 degrees F (60 C) while others require prolonged boiling. The need to gelatinize starch adjuncts means that the homebrewer must often cook cereal grains or vegetable starches before they are added to the mash.

Grains are available to homebrewers in a variety of forms, some of which are precooked (gelatinized) and can be added directly to the mash. The following list provides a short description of the various ways cereal grains are available to the homebrewer. They are listed in order of the degree of processing.

1. *Whole grains*—Whole grains are often the easiest and cheapest to find; however, their use presents problems for the homebrewer. Husks, bran, and the germ of the grain will still be intact. When whole grains are milled and cooked, undesirable flavors and other characteristics may be imparted to the beer. The husks will contribute phenolic and harsh flavors because of the presence of tannins. The bran and germ will contribute to poor head stability and inhibition of fermentation due to the presence of oils and fats. Old or improperly stored grain will have rancid (oxidized) oils that may detract from beer flavor.

    Whole grains, if used, must be ground into granules and cooked.

2. *De-husked grains*—Barley, brown rice, rye, oats, millet, triticale, and wheat berries often are available in the de-husked form. The harsh flavors produced by the husk are eliminated. However, oils and fats are still present, and with grains that have a great amount of oils the flavor of the beer will be influenced. De-husked grains are not gelatinized.

3. *De-branned grains*—Pearled barley and white rice are good examples of this degree of processing. With proper grinding or milling, these forms of grains can be easily utilized by the homebrewer. De-branned grains are not gelatinized.

4. *Grits*—Grains that have been de-husked, de-branned, de-germed, and then milled into small granules are called grits. Grits are useful to the homebrewer in that milling is not required. Grits are not gelatinized.

5. *Flakes*—Grits or forms of grains that have been moistened and passed between rollers are described as being flaked. The massive pressure involved in rolling wet grains creates heat. This heat along with the heat that is added to the rollers instantly gelatinizes these grains. Because flaked grains are gelatinized they can be added directly to the mash without precooking. The appearance of flaked grains is similar to uncooked oatmeal.

6. *Torrefied grains*—Grains that have undergone a process that gives them a character similar to puffed wheat, puffed rice, or popcorn are called torrefied. These grains are gelatinized and once they are crushed can be added directly to the mash.

7. *Refined starch*—Grain that has undergone extensive processing, including gelatinization, is called refined starch. A common example is cornstarch. Refined starch is very easy for the homebrewer to use and can be added directly to the mash.

## Adjuncts Commonly Used and Available to Homebrewers

BARLEY—As an adjunct, unmalted barley will contribute to foam (head) retention in the finished beer. The nitrogenous and complex proteins that contribute to head retention also contribute to chill haze problems. Traditionally barley was a classic ingredient used in the world-famous Guinness Stout. Clarity problems make it inappropriate for light beers, unless you desire the look of haze-infused beer.

Flaked barley is the easiest to use. If pearled or de-husked barley is used, it should be milled into small granules. Barley is gelatinized at low mashing temperatures, but homebrewers should cook all forms of barley (other than flaked barley) to ensure gelatinization and complete conversion during the mashing process.

Barley has a significant amount of vegetable gum and can inhibit runoff during lautering and sparging.

CASSAVA (TAPIOCA, MANIOC, YUCA, MACAXIERA)—This is one ingredient that has become more readily available to the American homebrewer through Asian and Latin ethnic food markets. Cassava is a starchy root easily grown in tropical climates. Its starchy character resembles potatoes.

I have tasted a native homebrew brewed with cassava in the Fiji Islands: *Vale vakaviti!* It was a 24-hour concoction of boiled cassava root, sugar, water, and yeast. Although cloudy and yeasty, its flavor was not all that objectionable. What surprised me the most was the announcement made in my honor the day before: "You want homebrew? Then tomorrow we will have homebrew." And so it was brewed to Pacific potency on the tiny and very remote island of Lakemba in 24 hours. (I wonder what the Pacific gravity was?)

If the opportunity ever presents itself to you and you are inspired, cook and physically crush the cassava before adding it to the mash for conversion.

CORN (MAIZE)—Fermentables that are derived from cornstarch will theoretically provide a neutral flavor to the beer. Their use will lighten the body and flavor of the finished beer. Some brewmasters claim that the use of corn (10 to 20 percent) will help stabilize the flavor of beer. This is logically true because all malt beer has more and "fuller" flavors from the all malt ingredients that can destabilize over a period of time. Corn contributes no flavor, therefore there is little character that can destabilize.

Regular cornstarch is the easiest form of corn to use (but usually the most expensive). It is easily converted in the mash without precooking. Flaked corn, if available (not the breakfast cereals, which have other ingredients added), can also be easily utilized in the mash. If corn grits or polenta are used they must be boiled in water for 30 minutes. After gelatinization, the starches may be added to the mash.

OATS—The high protein, fat, and oil content of oats is theoretically a deterrent to their use in brewing, but I have enjoyed many a fine brew with oats as an ingredient. Never mind the theory, make an oatmeal stout and gloat with oats. Oat malt is also available.

Oats have been used in the brewing process, particularly in the brewing of oatmeal stout. The character of this stout lingers as fond memories. There are several oatmeal stouts commercially produced today. It has been popularized by homebrewers and American craft brewers. Add 1 to 1 1/2 pounds (454–681 g) into your mash for a 5-gallon (19 l) batch.

POTATO—Potatoes, whether they are red, white, purple, sweet, or yam, are an easily gelatinized form of starch. Fermentables produced from potato starch (other than sweet potatoes or yams) do not contribute significantly to the character or flavor of beer, other than providing fermentables to be converted to alcohol. Sliced or chopped potatoes may be added directly to the mash. They are gelatinized at mashing temperatures. The homebrewer may choose to pre-cook potatoes to help assure complete conversion.

RICE—Rice is one of the more common adjuncts used by commercial breweries. It offers a clean source of fermentables, neutral flavor, and beer body lighteners.

White rice or rice grits are commonly available and are easily used. Whole white rice should be ground into small granules before cooking. It is absolutely necessary to cook the rice for 30 minutes in boiling water in order to gelatinize it. Black, sweet, purple, and red rice currently of Asian or South American origin offer intriguing possibilities for innovative brews. Black rice stout anyone?

RYE—The character that rye contributes to beer can be spicy, dry, and crisp. Unmalted rye, rye flakes, and malted rye are all available. Rye was primarily used in the process of making rye whiskey, but now with the popularity of rye ales and lagers brewed by homebrewers and commercial small brewers, rye has become more popular. It is a starch that can be gelatinized at mashing temperatures and converted to fermentable sugars, but the malting and mashing process usually produces "gooey" substances that result in "stuck" runoffs. Brewers who use rye usually add neutral and nonreactive rice husk/hulls to their mash. Rice husks/hulls are available at homebrew shops, specifically for the purpose of "loosening" the mash so liquid can more easily trickle through the mash during the straining process. Rye in brewing, particularly by homebrewers, is worth exploring.

SORGHUM, MILLET, MILO MAIZE—Sorghums, millet, and milo maize contain a great amount of oils and fats. These oils will go rancid with age or improper storage. Old and stale grain can detract from the flavor of the finished beer. The oils and fats can detract from the overall profile of the beer. Experiments have been done with special processing of these grains to remove oils and fats, making the grains more suitable for brewing.

A homebrewer is more likely to be able to utilize quality millet because the beer is fresh when consumed. My adventurous spirit has long invited me to experiment with this grain. There is much interest in these grains for brewing because they do not have gluten. Several gluten-free beers use sorghum, millet, milo maize, and/or sorghum (or millet) malt as their bases. These grains can also be toasted/roasted and added to beer, imparting a complex roast character.

Traditional and ceremonious beers are made with millet or sorghum in regions of the world where it grows in abundance, particularly the Himalayas, Pakistan, Nepal, and many parts of Africa.

TRITICALE—Triticale is a trademarked name of a grain hybrid that is a cross between rye and wheat. It has a low gelatinizing temperature. Its use by the homebrewer is largely unexplored. Anyone interested in "piobeering?"

WHEAT—Malted wheat, unmalted wheat, and torrefied wheat are often used for certain styles of beer.

Malted wheat can be milled and added to the mash grist in the same manner as malted barley. Because there are very few enzymes in malted wheat it is desirable but not necessary to mash it with malted barley of high enzymatic power.

Unmalted wheat in the form of wheat flakes or wheat flour is often used as an adjunct by brewers who wish to economize, enhance head retention and foam stability, lighten flavor and body, or brew a particular style of beer. The variety of wheat that is preferred as an adjunct is usually of the soft type (rather than "hard wheat"), low in protein (low gluten, low nitrogen).

Because of wheat's low gelatinizing temperatures, it can be added directly to the mash. Flaked wheat, wheat flour, or torrefied wheat can be added directly to the mash. Flaked wheat is already gelatinized. But again, I would advise homebrewers to precook any form of wheat in order that protein and starch conversion be assured during the mashing process.

Some chill haze problems may be experienced with the use of wheat as an adjunct. Amounts greater than 10 percent of any form of wheat will inhibit runoff during the lautering and sparging process. Rice hulls/husks can be added to the mash to alleviate this challenge.

QUINOA, TEFF, BUCKWHEAT, DINKEL, SPELT, KHOROSAN (KAMUT), AMARANTH, WILD RICE—These grains and others continue to attract experimentation by homebrewers and progressive small brewers. They are adventures in the waiting, but I am sure history would uncover a somewhere and a sometime people who have already done it. At least you may be "the first on your block. . . ."

Quinoa, from Peru; teff, from Ethiopia; buckwheat, from Asia; dinkel, spelt, and khorosan (Kamut) ancient varieties of wheat; amaranth, a nutritional grain from South American Indian cultures; and others offer some very interesting possibilities and the excitement of coming up with a truly unique beer. When in doubt, it will do little harm to boil these and other grains to gelatinize their starches and brew on.

Wild rice is not really rice. It is an indigenous grain first popularized as a specialty ingredient by craft- and homebrewers in Minnesota and Wisconsin, where it grows. Who'll be the first to brew with the starchy root of the cattail plant? Or revive the ancient Hawaiian brew called Okole, made from the roasted root of the ubiquitous ti plant?

For more detailed information about these and many more fermentable adjuncts see the "Fermentable Adjuncts" section of *The Homebrewer's Companion, Second Edition*.

# ADVANCED HOMEBREWING AND HOPS

Advanced homebrewers can choose to deal with fancy mathematical formulas to calculate bittering units and stage balancing acts, but by no means should any brewer substitute anything for quality, freshness, accurate information, and—most important—experience. Experience, more than anything else, will improve your ability to refine the artful balancing act between hop bitterness, flavor, aroma, and beer's sweetness and body.

There are methods by which homebrewers can match the bitter qualities of commercially made beer throughout the world, just by knowing the amount of International Bitterness Units in a given recipe. But before we get into these methods, a brief account of how hop bitterness can be lost in the beermaking process would be helpful.

## BITTERNESS

Not all of the bitterness potential from the alpha acid in the hop is utilized during the brewing and fermentation process. Under ideal conditions, when one boils all 5 gallons (19 l) of a 5-gallon batch of beer (as opposed to boiling a malt-extract-based concentrated wort, then adding cold water in the fermenter later), only 50 percent of the chemical conversion of alpha acid to isomerized (*iso-* for "short") alpha acid occurs. *The higher the specific gravity of your boiled wort the less efficient the extraction of bitterness will be.*

There is further loss of isoalpha acid bitterness as yeast and protein sediment have a natural tendency to attract isoalpha acid molecules. Bitterness compounds can ride on foam and be carried out or left behind during fermentation or transfer. After all is said and done, one can hope for about 30 percent utilization of the available potential bitterness in hops.

Percent utilization (% U) is equal to the amount of alpha acid present in the hop divided by the amount of alpha acid actually transferred into the finished beer multiplied by 100:

$$\% \ U = (\text{Isoalpha acid present} \div \text{alpha acid used}) \times 100$$

The "Hop Utilization Chart" on page 303 portrays examples of hop utilization based on density (original specific gravity) and length of boiling. Most homebrew recipe software will automatically calculate the utilization based on time and density and can quite accurately predict the final bitterness of your beer. If you're mathematically inclined and you are following a recipe and the desired bitterness is stated in terms of IBUs, you can use the following formula to calculate how much bittering hops to use when boiling your wort. (NOTE: Percentages are expressed as whole numbers, i.e., 15% = 15. Volumes are total volumes for recipe.)

*Metric units:*

$$\text{Weight}_{\text{grams}} = \frac{\text{Volume}_{\text{liters}} \times \text{IBU} \times 10}{\%\text{Utilization} \times \%\text{alpha acid of hops}}$$

Likewise:

$$\text{IBU} = \frac{\text{Weight}_{\text{grams}} \times \%\text{Utilization} \times \%\text{alpha acid of hops}}{\text{Volume}_{\text{liters}} \times 10}$$

*English units:*

$$\text{Weight}_{\text{ounces}} = \frac{\text{Volume}_{\text{gallons}} \times \text{IBU} \times 1.34}{\%\text{Utilization} \times \%\text{alpha acid of hops}}$$

Likewise:

$$\text{IBU} = \frac{\text{Weight}_{\text{ounces}} \times \%\text{alpha acid of hops} \times \%\text{Utilization}}{\text{Volume}_{\text{gallons}} \times 1.34}$$

For example, if I add 1 ounce of 5 percent alpha acid Hallertau hops during the last 15 minutes of the boil to a malt extract and water boil (I used 6 pounds of extract to 2 gallons of water for the boil, which gives me 6% utilization as indicated in the Hop Utilization Chart, page 303; but remember there are 5 gallons total for the recipe), then I would add bitterness to my beer in the amount of:

$$\text{IBU} = \frac{1 \times 5 \times 6}{5 \times 1.34} = 4.5$$

When using the International Bitterness Units equations, HBUs may be conveniently substituted in the formula for Weight$_{\text{ounces}} \times \%$ alpha acid of hops.

$$\text{IBU} = \frac{\text{HBU} \times \%\text{Utilization}}{\text{Volume}_{\text{gallons}} \times 1.34}$$

For 5 gallons (19 l) the formula is simplified to:

$$\text{IBU} = \frac{\text{HBU} \times \%\text{Utilization}}{6.7}$$

# Hop Utilization Chart
## Based on Density of Boiled Wort and Boiling Time

In Percent Utilization for Whole Hops (and Hop Pellets)

| APPROXIMATE SPECIFIC GRAVITY OF BOIL | 1.040 (10) | 1.070 (17.5) | 1.110 (28) | 1.130 (32.5) | 1.150 (37.5) |
|---|---|---|---|---|---|
| LBS. OF MALT EXTRACT PER GALLONS OF BOILING WATER | 1 lb./gal. 450g/3.8 l | 2 lbs./ga. 910g/3.8 l | 3 lbs./gal. 1.4kg/3.8 l | 4 lbs./gal. 1.8kg/3.8 l | 5 lbs./gal. 2.3 kg/3.8 l |
| **TIME OF BOIL** | | | | | |
| 15 minutes | 8% (9.6%) | 7% (8%) | 6% (7%) | 6% (7%) | 5% (6%) |
| 30 minutes | 15% (18%) | 14% (17%) | 12% (14%) | 11% (14%) | 10% (12%) |
| 45 minutes | 27% (30%) | 24% (29%) | 21% (25%) | 19% (23%) | 18% (21%) |
| 60 minutes | 30% (30%) | 27% (30%) | 23% (27%) | 21% (25%) | 20% (24%) |

For more information see the "Hops" section of *The Homebrewer's Companion, Second Edition.*

## ADVANCED HOMEBREWING AND WATER

The science of water and its significance in the brewing of beer can be a mind bender and become extremely involved. All of the important factors such as mineral content, pH, acidity, alkalinity, hardness, and temperature are influenced by one another.

The importance of brewing water becomes significant when brewing all-grain beer. Malt extract beers have already been properly balanced with minerals during the manufacturer's mashing process. When malt extract is made, evaporation removes only the water. However, when homebrewing all-grain beers, the important mineral balance necessary for proper enzyme activity may not be present; therefore, it would be prudent to learn the fundamentals of water and brewing. And for the homebrewer who wishes to duplicate traditional and world-classic beers, an even more thorough understanding of water chemistry is required.

Most homebrewers (even all-grain homebrewers) need not work themselves into a hydraulic frenzy over perfecting their water. There are so many other more important variables that require attention to ensure quality beer; the most important are sanitation and quality ingredients. Relatively speaking, so long as the water you use is potable and not extremely hard, then water becomes a lower priority. Where hard water (111 parts per million total hardness) or certainly very hard water (in excess of 200 parts per million total hardness) is used, mashing can be a frustrating affair. pH measurements of 8 and above are indications of both temporary and permanent hardness: a poor environment for diastatic enzymes to convert starches to sugars. Brewers with hard water will experience poor yields from their mash and harsh "husklike" and astringent flavors in their brew. To improve mash yields and reduce undesirable flavors you may treat the water with the addition of certain food-grade acids, acidified malt, or acids produced naturally with what is called a sour mash process.

If you use municipal water that is treated with chlorine, one of the simplest and most dramatic things you can do to improve your beers is to pass all brewing water through a countertop or more elaborate charcoal-type filter to remove chlorine. Chlorine will combine with organic compounds (beer worts included) and produce chlorophenols that even in parts per billion can lend a harsh flavor and aroma to your brew.

When the time comes and inspiration has evolved a desire for you to understand water and its relation to brewing, then you will need to know about the fundamental principles that concern water and beer brewing. What follows is a brief primer. For a continued discussion on water refer to *The Homebrewer's Companion, Second Edition.*

## WHAT IS HARD WATER? WHAT IS SOFT WATER?

The terms *hard* and *soft* were derived a long, long, long time ago when people began using soap. The ability of soap to lather is affected by the mineral content of the water. Generally, a high mineral content in water will inhibit lathering of soap; thus, it is "hard" to lather, ergo: hard water! Water having low mineral content is generally considered "soft" water.

Water hardness is measured in two ways: temporary hardness and permanent hardness. Total hardness is the combined effect of the two measurements. In the United States, total hardness is expressed in parts per million (ppm) of certain minerals and determines the degree of softness or hardness. Generally:

0 to 50 ppm is considered soft water
51 to 110 ppm is considered medium hard water
111 to 200 ppm is considered hard water
greater than 200 ppm is considered very hard water

## WHAT IS MEASURED TO DETERMINE TOTAL HARDNESS?

Essentially, total hardness is the measure of the bicarbonate, magnesium (Mg), and calcium (Ca) ions present in the water.

## WHAT IS TEMPORARY HARDNESS? HOW DOES IT AFFECT THE BREWING PROCESS?

In the United States temporary hardness is determined by a measure of bicarbonates [$2(HCO_3)$]. The hardness that bicarbonate ions contribute is temporary because it is easily precipitated (becomes solid) and is removed when water is boiled or treated with certain acids.

A measure of bicarbonates (temporary hardness) greater than 100 ppm is undesirable because of its contribution to the alkalinity (higher pH) of water and the harsh, bitter flavor that it imparts to beer. Alkalinity will inhibit the proper acid pH balance necessary during mashing, resulting in inadequate conversion of starch to fermentables. If used for sparging grains, alkaline water will extract undesirable harsh grainy flavors.

## WHAT IS PERMANENT HARDNESS?
## HOW DOES IT AFFECT THE BREWING PROCESS?

In the United States, permanent hardness is determined by a measure of calcium and magnesium ions, the calcium being more significant. It is that portion of total hardness remaining after the water has been boiled.

Generally, permanent hardness and the calcium ion raise the acidity (lower the pH) of water. A certain amount of permanent hardness is desirable in the homebrewing of all-grain beers. Enzyme conversion (starch to sugars) works best at a mash pH of 5.2 (acid).

## WHAT IS pH AND WHAT IS ITS SIGNIFICANCE IN BREWING?

pH is a measure of acidity and alkalinity of solutions and is measured on a scale of 0 to 14: 7.0 is neutral; less than 7.0 is acid; greater than 7.0 is alkaline.

Its measurement *is* affected by temperature. The pH of a solution at 150 degrees F (66 C) will be .35 less than at 65 degrees F (18 C). In other words, if a 150-degree mash measures 5.2, then a reading at 65 degrees F would indicate a pH of 5.55.

A measure of the pH of the brewing water *does not* give an indication of what the mash pH will be. The mineral content, particularly calcium, is more influential than the apparent pH of the water.

pH can be approximately measured with pH papers that are available at homebrew or chemical supply stores or pharmacies.

## WHAT MINERALS INFLUENCE THE BREWING PROCESS?

The calcium ion is by far the most significantly influential mineral in the brewing process. Its influence begins when the water in which it is dissolved is mixed with the malt grist. The calcium ion reacts and acidifies the mash with phosphates that are naturally present in malted barley. When calcium is present in quantities of 50 ppm or more, it will acidify the mash, usually dropping the pH to about 5.2. This process of "acidification" is often referred to as "buffering." The presence of the calcium ion is influential even in very small amounts. The small amount of calcium that is present in the malt will result in the acidification of distilled water (pH = 7.0) and malt grist to a pH value of 5.8.

In appropriate amounts the calcium ion also aids in protecting alpha-amylase from heat inactivation. It also helps reduce tannin and husk flavors from beer wort.

If there is an excessive amount of calcium, a harsh, thin flavor may characterize the beer. There also will be poor hop utilization due to inhibition of the necessary isomerization process (making hop-bittering resins soluble) during the boiling of the wort.

The bicarbonate $[2(HCO_3)]$ ion (temporary hardness) counters the positive effects of calcium ions. Its presence in excess of 100 ppm will alkalize the mash.

## HOW CAN THE pH OF THE MASH BE ADJUSTED?

The addition of calcium in the form of calcium sulfate ($CaSO_4$, gypsum) is the most acceptable way of influencing mash pH. If this is not available or if you would like to brew with very soft water (as some of the classic pilsener beers are), then a more sophisticated technique of adding lactic acid can accomplish acidification in the mash. A technique calling for an "acid rest" at about 90 degrees F (32 C) will also develop varying degrees of acidity. Additional information about acid rests is in *The Homebrewer's Companion, Second Edition*.

## WHERE CAN I FIND INFORMATION ABOUT MY WATER?

Consult your local town, city, or county water board or their Website. They will usually supply you with free information about the contents of your water.

## WHAT KINDS OF WATER ARE USED IN SOME OF THE FAMOUS (AND NOT-SO-FAMOUS) BREWING AREAS OF THE WORLD?

See accompanying examples: Pilsen, Munich, Dublin, Dortmund, Burton-on-Trent, Milwaukee in the illustrative chart on page 308. More cities can be found in *The Homebrewer's Companion, Second Edition*.

## CAN I ADJUST MY WATER?

It is much easier to add a mineral than to remove a mineral. The homebrewer who desires to make a variety of adjustments and has access to very soft or distilled water is most fortunate because adjustments are only a matter of adding certain minerals. If you have hard water and desire soft or mineral-free water, it is easiest to buy distilled, deionized or R/O (reverse osmosis) water and add minerals. For the waterlogged homebrew enthusiast there are a number of relatively inexpensive home water treatment systems; look in a directory of local businesses either online or in your phone book under Water Purification and Filtration Equipment. Other types of water filters that will remove select compounds including undesirable chlorine are readily available. These systems can be very cost-effective over the long term and can be used for other household water consumption.

## Water Used in Famous Brewing Areas of the World

| MINERAL (ION) | PILSEN | MUNICH | DUBLIN | DORTMUND | BURTON-ON-TRENT | MILWAUKEE | YOUR WATER |
|---|---|---|---|---|---|---|---|
| Calcium (Ca) | 7 | 70–80 | 115–120 | 260 | 260–352 | 35 | |
| Sulfate ($SO_4$) | 5–6 | 5–10 | 54 | 283 | 630–820 | 18 | |
| Magnesium (Mg) | 2–8 | 18–19 | 4 | 23 | 24–60 | 11 | |
| Sodium (Na) | 32 | 10 | 12 | 69 | 54 | ? | |
| Chloride (Cl) | 5 | 1–2 | 19 | 106 | 16–36 | 5 | |

Numerical values represent parts per million (ppm).

Various minerals can be added to water; however, caution and knowledge of water chemistry should be pursued by the homebrewer before adding *any* chemical to water used for consumption. The following information will give you an indication of the amounts of minerals needed in order to achieve an increase in ion concentrations:

1 teaspoon (5.2 g) of gypsum ($CaSO_4$) in 5 gallons (19 l) of water will increase (approximately) the concentration of:
Calcium ($Ca^{++}$) ion ....................................................................... 64 ppm
Sulfate [($SO_4$)$^{--}$] ion................................................................ 153 ppm

1 teaspoon (5.3 g) of pure table salt (NaCl) in 5 gallons (19 l) of water will increase (approximately) the concentration of:
Sodium ($Na^+$) ion ..................................................................... 110 ppm
Chloride ($Cl^-$) ion................................................................... 169 ppm

1 teaspoon (3.4 g) of Epsom salts ($MgSO_4$) in 5 gallons (19 l) of water will increase (approximately) the concentration of:
Magnesium ($Mg^{++}$) ion ............................................................... 17 ppm
Sulfate [($SO_4$)$^{--}$] ion.................................................................. 70 ppm

1 teaspoon (4.8 g) of calcium chloride flakes ($CaCl_2$) in 5 gallons (19 l) of water will increase (approximately) the concentration of:
Calcium ($Ca^{++}$) ion ..................................................................... 91 ppm
Chloride (2Cl)$^{--}$ ion.............................................................. 162 ppm

A more involved discussion of brewing water is presented in the "Water" section of *The Homebrewer's Companion, Second Edition.*

## ADVANCED HOMEBREWING AND YEAST

The homebrewer who has given proper attention to sanitation will be pleased with the results obtainable by using quality dried cultures of beer yeast. However, there is room for improvement and variety in your homebrews if you choose to undertake the culturing of your own liquid beer yeasts. But as with undertaking any new procedures that will improve your beer, more effort is needed on your part not only to do so, but also to understand and have a feeling of what is going on with your homebrew. If you haven't done so already, read "The Secrets of Fermentation," page 119.

Cultured pure liquid beer yeasts are available at almost all homebrew supply shops.

Once you have obtained a live culture of beer yeast and wish to maintain it for future uses you will want to do the following:

1. Prepare a culturing medium.
2. Propagate the yeast for storage.
3. Propagate the yeast for beer fermentation when ready to brew.

Culturing your own yeast and keeping it healthy is easier than you probably expected. Dismiss your anxiety. RDWHAHB. Granted, it is an extra effort some may choose not to bother with, especially as it is so easy to just go to your local homebrew supply store and buy a fresh package of liquid yeast culture, ready to pitch into your wort. But for those of you who are inspired, the reward of having your favorite yeast on hand will be comforting and reassuring.

## CULTURING YEAST OR YEAST HERDING

There are many methods of culturing yeast; all of them stress sanitation and sterile procedures. The method that I have been using for more than thirty years is extremely easy and requires no extra equipment other than a butane cigarette lighter, cotton swabs (Q-Tips), ethyl "grain" alcohol (or high-proof spirits), and rubber corks that will allow fermentation locks to be affixed to beer bottles.

Equipment and ingredients necessary to culture yeast:

1. 12 clean 12-ounce (355 ml) beer bottles*
2. 12 bottle caps
3. 2 to 3 fermentation locks with rubber corks that will allow them to be used on a beer bottle
4. 6 ounces (170 g) dried light malt extract
5. ⅛ teaspoon (1 ml) olive oil (this provides fatty acids and serves as a yeast nutrient for increased yeast reproduction)
6. ¼ ounce (7 g) bitter whole hops
7. 2½ quarts (2.5 l) water
8. household bleach (for sanitizing)
9. ethyl "grain" alcohol or high-proof vodka
10. small, fine strainer
11. cotton swabs (Q-Tips)
12. glass measuring cup with pouring spout

## PREPARATION OF CULTURING MEDIUM (WORT)

1. Boil 6 ounces (170 g) malt extract, ⅛ teaspoon (1 ml) olive oil, ¼ ounce (7 g) hops, and 2½ quarts (2.5 l) water for 30 minutes. This wort is highly

---

*You will be preparing and bottling small amounts of sterile beer wort and propagating yeast in these bottles as required.

hopped in order to help inhibit bacterial growth. Do not substitute other sugars for malt extract.

2. While wort is boiling, sanitize the already clean beer bottles. Place ¼ teaspoon (2 ml) of household bleach in each clean bottle and fill with cold water. Allow to sit for 15 minutes. Rinse well with hot tap water. Then preheat bottles by filling with hot tap water. Meanwhile . . .

3. Boil bottle caps (or immerse in high-proof vodka or ethyl "grain" alcohol) and glass measuring cup for at least 15 minutes, to sterilize.

4. After wort has boiled for 30 minutes, remove hops by pouring wort through a strainer into another pot or saucepan. Bring to a boil again and continue to boil for at least 10 more minutes.

5. Drain the hot water from the beer bottles.

6. Using the sterile measuring cup, pour about 6 ounces (170 g) of boiling hot sterile wort into each sanitized beer bottle. Don't breathe, and work in a dust-free and draft-free room.

7. Place the sterile bottle caps atop the bottles immediately, and cap.

8. Label the bottles "Sterile Beer Wort" and let cool slowly at room temperature, after which you should store them in your refrigerator for use as needed.

## CULTURING THE YEAST

Whenever you are in the process of culturing your own yeast, sanitation is extremely important. It is essential that you work in a draft-free, dust-free

*Burning lips! Yeast culturing requires very careful attention to sanitation and contaminant-free procedures. All surfaces that come in contact with yeast cultures and sterile wort must be contaminant-free. A butane lighter burns off surface contaminants, while boiling or chlorine bleach sanitizers disinfects the insides of the culturing bottles. If these procedures are used, yeast can be successfully cultured in bottles of sterile beer wort.*

environment. If you are using your kitchen, do not expose yeast to air that is smoky or filled with cooking oil vapors. Bacteria will "ride" on dust and other solids that are suspended in air and *will* contaminate your yeast should they be offered the opportunity.

In the proper environment:

1. Remove the bottled sterile beer wort from storage and shake vigorously in order to aerate the wort.
2. Prepare a solution of ½ teaspoon (8 ml) of household bleach per quart (1 l) of water and immerse rubber corks and fermentation locks in order to sanitize.
3. Carefully remove cap from bottle of wort.
4. Carefully open container of pure yeast culture and pour into the beer wort. If your container of yeast is glass (beer bottle?) and the surface of the opening through which the yeast will be poured has been exposed to the air, swab the lip and surrounding surfaces with disinfecting ethyl "grain" alcohol. Use the cotton swabs for this purpose, then use your butane cigarette lighter to "torch" the surface. (CAUTION: Grain alcohol is dangerously flammable. Do not use flame when containers are open.) This procedure will burn off bacteria that have surely come to rest on the surface and would have been carried into the sterile wort by the yeast. If your container is plastic or foil and the opening was unprotected, carefully swab the surface with alcohol.
5. After the yeast has been added to the beer wort, hot-water rinse and shake the excess sanitizing solution from the fermentation lock and cork and place atop the bottle. Appropriately fill the fermentation lock with a weak sanitizing solution.
6. Allow the inoculated wort to sit at room temperature until a good healthy fermentation is visible (usually seen within 6 to 18 hours, or less). Then place fermenting culture in a cold refrigerator. *Do not place in the refrigerator unless fermentation is active*; otherwise, the cooling of the air space in the bottle may create a vacuum and suck the liquid in the fermentation lock into the wort. If fermentation is active, the carbon dioxide gas produced is always pushing air out of the bottle. Refrigeration will slow fermentation and provide a better environment for the yeast to go dormant. You can be assured that the yeast will remain healthy, active, and ready to pitch into beer for at least 2 to 4 weeks, after which time you should propagate the yeast in another bottle of sterile beer wort. Through experience, I have discovered that if your bottle of yeast is not disturbed (no agitation or shaking), your yeast will survive for more than a year using this method, and still make excellent beer. Of course, after extended hibernation your yeast will certainly take a bit more time to

culture up to amounts useful for fermenting beer, but indeed it will. At no time should the fermenting wort be fully capped. One last caveat: Results will vary depending on the strain of yeast.

Your kitchen refrigerator is probably the most bacterially contaminated place in your house. Be absolutely certain to swab with alcohol and flame the pouring surfaces of your bottles of cultured yeast before transferring them from their storage container to anywhere else.

## Culturing Yeast for Pitching into Wort

As a homebrewer, you want enough yeast to pitch into your wort for quick, active fermentation. Ideally, the "rate" at which you would like to pitch into a 5-gallon (19 l) batch of beer would be 4 to 8 fluid ounces (120 to 240 ml) of yeast slurry (sediment). That's a lot of yeast! You can obtain this amount of yeast either by carefully removing and repitching the sediment from a primary fermentation (or, less ideally, from a secondary fermentation) or by pitching your yeast into an ever-increasing amount of wort and harvesting the sediment; starting with ½ to 1 pint (0.25 to 0.5 l) to 1 quart (1 l) to 1 gallon (4 l) to 2½ gallons (9 l) to 5 gallons (19 l).

Harvesting yeast from active primary (or secondary) fermentations is an easy way to obtain enough yeast for pitching into your beer. However, you must be certain that the yeast is not and will not get contaminated in the process. If in doubt, don't use it.

"Step-culturing" is laborious, time-consuming and very effective! However, on a practical level I have found that pitching active yeast that has been cultured from a bottle containing 16 to 20 ounces (480 to 600 ml) of fermenting wort has provided me with excellent results. Theoretically, I am certainly underpitching, but with the yeast that I am using the results are very satisfactory, even when visible fermentation is not evident for 12 to 18 hours. If the proper amount of yeast is pitched, visible fermentation will be evident within 12 hours—an ideal situation.

Let it be your choice and your experience that determine to what degree you want to step-culture your yeast.

## PROLONGED STORAGE OF YEAST

Once the yeast has gone through its fermentation cycle and its source of food is exhausted, the yeast will go into a period of dormancy. This life period will vary with the strain of yeast. After a prolonged period the yeast will begin to die. The period in which yeast will remain viable during the cells' hibernation will be dramatically shortened if the yeast is agitated.

Yeast can be stored for long periods by freezing. In order to freeze yeast without destroying the cell walls, glycerol should be added to the slurry in an amount equal to 10 percent of the total volume. If this is done correctly, the yeast may be frozen for up to one year before reculturing is necessary.

## CONTAMINATED YEAST

Your yeast can become contaminated with bacteria or wild yeast. Some of the most common indications of contaminated yeast are: 1) there is a visual deposit of yeast inside and on the glass at the surface of the beer, 2) fermentation often proceeds slowly for weeks, 3) the beer smells and/or tastes like Band-Aid plastic. The easiest and best solution to the problem of having contaminated yeast is to return to the original source of yeast and start over and make sure that all the brewing equipment that has come into contact with the contamination is cleaned and disinfected.

There are methods of "washing" yeast in weak acid solutions. These washes will inhibit or kill bacteria, but because yeast is more acid-resistant it will survive (though its qualities may suffer a little). If your yeast is contaminated with wild yeast it is virtually impossible for the homebrewer to separate the good from the bad. Your best bet is to replace the yeast. If this is not possible, sob (but don't let the tears fall into the beer).

## ADDITIONAL YEAST INFORMATION RESOURCES FOR THE HOMEBREWER

The November/December 1998 Special Issue and the 1989 Special Issue of *Zymurgy* magazine are both devoted to the subject of yeast and homebrewing. They are excellent resources for further reading on the subject of yeast, its culture, and its use in homebrewing. They are both available from the American Homebrewers Association, P.O. Box 1679, Boulder, CO 80306, USA, or at www.homebrewersassociation.org. Two excellent Websites are: www.wyeastlab.com and www.whitelabs.com. Additional discussion of yeast types and culturing is given in more detail in *The Homebrewer's Companion, Second Edition*.

> *"If the love of what you're doing exceeds the effort needed to do it, success is inevitable."*
> —Bob Beers and others

## LET'S GET PRACTICAL

### SPECIAL EQUIPMENT FOR THE ADVANCED HOMEBREWER

So, after all of this brew-haha you still want to brew your own beer from scratch. I admire your persistence. With that kind of attitude you are certainly more than likely to succeed.

You'll need some specialized equipment, some of which you may already have; otherwise, all items are available for purchase. The necessary equipment is simple enough so that it will be within your means to fabricate if necessary. If you can't personally do it, I am sure that some homebrew-appreciating friend will be happy to trade some brew for fabrication.

There are four essential pieces of equipment unique to all-grain mashing that you will have to procure:

1. A mill to grind your malt
2. A mash-tun to contain the malt grist and water at controllable temperatures
3. A lauter-tun to strain and separate the sweet wort from the spent grains
4. A cooling coil to "chill" the hot wort to fermentation temperatures as quickly as possible, or another means to chill your wort

This section first describes the kinds of equipment to buy or how to make them. The actual use of the equipment is described in detail later in this section.

## THE MILL

### Grinding the Grain

The purpose of a mill is to grind malted barley into small pieces so that the inner starches, sugars, and enzymes are exposed and accessible to the water that is added during the mash. At the same time, it is desirable to remove the husks from the grain, keeping them as intact as possible so they can help serve as a natural filter during the lautering process. The grain mill can double as a grinder of adjuncts such as rice, wheat, barley, etc.

By no stretch of the imagination should the malted barley be ground into flour.

Malted barley cannot be adequately ground with a rolling pin. Save the rolling pin for crystal, black, and chocolate malts; roasted barley; and pies. Commercial breweries use what is called a "roller mill" to grind all of their grains. Grain

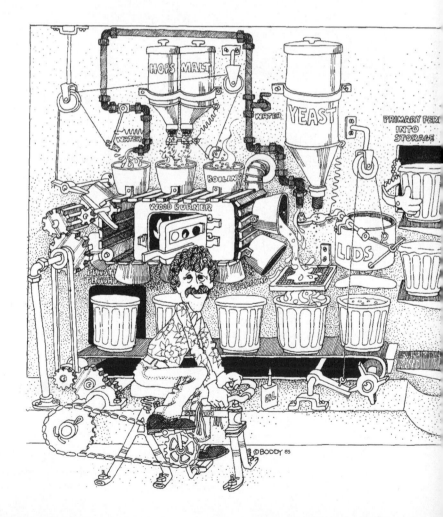

is crushed between two rotating, grooved rollers. This system enables the commercial brewer to retain the integrity of the husk as it is torn from the grain and crushed at the same time into granules with a minimal amount of dust.

Small roller-type mills can be purchased through your local homebrew supply store. Another option is the commonly available household hand-driven flour mill (not a meat grinder!). And with a little ingenuity it can easily be driven by an electric motor. A flour mill works on the principle that grains are forced between two plates, one of which is rotating. The grain is crushed as it passes between the plates. Adjustment of the space between the plates allows one to grind grain into flour or, for the homebrewer, into granules appropriate for brewing.

Most homebrew shops have a mill or two available for customer use. Simply crush your grains after you've bought exactly what you need. Crushed grains will keep for months in a stable, dry, bagged environment.

Whatever you do, don't grind your grains in the same area in which you brew. The dust that is created in the milling process is loaded with beer-spoiling lactobacillus bacteria.

### Don't Blame It on the Malt

For all-grain brewers or those who utilize a partial mash in their formulations, getting a good yield from grains is an important endeavor. Getting a good yield means getting a fair amount of fermentable sugars and other character-building carbohydrates from the grain. When good yields are not achieved and subsequent original gravities fall below expectations, brewers have a tendency to blame the ingredients and not the process. I've read many all-grain recipes, noting low yields. I have four simple suggestions for helping enhance your yields:

1. Test your efficiency by finely grinding (almost to flour) 1 pound of malt. Mash at 158 degrees F (70 degrees C) for 30 minutes to yield 1 gallon of sweet extract. Then follow the same procedure using your ordinary grind of malt. Note the difference in specific gravity. For homebrewing systems the regular grind should produce at least 80 percent of the fine-grind gravity. If yours is less, you should not blame your low yields on the malt, but rather on the nature of your grind.
2. Visit a brewery you have confidence in and ask if you can observe what properly ground malt looks like. There is no substitute for seeing this with your own eyes.
3. For greater extraction and yield, hold the mash at 158 degrees F (70 degrees C) for at least 10 minutes during the final mashing regime.
4. Investigate the hardness and pH of your water. If your pH is in the high 7s or higher and your hardness is more than 100 ppm, the water can contribute to reducing your yield. You will need to learn more about water before you can remedy the situation.

Admittedly these are four very simplistic approaches to improving your grain yields. They are meant to produce results with the least amount of hassle or in-depth scientific involvement on your part. At worst they are meant to be inspirational beginning steps toward improved yields. Yes, you can. Just brew it.

## THE MASH-TUN

### Holding the Water and Malt Grist at Controlled Temperatures

A mash-tun is a container whose purpose is to hold the combination of malt (and adjuncts) grist and water at desired temperatures. There are a variety of ways to mash and many systems and much specialized equipment designed for the homebrewer. Visit your local homebrew supply shop to see what is available, or pick up a copy of the American Homebrewers Association's *Zymurgy* homebrewing magazine, which often features articles about the latest innovations and methods on homebrewing. Check out the technical section on www .homebrewersassociation.org.

The methods of mashing that are most useful and practical for the homebrewer are called:

- Infusion system of mashing
- Temperature-controlled ("step infusion") system of mashing
- The decoction method of mashing, which is more sophisticated and discussed in *The Homebrewer's Companion, Second Edition.*

The *infusion mashing system* is a one-temperature mash, best used with fully modified malts that do not require a protein rest. It is essentially a process that involves the combination of a predetermined amount of grist and water (at a specific temperature). When combined, the temperatures of the grist and water stabilize. The object is to stabilize at the temperature and sustain a near-constant temperature during conversion of starch to sugar and dextrin. For the practical homebrewer, this will usually take 30 to 60 minutes.

The homebrewer can devise a system of infusion mashing in many different ways. Here are three methods that I have personally found to be practical, efficient, or economic.

1. The grist and water mash can be combined in an insulated "picnic cooler," the inner lining of which is food-grade plastic. Picnic coolers will sustain nearly constant temperatures inside for the period of time required for enzyme conversion of starch to dextrins and sugars.
2. The "monitored brewpot method" offers economy, simplicity, and excellent results to the homebrewer who would rather not have to buy any additional equipment. In this method the grist and water are combined in the brewpot. The temperature is carefully monitored every 15 to 20 minutes over a period of 30 to 60 minutes. The volume of mash that you are working with will maintain a fairly constant temperature. Any temperature drop will be very gradual. Heat can be easily added while stirring. When the temperature that you want to achieve is reached, remove the brewpot from the heat. You can even wrap a several towels or blanket around the pot to help insulate and stabilize the temperature.
3. Another very ingenious (if I say so, myself) way to maintain the temperature of the mash while it is in the brewpot is to place the entire brewpot in an insulated container large enough to accommodate it. Lining a large cardboard box with sheets of insulating foam is inexpensive and

*Having a crush! It may not be love at first sight, but with proper adjustments, the grinding plates on this type of flour mill can serve your malt-grinding needs.*

makes an insulated container. You will be surprised at how effective and convenient this system is in maintaining controlled temperatures. Prefabricated insulating foam boxes can be often found in metropolitan area seafood restaurants. These types of boxes are used to ship fresh seafood.

Going against the grain! Before and after. malted barley must be crushed into granular-size pieces, while maintaining the integrity of the husk.

*A grin reminder: Relax. Don't worry. Have a homebrew! Temperatures are easily maintained within insulated "picnic coolers" when undertaking an all-grain mash. The grain bag is easily fitted inside, while the sweet wort can be drawn out the spout upon starch-to-sugar conversion.*

## THE LAUTER-TUN

### Separating the Liquid from the Spent Grains

The object of the vessel called a lauter-tun is to separate the spent grains (and adjuncts) from the sweet liquor that has been created, leaving behind the grains and husks.

Some mash-tuns are designed so that they can be fit and adapted with what is called a "false bottom." A false bottom is a strainer that is positioned 1 or 2 inches (2.5 to 5 cm) above the real bottom of the mash-tun.

An outlet or spigot is positioned between the false bottom and real bottom. This false bottom creates a system whereby the grains are held 2 inches (5 cm) above the real bottom of a vessel, allowing sweet liquor to pass into the space below and flow out of the spigot (outlet) without the risk of clogging the "plumbing."

A false bottom can be created in any mash-tun or lauter-tun by containing the grains in a grain bag. Grain bags are made from cloth or synthetic fabric and have a screenlike weave for a bottom that allows liquid to flow from the bag while retaining the grains. If using a grain bag make sure that the grains are evenly heated throughout. Of course there must be a means of draining the mash-tun or lauter-tun of the liquid. Many picnic coolers have a convenient spigot that is perfect for the practical homebrewer.

An alternative to the picnic cooler and grain bag lautering system can be easily constructed from a 4- to 5-gallon (15 to 19 l) plastic food-grade bucket. The bottom of a bucket can be drilled with hundreds of holes ⅛ inch (0.3 cm)

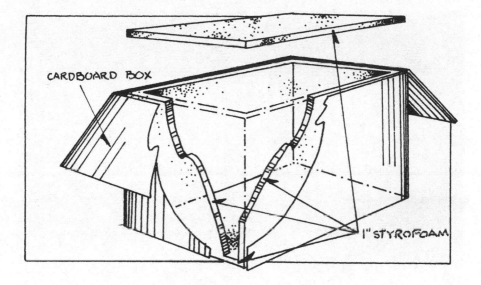

CARDBOARD BOX

1" STYROFOAM

in diameter, thus creating a strainer that will hold up to 15 pounds (6.8 kg) of grain. Grains and liquid can be added to this giant strainer, and a brewpot placed below can handily catch the sweet liquor.

## The Zapap Lauter-Tun

### A Most Versatile Lautering System

With a little bit more effort, a most versatile lautering system can be made with materials that are available anywhere. The "Zapap" lauter-tun is essentially constructed of two 5-gallon (19 l) plastic food-grade buckets (available from restaurant kitchens, hardware stores, or through your local homebrew supply shop). The bottom of one of the buckets is drilled with holes ⅛ inch (0.3 cm) in diameter, enough to give the appearance of a handmade strainer. The other bucket is fitted with a spigot or plastic hose 1 inch (2 cm) from the bottom of the bucket. The strainer bucket is inserted inside the bucket with the spigot. Voilà—you have just constructed a lauter-tun, complete with false bottom and controllable flow. You will need an electric drill to make holes. You will need a "spigot" (a ⅜-inch [1 cm] MPT [male pipe thread] drain cock—available at any hardware store—works great!) and a rubber gasket (inside diameter ⅜ inch [1 cm]; outside diameter ½ inch [1.3 cm]; thickness ¼ inch [0.64 cm]) that will line the hole in the bucket through which the spigot is inserted. If a spigot cannot be obtained, a ⅜-inch-outside-diameter plastic hose can be easily fitted into a ⁵⁄₁₆-inch (0.8 cm) hole drilled in the bucket. A hose clamp can be put on the hose to control flow.

The use of this lauter-tun is explained on page 322. For a more detailed

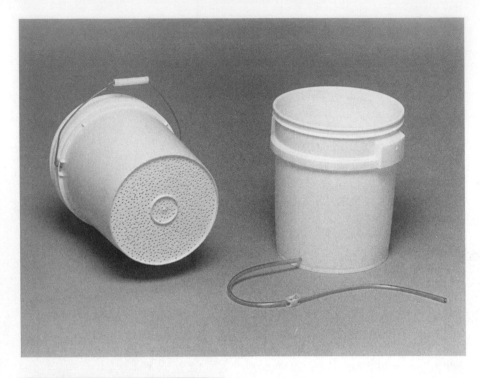

*There's a hole in the bucket! The Zapap lauter-tun; hundreds of holes are drilled in one of two 5-gallon (19 l) plastic food buckets. When inserted into the second bucket a "false bottom" is created, allowing grains to be suspended 2 to 3 inches above the outlet. The plastic clamp controls flow.*

discussion of sparging and many other lautering systems, consult *The Homebrewer's Companion, Second Edition.*

If all this seems to be too much work, simply stroll down to your local homebrew supply shop or visit the many homebrew supply shop Websites to see what prefabricated systems are available. One particular system called "Phil's Lauter

*This ain't my kitchen, but you get the picture. One of many user-friendly commercially available lautering and sparging systems specially designed for all-grain homebrewing. Note leisure time to relax, not worry, and have a homebrew. (System courtesy of Listermann Mfg., Norwood, Ohio, and T-shirt courtesy of BrewCo, Boone, North Carolina.)*

System" is essentially an elaboration of the Zapap lauter-tun with a few extra features that make homebrewing all the more fun at a reasonable price. While some systems are very reasonably priced, other stainless steel ones that may last several of your lifetimes can run into several hundreds and even thousands of dollars. Whatever you use will most certainly make excellent beer.

As homebrewers we can't claim, by any means, exclusivity on our hand-made creativity. I once discussed lautering systems with masterbrewers from the Anheuser-Busch and other large brewing companies. They explained a system that they fabricated in their pilot brewery to duplicate the hydrodynamics of sparge water flow through a 4- or 5-foot (1.2 to 1.5 m) bed of grain in their brewery mash-tun. They removed the lids from both ends of 9 or 10 large coffee cans, taped them together end to end with waterproof electrical tape, and attached a bottom can that had been punctured with holes. Voilà—your basic 5-foot-tall (1.5 m) lautering system! They said that it worked well, too.

## WORT CHILLERS

### COOLING THE BOILED WORT AS QUICKLY AS POSSIBLE

When brewing all-grain beers, the brewer must boil the entire wort. It is always important to cool the wort as quickly as possible, pitch the yeast when the wort is cool, and maintain sanitation.

The principle behind various configurations of wort chillers is that cold water is used to cool the hot wort without directly adding the water to the wort. This can be done in principle by immersing a lid-covered brewpot of hot wort in a bath of cold water so that the cold water can reduce the heat of the wort. Immersion of a brewpot in cold water, is effective, but slow.

There's one small catch that needs to be dealt with before chilling your wort using other methods. There are hops in your hot wort, so you'll need to separate the hops from the wort before passing into the cooling plumbing. You'll need to either put your wort into a vessel with a false bottom (like your lauter-tun) to separate the hops or have a screening device at the beginning of your exiting hot wort flow.

Many homebrewers devise a "closed" system by which the hot wort passes through copper tubing on its way to the fermenter. A portion of the copper tubing is coiled and that portion is immersed in a bath of cold water. Boiling-hot wort enters in one end and exits at temperatures between 50 and 70 degrees F (10 to 21 C), chilling 5 gallons (19 l) of wort in seconds as it passes through the coil.

A variety of wort chillers are available commercially. They are often advertised online, in homebrew magazines, or are available at homebrew supply shops. Some systems are fabricated from copper tubing that is inserted into a 15- to 20-foot (4.5 to 5 m) length of garden hose. Various plumbing fittings allow hot wort to pass through the copper tubing while allowing cold water to pass through the garden hose that envelops the copper tubing. Other systems are configured in such a manner that 15 to 25 feet (4.5 to 7.5 m) of coiled copper tubing is immersible in a moving cold-water bath.

By far, the easiest way to have a wort-chilling system is to buy one. If you are inclined to make your own, you'll need a length of soft copper tubing that has an inside diameter of ¼, ⅜, or ½ inch (0.6–1.4 cm) You do not want to even consider bending the copper tubing without a tube bender (ask your local plumber or go online). But if you are a homebrewer and want to try it anyway, fill the tube with water and temporary seal the ends. This will help reduce "crimping."

If you can't get a wort-chilling system together, don't let that deter you. You can still make all-grain beers by letting the wort cool to temperatures below 160 F (71 C). You can accomplish this by immersing the brewpot into a bath of cold water—either with a continuous in and out flow of water or by changing the water enough times to cool the wort inside the pot.

*Not a sci-fi chiller! This rather sophisticated wort chiller is a homebrew system that utilizes a two-stage coolant system. First, the hot wort exits the brewpot and flows through copper tubing that is inserted in a plastic hose. Cold water counterflows around the copper. As the cooler wort exits the first stage it enters another copper coil that is immersed (cutaway) in an ice-water bath. The temperature can be read as it exits into a fermenter or other receptacle. This system was made by Andrews Homebrewing Accessories, Riverside, California.*

You can also cool your wort while it is in the brewpot by immersing it in a large tub of cold water or in a pool, creek, river, or snowbank outside. Remove the hops by passing the cooled wort through a sanitized (boiled in water) strainer (through a funnel if using a carboy) on its way into your fermenter.

Try to figure out a way to cool the wort as quickly as possible for best results.

REMEMBER THAT MAINTAINING SANITATION IS EXTREMELY IMPORTANT AFTER THE TEMPERATURE OF THE WORT DROPS BELOW 160 to 170 DEGREES F (71 to 77 C).

## LET'S MASH!

Hold your horses. Not so fast, buster—and you, too, toots. I want to remind you of a few things.

Don't forget that you are a homebrewer and that the reason you are one is that you enjoy good beer and somehow have grown to enjoy the process of making beer. Some will even profess that since you are now going to mash your own grains it is time to get serious! Give yourself a break, and allow yourself to get concerned, but please, *not serious*. Being concerned will allow you to creatively work out the problems you may encounter. Being concerned will allow attention to quality. Being concerned will allow you to improve your skills with every batch of beer. Being concerned means allowing yourself to relax, not worry, and have a homebrew. Becoming serious will muddle your mind and mislead you from the real reason you are a homebrewer—enjoyment!

Enjoy the process, appreciate it, and savor it. Don't forget—you are a homebrewer. As time passes you will look back and cherish the memories of every batch of beer you've made.

## INTRODUCTION

There are three mashing procedures worth mentioning, two of which are of practical use to the homebrewer. Briefly they are:

1. *The Infusion Mash*—Infusion mashing is often referred to as a "one-step," one-temperature mash, in which grist and water are maintained at one temperature for a period of time allowing complete conversion. The infusion-mashing procedure is most appropriately used with fully modified malts. If undermodified malts are used in this system, complete conversion of starches to dextrins and sugars will result, but necessary yeast nutrients may not be adequately developed.
2. *The Temperature-Controlled (Step) Mash*—Sometimes referred to as "step infusion," this mashing procedure involves maintaining the

combination of grist and water at various temperatures for specific periods of time. This procedure is particularly suited for use with undermodified malted barley and adjuncts. It is also excellent for developing beer foam head quality and complete conversion of starches to sugars in a 30-minute saccharification "rest" at starch-to-sugar-conversion temperatures. It allows the degradation of proteins (for nutrients and head retention) when held at temperatures lower than those that are later necessary for starch conversion.

3. *The Decoction Mash*—This method of mashing achieves the same end as the temperature-controlled mash. The distinction of this method is that portions of the water and grist are brought to a boil and added to the main mash in order to raise the temperature through steps similar to the temperature-controlled mashing system. This system seems to have been developed in days predating the thermometer, when there was no accurate means of measuring temperature. Brewmasters devised this system in order to achieve much more consistency in their mashing process by using the known constant of boiling temperatures. This system is still used in Germany to get maximum extraction and perpetuate an age-old tradition. In the rest of the brewing world it is rarely used.

*Mix and mash!*

For those interested in learning more about the art and science of decoction mashing, Gregory Noonan's *New Brewing Lager Beer*, published by Brewers Publications, is one of the most comprehensive English-language resource on the subject. See also www.homebrewersassociation.org. The subject of decoction mashing is covered in more detail in the *The Homebrewer's Companion, Second Edition*.

The infusion and the temperature-controlled mashing procedures are the most practical for the homebrewer. The time involved in mashing with either method is about the same. If you organize your brewing session, you can figure that from mashing to boiling to sparging to cleaning and having that after-brewing beer will involve 4 to 5 hours of your time. Remember that cleaning both before and *afterward* is an unavoidable part of the brewing process and will take a considerable amount of your brew time. And maybe a beer or two.

## THE INFUSION MASH

If the malt you are using is highly modified, then this is the mash for you. It is the simpler of the two mashing systems and requires less attention. Once you've primed yourself with the preceding background information, you'll be surprised at how simple this process can be.

The situation that you want to achieve during the infusion mash is stabilizing the grist and water mash at a temperature between 150 and 158 degrees F (66 to 70 C) for 30 to 60 minutes. The higher temperatures will convert the starches more quickly and at the same time the mash will be more dextrinous, resulting in a more full-bodied beer. The lower temperatures will convert starches more slowly, resulting in a less full-bodied beer.

Desired temperatures are achieved by adding a measured amount of grain to water that is at a predetermined temperature. The following information will help you determine changes in temperature that will occur when the room-temperature grain is added to the hot water.

Here are some facts that will make your experience as an infusion masher as easy as eating pie.

1. The amount of water needed for every pound (454 g) of grain is 1 quart (.95 l).
2. There will be a temperature drop of 16 to 18 degrees F (-9 to -7 C) when the measured amount of water and grain are combined. For example, if 4 quarts (3.8 l) of water at a temperature of 168 degrees F (76 C) is added to 4 pounds (1.8 kg) of grain, the temperature of the mash will stabilize at 150 to 152 degrees F (66 to 67 C). If adjustments are necessary, heat can be added to raise the temperature or a small amount of cold water can be added to lower the temperature.
3. One-half gallon (1.9 l) of sparge water is (ideally) needed to sparge each pound (454 g) of grain. You will lose water along the way from mash to finished beer.

4. Each pound (454 g) of grain will absorb and retain approximately 0.1 (one-tenth) gallon (380 ml) of water.
5. Boiling will evaporate approximately ½ to 1 gallon (2 to 4 l) of water in 60 minutes. This depends on the vigor of the boil.
6. Sediments will account for ¼ to ½ gallon (1 to 2 l) of losses in volume.

Most homebrewers will brew in 5-gallon (19 l) increments. You will usually use between 6 and 10 pounds (2.7 to 4.5 kg) of grain (including adjuncts) for each 5 gallons (19 l) of homebrewed beer. The chart on page 332 provides practical information for the brewing of all-grain beers using an infusion mash procedure.

## THE TEMPERATURE-CONTROLLED STEP MASH

"STEP MASHING"
A temperature-controlled step mash is the most desirable method of mashing when undermodified malted barley is used. Since most malts available to home-brewers are fully modified, the temperature-controlled step mash is better im-plemented to improve foam quality . A temperature-controlled mash allows the homebrewer to more closely control the temperature of the mash. It promotes the development of yeast nutrients, more poetically referred to as "free amino nitrogens." Also, the controlled temperatures can aid in giving the beer more stability, less of a haze problem, and a more controllable balance of dextrins and fermentable sugars with starch conversion.

The practical method described here is easy to follow and also has the advantage of having a desirably thicker mash during the protein rest at 122 degrees F (50 C)—a condition that proteolytic enzymes enjoy or at temperatures between 130 and 135 degrees F (54 to 57 C), which will develop protein profiles for better foam quality and retention. The conversion of starch to dextrin and sugar occurs in a more diluted mash and at higher temperatures, developed during diastatic enzyme activity.

The temperature-controlled method of mashing will take the grist and wa-ter combination to either a nutrient-developing temperature of 122 degrees F (50 C) or a foam-quality-developing temperature of 133 degrees F (54.5 C) and maintain it for 30 minutes. The temperature is then raised to 150 to 158 degrees F (66 to 70 C) by adding a measured amount of boiling water. This temperature is then held 30 minutes. The temperatures that are chosen for starch conver-sion will determine the dextrin-sugar balance of the wort. Higher temperatures will produce beers with a fuller body. Lower temperatures will result in a beer with more alcohol and less body. A temperature rest at 150 degrees F (66 C) for 10 minutes followed by a boost in temperature to 158 degrees F (70 C) held for an additional 10 to 15 minutes (or until conversion) will produce a medium-bodied beer.

## Guidelines for Infusion Mashing

| GRAIN AND ADJUNCT POUNDS (KG) | MASH WATER GALLONS (LITERS) | WATER ABSORBED BY GRAIN GALLONS (LITERS) | SPARGE WATER AT 170°F (77C) GALLONS (LITERS) | WATER ADDED TO BOIL GALLONS (LITERS) | WATER EVAPORATION IN BOIL GALLONS (LITERS) | INITIAL YIELD TO PRIMARY GALLONS (LITERS) | YIELD TO SECONDARY GALLONS (LITERS) |
|---|---|---|---|---|---|---|---|
| 6 (2.7) | 1.5 (5.7) | 0.6 (2.3) | 3.0 (11.4) | 2.0 (7.6) | 0.5 (2) | 5.5 (21) | 5 (19) |
| 7 (3.2) | 1.75 (6.7) | 0.7 (2.7) | 3.5 (13.3) | 1.5 (5.7) | 0.5 (2) | 5.5 (21) | 5 (19) |
| 8 (3.6) | 2 (7.6) | 0.8 (3.1) | 4.0 (15.2) | 0.75 (2.9) | 0.5 (2) | 5.5 (21) | 5 (19) |
| 9 (4.1) | 2.25 (8.6) | 0.9 (3.5) | 4.5 (17.1) | 0.25 (1) | 0.5 (2) | 5.5 (21) | 5 (19) |
| 10 (4.5) | 2.5 (9.5) | 1 (3.8) | 5.0 (19) | 0 | 1.0 (3.8) | 5.5 (21) | 5 (19) |

NOTE: The "water added to boil" is added to the brewpot in order to obtain 6 gallons (23l) of wort. You will eventually boil this down to 5.5 gallons (21l) as indicated.

**Using undermodified malt and for developing nutrients**—For every pound of grains and adjuncts used, 1 quart (1 l) of water at a temperature of 130 degrees F (54 C) is necessary to decrease and stabilize the temperature of the mash to 120 to 124 degrees F (49 to 51 C).

**Using fully modified malt and for developing foam quality**—For every pound of grains and adjuncts used, 1 quart (1 l) of water at a temperature of 143 degrees F (61.5 C) is necessary to decrease and stabilize the temperature of the mash to 133 degrees F (54.5 C).

Stirring of the mash to evenly distribute the heat is helpful during each step-up of the temperature-controlled procedure.

In order to initiate starch conversion, the temperature of the mash needs to be raised to at least 150 degrees F (66 C). For every pound (450 g) of grain (and adjunct) that is in the mash, ½ quart (0.5 l) of water at 200 degrees F (93 C) will be needed to raise the temperature of the mash about 18 degrees F (10 C). (NOTE: In Colorado, I brew at an altitude of 5,300 feet. Water boils at 200 degrees F [93 C]. It would be safe to guess that water at 212 degrees F [100 C], which is boiling at sea level, would increase the temperature by about 25 degrees F [14 C]. Try it and record your observations for later use.) For example, if the temperature of the mash at the end of the protein rest is slightly raised to 132 degrees F (56 C), the 200-degree F (93 C) water that is added will raise the temperature to 150 degrees F (66 C).

If grain or other starch adjuncts need to be cooked, boil them in the water that you will ultimately add to raise the temperature of your malt mash from protein rest to starch conversion temperatures. Cooked adjuncts do not need to be in the mash during the protein rest.

If you wish to increase the temperature of your mash during the starch conversion, simply add heat (turn on the stove and stir) and raise to the desired temperature.

Most homebrewers will brew in 5-gallon (19 l) increments. You will use between 6 and 10 pounds (2.7 to 4.5 kg) of grain (including adjuncts) for each 5 gallons (19 l) of homebrewed beer. The chart on pages 334–335 provides practical information for the brewing of all-grain beers using a temperature-controlled procedure.

You may have thought that you've missed something, but all the practical essentials are here.

## IODINE TEST FOR STARCH CONVERSION

After you have finished your mashing procedures you may wonder whether or not you have completed the starch-to-sugar/dextrin conversion. You can do a simple test for starch by using tincture of iodine as an indicator. The test is based on the fact that tincture of iodine (available at any pharmacy) will turn a starch solution

# Guidelines for Temperature-Controlled Step

| GRAIN AND ADJUNCT POUNDS (KG) | MASH WATER AT 130°F (54 C) FOR NUTRIENT REST OR 140°F (60 C) FOR BEER HEAD/FOAM QUALITY REST GALLONS (LITERS) | WATER AT 200°F (93 C) TO RAISE TO 150°F (66 C) QUARTS (LITERS) | WATER ABSORBED BY GRAIN GALLONS (LITERS) | SPARGE WATER AT 170°F (77°C) GALLONS (LITERS) |
|---|---|---|---|---|
| 6 (2.7) | 1.5 (5.7) | 3 (3) | 0.6 (2.3) | 3.0 (11.4) |
| 7 (3.2) | 1.75 (6.7) | 3.5 (3.5) | 0.7 (2.7) | 3.5 (13.3) |
| 8 (3.6) | 2 (7.6) | 4 (3.8) | 0.8 (3.1) | 4.0 (15.2) |
| 9 (4.1) | 2.25 (8.6) | 4.5 (4.3) | 0.9 (3.5) | 4.5 (17.1) |
| 10 (4.5) | 2.5 (9.5) | 5 (4.8) | 1 (3.8) | 5.0 (19) |

NOTE: The "water added to boil" is added to the brewpot in order to obtain 6 gallons (23 l) of wort.

purple or black in color. If all of the starches in your mash have been converted to sugars or dextrins, the iodine will not display any color change.

To perform this test remove 1 tablespoon (15 ml) of the liquid mash and place it on a cool white saucer. Drip a drop of iodine into the puddle and observe. If there is a change in color to black or purple, then you should continue to mash until a repeat of this test indicates no or very little change in color.

## LAUTERING

### WORT SEPARATION AND SPARGING

Now that you've successfully converted your grains to the better things in life, it is necessary to stop the conversion process and separate the sweet liquor from the particulate matter (the spent grain and husk material). You accomplish this by raising the temperature of the mash to 170 degrees F (77 C) in order to deactivate enzymes, and then contain the spent grains in an oversized strainer while allowing the liquid to drain from the bottom. A measured amount of "rinse" (sparging) water is added to the surface of the grains to trickle through and carry remaining sugars away.

The major problem that you want to avoid is a "stuck runoff." A stuck runoff

## Mashing

| WATER ADDED TO BOIL QUARTS (LITERS) | WATER EVAPOR. IN BOIL GALLONS (LITERS) | INITIAL YIELD TO PRIMARY GALLONS (LITERS) | YIELD TO SECONDARY GALLONS (LITERS) |
|---|---|---|---|
| 5.5 (5.2) | 0.5 (2) | 5.5 (21) | 5 (19) |
| 2.5 (2.4) | 0.5 (2) | 5.5 (21) | 5 (19) |
| 1 (1) | 0.5 (2) | 5.5 (21) | 5 (19) |
| — | 1.0 (3.8) | 5.5 (21) | 5 (19) |
| — | 1.75 (6.7) | 5.5 (21) | 5 (19) |

You will eventually boil this down to 5.5 gallons (21 l) as indicated.

results from a compaction of the bed of grains in your lauter-tun and/or the clogging of the holes in the strainer section of the lauter-tun. In any case, the flow of liquid through the grains is hindered when a stuck runoff occurs. The possibility of a stuck or restricted runoff can be minimized by providing "foundation water" to the lauter-tun. Foundation water will provide a means of gently "floating" the grains onto the false bottom, avoiding compaction of the grain and clogging of the false-bottom strainer.

The principle of using foundation water in the lautering process can be demonstrated with an explanation of a double-bucket lauter-tun system (see page 322). The main points to remember are:

1. The sparge water should be 170 to 180 degrees F (77 to 82 C).
2. The level of liquid (sparge/foundation water and mash) should always be maintained above the surface of the grains that are gradually being added.

To begin, add enough hot water—170 degrees F (77 C)—so that the surface level exceeds the level of the false bottom by a good 2 or 3 inches (5 to 8 cm). Then alternately add the mash (grains and sweet liquor) and, if needed, more from the reservoir of sparge water while maintaining a level of liquid that is visibly above the surface of the grain bed. After all of the mash has been added to the lauter-tun, draining can commence.

If the mash were added to a dry lauter-tun, it would be more likely that the weight of the unsuspended grains would compact and clog the straining system.

When you begin, slowly drain the sweet wort, and continue to gently add hot sparge water until the supply of sparge water is depleted. Avoid pouring the sparging water onto the surface of the grains with abandonment; rather, gently spray or sprinkle the hot water over the surface. As the water gently flows through the "filter bed" of grains, it carries with it the desired sugars and dextrins.

If you are not using a double-bucket or false-bottom lautering system, do the best you can. There is a variety of ways to provide foundation water to the simplest lautering system, even if it is only temporarily. The principle remains the same: float the grains into your lautering system and retain a level of liquid above the grain bed.

**Helpful technique**: After runoff has flowed for about 5 minutes, take a long knife and cut the surface (about 2 inches deep into the grain bed) in several directions. This will break up the "mud" of malt dust that may settle atop your grain bed and prevent the flow of sparge water into and through the grain bed. Commercial brewers use "rakes" to do the same thing.

As you direct your sweet runoff into your brewpot, avoid excessive aeration of the hot liquid, as this could lead to the development of oxidized flavors later in the beermaking process.

## BOILING THE WORT

You are boiling a much greater volume of liquid than in a malt extract recipe boil because the wort is not concentrated. You will be able to boil your wort more vigorously, allowing for more or less evaporation, as required. The more vigorous boil will facilitate protein coagulation (the hot break) and more precipitation of sediment. The removal of this precipitate can be dealt with later.

## COOLING THE WORT

From 212 degrees F (100 C) to 70 degrees F (21 C) in 15 minutes!

In order to ensure healthy and contaminant-free fermentation (and beer), it is desirable to cool the hot wort as quickly as possible so that yeast can be pitched.

The cooling systems that have been described in the equipment section of this chapter are effective in reducing 5 gallons (19 l) of wort from boiling temperatures down to 60 degrees F (17 C) within 15 to 30 minutes.

The problems that need to be avoided are bacterial contamination and clogging due to the presence of hops.

*It takes two hands and with two beers everybody sings! The Zapap double-bucket lauter-tun demonstrates the ease of separating and sparging grains in an all-grain mash. The double-bucket configuration shown in operation strains the sweet wort from the spent grains. The flow is directed into the brewpot. The next step is boiling the wort with hops.*

It is extremely important that any piece of equipment be thoroughly sanitized if it is going to be in contact with the beer after the temperature has been reduced below 160 degrees F (71 C).

Clogging of cooling systems can be easily avoided if the hot wort is passed through a lauter system (called a hop-back at this stage of the process) and then introduced to the chiller system. The lauter-tun used during the mashing process can double as a hop-back with the added advantage that you can connect the drain spigot to the wort chiller with a piece of tubing.

If a lauter-tun system is unavailable, you must strain, sparge, and remove hops from the hot wort before the wort is allowed to enter the chilling system.

Once the wort enters the chilling system, the cold water that envelops the plumbing that is carrying the flow of hot wort should always be in motion for maximum efficiency. This is true no matter what method you devise.

In summary, the essential points to remember are:

1. You must remove the hops from the wort before it enters the chilling system.
2. Once temperatures drop below 160 degrees F (71 C), it is imperative that all equipment that comes in contact with the beer be sanitized.

If you simply do not want to deal with chilling systems you may "prechill" your hot wort by immersing your covered brewpot in a bath of cold water. Then you can sparge the warm wort—temperature must be below 160 F (71 C)—directly into a preheated fermenter. It is almost essential that your fermentation system be a closed system, one that allows you to lock the wort away from air and potential contaminants. After the hot wort has been put into your fermenter, you may have to wait many hours, perhaps overnight, before the wort drops to temperatures suitable for pitching yeast. Be forewarned that this procedure can result in beers that have a flavor character reminiscent of sweet corn (really dimethyl-sulfide) depending on the quality of the malt used. It is best to chill as quickly as possible. If a carboy fermenter is used, it may be immersed in a bath of cool water once the temperature is below 110 degrees F (43 C). CAUTION: If you are using a glass carboy for your fermenter, you must heat the glass sufficiently before adding hot wort to it. The shock of hot wort to cool glass will break the carboy. Never add boiling hot wort to a glass carboy.

NOTE: Remember that aeration of the cooled wort is important for healthy fermentation. Splashing the wort into your fermenter will accomplish adequate aeration.

## THE PROTEIN SEDIMENT (TRUB)

Once your wort has been added to the fermenter and allowed a quiet period of 30 minutes or so, you will notice the formation of sediment called "trub" on the bottom of the fermenter. This protein sediment was coagulated and precipitated (the hot-break) during the boil and further precipitated upon cooling (the cold-break). The use of a hop-back will filter out a significant amount of trub,

*A counterbalanced wort chiller! Leather hands hold what normally would be boiling hot copper tubing. (I don't know how she does it.) Boiling hot wort is added to the Zapap lauter-tun, which now serves as a "hop-back." As the hot wort separates from the hops, it passes into the coiled copper tubing, which is immersed in a bath of cold water (your sink). When the wort exits the tubing it flows, cooled, into the fermenter.*

in much the same way as the grains acted as a filter in your lauter-tun. If you wish, you may remove the wort from the trub by siphoning the clear wort off into another carboy, leaving the sediment behind.

In theory, the trub will inhibit fermentation and reduce the production of esters, often desirable in beer. In practice, the effect on fermentation is not significant to the homebrewer. If it bothers you, siphon the clear wort off and have a homebrew. If you can't be bothered, just have a homebrew.

For a more detailed discussion of equipment and process, see the "Making Beer: Equipment and Process" section in *The Homebrewer's Companion, Second Edition*.

## FERMENTATION

Ferment your beer to completion as you've done with all of your beers and don't forget to relax . . . don't worry . . . have a homebrew!

> *"It is not through knowledge, but through experience of the world that we are brought into relation with it."*
> —Albert Schweitzer,
> *My Life's Thoughts*

## 15 ALL-GRAIN RECIPES

### Pale Ales

### Light Lagers

### Amber Ales and Lagers

Weizenbier/Weissbier

**Notes on the following all-grain recipes:**

1. Most recipes are brewed to batch sizes that will yield a final 5 gallons (19 l) of beer. You'll notice original batch sizes ranging between 5 and 6 gallons (19 to 23 l). With primary to secondary and secondary to keg or priming vessel, a small amount of sediment and beer is left behind, thus reducing the volume of beer as you go through the various stages of fermentation and bottling/kegging.
2. If you are interested in kegging your homebrew, jump forward to Appendix 2, "Kegging Your Beer," page 405.
3. Straining systems for hops, vessels, ladles for cooled wort, spoons coming in contact with cooled wort—all must be sanitized before contacting cooled wort. The best and easiest way to sanitize smaller items is to steam or boil them. Sanitizing solution will not adequately sanitize wire mesh strainers.

## PALE ALES

*Humpty Dumpty English-Style Ordinary Bitter*
Quite possibly one of my all-time favorite recipes, Humpty Dumpty English-Style Ordinary Bitter is a full-flavored ale in the tradition of English real ale. Best brewed with ingredients of English origin, though, as usual, ingredients of American origin will make terrific ale as well. This is the kind of beer you'll seek when you're really in the mood to quench your thirst and enjoy the flavor of beer as it was always meant to be. Relatively light in alcohol, this beer has plenty of malt character without being sweet, plenty of hop character without being bitter. If you like beer, you won't be bitter about this bitter.

UK Kent Goldings hops are essential for the true character of this beer. British brewers will often use #2 invert sugar to add caramel character. A type of sugar becoming more readily available in the United States is dark Brazilian *rapadura*. This is dried and granulated pure cane sugar juice from Brazil. Sucanat is another type of more refined cane juice sugar, but not as full flavored as *rapadura*. Available at health food stores and ethnic food specialty stores or in the "natural sugar" section of more "natural-conscious" grocery stores.

Ingredients for 5¼ gallons* (20 l):

| | |
|---|---|
| 6 lbs. (2.7 kg) | English 2-row pale malt |
| ⅓ lb. (150 g) | English crystal malt (10 to 15 L) |
| ¼ lb. (110 g) | aromatic malt |
| 6 oz. (170 g) | *rapadura* (Brazilian dark cane sugar juice, dried or granulated) or British invert sugar #2 |
| 1½ tsp. (4 g) | gypsum as necessary for water lacking calcium and sulfate ions (optional) |
| 1 oz. (28 g) | UK Northdown hops or First Gold hops, or 1.6 oz. (45 g) UK Fuggles hops (boiling): 8 HBU (224 MBU) |
| 1 oz. (28 g) | Kent Goldings hops (5 minutes, flavor) |
| ½ oz. (14 g) | Kent Goldings hop pellets (dry hopping) |
| ¼ tsp. (1 g) | Irish moss powder |
| * | English ale–type yeast (Wyeast Thames Valley is excellent or White Labs English Ale work well) |
| ¾ c. (175 ml) | sugar (for bottling) or ⅓ c. (80 ml) corn sugar (for kegging) |

O.G.: 1.038–1.040 (9.5–10)
F.G.: 1.006–1.008 (1.5–2)
Bitterness: about 30 BU; Color: 6 SRM (12 EBC); Alcohol: 4.2% by volume

Add half the gypsum (if using) to 6½ quarts (6.2 l) of water. Add the crushed malts to this 6½ quarts (6.2 l) of 143-degree F (61.5 C) water and mix well. The temperature will stabilize between 130 and 135 degrees F (54.5–57 C). Add heat if necessary and hold the temperature at about 133 degrees F (56 C) for 30 minutes. Don't worry about a 3- to 5-degree F (2 to 3 C) temperature drop during this time.

Then add 3 quarts (3 l) of boiling water to this mash. This will raise the temperature to about or just below 155 degrees F (68 C). Hold at 149 to 155 degrees F (65–68 C) for 45 minutes. Complete conversion by raising the temperature to 158 degrees F (70 C) and holding for 10 to 20 minutes or until an iodine test indicates complete conversion. Then add more heat to raise the temperature to 167 degrees F (75 C). Then pour your mash into your lauter-tun and sparge with 3½ gallons (13 l) of hot water at 170 degrees F (76 C); add the other half of the gypsum (if using) to the sparge water. The sweet wort ends in your brewpot. The volume of the wort before boiling should be about 5½ gallons (21 l).

*A 6+-gallon fermenter is needed.

Bring the sweet wort to a boil and add the *rapadura* or invert sugar and boiling hops and boil for 60 minutes. Add the Irish moss for the last 10 minutes of the boil. Add the aroma hops for the final 5 minutes of the boil. Cool the wort to about 70 to 75 degrees F (21 to 24 C). This can be done simply by immersing the brewpot (with lid on) in a bath of cold running water for about 45 minutes. Other means of chilling can be used if desired.

Strain, sparge, and transfer immediately to your primary fermenter. The final primary batch size is 5¼ gallons (20 l). If necessary, add additional cold water to achieve this volume. Aerate the wort well and add yeast when the temperature of the wort is 70 to 75 degrees F (21–24 C). Preferably ferment at 70 to 72 degrees F (21–22 C) for 4 to 6 days or until fermentation is complete and appears to clear and darken. At this point, transfer the beer into a secondary fermenter and add the ½ ounce (14 g) Kent Goldings hop pellets. Let the fermentation complete and settle in the secondary for 7 days. For best results, secondary-"cellar" or age at 50 degrees F (10 C) to help drop yeast out of suspension, but this is not at all essential to the quality that you'll enjoy. Prime with sugar and bottle or keg when fermentation is complete. Age and carbonate/condition at about 70 degrees F (21 C).

## Good Life English Pale Ale

A terrific pale ale designed to balance hop character with malt character. Good Life has rich malty flavor without a heavy body and a great background of English hop character. American-grown Crystal hop pellets are used to add what is perceived as a hybrid of German Hallertau and Kent Goldings aroma and flavor to the finished ale. Why not celebrate serendipity with Good Life English Pale Ale? I have! I brew this ale three or four times a year to help assure the good life.

Ingredients for 6 gallons* (23 l):

| | |
|---|---|
| 9 lbs. (4.1 kg) | pale ale–type malt |
| 1.6 lbs. (0.73 kg) | Munich malt (: 7 L) |
| ½ lb. (225 g) | crystal malt (10–20 L) |
| 1.7 oz. (48 g) | UK Fuggles hops (boiling): 8 HBU (224 MBU) |
| 1 oz. (28 g) | UK Kent Goldings hops (30 minutes flavor): 6 HBU (168 MBU) |
| 1 oz. (28 g) | UK Kent Goldings hops (3 minutes aroma): 6 HBU (168 MBU) |
| ½ oz. (14 g) | American Crystal hop pellets (dry hopping) |
| ¼ tsp. (1 g) | Irish moss powder |
| * | English ale–type yeast |
| ¾ c. (175 ml) | sugar (for bottling) or ⅓ c. (80 ml) corn sugar (for kegging) |

O.G.: 1.052–1.056 (13–14)
F.G.: 1.012–1.014 (3–3.5)
Bitterness: 40–45 BU; Color: 8 SRM (16 EBC); Alcohol: 5.3% by volume

Add the crushed malt to 11 quarts (10.5 l) of 143-degree F (61.5 C) water and mix well. The temperature will stabilize between 130 and 135 degrees F (54.5–57 C). Add heat if necessary and hold the temperature at about 133 degrees F (56 C) for 30 minutes. Don't worry about a 3- to 5-degree F (2–3 C) temperature drop during this time.

Then add 5½ quarts (10.5 l) of boiling water to this mash. This will raise the temperature to about or just above 155 degrees F (68 C). Hold at 157 degrees F (69.5 C) for 30 to 45 minutes, stirring occasionally. Complete conversion by raising the temperature to 158 degrees F (70 C) and holding for 10 to 20 minutes or until an iodine test indicates complete conversion. Then add more heat to raise the temperature to 167 degrees F (75 C). Then pour your mash into your lauter-tun and sparge with 4 gallons (15 l) of hot water at 170 degrees F

*A 6+-gallon fermenter is needed.

(76 C). The sweet wort ends in your brewpot. The volume of the wort before boiling should be about 6½ gallons (24.5 l).

Bring the sweet wort to a boil, add the boiling hops, and boil for 60 minutes. Add 1 oz. (28 g) of the Goldings hops for the last 30 minutes of the boil. Add the Irish moss for the last 10 minutes of the boil. Add a final 1 oz. (28 g) of Goldings hops for the final 3 minutes of the boil. Cool the wort to 70 to 75 degrees F (21–24 C). This can be done simply by immersing the brewpot (with lid on) in a bath of cold running water for about 45 minutes. Other means of chilling can be used if desired.

Strain, sparge, and transfer immediately to your primary fermenter. The final primary batch size is 6 gallons (23 l). If necessary, add additional cold water to achieve this volume. Aerate the wort very well. Add yeast when the temperature of the wort is 70 to 75 degrees F (21–24 C). Preferably ferment at 70 to 72 degrees F (21–22 C) for 4 to 6 days or until fermentation is complete and appears to clear and darken. At this point transfer the beer into a secondary fermenter and add the ½ ounce (14 g) Crystal hop pellets. Let the fermentation complete and settle in the secondary for 7 days. For best results secondary "cellar" or age at 50 degrees F (10 C) to help drop yeast out of suspension, but this is not at all crucial to the quality. Prime with sugar and bottle or keg when fermentation is complete. Age and carbonate/condition at about 70 degrees F (21 C).

Prepare yourself for the Good Life.

## *Akka Lakka American Pale Ale*

Akka Lakka ching. Akka Lakka chow. Akka Lakka ching ching chow chow chow. Boom-a-lakka, Boom-a-lakka. Chow, chow, chow. Pine Island. Pine Island. Rah, rah, rah. Okay, enough of my nostalgic and mature behavior (hey, I'm having fun). Let's cut the shuck and jive and get on with the recipe for Akka Lakka Pale Ale—a light copper-colored pale ale with a childish squeak and pleasant twist of roast malt character provided by the Belgian Special-B malt and a toasted malt character provided by the Munich, Vienna, and Wheat malts. American hops and how they are used in this recipe help establish this beer as one you'll brew over and over again.

Ingredients for 5¼ gallons* (20 l):

|  |  |
|---|---|
| 7 lbs. (3.2 kg) | pale malt |
| 1½ lbs. (680 g) | Munich malt (10L) |
| 1 lb. (450 g) | Vienna malt |
| ¾ lb. (300 g) | wheat malt |
| ¼ lb. (110 g) | Belgian Special-B malt |

*A 6+-gallon fermenter is needed.

| | |
|---|---|
| 1 tsp. (4 g) | gypsum |
| 1 oz. (28 g) | Amarillo hops or ⅔ oz. (18 g) Citra hops (boiling): 7 HBU (196 MBU) |
| ½ oz. (14 g) | Horizon, Galena, or Sorachi Ace hops (boiling): 5 HBU (140 MBU) |
| 1 oz. (28 g) | Cascade or Sorachi Ace hops (1 minute, aroma) |
| ¼ tsp. (1 g) | Irish moss powder |
| * | American ale type yeast or White Labs Cry Havoc yeast |
| ¾ c. (175 ml) | sugar (for bottling) or ⅓ c. (80 ml) corn sugar (for kegging) |

O.G.: 1.052–1.056 (13–14)
F.G.: 1.012–1.016 (3–4)
Bitterness: 41 BU; Color 14 SRM (28 EBC); Alcohol: 5.3% by volume

Add half the gypsum to 10½ quarts (10 l) of water. Add the crushed malt to this 10½ quarts (10 l) of 143-degree F (61.5 C) water and mix well. The temperature will stabilize between 130 and 135 degrees F (54.5–57 C). Add heat if necessary and hold the temperature at about 133 degrees F (56 C) for 30 minutes. Don't worry about a 3- to 5-degree F (2–3 C) temperature drop during this time.

Then add 5 quarts (5 l) of boiling water to this mash. This will raise the temperature to about or just below 155 degrees F (68 C). Hold at about 155 degrees F (68 C) for 30 to 45 minutes, stirring occasionally. Complete conversion by raising the temperature to 158 degrees F (70 C) and holding for 10 to 20 minutes or until an iodine test indicates complete conversion. Then add more heat to raise the temperature to 167 degrees F (75 C). Then pour your mash into your lauter-tun and sparge with 3 gallons (11.5 l) of hot water (add the other half of the gypsum to the sparge water) at 170 degrees F (76 C). The sweet wort ends in your brewpot. The volume of the wort before boiling should be about 5½ gallons (21 l).

Bring the sweet wort to a boil and add the boiling hops and boil for 60 minutes. Add the Irish moss and boil for the last 10 minutes of the boil. Then add the aroma hops and boil during the final 1 minute of the boil. Cool the wort to 70 to 75 degrees F (21–24 C). This can be done simply by immersing the brewpot (with lid on) in a bath of cold running water for about 45 minutes. Other means of chilling can be used if desired.

Strain, sparge, and transfer immediately to your primary fermenter. The final primary batch size is 5¼ gallons (20 l). If necessary, add additional cold water to achieve this volume. Aerate the wort very well. Add yeast when the temperature of the wort is 70 to 75 degrees F (21–24 C). Preferably ferment at 70 to 72 degrees F (21–22 C) for 4 to 6 days or until fermentation is complete and appears to clear and darken. At this point transfer the beer into a secondary fermenter and let the fermentation complete and settle in the secondary fermenter for 7 days. For best results "cellar" or age at 50 degrees F (10 C) to help drop yeast out of suspension, but this is not at all crucial to the quality. Prime with sugar and bottle or keg when fermentation is complete. Age and carbonate/condition at temperatures at about 70 degrees F (21 C).

And as they say on the Great Pond, Akka Lakka!

## Dancing with Hops IPA

Here we go again. It's beer time for the eccentric, and getting out of bounds, out of "style," and getting to astonishingly tasty.

Dancing with Hops is a gorgeously fruity and aromatic IPA, with soothing bitterness and supporting malt foundation. It's a lesson in malt etiquette. The body is lightened with about 12 percent rice as part of the grain ingredients. Lightening the dance with rice actually enhances and brightens the character of this IPA.

The bittering units are about 80 BUs, yet the perception of the bitterness in Dancing with Hops is a smooth IPA of medium intensity. The frequent, diverse, and late hopping offers an explosive and uniquely balanced fruity and floral hop aroma and flavor. Citra: grapefruit, apricot, and passion fruit. Nelson Sauvin: passion fruit and sauvignon grapes. Simcoe: earthy base contrasting Citra and B Sauvin. You'll surprise all of your brewing pals when you serve them Dancing with Hops and afterward tell them it has rice as an ingredient.

Ingredients for 5½ gallons (21 l):

| | |
|---|---|
| 9½ lbs. (4.3 kg) | Maris Otter or other pale malt |
| 1 lb. (454 g) | English crystal malt (15 L) |
| ½ lb. (225 g) | Gambrinus honey malt |
| ½ lb. (225 g) | Belgian aromatic malt |
| 1½ lbs. (680 g) | rice flakes |
| ¼ lb. (114 g) | Maris Otter pale malt (for rice mash/boil) |
| ½ oz. (14 g) | Amarillo hops 8% alpha (boiling): 4 HBU (112 MBU) |
| ¼ oz. (7 g) | Columbus hops, whole or pellets, 14.5% alpha (boiling): 3.6 HBU (102 MBU) |
| ¼ oz. (7 g) | Columbus hops, whole or pellets, 14.5% alpha (30 minutes, flavor): 3.6 HBU (102 MBU) |
| ¼ oz. (7 g) | Simcoe hops 14% alpha (30 minutes, flavor): 3.5 HBU (98 MBU) |
| 1 oz. (28 g) | Cascade hops 5% alpha (30 minutes, flavor): 5 HBU (140 MBU) |
| ½ oz. (14 g) | Amarillo hops 8% alpha (10 minutes, flavor and aroma) |
| ¼ oz. (7 g) | Columbus hops 14.5% alpha (10 minutes, flavor and aroma) |
| ½ oz. (14 g) | Simcoe hops 14.5% alpha (10 minutes, flavor and aroma) |

½ oz. (14 g)    Citra hops (1 minute, aroma)
½ oz. (14 g)    Simcoe hops (1 minute, aroma)
⅓ oz. (10 g)    New Zealand Nelson Sauvin hop pellets (1 minute, aroma)
⅓ oz. (10 g)    New Zealand Nelson Sauvin or NZ Mouteka hop pellets (dry hopping in secondary)
⅓ oz. (10 g)    Citra hop or Sorachi Ace pellets (dry hopping in secondary)
⅓ oz. (10 g)    Simcoe or Columbus hop pellets (dry hopping in secondary)
¼ tsp. (1 g)    Irish moss powder
*               pale ale–type yeast or White Labs Cry Havoc yeast
¾ c. (175 ml)   sugar (for bottling) or ⅓ c. (80 ml) corn sugar (for kegging)

O.G.: 1.063–1.067 (15.4–16.4)
F.G.: 1.016–1.020 (4–5)
Bitterness: 80 BU; Color 11 SRM (22 EBC); Alcohol: 6.2% by volume

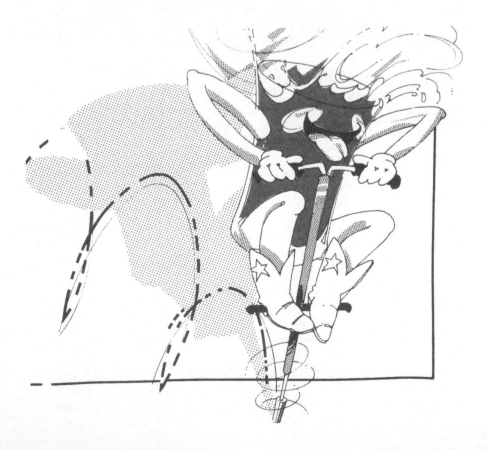

A step-infusion mash is employed to mash the grains. Add the crushed malted grain (reserve ¼ lb. malt for rice cooking) to 11½ quarts (11 l) of 143-degree F (61.5 C) water. Stir, stabilize, and hold the temperature at 132 degrees F (53 C) for 30 minutes. Meanwhile, add the rice flakes and ¼ pound of Maris Otter pale malt to 8 quarts (7.5 l) of cold water and bring to a boil, stirring to prevent scorching.

After the malt mash period has reached 30 minutes, add the boiling hot rice gruel and if needed add heat to bring the temperature up to 155 degrees F (68 C) and hold for about 30 minutes. Then raise the temperature to 167 degrees F (75 C), lauter and sparge with 3½ gallons (13.5 l) of 170-degree F (77 C) water. The sweet wort ends in your brewpot. Collect about 5½ gallons (21 l) of runoff.

Add the boiling hops, bring to a full and vigorous boil, and boil for 60 minutes. Add the 30-minute flavor hops for the last 30 minutes of the boil. Add the 10-minute aroma/flavor hops and Irish moss for the last 10 minutes of the boil. Add the 1-minute aroma hops for the last 1 minute of the boil. Turn off the heat and place the pot (with cover on) in a running cold-water bath for about 45 minutes or until the temperature is between 70 and 75 degrees F (21–24 C), or use other methods to chill your wort. Then strain and sparge the wort into a sanitized fermenter. Bring the total volume to 5½ gallons (21 l) with additional cold water if necessary.

Aerate the wort very well. Add the yeast when temperature of the wort is 70 to 75 degrees F (21–24 C). Ferment at about 70 degrees F (21 C) for about 1 week or when fermentation shows signs of calm and stopping. Rack from your primary to a secondary and add the hop pellets for dry hopping. If you have the capability, "cellar" the beer at about 55 degrees F (12.5 C) for about 1 week. Prime with sugar and bottle or keg when complete.

### *Hopotheosis Rosemary Xtra Pale Ale*

This recipe resulted after tasting a rosemary-infused IPA, called Rosemary Swamp Fox IPA, brewed by John Pinkerton, owner and brewmaster of the Moon River Brewing Company in Savannah, Georgia. This recipe is a transformation to somewhere in between an IPA and a Pale Ale with an intriguing light touch of rosemary, whose character suggests an exotic hop variety

Overdoing the rosemary will, well, make your beer taste more like rosemary. That's not necessarily a bad thing, but not what Hopotheosis is about. The recipe also includes a significant amount of fermentable agave syrup in the recipe to lighten the body and add a touch of caramel character.

As I've said a thousand times, so, let's cut the shuck and jive and get on with the recipe

Ingredients for 5½ gallons (21 l):

| | |
|---|---|
| 9 lbs. (4.1 kg) | Maris Otter pale malt |
| 1 lb. (454 g) | English crystal malt (10 L) |
| ½ lb. (225 g) | Belgian aromatic malt |
| 1¾ lbs. (795 g) | agave extract syrup |
| ¼ oz. (7 g) | Amarillo hops 9.5% alpha (boiling): 2.4 HBU (66 MBU) |
| ¼ oz. (7 g) | Citra or Centennial or Columbus hops 11% alpha (30 minutes, flavor): 9.6 HBU (269 MBU) |
| ½ oz. (14 g) | Amarillo or Simcoe hops (10 minutes, aroma) |
| ½ oz. (14 g) | freshly cut stem-end rosemary (dry "herbing") |
| ¼ oz. (7 g) | Nelson Sauvin hop pellets (dry hopping) |
| ¼ oz. (7 g) | Citra or Australian Galaxy or Sorachi Ace hop pellets (dry hopping) |
| ¼ tsp. (1 g) | Irish moss powder |
| * | pale ale–type yeast or White Labs Cry Havoc yeast |
| ¾ c. (175 ml) | sugar (for bottling) or ⅓ c. (80 ml) corn sugar (for kegging) |

O.G.: 1.061–1.065 (15–16)
F.G.: 1.014–1.018 (3.5–4.5)
Bitterness: 44 BU; Color 11 SRM (22 EBC); Alcohol: 6.4% by volume

A step-infusion mash is employed to mash the grains. Add 10½ quarts (10 l) of 143-degree F (61.5 C) water to the crushed grain. Stir, stabilize, and hold the temperature at 132 degrees F (53 C) for 30 minutes. Bring 5½ quarts (4.5 l) of water to a boil. When the malt mash has finished its 30-minute rest, add the boiling water to the mash and add heat to bring the temperature up to 155 degrees F (68 C) and hold for about 30 minutes. Then raise the temperature to 167 degrees F (75 C), lauter, and sparge with 3½ gallons (13.5 l) of 170-degree F (77 C) water. The sweet wort ends in your brewpot.

Collect about 5½ gallons (21 l) of runoff. Add the boiling hops, bring to a full and vigorous boil, and boil for 60 minutes. Add the 30-minute flavor hops for the last 30 minutes of the boil. Add the 10-minute aroma hops and Irish moss for the final 10 minutes of the boil. Turn off the heat and place the pot (with cover on) in a running cold-water bath for 45 minutes. Continue to chill in the immersion if needed to get to 70 to 75 degrees F (21–24 C) or use other methods to chill your wort. Then strain and sparge the wort into a sanitized fermenter. Bring the total volume to 5½ gallons (21 l) with additional cold water if necessary. Aerate the wort very well. Add the yeast when the temperature of the wort is about 70 degrees F (21 C). Ferment at about 70 degrees F (21 C) for about 1 week or when fermentation shows signs of calm and stopping. Rack from your primary to a secondary and add the rosemary and hop pellets for dry hopping. If you have the capability, "cellar" the beer at about 55 degrees F (12.5 C) for 1 week. Prime with sugar and bottle or keg when fermentation is complete.

## LIGHT LAGERS

### *Hanging Possum (Classic American) Pilsener*

Corn as an adjunct. The very notion will bring cringes and raised hair to many a homebrewer. In the name of purity, malt, hops, water, and the wholy ghost (yeast known as godisgood in former times), homebrewers yearning for the full flavor of beer often forsake nonmalted grains for all-malt beer. But with the skill of an open mind it is possible to maintain the full flavor of malted barley and add the character of other grain adjuncts. Grain adjuncts can brighten the character of many types of beers without compromising beer character, complexity, and flavorfully thirst-quenching drinkability.

Cheap shouldn't precede the word *adjunct* in this recipe or for the resulting great taste of this classic American Pilsener, which was commonly brewed in the earlier part of the American twentieth century. Hanging Possum Pilsener is a full-flavored, light-bodied beer brewed with corn and flavored adequately with hops that you'll love. Don't forget—it's alive, unfiltered, unpasteurized, and refermented in the bottle for conditioning.

Try this beer once and it'll be one of your regularly brewed beers. Disagree with me if you wish, but don't dare to debate until you've tried it yourself.

Ingredients for 6 gallons* (23 l):

| | |
|---|---|
| 8 lbs. (3.6 kg) | 2-row pale lager malt |
| ½ lb. (225 g) | aromatic malt |
| 1½ lbs. (680 g) | flaked corn |
| 1½ oz. (42 g) | French Strisselspalt or German Saphir hops (boiling): 6 HBU (168 MBU) |
| 1 oz. (28 g) | Hersbruck, Hallertau, or Tettnang hops (boiling): 3 HBU (84 MBU) |
| 1 oz. (28 g) | Hersbruck, Hallertau, or Tettnang hops (20 minutes, flavor) |
| ½ oz. (14 g) | Hersbruck, Hallertau, or Tettnang hops (10 minutes, finishing/flavor/aroma) |
| ½ oz. (14 g) | German Saphir or U.S. Tettnang hop pellets (2 minutes, finishing/aroma) |
| ¼ tsp. (1 g) | Irish moss powder |

*A 6+-gallon fermenter is needed.

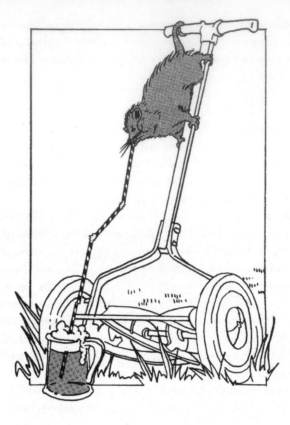

\*          American or German lager–type yeast or White Labs Cry
          Havoc yeast
¾ c. (175 ml)   sugar (for bottling) or ⅓ c. (80 ml) corn sugar (for kegging)

O.G.: 1.046–1.050 (11.5–12.5)
F.G.: 1.012–1.014 (3–3.5)
Bitterness: 31 BU; Color: 6 SRM (12 EBC); Alcohol: 4.5% by volume

Add the flaked corn and crushed malt to 10 quarts (9.5 l) of 143-degree F
(61.5 C) water and mix well. The temperature will stabilize between 130 and
135 degrees F (54.5–57 C). Add heat if necessary and hold the temperature at
about 133 degrees F (56 C) for 30 minutes. Don't worry about a 3- to 5-degree F
(2–3 C) temperature drop during this time.

Then add 5 quarts (5 l) of boiling water to this mash. This will raise the
temperature to about or just below 155 degrees F (68 C). Hold at about 155
degrees F (68 C) for 60 minutes, stirring occasionally. Complete conversion by
raising the temperature to 158 degrees F (70 C) and holding for 10 to 20 minutes
or until an iodine test indicates complete conversion. Then add more heat to

raise the temperature to 167 degrees F (75 C). Then pour your mash into your lauter-tun and sparge with 3 gallons (11.5 l) of hot water at 170 degrees F (76 C). The sweet wort ends in your brewpot. The volume of wort before boiling should be about 6½ gallons (24.5 l).

Bring the sweet wort to a boil, add the boiling hops, and boil for 60 minutes. Add the flavor hops for the last 20 minutes of the boil. Add the Irish moss and the flavor/aroma hops for the last 10 minutes of the boil. Add the finishing/aroma hops for the final 2 minutes of the boil. Cool the wort to 70 to 75 degrees F (21–24 C). This can be done simply by immersing the brewpot (with lid on) in a bath of cold running water for about 30 to 45 minutes. Other means of chilling can be used if desired.

Strain, sparge, and transfer immediately to your primary fermenter. The final primary batch size is 6 gallons (23 l). If necessary, add additional cold water to achieve this volume. Aerate the wort very well. Add the yeast when the temperature of the wort is 70 to 75 degrees F (21–24 C). If you have the capacity to primary ferment at about 55 degrees F (13 C), then do so once you see visible signs of fermentation. Regardless of what temperature you ferment at, after primary fermentation is complete, and there is little sign of fermentation activity, transfer the beer to a closed secondary fermenter and lager at temperatures between 35 and 55 degrees F (2–13 C) for 3 to 4 weeks. Prime with sugar and bottle or keg when lagering is complete. Let condition at room temperature for about a week before storing at colder temperatures

And remember, if you don't have the capacity to cold ferment Hanging Possum Pilsener it will still be an excellent beer bottled right after fermentation is complete.

### RU Kidding Me? Czech-Style Pils

Are you kidding me? That's the reaction you'll get from friends who love the taste of true Czech-style original pilsener. RUK Me for short, but the long of it is this simple yet elegant recipe that won't be short on the full aromatic flavor of malt and great crisp flavor of hops that were meant for this style. Sure you could use traditional Saaz, but the blend of the hops in this recipe is tried and true on my palate and that of many a friend. As I write, it'll be one of my very next batches of lager beers for the months of beerjoyment ahead.

Ingredients for 5 gallons (19 l):

| | |
|---|---|
| 8½ lbs. (3.9 kg) | Bohemian (floor) or German Pilsener malt |
| ½ lb. (225 g) | aromatic malt |
| 1½ oz. (42 g) | Mt. Hood hops or Liberty hops (boiling): 7–8 HBU (210 MBU) |
| 1½ oz. (42 g) | Czech Saaz hops (30 minutes, flavor): 6 HBU (168 MBU) |

| | |
|---|---|
| ½ oz. (14 g) | American Crystal or Czech Saaz hops (1 minute, finishing/aroma) |
| ¾ oz. (21 g) | American Crystal or Czech Saaz hop pellets (dry hopping) |
| ¼ tsp. (1 g) | Irish moss powder |
| * | Czech Pilsener lager–type yeast or White Labs Cry Havoc yeast |
| ¾ c. (175 ml) | sugar (for bottling) or ⅓ c. (80 ml) corn sugar (for kegging) |

O.G.: 1.046–1.050 (11.5–12.5)
F.G.: 1.010–1.012 (2.5–3)
Bitterness: 33 BU; Color: 6 SRM (12 EBC); Alcohol: 4.7% by volume

Add the crushed malt to 9 quarts (8.5 l) of 143-degree F (61.5 C) water and mix well. The temperature will stabilize between 130 and 135 degrees F (54.5–57 C). Add heat if necessary and hold the temperature at about 133 degrees F (56 C) for 30 minutes. Don't worry about a 3- to 5-degree F (2–3 C) temperature drop during this time.

Then add 4½ quarts (4.3 l) of boiling water to this mash. This will raise the temperature to about or just below 155 degrees F (68 C). Hold at about 155 degrees F (68 C) for 30 to 45 minutes, stirring occasionally. Complete conversion by raising the temperature to 158 degrees F (70 C) and holding for 10 to 20 minutes or until an iodine test indicates complete conversion. Then add more heat to raise the temperature to 167 degrees F (75 C). Then pour your mash into your lauter-tun and sparge with 3 gallons (11.5 l) of hot water at 170 degrees F (76 C). The sweet wort ends in your brewpot.

Bring the sweet wort to a boil, add the boiling hops, and boil for 60 minutes. Add the flavor hops for the last 30 minutes of the boil. Add the Irish moss for the last 10 minutes of the boil. Add the finishing/aroma hops for the final 1 minute of the boil. Cool the wort to 70 to 75 degrees F (21–24 C). This can be done simply by immersing the brewpot (with lid on) in a bath of cold running water for about 45 minutes. Other means of chilling can be used if desired.

Strain, sparge, and transfer immediately to your primary fermenter. The final primary batch size is 5 gallons (19 l). If necessary, add additional cold water to achieve this volume. Aerate the wort very well. Add the yeast when the temperature of the wort is 70 to 75 degrees F (21–24 C). If you have the capacity to primary ferment at about 55 degrees F (13 C), then do so once you see visible signs of fermentation. Regardless of what temperature you ferment at, after primary fermentation is complete and there is little sign of fermentation activity, transfer the beer to a closed secondary fermenter, add the dry hop pellets, and lager at temperatures between 35 and 55 degrees F (2–13 C) for 3 to 4 weeks.

Prime with sugar and bottle or keg when lagering is complete. Let condition at room temperature for about a week before storing at colder temperatures.

And remember, if you don't have the capacity to cold ferment RU Kidding Me? pilsener it will still be an excellent beer bottled right after fermentation is complete.

### Siam Pils

There are some excellent German-style pilseners brewed with rice in Southeast Asia. That's right, I said German-style with rice. Now there'll be none of that in Germany, for it's all malt without a doubt in Germany. But in other parts of the world German brewmasters have adapted to the climate and some of the local preferences for a lighter crisper beer. Without compromising the hop and malt character of the German Pils tradition, these German brewmasters have developed a winner for my repertoire.

I could simply refer you back a few pages to Hanging Possum Pilsener and recommend you substitute flaked rice for flaked corn, but rice has a lighter palate and I've created a slightly more floral blend of hops that contributes to the delicate yet satisfying palate of Siam Pils.

Ingredients for 5 gallons (19 l):

| | |
|---|---|
| 8½ lbs. (3.9 kg) | German Pilsener lager malt |
| ½ lb. (225 g) | aromatic malt |
| 1 lb. (450 g) | flaked rice |
| 2 oz. (56 g) | Saaz hops (boiling): 8 HBU (224 MBU) |
| ¼ oz. (7 g) | New Zealand Hallertau hop pellets (boiling): 2 HBU (56 MBU) |
| ½ oz. (14 g) | Santiam hops (2 minutes, aroma) |
| ½ oz. (14 g) | Crystal hop pellets (dry hopping) |
| ¼ tsp. (1 g) | Irish moss powder |
| * | German lager–type yeast |
| ¾ c. (175 ml) | sugar (for bottling) or ⅓ c. (80 ml) corn sugar (for kegging) |

O.G.: 1.050–1.054 (12.5–13.5)
F.G.: 1.012–1.014 (3–3.5)
Bitterness: 42 BU; Color: 6 SRM (12 EBC); Alcohol: 5% by volume

Add the flaked rice and crushed malt to 10 quarts (9.5 l) of 143-degree F (61.5 C) water and mix well. The temperature will stabilize between 130 and 135 degrees F (54.5–57 C). Add heat if necessary and hold the temperature at about 133 degrees F (56 C) for 30 minutes. Don't worry about a 3- to 5-degree F (2–3 C) temperature drop during this time.

Then add 5 quarts (5 l) of boiling water to this mash. This will raise the temperature to about or just below 155 degrees F (68 C). Hold at about 155 degrees F (68 C) for 60 minutes, stirring occasionally. Complete conversion by raising the temperature to 158 degrees F (70 C) and holding for 10 to 20 minutes or until an iodine test indicates complete conversion. Then add more heat to raise the temperature to 167 degrees F (75 C). Then pour your mash into your lauter-tun and sparge with 3 gallons (11.5 l) of hot water at 170 degrees F (76 C). The sweet wort ends in your brewpot.

Bring the sweet wort to a boil, add the boiling hops, and boil for 60 minutes. Add the Irish moss for the last 10 more minutes of the boil. Add the aroma hops for the final 2 minutes of the boil. Cool the wort to 70 to 75 degrees F (21–24 C). This can be done simply by immersing the brewpot (with lid on) in a bath of cold running water for about 30 to 45 minutes. Other means of chilling can be used if desired.

Strain, sparge, and transfer immediately to your primary fermenter. The final primary batch size is 5 gallons (19 l). If necessary, add additional cold water to achieve this volume. Aerate the wort very well. Add the yeast when the temperature of the wort is 70 to 75 degrees F (21–24 C). If you have the capacity to primary ferment at about 55 degrees F (13 C), then do so once you see visible signs of fermentation. Regardless of what temperature you ferment at, after primary fermentation is complete and there is little sign of fermentation activity, transfer the beer to a closed secondary fermenter, dry hop with the dry hopping hop pellets, and lager at temperatures between 35 and 55 degrees F (2–13 C) for 3 to 4 weeks. Prime with sugar and bottle or keg when lagering is complete. Let condition at room temperature for about a week before storing at colder temperatures.

And remember, if you don't have the capacity to cold ferment Siam Pils it will still be an excellent beer bottled right after fermentation is complete.

## AMBER ALES AND LAGERS

### Gopher Greatness Oktoberfest

First introduced at the Gopher Greatness Forest and Field Golf Tournament. A keg of brew at every hole. Tennis balls for golf balls. And the hole—well, that was about 100 square feet (10 square meters) outlined with a rope. Each hole picturesquely perfected by inspired homebrewers. Watch out for the gophers! Lost ball? Oh well, go for greatness with a Gopher Greatness German-style Oktoberfest. It's another lesson in the etiquette of malt.

You'll experience a deep golden, malty, and luscious lager with plenty of toasted Munich malt and a touch of aromatic malt. Brew an Oktoberfest lager the way it used to be brewed before the 2000 millennium, when German Oktoberfest prided itself with expressing its malt and hops.

Ingredients for 5¼ gallons* (20 l):

| | |
|---|---|
| 6 lbs. (2.7 kg) | pilsener-style malted barley |
| 4 lbs. (1.8 kg) | Munich malt |
| ½ lb. (225 g) | aromatic malt |
| ½ oz. (14 g) | Perle or German Tradition hops (boiling): 4 HBU (112 MBU) |
| 1 oz. (28 g) | Hallertau or Saphir hop pellets (10 minutes, flavor and aroma) |
| ¼ tsp. (1 g) | Irish moss powder |
| * | German lager or Oktoberfest/Maerzen type–lager yeast or White Labs Cry Havoc yeast |
| ¾ c. (175 ml) | sugar (for bottling) or ⅓ c. (80 ml) corn sugar (for kegging) |

O.G.: 1.052–1.056 (13–14)
F.G.: 1.012–1.016 (3–4)
Bitterness: 20 BU; Color: 10 SRM (20 EBC); Alcohol: 5.3% by volume

Add the crushed malt to 10½ quarts (10 l) of 143-degree F (61.5 C) water and mix well. The temperature will stabilize between 130 and 135 degrees F (54.5–57 C). Add heat if necessary and hold the temperature at about 133 degrees F (56 C) for 30 minutes. Don't worry about a 3- to 5-degree F (2–3 C) temperature drop during this time.

Then add 5 quarts (5 l) of boiling water to this mash. This will raise the temperature to about or just below 155 degrees F (68 C). Hold at about 155 degrees F (68 C) for 30 to 45 minutes, stirring occasionally. Complete conversion by raising the temperature to 158 degrees F (70 C) and holding for 10 to 20 minutes or until an iodine test indicates complete conversion. Then add more heat to raise the temperature to 167 degrees F (75 C). Then pour your mash into your lautertun and sparge with 2½ gallons (9.5 l) of hot water at 170 degrees F (76 C). The sweet wort ends in your brewpot. The volume of the wort before boiling should be about 5½ gallons (21 l).

Bring the sweet wort to a boil, add the boiling hops, and boil for 60 minutes. Add the Irish moss and flavor/aroma hops and boil for the final 10 minutes of the boil. Cool the wort to 70 to 75 degrees F (21–24 C). This can be done simply by immersing the brewpot (with lid on) in a bath of cold running water for about 30 to 45 minutes. Other means of chilling can be used if desired.

*A 6+-gallon fermenter is needed.

Strain, sparge, and transfer immediately to your primary fermenter. The final primary batch size is 5¼ gallons (20 l). If necessary, add additional cold water to achieve this volume. Aerate the wort very well. Add the yeast when the temperature of the wort is 70 to 75 degrees F (21–24 C). If you have the capacity to primary ferment at about 55 degrees F (13 C), then do so once you see visible signs of fermentation. Regardless of what temperature you ferment at, after primary fermentation is complete and there is little sign of fermentation activity, transfer the beer to a closed secondary fermenter and lager at temperatures between 35 and 55 degrees F (2–13 C) for 3 to 4 weeks. Prime with sugar and bottle or keg when fermentation is complete. Let condition at room temperature for about a week before storing at colder temperatures.

And remember, if you don't have the capacity to cold ferment Gopher Greatness, then go for greatness and do it any way you can and still enjoy an excellent beer bottled right after fermentation is complete.

### Spider's Tongue German Rauchbier (Smoked Beer)

As fine as the finest gossamer, Spider's Tongue smoked lager will be one of your crowning achievements if you like smoke-flavored foods. In the tradition of Bamberg, Germany, this brew is equal to the best you can find in Bamberg. The amount of smoke malt may seem like a lot, but this is quite close to the recipe used in Bamberg, though brewers there use colored malt rather than crystal malt to add an amber hue. The secret to German-style smoked beer is to go easy on the hops. Too much hop bitterness will intensify the smoke character and put it out of balance.

Ingredients for 5¼ gallons* (20 l):

    10 lbs. (4.5 kg)   German Rauchmalt (beechwood-smoked pale malt)
    ½ lb. (225 g)      crystal malt (40 L)
    1 oz. (28 g)       German Hersbrucker-Hallertau hops (boiling):
                       4 HBU (112 MBU)

*A 6+-gallon fermenter is needed.

¾ oz. (21 g)    Crystal hop pellets (20 minutes, flavor): 4 HBU (112 MBU)
¼ oz. (7 g)     Crystal hop pellets (dry hopping)
¼ tsp. (1 g)    Irish moss powder
*               German lager or Oktoberfest/Maerzen lager–type yeast
                or White Labs Cry Havoc yeast
¾ c. (175 ml)   sugar (for bottling) or ⅓ c. (80 ml) corn sugar (for kegging)

O.G.: 1.052–1.056 (13–14)
F.G. 1.012–1.016 (3–4)
Bitterness: 22 BU; Color: 14 SRM (28 EBC); Alcohol: 5.3% by volume

Add the crushed malt to 10½ quarts (10 l) of 143-degree F (61.5 C) water and mix well. The temperature will stabilize between 130 and 135 degrees F (54.5–57 C). Add heat if necessary and hold the temperature at about 133 degrees F (56 C) for 30 minutes. Don't worry about a 3- to 5-degree F (2 to 3 C) temperature drop during this time.

Then add 5 quarts (5 l) of boiling water to this mash. This will raise the temperature to about or just below 155 degrees F (68 C). Hold at about 155 degrees F (68 C) for 30 to 45 minutes, stirring occasionally. Complete conversion by raising the temperature to 158 degrees F (70 C) and holding for 10 to 20 minutes or until an iodine test indicates complete conversion. Then add more heat to raise the temperature to 167 degrees F (75 C). Then pour your mash into your lauter-

tun and sparge with 2½ gallons (9.5 l) of hot water at 170 degrees F (76 C). The sweet wort ends in your brewpot. The volume of the wort before boiling should be about 5½ gallons (21 l).

Bring the sweet wort to a boil, add the boiling hops, and boil for 60 minutes. Add the flavor hops and boil for the last 20 minutes of the boil. Add the Irish moss and boil for the final 10 minutes of the boil. Cool the wort to 70 to 75 degrees F (21–24 C). This can be done simply by immersing the brewpot (with lid on) in a bath of cold running water for about 30 to 45 minutes. Other means of chilling can be used if desired.

Strain, sparge, and transfer immediately to your primary fermenter. The final primary batch size is 5¼ gallons (20 l). If necessary, add additional cold water to achieve this volume. Aerate the wort very well. Add the yeast when the temperature of the wort is 70 to 75 degrees F (21–24 C).

If you have the capacity to primary ferment at about 55 degrees F (13 C), then do so once you see visible signs of fermentation. Regardless of what temperature you ferment at, after primary fermentation is complete and there is little sign of fermentation activity, transfer the beer to a closed secondary fermenter, add the ¼ ounce (7 g) of dry hop pellets and lager at temperatures between 35 and 55 degrees F (2–13 C) for 3 to 4 weeks. Prime with sugar and bottle or keg when fermentation is complete. Let condition at room temperature for about a week before storing at colder temperatures.

And remember, if you don't have the capacity to cold ferment Spider's Tongue, what you'll have brewed is an alelike version of the same beer—an excellent brew, but different.

### Carla's Oat Brown Ale

Something new, "out-of-style," different, unique, and refreshing with hints of dry and satisfying toastiness from English mild malt and a hop character that balances a reassuring bitterness with hop flavor and aroma. A bit of Brazilian dark *rapadura* sugar for mystery. Oats for smoothness. Aromatic and crystal malts for a swish of malt sweetness. It's a low-alcohol brew often referred to as a session beer, commemorating our family's joy and welcoming our daughter Carla Vitoria into our lives.

Ingredients for 5½ gallons (21 l):

| | |
|---|---|
| 4 lbs. (1.8 kg) | Maris Otter pale malt |
| 3 lbs.(1.4 kg) | English mild malt |
| 1 lb. (454 g) | rolled oats |
| ½ lb. (225 g) | English crystal malt (10 L) |
| ½ lb. (225 g) | honey malt |
| ¼ lb. (113 g) | aromatic malt |
| 9 oz. (250 g) | dark *rapadura* sugar |
| 1 oz. (28 g) | UK Fuggles or Styrian Goldings hops (boiling): 4.7 HBU (132 MBU) |
| 1 oz. (28 g) | UK Kent Golding hops (5 minutes, aroma) |
| 2 drops | Styrian Goldings hop oil |
| 1 Tbsp. (15 ml) | grain alcohol or 100+ proof vodka/neutral spirits |
| 4 oz. (118 ml) | cheap pasteurized light lager beer |
| ¼ tsp. (1 g) | Irish moss powder |
| * | English Ale yeast or White Labs Cry Havoc yeast |

¾ cup (175 ml)   sugar (for bottling) or ⅓ c. (80 ml) corn sugar
(for kegging)

O.G.: 1.046–1.050 (11.5–12.5)
F.G. 1.014–1.018 (3.5–4.5)
Bitterness: 37 BU; Color: 10 SRM (20 EBC); Alcohol: 4.2% by volume

A step-infusion mash is employed to mash the grains. Reserving 1 cup of crushed pale malt (for boiling with the oats), add the rest of the crushed grains to 8½ quarts (8.1 l) of 143-degree F (61.5 C) water. Stir, stabilize, and hold the temperature at 133 degrees F (53 C) for 30 minutes. Meanwhile, add the rolled oats and the reserved 1 cup crushed pale malt to 5½ quarts (4.3 l) cool water, bring to boil, and boil for 15 minutes. After the 133-degree all-malt mash has done its 30 minutes of time, add the boiling oat-malt mixture. Add heat if necessary to bring the temperature up to 155 degrees F (68 C) and hold for about 30 minutes. Then raise the temperature to 167 degrees F (75 C), lauter, and sparge with 3½ gallons (13.5 l) of 170-degree F (77 C) water. The sweet wort ends in your brewpot. Collect about 5½ gallons (21 l) of runoff.

Add the boiling hops and *rapadura* sugar and bring to a full and vigorous boil. Boil for 60 minutes. Add the Irish moss for the last 10 minutes of the boil. Add the aroma hops for the final 5 minutes of the boil. Turn off the heat and place the pot (with cover on) in a running cold water bath for 45 minutes. Continue to chill in the immersion or use other methods to chill your wort. Then strain and sparge the wort into a sanitized fermenter. Bring the total volume to 5½ gallons (21 l) with additional cold water if necessary.

Rack from your primary to a secondary. Prepare the hop oil by using a pipette to carefully add 2 drops (don't overdo it) of oil into a sanitized beer glass into which you've added the grain alcohol or 100+ proof vodka/neutral spirits. Swirl and blend the hop oil into the alcohol. Add the pasteurized light lager beer to further disperse the oil into the mixture. Add the dispersed oil/beer/alcohol mixture into your secondary fermenter and then rack the beer from the primary into the secondary. If you have the capability, "cellar" the beer at about 55 degrees F (12.5 C) for about 1 week. Prime with sugar and bottle or keg when complete.

Read more about hop oils in *The Homebrewer's Companion, Second Edition.*

## Monkey's Paw Brown Ale

A rich, satisfying, chocolaty brown ale with a pleasant sweetness balanced with a classic, crisp, and earthy English hop finish. Monkey's Paw will make you wish you had another, but that won't be necessary because this recipe, like all the others, is for 5 gallons (19 l)—5 gallons of many "another" glasses of your medium-bodied brown ale in the English tradition.

Ingredients for 5¼ gallons* (20 l)

| | |
|---|---|
| 8½ lbs. (3.9 kg) | pale malted barley |
| ¼ lb. (110 g) | chocolate malt |
| ¼ lb. (110 g) | black malt |
| 1 lb. (450 g) | crystal malt (10–15 L) |
| 1 tsp. (4 g) | gypsum |
| 1 oz. (28 g) | Fuggles hops (boiling): 5 HBU (140 MBU) |
| 1 oz. (28 g) | English Kent Goldings hops (10 minutes, flavor/aroma) |
| ¼ tsp. (1 g) | Irish moss powder |
| * | English or American ale–type yeast or White Labs Cry Havoc yeast |
| ¾ c. (175 ml) | sugar (for bottling) or ⅓ c. (80 ml) corn sugar (for kegging) |

O.G.: 1.048–1.052 (12–13)
F.G.: 1.012–1.016 (3–4)
Bitterness: 41 BU; Color: 14 SRM (28 EBC); Alcohol: 4.7% by volume

Add the crushed malt and half the gypsum to 10 quarts (9.5 l) of 143-degree F (61.5 C) water and mix well. The temperature will stabilize between 130 and 135 degrees F (54.5–57 C). Add heat if necessary and hold the temperature at about 133 degrees F (56 C) for 30 minutes. Don't worry about a 3- to 5-degree F (2–3 C) temperature drop during this time.

Then add 5 quarts (5 l) of boiling water to this mash. This will raise the temperature to about or just below 155 degrees F (68 C). Hold at about 155 degrees F (68 C) for 30 to 45 minutes, stirring occasionally. Complete conversion by raising the temperature to 158 degrees F (70 C) and holding for 10 to 20 minutes or until an iodine test indicates complete conversion. Then add more heat to raise the temperature to 167 degrees F (75 C). Then pour your mash into your lauter-tun and sparge with 3 gallons (11.5 l) of hot water (add the other half of the gypsum to the sparge water) at 170 degrees F (76 C). The sweet wort ends in your brewpot. The volume of the wort before boiling should be about 5½ gallons (21 l).

Bring the sweet wort to a boil, add the boiling hops, and boil for 60 minutes. Add the Irish moss and flavor/aroma hops and boil for the final 10 minutes of the boil. Cool the wort to 70 to 75 degrees F (21–24 C). This can be done simply by immersing the brewpot (with lid on) in a bath of cold running water for about 45 minutes. Other means of chilling can be used if desired.

Strain, sparge, and transfer immediately to your primary fermenter. The final primary batch size is 5¼ gallons (20 l). If necessary, add additional cold

*A 6+-gallon fermenter is needed.

water to achieve this volume. Aerate the wort very well. Add the yeast when the temperature of the wort is 70 to 75 degrees F (21–24 C). Preferably ferment at 70 to 72 degrees F (21–22 C) for 4 to 6 days or until fermentation is complete and appears to clear and darken.

At this point transfer the beer into a secondary fermenter and let the fermentation complete and settle in the secondary fermenter for 7 days. For best results "cellar" or age at 50 degrees F (10 C) to help drop yeast out of suspension, but this is not at all crucial to the quality. Prime with sugar and bottle or keg when fermentation is complete. Age and carbonate/condition at temperatures at about 70 degrees F (21 C).

Beware of what you wish for when you are enjoying a Monkey's Paw; things could get out of hand.

## WEIZENBIER/WEISSBIER

### NoopleTucker Dunkel Weizen or Weizen (Dark or Pale Bavarian-Style Wheat Beer)

It takes two sides to play NoopleTucker, so pick yours, dark or pale. The subtleness of German hops and special German-style wheat beer yeast conspire to create the profound authentic German character enjoyed throughout the world. Now available in your home beer garden. The pale version is lighter and and lively. If you want more complexity try the dark "Dunkel" version. *Dunkel* is "dark" in German, and the dignified contribution of roasted malts bring out a hint of cocoa character to an otherwise fruity, refreshing wheat beer. Afraid of the dark? The pale version omits the dark roasted malts from the recipe.

Now about NoopleTucker: It's a unique game that is by far Maine's Whitehead Island's most popular sporting event. You might at first describe it as "blind volleyball," but it is much more strategic than one might assume. It's played with a volleyball, but instead of a net, a large opaque sheet of plastic separates the two teams. No peeking. Now get brewing.

Ingredients for 5¼ gallons* (19 l):

| | |
|---|---|
| 7 lbs. (3.2 kg) | pale malted barley (for Dunkel Weizen, use 4 lbs. [1.8 kg] pale malt and 3 lbs. [1.4 kg] Munich-style malt [10–15 L]) |
| 3 lbs. (1.4 kg) | wheat malt (for Dunkel Weizen, add 2 oz. [56 g] debittered black malt) |
| ¾ oz. (21 g) | Hallertau or Spalt hops (boiling): 3.5 HBU (98 MBU) |
| ¼ oz. (7 g) | Hallertau or Saphir hops (2 minutes, finishing/aroma) |

*A 6+-gallon fermenter is needed.

¼ tsp. (1 g)    Irish moss powder
*               German-style Bavarian wheat ale–type yeast
¾ c. (175 ml)   sugar (for bottling) or ⅓ c. (80 ml) corn sugar (for kegging)


O.G.: 1.048–1.052 (12–13)
F.G.: 1.010–1.012 (2.5–3)
Bitterness: 12 BU; Color: 6 SRM (12 EBC) & Dunkel: 15 SRM (30 EBC);
Alcohol: 5% by volume


Add the crushed malt to 10 quarts (9.5 l) of 143-degree F (61.5 C) water and mix well. The temperature will stabilize between 130 and 135 degrees F (54.5–57 C). Add heat if necessary and hold the temperature at about 133 degrees F (56 C) for 30 minutes. Don't worry about a 3- to 5-degree F (2–3 C) temperature drop during this time.

Then add 5 quarts (4.5 l) of boiling water to this mash. This will raise the temperature to about or just below 155 degrees F (68 C). Hold at 149 to 155 degrees F (65–68 C) for 45 minutes, stirring occasionally. Complete conversion by raising the temperature to 158 degrees F (70 C) and holding for 10 to 20 minutes or until an iodine test indicates complete conversion. Then add more heat to raise the temperature to 167 degrees F (75 C). Then pour your mash into your lauter-tun and sparge with 3½ gallons (13 l) of hot water at 170 degrees F (76 C). The sweet wort ends in your brewpot. The volume of the wort before boiling should be about 5½ gallons (21 l).

Bring the sweet wort to a boil, add boiling hops, and boil for 60 minutes. Add the Irish moss for the last 10 minutes of the boil. Add the finishing/aroma hops for the final 2 minutes of the boil. Cool the wort to 70 to 75 degrees F (21–24 C). This can be done simply by immersing the brewpot (with the lid on) in a bath of cold running water for about 30 to 45 minutes. Other means of chilling can be used if desired.

Strain, sparge, and transfer immediately to your primary fermenter. The final primary batch size is 5¼ gallons (20 l). If necessary, add additional cold water to achieve this volume. Aerate the wort very well. Add the yeast when the temperature of the wort is 70 to 75 degrees F (21–24 C). Preferably ferment at 70 to 72 degrees F (21–22 C) for 4 to 6 days or until fermentation is complete and appears to clear and darken.

At this point transfer the beer into a secondary fermenter. Let the fermentation complete and settle in the secondary fermenter for 7 more days at 70 to 72 degrees F (21–22 C). When fermentation appears to be complete you may then "cellar" or age at 50 degrees F (10 C) to help drop yeast out of suspension, but this is not at all crucial to the quality. Prime with sugar and bottle or keg when fermentation is complete. Age and carbonate/condition at temperatures at about 70 degrees F (21 C).

## PORTERS AND STOUTS

### Silver Dollar Porter

This is the best porter either side of a silver dollar can buy—but you can't buy it because it ain't for sale. It's homebrew and it's yours—lucky for you, because there won't be enough to go around as it is.

A full-bodied, bittersweet version of black heaven, this is the homebrewer's best shot at duplicating the famous Anchor Porter of San Francisco fame. It'll bring tears of joy to your eyes.

Ingredients for 5 gallons (19 l):

| | |
|---|---|
| 8 lbs. (3.6 kg) | pale malted barley |
| 1 lb. (450 g) | Munich malt |
| ½ lb. (225 g) | crystal malt (10–15 L) |
| ½ lb. (225 g) | black malt |
| ½ lb. (225 g) | chocolate malt |
| 1 tsp. (4 g) | gypsum |
| 1 oz. (28 g) | Northern Brewer or Perle hops (boiling): 8 HBU (224 MBU) |
| ½ oz. (14 g) | Cascade hops (boiling): 3 HBU (84 MBU) |
| ½ oz. (14 g) | Cascade hops (2 minutes, finishing/aroma) |
| ¼ tsp. (1 g) | Irish moss powder |
|  | American ale–type yeast or White Labs Cry Havoc yeast |
| ¾ c. (175 ml) | sugar (for bottling) or ⅓ c. (80 ml) corn sugar (for kegging) |

O.G.: 1.052–1.056 (13–14)
F.G.: 1.012–1.016 (3–4)
Bitterness: 43 BU; Color: 40 SRM (80 EBC); Alcohol: 5.3% by volume

Add half the gypsum to 10 quarts (9.5 l) of water. Add the crushed malt to the 10 quarts (9.5 l) of 143-degree F (61.5 C) water and mix well. The temperature will stabilize between 130 and 135 degrees F (54.5–57 C). Add heat if necessary and hold the temperature at about 133 degrees F (56 C) for 30 minutes. Don't worry about a 3- to 5-degree F (2–3 C) temperature drop during this time.

Then add 5 quarts (5 l) of boiling water to this mash. This will raise the temperature to about or just below 155 degrees F (68 C). Hold at about 155 degrees F (68 C) for 45 minutes, stirring occasionally. Complete conversion by raising the temperature to 158 degrees F (70 C) and holding for 10 to 20 minutes or until an iodine test indicates complete conversion. Then add more heat to raise the temperature to 167 degrees F (75 C). Then pour your mash into your lauter-tun and sparge with 3 gallons (11.5 l) of hot water (add the other half of the gypsum to the sparge water) at 170 degrees F (76 C). The sweet wort ends in your brewpot.

Bring the sweet wort to a boil, add both of the boiling hops, and boil for 60 minutes. Add the Irish moss and boil for the last 10 minutes of the boil. Add the finishing/aroma hops and boil for the final 2 minutes of the boil. Cool the wort to 70 to 75 degrees F (21–24 C). This can be done simply by immersing the brewpot (with lid on) in a bath of cold running water for about 45 minutes. Other means of chilling can be used if desired.

Strain, sparge, and transfer immediately to your primary fermenter. The final primary batch size is 5 to 5½ gallons (19–21 l). If necessary, add additional cold water to achieve this volume. Aerate the wort very well. Add the yeast when the temperature of the wort is 70 to 75 degrees F (21–24 C). Preferably ferment at 70 to 72 degrees F (21–22 C) for 4 to 6 days or until fermentation is complete and appears to clear and darken.

At this point transfer the beer into a secondary fermenter and let the fermentation complete and settle in the secondary fermenter for 7 days. For best results "cellar" or age at 50 degrees F (10 C) to help drop yeast out of suspension, but this is not at all crucial to the quality. Prime with sugar and bottle or keg when fermentation is complete. Age and carbonate/condition at temperatures at about 70 degrees F (21 C).

### Dusty Mud Irish Stout

Dusty Mud revisits the simplicity with which you can brew a classic Irish-style stout. After 7 to 14 days of fermentation you will discover that it *tastes great* at bottling time! This smooth stout has hints of caramel, roasted barley, and cocoa, climaxing to stout perfection—smooth as silk and easy drinking. Making the world mud-lucious one beer at a time. This is as close as it gets to the twentieth-century Guinness character of yesteryear, when real hops were used and roasted malt and barley character surfaced. In comparison, and I think you will agree after making Dusty Mud Irish Stout, today's Guinness is like a cat without a meow.

Ingredients for 5¼ gallons* (20 l):

| | |
|---|---|
| 6 lbs. (2.7 kg) | English or American 2-row pale malt |
| 1 lb. (450 g) | English crystal malt (10 L) |
| ¾ lb. (340 g) | roasted barley |
| ½ lb. (225 g) | black malt |
| 1 tsp. (4 g) | gypsum |
| ¼ oz. (7 g) | First Gold hops (boiling): 2 HBU (56 MBU) |

*A 6+-gallon fermenter is needed.

½ oz. (14 g)    Kent Goldings hops (boiling): 2 HBU (56 MBU)
½ oz. (14 g)    Willamette or Fuggles hops (boiling): 3 HBU (84 MBU)
¼ tsp. (1 g)    Irish moss powder
*               Irish ale–type yeast
¾ c. (175 ml)   sugar (for bottling) or ⅓ c. (80 ml) corn sugar
                (for kegging)


O.G.: 1.038–1.040 (9.5–10)
F.G.: 1.006–1.008 (1.5–2)
Bitterness: about 28 BU; Color: 44 SRM (88 EBC); Alcohol: 4.2%
by volume

Add half the gypsum to 8 quarts (7.5 l) of 143-degree F (61.5 C) water. Then add the crushed malt and mix well. The temperature will stabilize between 130 and 135 degrees F (54.5–57 C). Add heat if necessary and hold the temperature at about 133 degrees F (56 C) for 30 minutes. Don't worry about a 3- to 5-degree F (2–3 C) temperature drop during this time.

Then add 4½ quarts (4 l) of boiling water to this mash. This will raise the temperature to about or just below 155 degrees F (68 C). Add heat and increase the temperature to about 158 degrees F (70 C) and hold for 45 minutes, stirring occasionally. Then add more heat to raise the temperature to 167 degrees F (75 C). Then pour your mash into your lauter-tun and sparge with 3½ gallons (13.5 l) of hot water (add the other half of the gypsum to the sparge water) at 170 degrees F (76 C). The sweet wort ends in your brewpot.

Bring the sweet wort to a boil, add all of the boiling hops, and boil for 60 minutes. Add the Irish moss and boil for the final 10 minutes of the boil. Cool the wort to 70 to 75 degrees F (21–24 C). This can be done simply by immersing the brewpot (with lid on) in a bath of cold running water for about 30 to 45 minutes. Other means of chilling can be used if desired.

Strain, sparge, and transfer immediately to your primary fermenter. The final primary batch size is 5¼ gallons (20 l). If necessary, add additional cold water to achieve this volume. Aerate the wort very well. Add the yeast when the temperature of the wort is 70 to 75 degrees F (21–24 C). Preferably ferment at 70 to 72 degrees F (21–22 C) for 4 to 6 days or until fermentation is complete and appears to clear and darken.

At this point transfer the beer into a secondary fermenter and let the fermentation complete and settle in the secondary fermenter for 7 days. For best results "cellar" or age at 50 degrees F (10 C) to help drop yeast out of suspension, but this is not at all crucial to the quality. Prime with sugar and bottle or keg when fermentation is complete. Age and carbonate/condition at temperatures at about 70 degrees F (21 C).

## RESOURCES FOR 91 ALL-GRAIN RECIPES

*Other all-grain recipes can be found in* The Homebrewer's Companion, Second Edition, Microbrewed Adventures, *and* Home Brewer's Gold.

### ALL-GRAIN RECIPES IN *THE HOMEBREWER'S COMPANION, SECOND EDITION:*

Jack Union's Classic Pale Ale
Quite Contrary American IPA
Zymurgific English-Style Summer Ale
Jokester Mild Ale
Golden Valley (or Val) Epiphany Ale
Leftmalle Dubbel
Mr. Kelly's Coconut Curry Hefeweizen
Rye Not?
Buzzdigh Moog Double Brown Ale
Someplace You Gotta Go Coconut Porter
Barrel of Monkeys Wheat-Oatmeal Nut Stout
Black Samba Imperial Baltic Porter
A Return to Innocence Juniper-Cherry Bock
The Horse You Rode In On Apricot Honey Spiced Ale
Mile High Green Chile Ale
Pumpkin (Cucurbito Pepo) Ale
Speltbrau
Sikaru Sumerian Beer
Come Helles or High Water
A Fine Time to Be Me Czech Pils
Creede Lily German Pils
Swingtop American Pre-Prohibition Pilsener
St. Louis Golden Lager
Dork's Torque Mexican Crown Lager
Claude of Neptune Amaizeing CopperBock
Princess of Peace Märzen
Sweet Mischief Vienna-Mild Lager
Jump Be Nimble, Jump Be Quick German Dunkel
Ivan the Wonderful's Czech Dark Lager
Blinking Star Dark Lager
Shineblast Imperial Helles
My Goodness My Bock
Rogerfest Cherrywood Lager

ALL-GRAIN RECIPES IN *MICROBREWED ADVENTURES:*

Samuel Adams 1880 (amber lager)
Vienna-Style Ouro de Habanera (Havana Gold)
George Killian's Irish Red Ale from Pellforth
1447 Belgium Zwarte Rose (black) Ale
Irish Cocoa Wood Porter
Quingdao Dark Lager
Switch and Toggles Preposterous Porter
Zaltitis Baltic Porter
Andech's Weekday Bock
Original Dogbolter Ale—Goose & Firkin (brown ale)
Puritanical Nut Brown Ale
English-Style Bitter
Beyond the Ordinary Ordinary Bitter
"Original" Ballard Bitter
Belgian-Style Cherry–Black Currant (Kriek-Cassis) Lambic
Magic Bolo #9.1300 (apricot ale)
New Wisconsin Apple/Raspberry/Cherry Beer
Crazy Old Man Altbier
65-65-65-65 India Pale Ale
Telluride India Pale Ale
Czech-Mex Tijuana Urquell
Klibbety Jibbit (light lager)
MickViRay Papazian Pilsener
Printz Helles German Lager
Swakapmund Cowboy (light) Lager
1982 Original Sierra Nevada Pale Ale
Piozzo Italian Pale Ale
1981 Boulder Christmas Stout
Bert Grant's Planet Imperial Stout
Brooklyn's Original Chocolate Stout
Felicitous Stout
Pumpernickel Rye Stout
Wolaver's Organic Oatmeal Stout
Jeff Bagby's Hop Whompus 2004
John 1981—a homebrewed version of Charlie 1981
Monastic Bleue Strong Belgian-Style Ale
Old Lighthouse in the Fog Barleywine Ale
Stone 03 Vertical Epic (specialty ale)
19th-Century Leipziger Gose

Alaskan Winter Spruce Old Ale
Flying Fish Baby Saison Farmhouse Ale
Frog & Rosbif's Brown Wheat Coriander (mild)
Mile High Green Chile Ale
Poetic Brighella Italian-Belgian-German-English-American Ale
Vello's Gotlandsdricke (specialty ale)
Zeezuiper Spiced Nederlander Strong Ale
Zimbabwe Zephyr Sorghum beer
Hans Weissbier
Original Pyramid Wheaten Ale

## ALL-GRAIN RECIPES IN *HOME BREWER'S GOLD:*

Aecht Schlenkerla Rauchbier, Brauerei Heller-Trum, Bamberg,
    Germany
Aventinus, Private Weissbierbrauerei G. Schneider & Son K.G.,
    Munich, Germany
B&H Breakfast Toasted Ale, Barley & Hopp's, San Mateo, California
    USA
Bow Valley Premium Lager, Bow Valley Brewing Co., Canmore,
    Alberta Canada
Brick Red Baron, Brick Brewing Co. Ltd., Waterloo, Ontario Canada
California Blonde Ale, Coast Range Brewing Co., Gilroy, California
    USA
Capstone ESB, Oasis Brewery, Boulder, Colorado USA
Cascade Pale Ale, Cascade Brewery, Hobart, Tasmania, Australia
Coriander Rye Ale, Bison Brewing Co., Berkeley, California USA
Delaney's Ale, South China Brewing Co. Ltd, Aberdeen, Hong Kong
Derailer Doppelbock, Tabernash Brewing Co., Denver, Colorado USA
Dos Equis Special Lager, Cerveceria Cuauhtémoc, Monterrey,
    Mexico
Edelweiss Dunkel, Österreichische Bräu-Aktiengesellschaft, Linz,
    Austria
Founders Stout, Mishawaka Brewing Co., Mishawaka, Indiana USA
Grain D'Orge, Brasserie Jeanne D'Arc, Ronchin-Lille, France
Griffon Extra Pale Ale, McAuslan Brewing Inc., Montreal, Quebec
    Canada
Hoegaarden, Brouwerij de Kluis, Hoegaarden, Belgium
Icehouse, Plank Road Brewery, Milwaukee, Wisconsin USA
Leinenkugel's Red Lager, Jacob Leinenkugel Brewing Co., Chippewa
    Falls, Wisconsin USA
Liefmans Frambozen, Brouwerij Liefmans, Oudenaarde, Belgium
Liefmans Goudenband, Brouwerij Liefmans, Oudenaarde, Belgium

Lindemans' Cuvée René, Lindeman's Farm Brew, Blezenbeek,
    Belgium
Mackeson XXX Stout, Whitbread Beer Co., London, England
Miller Lite, Miller Brewing Co., Milwaukee, Wisconsin USA
OB Lager, Oriental Brewery Co. Ltd., Seoul, Korea
Old Rasputin Russian Imperial Stout, North Coast Brewing Co. Inc.,
    Fort Bragg, California USA
Olde English 800 Malt Liquor, Pabst Brewing Co., Milwaukee,
    Wisconsin USA
Ozone Ale, Hubcap Brewery/Brewing Co. of Vail, Vail, Colorado USA
Pauwel Kwak, Brewery Bosteels, Buggenhout, Belgium
Point Amber Lager, Barton Beers Ltd., Chicago, Illinois USA
Radegast Birell, Radegast Brewery J.S.C., Nosovice, Czech Republic
Redwood Coast Alpine Gold Pilsner, Redwood Coast Brewing Co.,
    Alameda, California USA
Redwood Coast Brown, Redwood Coast Brewing Co., Alameda,
    California USA
Ruddles Best Bitter, Ruddles Brewery, Rutland, United Kingdom
Ruffian Mai-Bock, Mountain Valley Brew Pub, Suffern, New York
    USA
Ruffian Pilsner, Mountain Valley Brew Pub, Suffern, New York USA
Saint Brigid's Porter, Great Divide Brewing Co., Denver, Colorado USA
San Quentin's Breakout Stout, Marin Brewing Co, Larkspur, California
    USA
Scotch Ale, Samuel Adams Brewhouse, Philadelphia, Pennsylvania
    USA
Seabright Session Ale, Seabright Brewery, Santa Cruz, California USA
Slow Down Brown Ale, Il Vicino Inc., Albuquerque, New Mexico USA
Snake River Pale Ale, Snake River Brewing Co., Inc., Jackson,
    Wyoming USA
St. Charles Porter, Blackstone Restaurant & Brewery, Nashville,
    Tennessee USA
Star Brew 1000 (Wheat Wine), Marin Brewing Co., Larkspur,
    California USA
Stoddards ESB, Stoddard's Brewhouse and Eatery, Sunnyvale,
    California USA
Stoddards Kölsch, Stoddard's Brewhouse and Eatery, Sunnyvale,
    California USA
Stoudt's Export Gold, Stoudt Brewing Co., Adamstown, Pennsylvania
    USA
Sundance Hefe-Weizen, Palmer Lake Brewing Co., Palmer Lake,
    Colorado USA

Tabernash Munich Dark Lager, Tabernash Brewing Co., Denver,
   Colorado USA
Thomas Kemper Hefeweizen, Thomas Kemper Lagers, Seattle,
   Washington USA
Wet Mountain India Pale Ale, Il Vicino, Salida, Colorado USA
Zoser Oatmeal Stout, Oasis Brewery, Boulder, Colorado USA

## SOUR BEERS AND BELGIAN LAMBIC

For many, sour beer is "in." You either love it or you don't. In the United States, homebrewers, craft brewers, and their beer-drinking fans have popularized the type of beer many simply describe as "sour beer." A well-known and respected lambic brewer from the Brussels area once asked me, "Why do Americans describe many of their beers as sour? We don't describe our beers as sour here in Belgium." His question was thought-provoking. We are only introducing a one-dimensional thought to the discussion when we describe "sour" beers in a singular term. "Sour" is a literal sensation and a general descriptor of a genre of beer. Actually life and beer are much more complex. Sometimes in our passion to describe what we love, we don't do justice to the true nature of a beer's character and nuances. If you're a fan of Belgian lambics, Gueuze, Flanders (sour) red ales, and the growing availability of American-made wood- and aged specialties, think about what you really like about those beers. What they have in common is their acidity or sourness, but lambic, Gueuze, and all the other sour fermented beers you love and cherish are not just sour. They are wild, complex, and full of unusual flavors that have little to do with sourness.

Sour mash brewing is an unusual method resulting in beers that have varying degrees of sourness in their character. The sourness is a result of bacterial activity, but the end product is microbiologically stable. What this means for the brewer is that there is a method by which one can achieve any degree of naturally produced sourness in any type of beer and the stabilizing effect that acidity imparts to the end product.

Why would anyone want to make sour beer? This question used to be relevant, but now with the established and growing popularity of sour beers, a certain amount of sourness in beer is attractive to many beer drinkers. For certain beer styles such as Belgian lambic, other Belgian ales, Berliner Weisse, and even Guinness Stout, acidity is part of the character. An enhanced level of acidity can create a pleasant balance and finesse in your fruit beers. Achieving sourness in beer without the introduction of wild microorganisms to wort fermentation is now explored by both homebrewers and craft brewers. Acid-creating bacteria can also be introduced in the mash and before the boil.

At issue, and more challenging, is the concern with introducing wild microcreatures into the fermention. Our wild friends are difficult to control. Wild fermentations can produce unpredictable results. Sometimes the beer heads off in a direction we'd rather not pursue. But with growing availability of special cultures of wild yeast and bacteria, homebrewers can explore these options with knowledgeable expectations. That frontier is covered in more detail in the *The Homebrewer's Companion, Second Edition*. Here, we'll explore a unique way in which to naturally create acidity in your special beers without having to introduce bacteria to your fermentation—it's called "sour mashing."

My first sour mash beer was tasted in Kentucky in 1989. It offered much inspiration for experimentation and thoughts on how this technique could be applied to homebrewing to approximate some of the wilder and more sour beer styles of the world.

## THE PRINCIPLES OF SOUR MASH BREWING

Bacteria that produce sourness and increase acidity of mashes and worts are ever-present on grains of malted barley. By introducing crushed malted barley to sweet diluted malt extract or warm mashes, the conditions are optimal for bacterial (especially lactobacillus) activity resulting in the souring of the mash. The degree of sourness can be controlled by temperature and time of activity.

After the souring activity is complete, the sweet-and-sour extract can be boiled with hops and the brewing process carried through to completion. The bacterial activity is killed with wort boiling. The sourness remains, but further bacterial activity is stopped.

Cultured lager or ale yeast can be used to produce almost any style of beer with a "twang" from the sour mash. But even more interesting, homebrewers can use "lambic-style" yeast cultures which include among other microorganisms *Brettanomyces lambicus* or *Brettanomyces bruxellensis*. With skill and access to great ingredients, homebrewers can come pleasantly close to duplicating many of the characters that make Belgian ales and lambics so unique.

### Basic Procedures for Producing Sour Extract from Malt Extract or All-Grain Mash

*Malt extract method* for producing sourness in beer, for 5 gallons (19 l):

    5–6 lbs. (2.3–2.7 kg)    malt extract
    ½ lb. (225 g)            crushed pale malted barley

Dissolve the malt extract in 1½ gallons (5.7 l) of hot water and stabilize the temperature at about 130 degrees F (54 C). Pour this hot, sweet malt extract into an odorless, sanitized, food-grade, 5-gallon (19 l) bucket. Add the crushed

malted barley. Stir to mix. Place a sheet of aluminum foil in contact with the surface of the liquid to form a complete barrier from the air. Fit lid snugly on the
pail. Insulate the pail on all sides with a sleeping bag and/or blankets to help
maintain the warm temperature and promote lactic bacterial activity and souring. The lactobacillus will sour the extract very dramatically and will be noticeable after about 15 hours; 15 to 24 hours should be adequate for your first
experiment with this process.

When you open the container, you may notice some mold growing on the
surface. Don't worry. Skim off and discard the mold. The aluminum foil helped
minimize this in the first place. You will definitely notice the absolutely abomi-
nable, putrid odor the bacteria have caused. Don't worry. It's supposed to smell
awful—almost awful enough to throw out. *But don't!*

Strain and transfer your sour extract to your brewpot, add and process any
specialty grains, and then bring the sweet wort to a boil. Don't forget to remove
the grains with a strainer and then add hops according to whatever recipe you
are following. Most of the foul-smelling aroma will be driven off during boiling. Taste the wort. It will be sour, but fermentation and dilution with more
water will lessen the sourness.

*All-grain mash method* for producing sourness in beer, for 5 gallons (19 l):

6–8 lbs. (2.7–3.6 kg)   pale malted barley and specialty malts of your choice

Using an infusion, step-infusion, or decoction method, mash all but ½ pound
(225 g) of the pale malted barley. Transfer the full mash into an odorless, sanitized, food-grade, 5-gallon (19 l) bucket. Let the mash cool to 130 to 135 degrees
F (54–57 C) and add the ½ pound of reserved crushed malted barley. My experimentation has taught me that mash temperatures, while not completely
killing all lactobacillus, will kill enough to prevent a good start on the souring
process; therefore cooling to 130 to 135 degrees F (54–57 C) is recommended.

Stir to mix. Place a sheet of aluminum foil in contact with the surface to form
a complete barrier from the air. Fit lid snugly on the pail. Insulate the pail on all
sides with a sleeping bag and/or blankets to help maintain the warm temperature
and promote lactic bacterial activity and souring. The lactobacillus will sour the
mash and will be noticeable after about 15 hours; 15 to 24 hours should be adequate for your first experiment with this process. More time will produce more
sourness.

After the souring process, open the container (hold your nose), remove the
aluminum foil, and skim the scum from the surface and discard. Transfer the
sour mash to a lauter-tun, drain, and sparge with 180-degree F (82 C) water.
Proceed as you would with an all-grain batch of beer, adding hops as called for
in your recipe.

## RECIPES FOR LAMBIC-TYPE BEERS AND SOUR BEER

Lambic-Type Beers and Sour Beer

## LAMBIC-TYPE BEERS AND SOUR BEER

### Vicarious Gueuze Lambic

Vicarious Gueuze Lambic achieves its sourness from bacterial contamination of diluted malt extract syrup or powder. Then ale yeast is added to the finished sour wort before or along with the specially cultured yeast strains of *Brettanomyces bruxellensis* and *Brettanomyces lambicus*. (If you culture these strains yourself, know that they are difficult to handle and culture because they will kill themselves with the acidity they produce. They can be cultured on special mediums that neutralize their acidity—for a while.) These "Brett" yeasts do produce some acidity, but the special character of true Belgian-style lambics are a result of the introduction of several types of bacteria. The sour mash produces a substitute level of acidity that resembles the complexity of wild fermentation. "Lambic-style" yeast cultures are readily available at most homebrew supply stores and work very well. Fermentation by-product aromas and flavors will resemble the pungent, unhinged character of a Belgian lambic.

Try a commercially available imported Gueuze from Belgium or go there yourself and try this style before you brew it. It is not a style for every beer enthusiast, but for those who are hooked, it is liquid gold.

Ingredients for 5 gallons (19 l):

6 lbs. (2.7 kg)   light malt extract syrup
½ lb. (225 g)    crushed pale malted barley
½ lb. (225 g)    crystal malt (10 L)
½ oz. (14 g)     stale old hops: 1–2 HBU (28–55 MBU)
*                American-style ale yeast in combination with lambic-style bacteria/yeast culture (which includes *Brettanomyces bruxellensis* yeast and *Brettanomyces lambicus* yeast cultures)
¾ c. (175 ml)    corn sugar (for bottling)

O.G.: 1.048–1.052 (12–13)
F.G.: 1.006–1.012 (1.5–3)
Bitterness: very low; Color: 8 SRM (16 EBC); Alcohol: 5.5% by volume

Steep the crystal malt in 1½ gallons (5.7 l) of water at 150 degrees F (65.5 C) for 30 minutes. Remove the crystal malt from the liquid. Add the malt extract. Dissolve the malt extract into solution and stabilize temperature between 120 and 130 degrees F (49–54 C). Gently pour this warm extract into a 4- to 5-gallon (15–19 l), food-grade, odor-free plastic pail fitted with a lid. Begin the souring process with the addition of the crushed pale malt as described on page 373.

After you have soured your sweet wort, strain out the grains. The sweet and sour wort ends in your brewpot. Add water to have about 2½ gallons (9.5 l) of wort in your brewpot. Add the hops and boil for 60 minutes. Sparge and transfer to your fermenter in which you have added about 2 gallons (7.8 l) of cold water. The final volume should be 5 gallons (19 l). Add ale yeast and lambic-style yeast (and bacteria) when the temperature is below 75 degrees F (24 C).

Transfer the beer to a closed secondary fermenter after 7 days of fermentation.

With the *Brettanomyces* yeast strains you will notice that once most ale yeast fermentation is complete and becomes "quiet," the surface of your fermentation will slowly develop a cover appearing as a white fuzzy skin. This is normal and a consequence of these *Brettanomyces* yeasts. There's no need to disturb (and it is actually beneficial to *not* disturb) this intriguing (to say the least) white landscape. Using a clear glass or plastic fermenter will enable you to watch this interesting phenomenon.

Belgian lambics are traditionally aged for more than a year before bottling. Don't worry, and go along the way your beer wishes to take you. Prime with sugar and bottle when fermentation is complete and the mood strikes you as right. If bottling after 6 months or more of aging, rehydrate some fresh dried ale yeast in warm water for 15 minutes and add to your just-about-to-be-bottled beer. This will help assure enough active yeast for adequate bottle refermentation and carbonation. The intense acidity of some of these brews can mellow with age, somewhat.

As a related exercise you may find a commercial sour or lambic-style beer you really love, whose yeast and bacteria sediment is worthy of adding to your ferment. Most of the time there's no harm done in adding the sediment and a "ta-da" portion of the beer at middle or latter stages of a long ferment. Though prepare yourself for a bit of unpredictability. Remember, there are no known pathogens that can survive in beer. There is no evil lurking about.

## *Loysenian Cherry Kriek*

Belgian Kriek lambic is a style of lambic infused with strongly flavored and intensely colored Belgian red cherries during aging. The later addition of cherries (or any fruit) causes a secondary fermentation due to the addition of fruit sugars. The sourness of the sour mash/extract process produces sharp acidity. The *lambicus* and *bruxellensis* yeasts produce fruity, pungent, and acidic aromatics and make some contribution to flavor. The cherries offer a ripe, refreshing fruitiness. All climax together, bringing the homebrewer closer to the real thing.

Ingredients for 5 gallons (19 l):

| | |
|---|---|
| 6 lbs. (2.7 kg) | light malt extract syrup |
| ½ lb. (225 g) | crushed pale malted barley |
| ½ lb. (225 g) | crystal malt (10 L) |
| ½ oz. (14 g) | stale old hops: 1–2 HBU (28–55 MBU) |
| 10–12 lbs. (4.5–5.4 kg) | sour cherries (if chokecherries or edible wild cherries can be found, substitute 3–4 lbs. [1.4–1.8 kg] of these for 3–4 lbs. of the sour cherries) |
| * | American-style ale yeast in combination with lambic-style bacteria/yeast culture (which includes *Brettanomyces bruxellensis* yeast and *Brettanomyces lambicus* yeast cultures) |
| ¾ c. (175 ml) | corn sugar (for bottling) |

O.G.: 1.048–1.052 (12–13)
F.G.: 1.006–1.012 (1.5–3)
Bitterness: very low; Color: red; Alcohol: 5.5% by volume

Steep the crystal malt in 1½ gallons (5.7 l) of water at 150 degrees F (65.5 C) for 30 minutes. Remove the crystal malt from the liquid. Add the malt extract. Dissolve the malt extract into solution and stabilize the temperature between 120 and 130 degrees F (49–54 C). Gently pour this warm extract into a 4- to

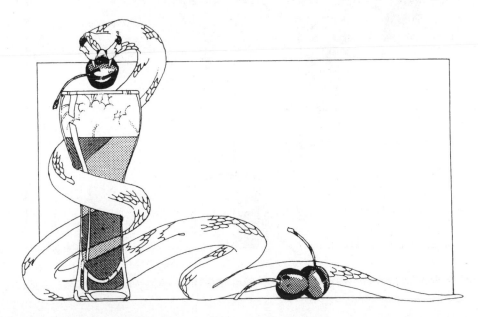

I would like to have the men of Heaven
In my own house;
With vats of good cheer
Laid out for them.

I would like to have the three Marys
Their fame is so great.
I would like people
From every corner of Heaven.

I would like them to be cheerful
In their drinking,
I would like to have Jesus, too
Here amongst them.

I would like a great lake of beer
For the King of Kings.
I would like to be watching Heaven's family
Drinking it through all eternity.

—anonymous Gaelic poet

5-gallon (15–19 l), food-grade, odor-free plastic pail fitted with a lid. Sour with the addition of the crushed pale malt as described on page 373.

After you have soured your sweet wort, strain out the grains. The sweet wort ends in your brewpot. Add water to have about 2½ gallons (9.5 l) of wort in your brewpot. Add the hops and boil for 60 minutes. Sparge and transfer to a fermenter in which you have added about 2 gallons (7.8 l) of cold water. The final volume should be 5 gallons (19 l). Add the yeast and bacteria when the temperature is below 75 degrees F (24 C).

After 1 to 2 weeks, whenever vigorous primary fermentation has slowed down, siphon the fermented brew to a 6½-gallon (25 l) glass carboy fermenter. Meanwhile, crush the cherries (but do not crush the pits) and add to the fermentation. Be reasonably sanitary when crushing the cherries, but it isn't necessary to sanitize them. Any wild microorganisms on the cherries will add tempered and natural complexity to the fermentation, which is typical of this style of brew. Secondary ferment for about 1 month.

After 1 month, siphon the beer to a third fermenter, leaving behind spent cherries, pits, and yeast sediment. Continue to ferment. These beers are traditionally aged for more than a year before bottling. Don't worry and go along the way your beer wishes to take you. Prime with sugar and bottle when fermentation is complete and the mood strikes you as right. If bottling after 6 months or more of aging, rehydrate some fresh dried ale yeast in warm water for 15 minutes and add to your just-about-to-be-bottled beer. This will help assure adequate bottle refermentation and carbonation. Age well before serving.

Raspberries, peaches, blueberries, black currants, and other fruits can be substituted for cherries.

### Brighella Milano Sour Golden Ale

In Milan, Italy, there is a brewpub called Birrificio Lambrate. There they brew a variety of beers, many hybrids of the English, Belgian, Irish, German, and American beer cultures. I once tasted their Christmas beer, then called Brighella. It was a high-alcohol golden ale with a balanced and mercifully sour magnificence. Their formulation creatively borrowed elements of Belgian, English, and German brewing techniques. Their principal innovation involved using German *sauer* malt to add sourness and acidity to the beer.

The German-made sauer malt (soured by natural lactic fermentation and often used in very small percentages by German brewers in order to naturally acidify brewing water) contributes remarkably soft acidity without the sometimes aggressive complexity of bacterially fermented Belgian ales, from which this beer's pedigree emerged. English ale yeast was used in this brew as it is used in all of Birrificio Lambrate's beers. This beer is refreshing with a high degree of drinkability.

Ingredients for 5 gallons (19 l):

| | |
|---|---|
| 9 lbs. (4.1 kg) | pale ale-type malt |
| 1½ lbs. (0.73 kg) | German sauer malt |
| ½ lb. (225 g) | honey malt |
| ¼ lb. (114 g) | Belgian Special-B malt |
| 1¼ oz. (35 g) | Styrian Goldings or Willamette hops (boiling): 6 HBU (168 MBU) |
| ¾ oz. (21 g) | New Zealand Nelson Sauvin hop pellets (dry hopping) |
| ¼ tsp. (1 g) | Irish moss powder |
| * | well-attenuating English ale–type yeast or SafAle dried ale yeast |
| ¾ c. (175 ml) | sugar (for bottling) or ⅓ c. (80 ml) corn sugar (for kegging) |

O.G.: 1.066–1.070 (16.1–17.1)
F.G.: 1.014–1.018 (3–3.5)
Bitterness: 40–45 BU; Color: 13 SRM (26 EBC); Alcohol: 7% by volume

Add the crushed malt to 11 quarts (10.5 l) of 143-degree F (61.5 C) water and mix well. The temperature will stabilize between 130 and 135 degrees F (54.5–57 C). Add heat if necessary and hold the temperature at about 133 degrees F (56 C) for 30 minutes. Don't worry about a 3- to 5-degree F (2–3 C) temperature drop during this time.

Then add 5½ quarts (10.5 l) of boiling water to this mash. This will raise the temperature to about or just above 155 degrees F (68 C). Hold at 157 degrees F (69.5 C) for 30 to 45 minutes, stirring occasionally. Complete conversion by raising the temperature to 158 degrees F (70 C) and holding for 10 to 20 minutes or until an iodine test indicates complete conversion. Then add more heat to raise the temperature to 167 degrees F (75 C). Then pour your mash into your lauter-tun and sparge with 4 gallons (15 l) of hot water at 170 degrees F (76 C). The sweet wort ends in your brewpot. The volume of the wort before boiling should be about 6½ gallons (24.5 l).

Bring the sweet wort to a boil, add the boiling hops, and boil for 60 minutes. Add the Irish moss for the final 10 minutes of the boil. Cool the wort to 70 to 75 degrees F (21–24 C). This can be done simply by immersing the brewpot (with the lid on) in a bath of cold running water for about 45 minutes. Other means of chilling can be used if desired.

Strain, sparge, and transfer immediately to your primary fermenter. The final primary batch size is 5 gallons (19 l). If necessary, add additional cold water to achieve this volume. Aerate the wort very well. Add the yeast when the temperature of the wort is 70 to 75 degrees F (21–24 C). Preferably ferment at 70 to 72 degrees F (21–22 C) for 4 to 6 days or until fermentation is complete and appears to clear and darken.

At this point transfer the beer into a secondary fermenter and add the ¾ ounce (21 g) Nelson Sauvin hop pellets. Let the fermentation complete and settle in the secondary for 7 days. For best results secondary "cellar" or age at 50 degrees F (10 C) to help drop yeast out of suspension, but this is not at all crucial to the quality. Prime with sugar and bottle or keg when fermentation is complete. Age and carbonate/condition at about 70 degrees F (21 C).

## MAKING HONEY MEAD

*Mead*—The mere mention of the word conjures visions of drinking vessels swaying high in the air. It is the nectar of nectars and one of the most natural drinks ever made by man.

Predating all other forms of concentrated sugars, honey, diluted to honey water, was in all probability one of the first fermented beverages ever concocted by man. With its fermentation came the alcoholic drink we know as mead.

The ancient Greeks, Romans, Egyptians, Scandinavians, and Assyrians procured this legendary drink as a vehicle for saturnalian revelry unmatched today. The Inca and Aztec Indians also brewed mead and held it in reverence.

Imbued with legendary intoxicating and aphrodisiacal qualities, mead heralded in and out many a fascinating orgy. Tales, stories, and lies abound of the joy, happiness, and tragedy mead has brought to its imbibers. Presently, most modern-day social gatherings are simply not of the unbounded caliber they once were. As for mead's aphrodisiacal character— well, the earth rotates more slowly and perhaps we know a bit too much. . . . You'll never know until you check it out.

### WHAT IS MEAD?

In essence, mead is defined as yeast-fermented honey water. Now if one should do an imaginative thing such as add fruit to the honey water, the resulting fermentation is technically called a *melomel*. With the addition of grapes, you have a melomel called *pyment*. Becoming intrigued? Well, hold on, there's more. Mead infused with herbs and/or spices is called a *metheglin*. Honey and apple juice combine to ferment and make *cyser*. Mead made with caramelized honey is called *bochet*. Finally, a spiced pyment (melomel) is called *hippocras*.

Getting back to simple mead and present-day palates, one is likely to find that haphazardly fermented honey water is not to one's liking. Traditionally, mead has been and still is a fermented beverage brewed with the ratio of 1 gallon (4 l) of water to 2½ to 4 pounds (1.1 to 1.8 kg) of honey, often resulting in a prolonged fermentation and an intoxicatingly sweet and very enjoyable honey wine–like beverage. As the amount of honey is increased, more of the sugar content of the mead "wort" will not ferment because higher alcohol levels inhibit yeast fermentation.

If you can find commercially made mead, it's often sweet, old, and stale, smelling like wet cardboard or old garbage. Rare is the find of freshly made mead in good "health." But, finding commercially made mead in your neighborhood store is improbable. To locate a commercially made "spiced" or "fruit" mead was impossible up until the early 1990s, when meads began to catch the fancy of some small breweries and brewpubs. Mead from Poland can be quite fine indeed, if you can find it. Also there may be a micromeadery starting up in a community near you—soon. Keep your eyes alert. Sometimes you may be fortunate enough to sample some at a local small brewery. And what a treat it is. A simple search on the Internet for "mead" or "mead lovers" will get you in the right direction. Try also www.talisman.com/mead/ and www.gotmead.com .

It's another kind of "Relax. Don't worry."

### Well, all right!

You say that you can brew beer? Well, then, if you can do that, you are able to make some excellent mead, metheglin, pyment, hippocras, cyser, spice, herbed, fruited, or whatever you'd like to call it—EASILY!

## BUT FIRST . . . ABOUT HONEY

Honey is derived from the nectar of flowers, processed and ripened with the aid of enzymes secreted by the honeybee. Because the source of nectar can vary, so does the quality and flavor of the honey. There are hundreds of different kinds, but mostly they are comprised of glucose and fructose sugars with trace amounts of sucrose and maltose. The water content of honey is usually less than 15 percent. The color and flavor are the most significant and recognizable characteristics to the mead maker.

Lighter honeys such as clover, mesquite, orange blossom, linden, basswood, and alfalfa are only a few of many that are considered to be some of the best for mead making because of their minimal contribution of strong flavors. This view of "best" may be debatable, because traditional mead was most likely made with whatever honey was available, usually wild and mixed blossoms. I've had some exceptionally fine meads made with dark and strong buckwheat honey, so I have a legitimate hesitancy to generalize.

There are many qualities of honey that help it preserve itself. Quality honey will keep for decades without spoiling.

## About Boiling Honey

Mead makers often will debate whether or not honey should be boiled before it is fermented. Boiling drives off some of the delicate floral character of the honey. Yes, I'm sure something is lost in the boiling process, but what is gained is a sweet mead "wort" free of wild microorganisms that may or may not contribute to strange flavors. Also, boiling coagulates protein and aids in the natural clarification of the mead after fermentation.

A good compromise is to either bring the honey/water mix just to a visible boil and stop or boil for only 15 minutes. Or simply don't worry about it and do what feels right.

## Fermentation Temperature

Unlike beer, mead is best fermented above 70 degrees F (21 C) and below 78 degrees F (26 C). Undesirable by-products common with high temperature beer fermentation are minimal with honey fermentations. Cooler fermentations are not detrimental to mead flavor. It just takes longer to ferment.

## Nutrients

Of most importance, one should realize that honey lacks nutrients that are necessary for healthy yeast fermentation. The mead maker often adds nutrients to the ferment to help yeast do its thing more quickly. Without the addition of nutrients, mead still can be made, but the fermentation may take 3 months to a year before completion, rather than less than 6 weeks.

Commercially prepared "yeast nutrients" are available at all home wine- and beermaking supply stores. When added to the mead "wort" before fermentation begins, they will provide needed nutrients for the yeast. Caution: Do not overdo the addition of these powdered compounds of yeast nutrient. If too much is used, a vitaminlike flavor will persist in your mead.

An excellent and all-natural source of complete nutrients for yeast is a product derived from yeast, called "yeast extract." It is often used as a vitamin supplement in the food industry and as a yeast nutrient in the wine industry. Yeast extract is basically the "guts" of yeast cells. Yeast is cultured specifically for this purpose, and is centrifuged, leaving behind the cell wall "skeletons." What is extracted is high in all of the nutrients that yeasts need for healthy fermentation. Yeast extract is all natural and not derived from manufactured chemical compounds. You are not adding anything to your mead that isn't already there. One-quarter ounce (7 g) of yeast extract per 5 gallons (19 l) of mead will be adequate for healthy and quick fermentation.

Of course, yeast nutrients would have no place in traditionally made mead. Excellent mead can be made without the addition of nutrients of any kind. You just may have to wait a little longer, that's all. Patience has its virtue.

### *Acidity*

When making traditional mead, you can add a small quantity of "acid blend" (a combination of 25 percent citric, 30 percent malic, and 45 percent tartaric acids) to the ferment to give it a subtle fruity character and lessen the "hotness" of the alcohol flavor. Honey alone lacks acidity. A small amount of acid blend in the traditional mead recipes is included as optional for those who may prefer this character.

### *Stuck Fermentation*

It can happen to the most experienced mead maker, though with improved yeast cultures it happens less frequently. But yeast may simply poop out, without warning, in the middle of or close to the end of fermentation. Activity stops and specific gravity indicates that surely there is much more sugar to ferment. The causes of stuck fermentation are numerous, but the most common may be lack of nutrients at the onset of fermentation, lack of oxygen in the honey wort before fermentation begins, or the inhibition of fermentation by the presence of alcohol.

There is a naturally derived product available to homebrewers and winemakers that has been found to help "unstick" stuck fermentations. Called "yeast hulls," "yeast ghosts," or "yeast skeletons," they are essentially the cell walls left behind during the extraction process discussed earlier in the "Nutrients" section. How they work when added to a stuck fermentation is not fully understood, but it is believed that the cell wall material adsorbs yeast "poisons" produced by yeasts that inhibit fermentation.

Adding yeast hulls in the amount of $\frac{1}{4}$ to $\frac{1}{2}$ ounce (7 to 14 g) per 5 gallons (19 l) along with fresh yeast can unstick stuck fermentation.

## TRADITIONAL MEADS

Making basic unflavored mead is one of the most challenging and satisfying endeavors for the mead maker. Challenging, because you, your honey, water, and yeast are out there all alone, without the support of the fascinating flavors of fruits and spices. Making clean, smooth, and gentle-tasting pure mead is to connect yourself to the roots of all alcoholic beverages. While gazing up at the stars some

evening, mead in hand, imagine that this is what it might have been like eight thousand years ago.

Traditional mead is a treasure capturing the essence of honey and the nectar of blossoms. It can be dry or sweet, but always 12 to 15 percent alcohol.

I owe a debt of gratitude to Leon and Gay Havill for introducing me to the experience of tasting fresh, pure, and traditional mead. They run a small meadery in the south of New Zealand in Rangiora, a small town outside Christchurch, and make mead called Havill's Mazer Mead. The Havills always enjoy visitors, should you be traveling in the area. And Havill's Mazer Mead is some of the best I've ever had.

I also owe much gratitude to Lieutenant Colonel Robert Gayre of Gayre and Nigg. When I knew him he was a retired gentleman and the world's most knowledgeable person on the history and production of mead. He inspired in me an appreciation of mead's tradition and importance in world history. Lieutenant Colonel Gayre owned and operated a meadery in Cornwall, England, in the 1940s and in 1948 published a book, *Wassail in Mazers of Mead,* reprinted by Brewers Publications, Boulder, Colorado, under the title *Brewing Mead: Wassail in Mazers of Mead,* with a how-to chapter that I wrote. Lieutenant Colonel

## Mead, Honeymoons, and Love

Who would have thought that the bees, the moon, and the magical brews of man could combine to add to the bliss, luster, and memories of weddings?

Mead is a beverage of love. The drinking of mead has been held responsible for fertility and the birth of sons. This is where the tradition of the honeymoon got its start. If mead were consumed for one month (one moon) after a wedding, then in nine months a son would be born and the mead maker congratulated. The custom of drinking mead at weddings and for one month after initiated our present-day custom of the honeymoon.

Interestingly, mead drinking developed quite a reputation for its ability to increase the chances of bearing sons, so much so that a special drinking cup, called the Mazer Cup, was handed down from generation to generation. The couple that drank from the cup would bear sons to carry on the family name and increase the male birth rate, important in the days of constant war.

Fact or folly? Scientists have been doing animal experiments and have found they can increase the chances of bearing males by altering the body's pH. It is known that the acidity or alkalinity of the female body during conception can influence the sex of the newborn. Blood sugar levels do alter pH.

Mead is indeed a noble drink. For more than five thousand years, Virgil, Plato, Plutarch, Zeus, Venus, Jupiter, Odysseus, Circe, the Argonaut, Beowulf, Aphrodite, Bacchus, Odin, Valhalla, the Sanskrit Rig-Veda, Thor, King Arthur, Queen Elizabeth I, the French, Greeks, Mayans, Africans, English, Irish, Swedes, Poles, Hungarians, Germans, present-day homebrewers, and even the Australian Aborigines all likened part of their enjoyment of life to mead.

Centuries ago the making of mead was art, regulated by custom and statutes. The brewing of mead was not done by just anyone. Certain individuals were trained and held in the highest esteem for turning honey into the magic of mead.

Today every homebrewer has the know-how to become a dignitary and the maker of mead for special occasions or for any occasion. The stronger versions keep for years, as does a good marriage.

And as for having sons, you will have to experiment on your own.

Gayre resided at Minard Castle, Argyll, Scotland, and passed away in 1994. In 2008 I had the pleasure of trying several of his 60-plus-year-old experimental and Gulval (Cornwall) meads. They were exceptional. An account of the experience, flavors, aromas, and character of those meads can be found in *The Homebrewer's Companion, Second Edition*.

## MEAD RECIPES

### *Antipodal Mead (Traditional)*
There are islands on the almost exact opposite side of the world from where I live. They are called the Amsterdam and St. Paul Islands and they are located in the Indian Ocean. Where is your antipode?

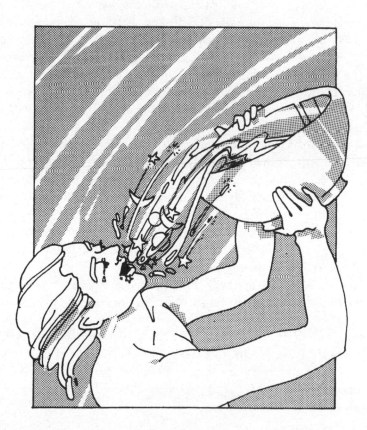

Ingredients for 5 gallons (19 l):

> 15 lbs. (6.8 kg)   light honey
> 1 Tbsp. (8 g)      gypsum
> 4 tsp. (20 g)      acid blend (optional)
> ¼ tsp. (1 g)       yeast extract as a nutrient
> ¼ tsp. (1 g)       Irish moss powder
> 1 oz. (28 g)       dried champagne yeast or Pris de Mousse wine yeast

O.G.: 1.120–1.130 (28–30)
F.G.: 1.020–1.035 (5–9)
Alcohol: about 14% by volume

Add the honey, gypsum, acid blend (if using), and Irish moss to 1½ gallons (5.7 l) of water and bring to a boil for 15 minutes. Skim the coagulated meringue-like foam off the surface (this is albumin-type protein). Be careful, honey worts will boil over just like beer worts. Leave the lid ajar and monitor the onset of boiling very carefully.

Transfer the hot mead "wort" to a closed fermenter system and 1½ gallons (5.7 l) of cold water. Seal the carboy briefly and shake the contents to aerate the wort. If necessary, add cold water to make 5 gallons total. Glass carboys are ideal for mead fermentation. Rehydrate the dry yeast in preboiled and then cooled 105-degree F (41 C) water for 10 minutes before pitching. Pitch the yeast when temperature of the mead wort is below 80 degrees F (27 C). Ferment to completion, then carefully rack into a secondary (carboy) fermenter and let clear. Bottle at least 3 months after the mead has cleared. It is ready to drink as soon as it has cleared.

Antipodal Mead may be flavored with fruit or herbs and spices to make melomels, pyments, or metheglins. Use fruit in addition to all of the above ingredients but do not boil fruit, rather add it at the end of the boil and steep at pasteurizing temperatures at about 160 degrees F (71 C) for about 20 to 30 minutes before adding to the fermenter. If adding fruit in the pasteurizing "wort," then after 1 week in an open fermenter siphon the fermenting mead off the fruit, which has either settled to the bottom or is floating on the surface. Proceed with a closed system for the secondary fermentation.

You may also add fruit and/or herbs to the secondary fermenter at the stage in which fermentation is nearly finished. Be sure to leave plenty of head space in the secondary fermenter because when fruit is added fermentation will probably begin again. In this case a 6½-gallon (25 l) glass fermenter will be needed for a 5-gallon (19 l) batch. One to 2 weeks after having added fruit to a closed fermenter, siphon off above the sediment and under the remaining floating bits of fruit into a 5-gallon (19 l) closed fermenter. Proceed with the closed system until ready to bottle as instructed above.

## Chief Niwot's Mead

This traditional mead is not quite as sweet as Antipodal Mead. It is also carbonated to give the traditional flavor a bubbly and champagnelike disposition.

Ingredients for 5 gallons (19 l):

| | |
|---|---|
| 13 lbs. (5.9 kg) | light honey |
| 1 Tbsp. (8 g) | gypsum |
| 4 tsp. (20 g) | acid blend (optional) |
| ¼ tsp. (1 g) | yeast extract as a nutrient |
| ¼ tsp. (1 g) | Irish moss powder |
| 1 oz. (28 g) | dried champagne yeast or Pris de Mousse wine yeast |
| ⅓ c. (80 ml) | corn sugar (for bottling) |

O.G.: 1.110–1.120 (26–28)
F.G.: 1.015–1.025 (4–6)
Alcohol: about 14% by volume

Add the honey, gypsum, acid blend (if using), and Irish moss to 1½ gallons (5.7 l) of water and bring to a boil for 15 minutes. Skim the coagulated meringue-like foam off the surface. Be careful, honey worts will boil over just like beer worts. Leave the lid ajar and monitor the onset of boiling very carefully.

Transfer the hot mead "wort" to a closed fermenter system and 1½ gallons (5.7 l) of cold water. Seal the carboy briefly and shake the contents to aerate the wort. If necessary, add cold water to make 5 gallons. Glass carboys are ideal for mead fermentation. Rehydrate the dry yeast in preboiled and then cooled to 105-degree F (41 C) water for 10 minutes before pitching. Pitch the yeast when temperature of the mead wort is below 80 degrees F (27 C). Ferment to completion and bottle as you would beer, with the addition of corn sugar. It is ready to drink as soon as it has cleared.

## Melimiguelenium Ginger Mead

Originally brewed for the new millennium, the mead wasn't ready for a year and a half. 'Twas a long wait, but so was the millennium. We can't be sure about what this century will bring, but for sure this medium-sweet mead has an unzipped ginger flavor that will help celebrate every single day of whichever century by just knowing that there is a stash waiting to be enjoyed. Worth making a double batch, this is as fine as the finest liqueur and ages supremely.

Ingredients for 5 gallons (19 l):

| | |
|---|---|
| 17½ lbs. (7.9 kg) | light honey |
| ¾ lb. (340 g) | grated fresh ginger |

¼ tsp. (1 g)        yeast extract as a nutrient
¼ tsp. (1 g)        Irish moss powder
1 oz. (28 g)        dried champagne yeast or Pris de Mousse wine yeast

O.G.: 1.126–1.130 (29.5–30)
F.G.: 1.020–1.035 (5–9)
Alcohol: about 14% by volume

Add the honey, grated ginger, and Irish moss to 1½ gallons (5.7 l) of water and bring to a boil for 15 minutes. Skim the coagulated meringuelike foam off the surface (this is albumin-type protein). Be careful, honey worts will boil over just like beer worts. Leave the lid ajar and monitor the onset of boiling very carefully.

Transfer the hot mead "wort" with the grated ginger to a closed fermenter system and 1½ gallons (5.7 l) of cold water. Seal the carboy briefly and shake the contents to aerate the wort. If necessary, add cold water to make 5 gallons. Glass carboys are ideal for mead fermentation. Rehydrate the dry yeast in preboiled and then cooled to 105-degree F (41 C) water for 10 minutes before pitching. Pitch the yeast when temperature of the mead wort is below 80 degrees F (27 C). Ferment for 1 month, then siphon the mead into a second fermenter while avoiding the ginger. Discard the spent ginger. Continue to ferment for an additional 1 to 2 months or until the mead begins to clear. Then siphon the mead into another fermenter, leaving the yeast behind. Continue to ferment to completion. Let it sit, then bottle after the mead has been clear for at least 6 months. It is ready to drink as soon as it has cleared.

### Prickly Pear Cactus Fruit Mead

Prickly pear mead is the most seductively delicious mead I have ever had—*ever*. Its color can be as dramatic as a sunset. The fluorescent crimson of ripe prickly pear fruit, the titillatingly soft character of light mesquite honey, a floral bouquet of the Sonoran desert freshly washed by rain, and, finally, the sweet delicate currant nature of the world's finest sherry all combine to stun your senses in appreciation of one of the greatest gifts to this world.

This recipe was inspired by Dave Spaulding's (Tucson, Arizona) award-winning mead I tasted in 1986. Since 1987 I have not let a year go by without brewing at least 5 gallons (19 l). At 14.5 percent alcohol, Prickly Pear Cactus Fruit Mead ages exceptionally well. Years bring out the best in it.

Prickly pear cacti grow in drier areas from Canada to the Equator. In North America each fall, the plant produces dozens of fruits that ripen to a crimson-purple-red. The fruits are covered with fuzzy thorns and should be picked with tongs. They can be frozen until used. Their size varies from about 2 to 6 inches (5–15 cm). The red color is sometimes difficult to maintain through the finish of the fermentation. Don't worry if your mead turns from red to deep gold. If you wish to maintain the color, add 2 or 3 peeled, washed, and sliced deep-red beets to the secondary fermenter. This mead will still take on all the character of the finest sweet mead you've ever made.

As you may have ascertained by now, I have a special place in my life for prickly pear mead. There is a tradition I began in 1987, the year of my first prickly pear mead. For decades, each year I took at least one bottle up to Mead Mountain (on a map it's really named something else, but I have personally renamed this peak Mead Mountain). I have taken the liberty of burying these meads within 100 yards (91 m) of the nearly 9,000-foot (2,743 m) summit. There they have weathered temperature extremes from 40 degrees below zero F (-40 C) to 80 degrees F (27 C).

In October 1992, two friends and I had the privilege of enjoying a bottle of prickly pear mead that had been aged on a mountaintop. Among the clouds swirling around us, threatening rain and snow, we opened one well-aged bottle and cautiously sipped. There never has been nectar tasting as close to godliness as that mead. Without any exaggeration, I must confide that we all agreed

that this mead, on this day, on Mead Mountain was unanimously "the best drink we had ever had." And as we felt the warmth of the alcohol reach our hearts, the clouds, which had enveloped us the entire day during our two-hour journey to the peak, parted. To the east we could clearly see our town 3,500 feet (1,066 m) below. To the west a storm wall of clouds stood miles high, suspended over the Continental Divide. Pieces of clouds and misty vapors swirled around us.

Friends Jeff Markel, Chris Webster, and I shared 12 ounces of prickly pear mead, but it felt as if we had partaken of the mountain and all it had endured over the thousands of years it had been there. I will continue to bury more mead on that mountain as the years permit me. So far I have left far more than I have taken. I'll know when the time is right to open another bottle.

Ingredients for 5 gallons (19 l):

| | |
|---|---|
| 5–8 lbs. (2.3–3.6 kg) | red, ripe prickly pear cactus fruit |
| 20 lbs. (9.1 kg) | light honey (mesquite is preferred, but clover, alfalfa, or other light honeys will produce superb results) |
| 1 oz. (28 g) | dried sherry, wine, or champagne yeast (Prise de Mousse champagne yeast works very well in combination with sherry yeast) |
| ¼ tsp. (1 g) | yeast extract as a nutrient |
| 1 tsp. (4 g) | pectin enzyme (optional) |

O.G.: 1.130–1.150 (30–32)
F.G.: 1.025–1.050 (6–12.5)
Alcohol: 14% by volume

Slice the fruit or, easier, chop in a food processor and boil with 2½ gallons (9.5 l) of water for 2 hours. Meanwhile, combine the honey with 1 gallon (3.8 l) of water and boil for 15 minutes. Skim off the coagulated white albumin protein as it forms on the surface of the boil. Turn the heat off. Strain the boiled juice of the fruit into the honey brewpot. Then add this concentrated honey "wort" to a sanitized fermenter with enough cold water to make 5 gallons. Rehydrate the dry yeast in preboiled and then cooled to 105-degree F (41 C) water for 10 minutes before pitching. Pitch the yeast when the temperature of the mead wort is below 76 degrees F (24.4 C).

Ferment at temperatures between 70 and 77 degrees F (21–25 C). Fermentation may last anywhere from 3 months to 1 year. Bottle at least 6 months after both fermentation is complete and mead is clear. Fermentation may stop months before the mead clears. Rack the mead from a primary fermenter to a secondary fermenter when fermentation appears almost finished. If available, use carbon dioxide gas to purge the secondary carboy of oxygen before transferring the mead into it in order to minimize oxidation.

The type and batch of honey, the character of the fruit, and the strain of yeast are but a few of several factors that affect the behavior and duration of fermentation. One batch of Prickly Pear Cactus Fruit Mead may take less than 6 months to finish and clarify, while another batch may take 2 years! Nevertheless, this mead always does clear and always is spectacular.

Note that there is good reason to boil the fruit, even though it sets the pectin in it and causes haze to form in the mead. Prickly pear fruit juice is very mucilaginous and even more so if the juice is not boiled. The haze eventually settles out. You may add 1 teaspoon (4 g) of pectin enzyme (follow instructions that come with the enzymes if contrary to this recommendation) to the fermenter to aid in clarification.

When the mead is clear and fermentation has stopped, it is ready to drink and bottle. If you find that a batch of Prickly Pear Cactus Fruit Mead is too sweet for your taste and you haven't bottled it yet, endeavor to make another batch by using only 14 pounds (6.4 kg) of honey and blend the two batches at a ratio that suits your taste. Let this blend rest in the fermenter for a few months in case fermentation begins anew; if this happens, let rest until the referment is complete.

### Barkshack Sparkling Gingermead

A twentieth-century legend. Unlike traditional mead, Barkshack Sparkling Gingermead and its variations are brewed with less honey per gallon, happily resulting in a dry, effervescently clear beverage with a 9 to 12 percent alcoholic sparkle, reminiscent of white champagne, or more accurately, like a dry (not sweet), alcoholic "ginger ale." Barkshack Sparkling Gingermead will take many brewers and friends by storm. In fact, 99 percent of the people who have tasted Barkshack Sparkling Gingermead (or variations thereof) have pursued it as if it were a love affair. There are hundreds of brewers today who began their brewing endeavors because of the thrill of Barkshack Sparkling Gingermead. It is wonderful. It is glorious. It is well worth waiting for. And wait you must.

Barkshack Sparkling Gingermead is a brew that should be allowed to mature in a secondary fermenter for 1 to 1½ months before bottling. Then, depending on ingredients, it needs to mature for 3 months to a full year in order to reach its full taste potential and to allow immature flavors to disappear. Patience is indeed a virtue that, in this case, is well rewarded.

The recipe and procedures for brewing the basic Barkshack Sparkling Gingermead are simple and should make sense to even the beginning homebrewer.

Points that are emphasized in the brewing of this recipe or variations are:

1. Honey should be boiled with water, briefly or for 15 to 30 minutes.
2. Champagne yeasts should be used for the more alcoholic versions of mead (percent alcohol in excess of 10 percent); otherwise, lager or ale yeast will suffice.
3. Slow primary fermentation is sometimes experienced with mead fermentation. Under no circumstances should the mead remain in an open primary fermenter for more than 7 days. Use a secondary fermenter with a fermentation lock.
4. Pasteurize all fruit that you may use. This can be done by adding fruit to the hot sparged or partially strained "wort." Do not boil the fruit as this may sometimes cause unsettling (pectin) haze.
5. When adding spice or herbs to the mead as flavoring, you may prepare a strong fresh "tea" and add it at bottling time or add these flavorings during the secondary aging period; flavors will be cleaner and fresher if not added during primary fermentation. "Strong, fresh tea" is hard to quantify. Some herb and spice teas are powerful in small amounts, while others may warrant a heavy-handed dose in order to manifest themselves in 5 gallons (19 l) of mead. Use your personal experience with teas, herbs, and spices to guide you and if in doubt go light and increase in the next batch if needed. If you want to experiment, brew a tea with a given amount of herbs or spices and blend it in one quart of water. Assess the strength and increase, decrease, or hold the ratio and increase proportionally from one quart to 20 quarts; there are 20 quarts in 5 gallons. This method can help approximate if you want to take the time to experiment.

Ingredients for 5 gallons (19 l):

| | |
|---|---|
| 7 lbs. (3.2 kg) | light honey |
| 1½ lbs. (680 g) | corn sugar |
| 1–6 oz. | |
| (28–168 g) | grated fresh ginger |
| 1 tsp. (4 g) | gypsum |
| 1 tsp. (4 g) | citric acid or acid blend (a mix used in winemaking) |
| ¼ tsp. (1 g) | yeast extract as a nutrient |
| ¼ tsp. (1 g) | Irish moss powder |
| 1–6 lbs. | |
| (450 g–2.7 kg) | crushed fruit such as sour cherries, blackberries, raspberries (my favorite), blueberries, rhubarb, grapes, grape concentrate, cranberries, chokecherries, etc. (all optional) |

3 oz. (84 g)     lemongrass or other herb or spice flavorings—but go easy
                 on the cloves, cinnamon, mint, hops; lemon or orange peel
                 is also nice (all optional)
1 oz. (28 g)     dried champagne yeast
¾ c. (175 ml)   corn sugar (for bottling)

O.G.: 1.060–1.066 (15–16)
F.G.: 0.992–0.996
Alcohol: 9% by volume

Hey, now! Relax, don't worry, have a homebrew.

Add the honey, corn sugar, ginger, gypsum, citric acid, Irish moss, and yeast nutrient to 1½ gallons (5.7 l) of water and boil for 15 minutes. Turn the heat off. If you are going to add fruit, take a small strainer and fish out as much of the ginger shavings as you can, but don't worry. Then add your crushed fruit to the pot of hot "wort" and let it steep for 10 to 15 minutes.

If adding fruit, pour the entire contents of the "wort" (unsparged if fruit is added) into an open plastic 7- to 10-gallon (26.5–38 l) primary fermenter to which about 3 gallons (11.5 l) of cold water has been added (or enough to make 5 gallons [19 l]). If not adding fruit, you have the option of putting the fermentation into a glass or plastic carboy.

Rehydrate the dry yeast in preboiled and then cooled to 105-degree F (41 C) water for 10 minutes before pitching. Pitch the yeast when the temperature of the mead wort is 70 to 78 degrees F (21–26 C).

If there is fruit in your primary fermenter, then after specific gravity has fallen to 1.020 (5), or within 7 days, whichever comes first, rack the brew into a secondary fermenter. Remove the fermented fruit with a sanitized strainer, or carefully manipulate the siphon hose so that no fruit (or very little) passes to the secondary fermenter. If no fruit has been added to your primary fermenter and you are using a closed fermentation system, you can leave the mead to ferment until it begins to slow down and sediment settles. Relax and don't worry.

Age for 1 to 2 months in the secondary fermenter.

Bottle with ¾ cup (175 ml) of corn sugar. If herb, spice, or tea flavoring is desired, add a strong strained tea to the finished mead at bottling time. In this manner, you may add the "tea" halfway through the bottling process, enabling you to bottle 2 flavors of mead!

The flavor of mead will change with age. Harsh and sharp flavors will mellow. A tasting after 6 months will give some indication of your results. But a sparkling cold Barkshack Gingermead of 1 year or more—now that's heaven.

More mead recipes can be found in both *The Homebrewer's Companion, Second Edition,* and *Microbrewed Adventures.*

## RESOURCES FOR 13 MEAD RECIPES

### MEAD RECIPES IN *THE HOMEBREWER'S COMPANION, SECOND EDITION:*

Waialeale Chablis Mead
A Taste of Happiness Sparkling Apple Cyser
White Angel Still Mead
Love's Vision—Honey & Pepper Still Mead
Aloi Black Raspberry Still Mead
Ruby Hooker Raspberry Still Mead
Acermead
Lavender & Roses Still Mead
1944 Sack Metheglin

### MEAD RECIPES IN *MICROBREWED ADVENTURES:*

Castle Metheglin
Sparkling Mead—Tropical Champagne
St. Bartholomew's Mead

An additional resource for any mead maker is Ken Schramm's excellent book *The Compleat Meadmaker* (Brewers Publications, 2003).

# APPENDICES
# APPENDIX 1

## HOMEBREWER'S GLOSSARY

For a comprehensive guide to beer terms see *Dictionary of Beer & Brewing,* by Dan Rabins and Carl Forget (Brewers Publications, 1998).

**adjuncts**—Usually any additional fermentable ingredient, other than malted grain, added to beer.

**aerobic**—Processes requiring oxygen.

**ale**—A style of beer. Traditionally a "top-fermented" beer brewed at temperatures between 60 and 70 degrees F (16–21 C) using ale yeast.

**ale yeast**—*Saccharomyces cerevisiae* type of yeast. Generally speaking, it produces the desired type of beer best at fermentation temperatures between 55 and 70 degrees F (12.5–21 C). It is also known as "top-fermenting yeast" because of some varieties' ability to form a layer of yeast on the surface during primary fermentation. Top-fermenting yeast is anaerobic and will always form sediment on the bottom.

**alpha acid**—The bittering acid of hops, usually measured in percent by weight: 2–4 percent is low; 5–7 percent is medium; 8–10 percent is high; and 11–15 is very high. Above 15 is ridiculously high.

**Alpha Acid Units (AAUs)**—Another measurement of potential bitterness in hops. Homebrew Bitterness Units (HBUs) are the same as Alpha Acid Units, the system first devised by the late British homebrew author and pioneer, Dave Line. One HBU is equal to a 1 percent alpha acid rating of 1 ounce (28.4 g) of hops. HBUs are calculated by multiplying the percent of alpha acid in the hop by the number of ounces of hops.

**alpha-amylase**—One of two principal diastatic enzymes that convert starches to fermentable sugars; often referred to as the "liquefying" enzyme, converting soluble starch to dextrin.

**anaerobic**—Processes that do not require dissolved oxygen.

**apparent degree of actual fermentation (or attenuation)**—Measured as a percent. This measures the degree to which the original extract has been converted to alcohol and other fermentation by-products. It is a measure of the change in density. The *apparent degree* is not real, for the same reason apparent extract is not real extract (see below). *Apparent degree* of fermentation is more easily measured than real degree, and for the purpose of determining residual fermentation extract, it is sufficient.

**apparent extract and real extract**—Measured in degrees Balling (or Plato) (specific gravity). This is a measure of the final gravity or weight of the final extract. Because alcohol is lighter than water, the extract of finished beer will appear to be less if it is measured with the alcohol in it as it naturally occurs. *Apparent extract* is measured reasonably accurately with a hydrometer. To measure the real extract, one can boil off the alcohol and replace the lost volume with distilled water and then take a measurement. The *real extract* reading will be higher and will indicate true percentages.

**apparent limit of fermentation (or attenuation)**—Measured as a percent. This measures the absolute limit of fermentation. A portion of the wort used for brewing is subjected to ideal fermentation conditions and inoculated with more than enough yeast to assure maximum fermentation of the wort.

**attenuation**—The measure of how much of the dissolved fermentable sugars in beer wort is converted by the fermentation process to alcohol and $CO_2$, indicated by the difference between starting specific gravity and final specific gravity.

**Balling**—A scale of measurement used by professional brewers worldwide to measure of the density of a liquid as compared to water. Degrees Balling is also known as degrees Brix. For practical purposes degrees Balling/Brix is equal to degrees Plato. One degree B is a measure of 1 gram of sucrose in 100 grams of solution. *See also* Specific Gravity and Plato.

**barm**—Verb: to add yeast; pitch. Noun: the foam or froth atop fermenting beer (kraeusen) or foam on top of a glass of beer.

**beer**—Any alcoholic beverage made from the fermentation of sugars derived from grain. That which is meant to be enjoyed. *Birra* in Italian, *cerveja* in Portuguese, *cerveza* in Spanish, *piwo* in Russian, *pivo* beer in Czech, *bière* in French, *bier* in German and Dutch.

**beta-acid**—Bitter acid of hops. Its contribution to beer's bitterness is negligible due to its insolubility.

**beta-amylase**—One of the two principal diastatic enzymes. Often referred to as the saccharifying enzyme, converting dextrins and soluble starches to fermentable sugars.

**bitterness perception**—Measured subjectively: none, very low, low, medium, medium-high, high, very high. Measures the actual degree of bitterness one is likely to perceive, relative to the overall bitterness range of all beer styles listed.

**Bitterness Units (BUs)**—Also known as International Bitterness Units. One

Bitterness Unit is equal to 1 milligram of iso(merized) alpha acid in 1 liter of wort or beer. This is a system of measuring bitterness devised by brewing scientists and is an accepted standard throughout the world. Homebrewers usually do not have the sophisticated equipment to measure actual BUs and often use a system of Homebrew Bitterness Units (HBUs) to closely approximate the desired bitterness in their beer.

**body**—The "mouthfeel" of beer; "thicker" beers are said to have a fuller body.

**bottom-fermenting**—*See* Lager Yeast.

**break**—The phase during the boiling and cooling of beer wort when proteins precipitate; also hot-break, cold-break.

**Brix**—*See* Balling.

**bung**—Usually a wooden stopper used to seal old-fashioned kegs.

**carbonation level**—Measured in volumes (i.e., percent carbon dioxide by volume).

**carboy**—A 5- or 6½-gallon (19–25 l) glass bottle with a narrow opening on top. Properly cleaned, carboys can be used as primary or secondary fermenters.

**cellaring**—The tradition of storing ales at cool temperatures in the 50–55 degrees F (10–12.5 C) range.

**chill haze**—Haze caused by precipitation of protein-tannin compounds at cold temperatures. Does not affect flavor. Reduction of proteins or tannins in brewing or fermenting will reduce haze.

**cold-break**—*See* break.

**cold fermentation**—Lager-style beers are typically cold fermented at temperatures below 55 degrees F (13 C) in order to minimize fruity ester character and develop typically smoother flavors associated with lager beers.

**color**—Describes the actual color of the beer.

**color (SRM)**—Measured in Standard Reference Method units, expressed as degrees SRM. For the purposes of general beer style guidelines, degrees SRM are assumed to be equivalent to degrees Lovibond. Also assumed is the general conversion of European Brewing Convention (EBC) color to SRM using the equation $SRM = (0.375 \times degrees\ EBC) + 0.45$.

**conditioning**—The process of developing $CO_2$ (carbonation) in beer by the addition of fermentable sugars during the final stage of fermentation in the bottle or keg.

**copper**—An old term that refers to the brewpot or boiling kettle, which used to be made from copper; some brewers still use coppers.

**dextrins**—Unfermentable and tasteless carbohydrates that contribute body to beer. Technically, 4 or more glucose molecules linked together.

**dextrinization**—The enzymatic process of degrading soluble starch molecules to dextrin molecules.

**diacetyl**—A chemical naturally produced during fermentation, characterized by a butterscotch flavor.

**diastase (diastatic)**—Referring to enzymes in malt that convert starch to sugars and dextrins.

**dimethyl-sulfide (DMS)**—A compound developed in beer during fermentation. In excess its aroma and flavor are similar to sweet corn.

**drunk**—Past participle of "drink."

**Dunkel**—German word for "dark" (as in color).

**ester**—Term used to describe the "fruity" aromatics and flavors of beer. Apple, pear, grapefruit, strawberry, raspberry, and banana esters are often produced during the respiration cycle of yeast.

**fermentation**—The conversion by metabolism of sugar to alcohol and carbon dioxide by yeast. It is an anaerobic process.

**fermentation lock**—A simple water-and-bubble-type device used during closed or secondary fermentation that prevents ambient air from coming in contact with the fermenting brew. At the same time, the fermentation lock permits the escape of carbon dioxide (a by-product of fermentation). It fits into a rubber cork atop a carboy being used as a secondary fermenter.

**fining**—A procedure used by some brewers to aid in the clarification of their brews. Usually a gelatinous ingredient such as gelatin or isinglass is added during the final stages of fermentations and Irish moss is added at the end of the boiling process.

**finishing hops**—Fresh aromatic hops that are added to the boiling wort during the final 1 to 2 minutes of boiling. Clean hops can be added during secondary fermentation. This is called "dry hopping." Care should be taken to ensure cleanliness. Finishing or dry hopping impart hop aroma and flavor to beer.

**flocculation**—The tendency of yeast to gather and migrate to the surface or bottom of fermenting beer. Usually refers to the sedimentation phase of fermentation that follows yeast suspension.

**gelatinization**—In mashing, the process of making starch soluble, usually in reference to cooking (boiling) adjuncts.

**grist**—Ground (milled) malt and/or adjuncts.

**gyle**—That portion of unfermented beer wort that is reserved for or added to finished beer for conditioning (carbonation).

**Helles**—German word for "light" (as in color).

**homebrew**—That which is to be enjoyed.

**Homebrew Bitterness Units (HBUs)**—Homebrew Bitterness Units are a measure of the total amount of bitterness potential in a given volume of beer. HBUs are calculated by multiplying the percent of alpha acid in the hops by the number of ounces. For example, if 2 ounces of Northern Brewer hops (9% alpha acid) and 3 ounces of Cascade hops (5% alpha acid) were used in a 10-gallon batch, the total amount of bitterness units would be 33: $(2 \times 9) + (3 \times 5) = 18 + 15$. Bitterness units per gallon would be 3.3 in a 10-gallon batch or 6.6 in a 5-gallon batch, so it is important to note volumes whenever expressing HBUs. HBUs are not related to International Bitterness Units (IBUs) except that they both help measure bitterness in beer. *See also* Metric Bitterness Units (MBUs).

**hop aroma**—Intensity measured subjectively: none, very low, low, medium, medium-high, high, very high. Measures the actual degree of hop aroma one is likely to perceive, relative to the overall aroma intensity range of all beer styles listed. A comment describing the character/variety may be included.

**hop back**—Piece of equipment resembling a strainer. After the boiling of the wort, the hot wort is passed through a bed of fresh hops to impart hop flavor and aroma to the brew.

**hop flavor**—Measured subjectively: none, very low, low, medium, medium-high, high, very high. Measures the actual degree of hop flavor one is likely to perceive, relative to the overall flavor intensity range of all beer styles listed. A comment describing the character/variety may be included.

**hot-break**—The time at which the protein trub coagulates during boiling.

**hydrometer**—A very simple device to measure the specific gravity of liquids.

**International Bitterness Units (IBUs)**—*See also* Bitterness Units. One International Bitterness Unit is equal to 1 milligram of iso(merized) alpha acid in 1 liter of wort or beer. This is a system of measuring bitterness devised by brewing scientists and is an accepted standard throughout the world. Homebrewers usually do not have the sophisticated equipment to measure actual BUs and often use a system of Homebrew Bitterness Units (HBUs) to closely approximate the desired bitterness in their beer.

**isinglass**—A high-molecular protein derived from the swim bladders of certain fish. It is traditionally added to English-style real ale after it has been "cellared" to help clear the beer by hastening yeast sedimentation.

**kraeusen**—The billowy, rocky, foamy head that develops on the surface of the wort during the first days of fermentation.

**kraeusening**—A priming process that substitutes unfermented wort for sugar at bottling time.

**lager**—From the German word meaning "to store." Also a style of beer. Traditionally a "bottom-fermented" beer brewed at temperatures of 40 to 50 degrees F (4–10 C) and stored for a period of time at temperatures as low as 32 degrees F (0 C).

**lagering**—The period during which lager beer is aged.

**lager yeast**—*Saccharomyces uvarum* (formerly known as *S. carlsbergensis*) type of yeast. Generally speaking, true lager yeast does best at fermentation temperatures of 33 to 50 degrees F (0.5–10 C). It is also known as "bottom-fermenting yeast" because of its tendency not to flocculate, or form a head of yeast on the surface of the brew.

**lambic**—A style of Belgian beer that is brewed with wild yeast and beer-souring bacteria.

**lautering**—Process of removing spent grains or hops from wort. This is simply done by the utilization of a strainer and a subsequent quick hot-water rinse (sparging) of the caught spent grains and hops.

**lauter-tun**—The brewing vessel that is used to separate grains from sweet wort by a straining process.

**liquefication**—*See* dextrinization.

**malt**—*See* malted barley.

**malted barley**—Barley that has been partially germinated (sprouted) and then dried. Sugars, soluble starches, and starch-converting enzymes are developed during the malting process.

**malt extract**—A sugary liquid, syrup, or powder that has been derived by mashing malted barley (grain) and dissolving evolved sugars in water. This malt extract can be reduced to syrup or a dry form by removing water by evaporation.

**mashing**—The process of converting grain starches to fermentable sugars by carefully sustaining a water and grain "soup" at temperatures ranging from 140 to 160 degrees F (60–71 C) for a period of time.

**Metric Bitterness Units (MBUs)**—Are equal to the number of grams of hops multiplied by the percent alpha acid. *See also* Homebrew Bitterness Units (HBUs).

**original extract**—Measured in degrees Balling (specific gravity). This is a measure of the weight of fermentable and unfermentable extracts dissolved in solution as compared to the total weight of the solution.

**percent alcohol**—Measured in terms of percentage by volume or percentage by weight.

**pH**—A measure of the acidity or alkalinity of a solution on a scale of 1 to 14. Distilled water is neutral; it is neither acid nor alkaline. The measure of neutrality on the pH scale is 7.0. A pH of less than 7.0 is acidic, while a pH greater than 7.0 is alkaline (also called "basic"). The scale is a logarithmic scale. The numerical measures are not based on a linear scale. Simply speaking, the difference between 6 to 5 is ten times greater than 7 to 6.

**phenolic**—Can be any one or a combination of a medicinal, plastic, electrical-fire, Listerine-like, Band-Aid-like, smoky, or clovelike aromas or flavors. Most often caused by wild strains of yeast or bacteria. Can be extracted from grains. Sanitizing residues left in equipment can contribute.

**pitch(ing)**—The "throwing in" or addition of yeast to the wort.

**Plato**—A scale of measurement used by professional brewers worldwide to measure the density of a liquid as compared to water. *See* Balling for a full explanation. *See also* Specific Gravity.

**primary fermentation**—Process of initial fermentation. It is generally considered to be the first 60 to 75 percent of the fermentation process.

**primary fermenter (the primary)**—Any vessel in which primary fermentation occurs.

**priming**—The process of adding sugar at bottling time. Three-fourths cup (175 ml) of corn sugar to 5 gallons (19 l) is standard.

**protease (proteolytic)**—Referring to enzymes in malt that degrade proteins.

**rack (racking)**—Process of transferring unfinished homebrew from a primary fermenter to a secondary fermenter. A siphon is often used by homebrewers so that yeast sediments remain undisturbed in the primary.

**relax**—To ease the mind. Homebrew helps.

**residual fermentation extract**—Measured as a percentage. This is a measure of the difference between the apparent limit of fermentation and the apparent degree of fermentation. This is a measure of degree, not of content. (It is not to be confused with real extract.) This measurement can help give the brewer an indication of residual sweetness and body/mouthfeel.

**respiration**—An aerobic and metabolic cycle that yeast performs prior to its fermentation cycle, during which oxygen is stored as energy for later use.

**secondary fermentation**—Closed fermentation, which occurs after the brew has been transferred from the primary fermenter into a second (or secondary) fermenter, usually a carboy. It is the final 25 to 40 percent of fermentation, which precedes bottling. This later stage of fermentation is much less active than primary fermentation. It is desirable to protect the brew with a fermentation lock.

**secondary fermenter (the secondary)**—Any vessel in which secondary fermentation occurs. It is desirable to use a carboy. Carboys have the advantage of a small opening on the top to which a fermentation lock can easily be secured.

**sparge (sparging)**—*See* lautering.

**specific gravity**—A measure of the density of a liquid as compared to water. Readings above 1.000 indicate a density higher than plain water. Adding fermentable sugar to water will increase density. Fermentation will decrease density. Degrees Balling/Brix or degrees Plato are other scales of measuring the density of the wort. *See* Balling.

**sterile**—Impossible condition to achieve. There will always be microorganisms in your wort. Sanitization is the best situation that can be achieved.

**top-fermenting**—*See* ale yeast.

**trub (pronounced "troob")**—Proteins that precipitate out of the malt wort during boiling with hops. Trub is removed from the wort by professional and sophisticated brewers. Its presence in homebrewing is less significant and should not be worried about.

**worry**—Something to be avoided. Homebrew helps in avoiding this. Like a debt that you paid that you may never have owed.

**wort (pronounced "wert")**—Lovingly prepared liquid that will ferment to homebrew.

**yeast**—Microorganisms that convert fermentable sugars to alcohol, $CO_2$, and various by-products that contribute to the taste of beer. All yeast fermentation is anaerobic. And all yeast types will suspend themselves throughout the fermenting beer.

**zymurgy**—The science/art of yeast fermentation. Also, the last word in my dictionary. Also, the magazine of the American Homebrewers Association.

# Appendix 2

## KEGGING YOUR BEER

"Draft beer always tastes better." How many times have you heard this? There's some science to support this observation. Most commercial breweries do not pasteurize their keg beer. Furthermore, brewers who care about the quality of their beer will insist that their keg beer be refrigerated to preserve the freshness. So there you have it: the two main reasons why keg beer almost always has a fresher, more enjoyable flavor than smaller bottled or canned beer.

Naturally, homebrew in bottles or kegs is not pasteurized and if we can, we keep it refrigerated or at least store it in a cool and calm environment. Yet, homebrewers also notice that their keg versions are often a bit fresher tasting than the bottle versions. There's some science here, too. The airspace in the bottle or can gradually reacts with beer and creates changes called oxidation. Some oxidation in certain types of beer can be desirable, but most of these changes reduce the fresh-tasting character. The ratio of air volume to beer is much less in a keg of beer than it would be in a bottle. Thus, you minimize oxidative changes in your beer when you keg.

Keep in mind that everything is relative. Breweries ship beer in bottles and kegs by road, rail, and sea, enduring fluctuating temperatures, exposure to bright light, and agitating motion. Even the trip from the store to your home creates conditions that accelerate beer flavor change. Homebrew is made at home. The conditions your homebrew experiences from your brewery to your glass of enjoyment are minimally insignificant compared to what commercial beers go through.

So the big question is: Can you put your homebrewed beer in kegs and serve it "on draft"? The answer is Yes. There are many advantages to kegging your beer; one not mentioned yet is quite obvious. There are no bottles to wash! Kegging beer is an incredibly simple process, but it does require an investment in kegs and tapping system apparatus. The cash you will spend in order to get set up may bother you a bit, but once that expenditure is a memory, you'll wonder why you didn't do it sooner. There are *no* homebrewers out there who have ever regretted making kegging an option.

The actual process of kegging is simple. Finished beer is siphoned directly into a sanitized keg; then priming sugar is added at a rate of 1/3 cup (80 ml) corn sugar per every 5 gallons (19 l). NOTE: Less priming sugar is required for draft beer. Excessive foaming will result if the normal bottling rate of ¾ cup (175 ml) of corn sugar per 5 gallons (19 l) is used. The keg is then sealed and set aside for conditioning for 1 to 2 weeks.

The beer can be dispensed with tapping systems that are designed for the type of keg used. The first few glasses may contain a small amount of sediment; after that, it's all clear aleing. If a $CO_2$ dispensing system is used, the beer can be dispensed over a period of weeks or even months (if you are a slow savorer). $CO_2$ tapping systems allow you to draw a pint whenever you like because the beer is being displaced with carbon dioxide. The pressure required to dispense beer through a hose 3 feet (1 m) or shorter is only 5 to 8 pounds (per square inch). The valves and pressure gauges that come with a $CO_2$ system are adjustable and will indicate the amount of pressure being used. $CO_2$ does not adversely react with the beer inside the keg unless you inadvertently overpressurize the keg and the beer becomes overcarbonated.

If a British-style real ale hand pump is used to push out the beer, the beer will be displaced with air (containing oxygen and potential airborne contaminants). The oxygen will oxidize the beer over a short period of time. So, if a hand-pump tapper system is used, invite your friends over and drink it up. Keeping the beer cold will slow down the oxidation process, but will not prevent it.

## Kegging Systems

### The Brewery Keg

Commercial breweries use a variety of keg sizes. The traditional commercial American sizes are half (15½ gallons/59 l) or quarter (7¾ gallons/30 l) barrels. More recently approximately 5-gallon (19 l)-sized kegs, called "sixtels" have become popular. They are called sixtels because they are close to being one-sixth of a 31-gallon U.S. barrel. Most of the commercially used types of kegs cannot be used by homebrewers because they can only be cleaned and filled with sophisticated brewery equipment. CAUTION: Commerical kegs should never be taken apart because they can vent pressurized contents and hardware with explosive and deadly force.

There is one type of brewery keg that can be used, but it is no longer used by most breweries and difficult to find. It is called a Golden Gate keg. If you can get your hands on any of these kegs, be sure you can find the tapping fixtures needed to get the beer out and push the gas in. CAUTION and BEWARE: Any keg with a brewery name still on it is considered stolen property. In some states it is a felony to possess any form of used brewery kegs. If you buy one from the

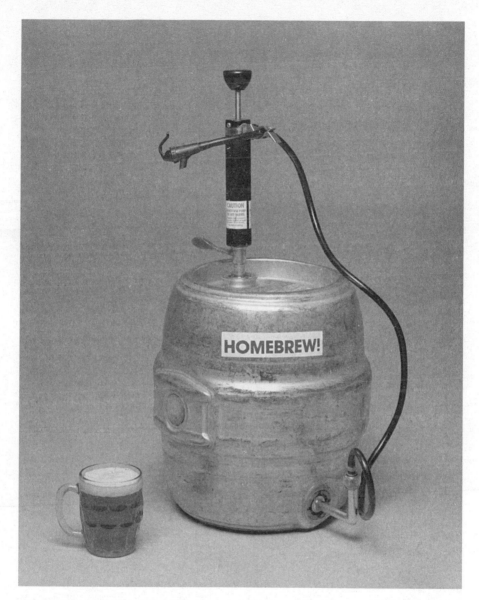

*Don't roll out this barrel! Rarely used or available, this Golden Gate type brewery keg was used to hold draft homebrew. The sediment was drawn off with the first pint of brew. A hand pump or tapper system can be attached. Now, any keg with a brewery name still on it is considered stolen property. In some states it is a felony to possess any form of used brewery kegs. If you buy one from the brewery, save the receipt.*

brewery, save the receipt. There are other options that are safer and more reliable. See below.

Golden Gate kegs are hard to find now, but if you use them they must be thoroughly cleaned and sanitized. In order to accomplish this, first release all pressure from the keg. Then remove the wooden (or in some cases, plastic) bung from the side of the keg, empty the remaining contents, and clean and sanitize with 1 ounce (30 ml) per 5 gallons (19 l) of household bleach solution for at least an hour. The solution should then be be drained through the keg's internal plumbing. This will sanitize everything that comes in contact with the beer.

Priming sugar is boiled with a small amount of water and added directly to the empty keg. Beer is siphoned directly into the keg with a minimum amount of aeration. The keg is then rebunged with a new bung. You will have to find a source of new bungs. They are often accessible through your local homebrew supply shop or through mail-order outlets advertised in homebrew magazines.

## THE CORNELIUS "KEG" (THE CORNY KEG)

The Cornelius draft system is one of the most versatile systems for the homebrewer. Cornelius "kegs" are actually stainless steel canisters that originally were meant to serve as containers for the soft drink industry. Now they are common and known in the beer business. They come in $2\frac{1}{2}$-, 3-, 4- ,5-, and even 10-gallon (9–38 l) sizes. The most commonly used by homebrewers is the 5-gallon (19 l) size (also known as a "sixtel" size), perfect for your 5-gallon batch of beer and small enough to fit in a refrigerator. The difference between Corny kegs used by homebrewers and sixtels used by breweries is that the Corny keg has a large and easily removed plug opening at the top; it is not fitted with commercial hardware that adapts to commercial tapping systems. It is very easy to clean and sanitize. Beer can be dispensed as needed with a $CO_2$ tapping system.

As always, sanitation is important. All the fittings should be taken apart (and occasionally replaced with new gaskets), cleaned, and sanitized (as well as the inside surface of the keg) after it is empty. There is only one small, though solvable, problem that I have encountered in using these containers. The gasket that seals the top of the container will sometimes leak unless a small amount of pressure (5 lbs.) is injected immediately after the keg is filled. The small amount of pressure will force a seal and prevent $CO_2$ from escaping while the beer is conditioning. The Cornelius (Corny keg) draft system is a joy to use.

The containers and tapping fixtures are available through most homebrew supply shops, while others will be able to direct you to sources where you can obtain them.

*Better than soda pop! This draft beer system uses a canister normally used for soft drinks, dispenses with $CO_2$ pressure, and conveniently fits in most refrigerators. Canisters come in 2½-, 3-, 4- and 5-gallon (9–38 l) sizes.*

## THE PARTY PIG

This system involves filling a durable and reusable 2¼-gallon (8.5 l) PET plastic "keg" and having the beer dispense itself without the use of expensive $CO_2$ apparatus. The Party Pig is so called because it kind of resembles a cute little pig, filled with beer and a nose you push to dispense it. How does it work? It's quite easy. You clean and sanitize the inside of the keg. You prime and siphon your beer into the Party Pig. You insert a plastic "pressurizing bag" into the keg. You seal it with a special screw cap that also serves as a tapping device. Then you activate the system by applying a small amount of pressure into the keg. Wait for the beer to condition and carbonate. Chill and serve by pressing the "nose" of the pig. The pressurizing bag begins to mix baking soda with a food-grade acid solution, producing gas *inside the bag only*. The bag slowly inflates, pushing the beer out as you dispense it. It's that simple. See the system on www.partypig.com.

*All it needs are ears and a wiggly tail and your homebrew. The Party Pig is a low-cost option worth considering for tapping out your own draft beer.*

## QUICK DRAFT BEER

Need carbonated draft beer in a hurry and all you have is finished beer resting in carboys? Need sediment-free beer for traveling? Here's a way to do it that is so easy you'll wonder why you didn't think of it yourself.

Simply siphon unprimed clear, finished beer from your fermenter into your Cornelius or stainless steel keg. Seal it off. Chill to below 40 degrees F (4 C) and apply 25 to 30 pounds per square inch of $CO_2$ pressure to the flat, cold beer. Shake it vigorously for 5 to 10 minutes with live pressure on or let it set for 2 days. The carbon dioxide gas will dissolve into the beer and you'll have sediment-free, "artificially" carbonated draft beer.

## POINTS TO REMEMBER WHEN KEGGING

1. Prime at a rate of ⅓ cup (80 ml) of corn sugar for every 5 gallons (19 l) of beer.
2. A small amount of sediment will be drawn off with the first few glasses of beer—after that, it's clear aleing!
3. Sanitize all equipment. Use a long-handled brush to clean inside tubes along with a santitizing cleaner/cleanser.

4. Pressure should be applied only after the initial natural pressure is relieved. Only 5 pounds of $CO_2$ pressure is required to dispense beer through a 3-foot (1 m) hose with spigot.

5. Do not aerate beer as it goes into the keg. Siphon quietly. For added protection, you may wish to "purge" (displace) the air with $CO_2$ from your tapper system. This will eliminate oxygen from inside the keg and prevent its combination with the beer.

6. Kegs should be allowed to condition at temperatures no less than 60 degrees F (16 C) for quick carbonation. If pure lager yeast cultures are used and you know that the yeast works well at lower temperatures, then kegs can be conditioned at lower temperatures; otherwise keep the keg at room temperature for 1 to 2 weeks before refrigeration.

7. Excessive pressure may inhibit yeast activity during the conditioning period.

For an advanced discussion on kegging and draft beer equipment, see "Kegging and Draft Equipment" in *The Homebrewer's Companion, Second Edition*.

# APPENDIX 3

## KRAEUSENING YOUR BEER

## NATURAL CARBONATION WITHOUT CORN SUGAR

Kraeusening (besides being difficult to spell) is the process of priming beer with a measured amount of gyle. Gyle is the amount of unfermented wort a brewer uses to prime the finished beer for carbonation purposes. Gyle can be used instead of the simpler homebrewing procedure of adding ¾ cup (175 ml) of corn sugar for every 5 gallons (19 l) of finished beer. It allows the homebrewer to make a brew from 100 percent barley malt, hops, water, and yeast.

Kraeusening, a process using natural ingredients, is used by many commercial brewers to naturally condition beer. On any given day, breweries are always brewing and packaging one batch of beer or another. It is convenient for commercial breweries to add a small amount of the new beer to the finished beer. But for the homebrewer, brewing and bottling in the same day is often more time-involving than desirable (it doesn't leave you with as much chance to relax and enjoy. . . . . . . ).

## A PRACTICAL METHOD FOR THE HOMEBREWER

Aha! You don't have to brew the same day as you are bottling in order to kraeusen your beer. There is an easier, more convenient way. A homebrewer only has to save a measured amount of unfermented sterile wort stored in a sealed container in the refrigerator. The gyle must be taken from the wort *before* yeast has been added. When it is time to bottle, the stored gyle is added to the finished beer.

The big question is: How much wort should be saved as gyle? The sugar content and specific gravity of worts will vary with every batch. Keeping that in mind, I have reduced an involved mathematical equation to a simple formula that anyone can use. This formula will allow you to calculate accurately the amount of gyle to save in order to prime any amount of beer being brewed. There is one assumption that I make: that priming is based on a priming rate of about ¾ cup (175 ml) of corn sugar per 5 gallons (19 l). The formula is:

$$\text{Quarts of gyle} = \frac{(12 \times \text{gallons of wort})}{[(\text{specific gravity} - 1) \times 1000]}$$

For example, for 5 gallons (19 l) of wort that has a specific gravity of 1.040:

$$\text{Quarts of gyle} = \frac{(12 \times 5)}{[(1.040 - 1) \times 1000]} = \frac{60}{40}$$

NOTE: The denominator is simply equal to the last 2 digits of the specific gravity.

$$\text{Quarts of gyle} = 1\frac{1}{2}$$

If the Balling scale is used instead of specific gravity, then the formula becomes:

$$\text{Quarts of gyle} = \frac{(3 \times \text{gallons of wort})}{\text{degrees Balling}}$$

NOTE: The gyle *must* be removed from your batch of wort before yeast is pitched. It is important that gyle be sealed in a sterile jar and kept cold in the refrigerator.

# APPENDIX 4

## ALCOHOL, YOUR BEER, AND YOUR BODY

What is the effect of alcohol on your body, particularly with overindulgence?

Those of us who have made the switch from commercial to homebrewed beer agree that, compared to commercial overindulgence, homebrew overindulgence leaves one with a minimal hangover.

There are many reasons why you feel better after drinking homebrew. One important reason is the intake of brewer's yeast and the vitamin B complex that is naturally in unfiltered homebrew. Brewer's yeast is one of the richest and most complete sources of the vitamin B complex. Even with homebrew appearing clear, there is a small amount of yeast in suspension and more as sediment. A dose of the yeast sediment in the bottom of the bottle also provides the tonic, which provides vitamins that make you feel better.

It is a known fact that alcohol consumption depletes our body of the vitamin B complex (B complex refers to all of the B vitamins). The vitamin B complex is important for the metabolism of fats, carbohydrates, and protein. In other words, without it we cannot convert the food we eat into usable energy. The energy or fuel our body synthesizes from food is glucose (blood sugar). Ever wonder why you have a hangover headache? It's due in part to the lack of glucose reaching your brain. Ever wonder why you feel shaky or have very low energy? It's due in part to a deficiency of the vitamin B complex, which, in turn, decreases the digestion of food and inhibits the orderly functioning of the nervous system. Ever feel dehydrated? That's in part due to the deficiency of vitamin B complex. The B complex helps maintain fluid levels in our bodies.

There is an advantage to drinking unfiltered homebrew with a small amount of yeast as opposed to filtered commercial beer. The yeast in homebrew helps balance our body's deficiencies and helps in its quest for normalcy.

It's quite obvious that the cure for a hangover, no matter how bad, is not the consumption of more homebrew. What follows are a few effective suggestions and the reasoning behind them.

First of all, come to grips with the fact that our bodies do not enjoy the presence of a lot of alcohol; sometimes we *think* our minds may, but our bodies certainly do not! When healthy, we have a built-in chemistry that is exceptionally

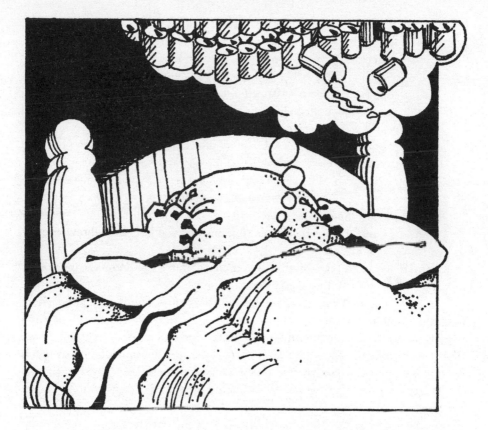

efficient in the elimination of moderate amounts of alcohol. Bless your bottles; otherwise, we'd remain forever inebriated. Our body's metabolic systems burn a considerable amount of energy in the process of elimination and use an inordinate quantity of water. Furthermore, the wastes from this process shellac our feelings.

What follows is a surefire means of helping our bodies rid themselves of alcoholic wastes and replace essential vitamins that have been destroyed.

1. Before drinking and before going to sleep partake of the vitamin B complex. Two teaspoons of brewer's yeast in a glass of juice is the cheapest and most effective way to provide you with the B complex. Vitamin B complex pills are simpler and can also be taken.

   If you have a notion that doesn't jibe with what I'm saying about vitamin B or it's not convenient at the time, take two aspirin or ibuprofen before retiring. Do not use Tylenol or its generic acetaminophen—it will damage your liver if you have alcohol in your system. Aspirin or ibuprofen won't really help your body, but it will hide some of the pain.

2. Drink at least a pint of water *before* retiring. One of the reasons for feeling lousy is dehydration. If you haven't minded your p's and q's and have downed several quarts of homebrew, it may not make much sense that you need more liquid, but believe me, you need water! Much of this water will be used in the process of waste elimination other than through urination; so don't worry about necessary middle-of-the-night trips to the potty. Obviously if you gotta go—go!

3. Shower in the morning. Your skin pores are clogged with waste by-products from the breakdown of alcohol. It's as though your body were wrapped in dirty plastic wrap. When your skin can breathe, you will feel exceptionally better.

4. Eat breakfast. Settle your stomach. This is especially effective if you replace some of those B complex vitamins that you lost the night before.

So take heed and take vitamin B complex (brewer's yeast or vitamin pills), lots of water, a shower, and a light breakfast.

And take caution: There are no general rules applicable to everyone. Most individuals can implement the above suggestions. But realize that each person's body is unique and can react differently to the food and beverage enjoyed. Some may have an allergic reaction to yeast or may not be able to metabolize as much yeast as in homebrew. So when in doubt, consult a doctor and your health specialist to make sure you are not experiencing allergic reactions to food and/or beverages.

Moderation is always recommended. If you practice it, you are much more likely to enjoy beer responsibly into ripe old age.

## MAGIC?

Yeast produces alcohol. When we consume alcohol it destroys our body's store of the vitamin B complex. The yeast that made the alcohol that depletes the vitamin B complex replenishes the vitamin B complex. Think about that. Isn't this part of the magic that we are all involved in?

# APPENDIX 5

## GROWING YOUR OWN HOPS

If you have an area that gets a reasonable amount of sunlight, growing hops is a great way to expand the enjoyment of your homebrewing hobby. Hop cuttings are readily available in early springtime through Internet sites such as www.freshops.com. Many varieties are quite hardy, easy to grow, and fun to have around

Hops can be grown with relative ease anywhere between the 40th and 50th parallels, both north and south of the equator. They have been grown with varying degrees of success in every state of the United States and probably will do well in your area with a reasonable amount of attention.

## Essentials of Hop Growing

Hop plants will need plenty of sunshine and something to climb, as their vine-like growth will reach lengths of 20 to 35 feet (6.1 m to 10.7 m) in 4 months. It is not uncommon for well-tended plants to grow 1 to 2 feet (30 cm to 60 cm) in one day during the peak of the growing season.

Following harvest in August to September in the northern hemisphere (February to March in the southern hemisphere) the vines will completely die off and new shoots will rise the following spring from the ever-expanding deep root system.

## Soil

The soil in which hops are grown needs to be loamy, free of weeds, well drained, and fertilized with potash, phosphates, and nitrogen. Manure compost and/or commercial fertilizer may be used for this purpose. During the growing season, the soil needs to be constantly moist for best results. It is important that the soil not be hard or claylike, as moisture will evaporate more readily from hard-packed soil.

## PROPAGATION

Hops grown commercially in the United States are cultivated from root cuttings rather than propagated by seed. Each year tens of thousands of experimental varieties are grown by farms devoted to research and development, but only root cuttings from a few dozen varieties become considered for commercially availability (see the Hop Variety Guide chart on page 76). Grow what you can get, but it is desirable to obtain root cuttings 8 to 12 inches (20 cm to 30 cm) long from the female type of whatever variety you find. In the United States, females almost exclusively are cultivated without male plants, hence the lack of viable seeds. On the other hand, wild hops, common in many mountain and rural areas, may be either male or female. Male varieties do not produce the hop cones used in brewing. Hops from wild plants make a brew of variable quality. I have tried beers brewed with wild hops, some of which were poor and some of which were excellent. The aroma that the hops exude gives you some indication of whether you want to brew with them. Experiment with small batches if in doubt and proceed from there.

I continue to grow with great success both the Cascade and Mt. Hood varieties of hops. They are hearty and give a good yield year after year. In their second year, there was a considerable mass of roots from which I dug, cut, and further propagated. But it is best to wait until the third year before removing portions of the root to not risk diminishing the yield.

In addition to www.freshops.com, hop roots are commercially available through many seed and nursery catalogs or sometimes through your local homebrew supply shop during the months of February and March only.

*Hops, relaxing in the sun; not worrying and wanting to be in your homebrew.*

## PLANTING AND CARE

Lay the roots 6 inches (15 cm) beneath the ground and at intervals of 2 to 3 feet (60 cm to 90 cm). This should be done in early March or April (or whenever your soil thaws from winter's freeze) along with your peas, radishes, and other very early spring crops.

Wooden stakes need to be well driven into the ground close to the root. This should be done before any growth begins. Heavy string or cord should be tied to the stake and led to trellises, poles, fences, or your own unique network of macramé. Remember that hops grow extensively and need something on which to climb.

When the growing season begins, many shoots will emerge. All but the strongest 4 or 5 should be thinned out. These shoots will quickly grow to 4- to 5-foot (1.2 m to 1.5 m) lengths in a matter of weeks. When they reach 2 to 3 feet (60 cm to 90 cm) it will be necessary to "train" the hops onto the cord. Wind them clockwise around the cord that leads from the stake. Be sure it is clockwise so it will follow the sun across its southeast-to-southwest path (in the southern hemisphere train the hops counterclockwise).

As the hops race up the vine, keep the soil moist at all times. Irrigation is best because the excessive wetting of leaves may promote mildew in some varieties. Continue to thin out new shoots as they appear.

## PESTS AND PROBLEMS

At midseason, in especially damp climates, leaves are removed from the ground level to the 5-foot (1.5 m) level. This prevents the upward spread of leaf wilt, which can completely defoliate a hop vine.

Fungus and mildew are problems that may also arise if climatic conditions are unfavorable and precaution is not taken.

Aphids are pests that are attracted to hops. They can be controlled with lady bugs, nicotine, pyrethrum, or other nonpersistent insecticides. Use caution when choosing insecticides, even though the harvestable whole hops do not begin to present themselves until late July and early August.

## HARVEST

The green conelike whole hop is harvested toward the middle of August and into September, depending on the growing season and variety of hops. Hops should be harvested just before or as they begin to turn brown on the tips. Their ripeness is evident when the whole hop begins to fluff and an abundance of

fine, yellow, resinous powdery-looking glands (like tiny sacs) called lupulin are present at the base of the whole hop's flowerlike petal. Ripe hops emit a pleasing and pungent aroma when crushed between the fingers.

The lupulin is actually thousands of tiny sacks of fragrant, bitter resins and oil. Exercise gentle care in harvesting and drying to preserve the best qualities of the hop. Hops are best air-dried until slightly crisp but still springy to the touch. Sun drying is too harsh and is not recommended.

After drying, it is important that the hops be stored in airtight bags and best kept at freezing temperatures. The very best way to store hops is to place the dried hops into Food Saver® type bags and then vaccum- and heat-seal the package. The process not only compresses the hops, but also seals the bag airtight. Store in a freezer for years or in your refrigerator. Hops eventually will spoil when the bitter resins and aromatic oils are exposed to heat and oxygen.

With the first frost, the vines will die and can be removed to the ground. You will find that with proper care, every year will produce an astounding amount of root crop for your fellow brewers. A more abundant crop will ensue with every harvest.

# APPENDIX 6

## TROUBLESHOOTING—PROBLEM SOLVING

## AND UNDESIRABLE BEER

Every masterbrewer, whether amateur or professional, eventually encounters undesirable flavors in beer. There is a saying in the brewers' world: "There is no bad beer, only beers less desirable than others." That's the nice way we talk to help each other out. In fact, undesirable flavors, aromas, colors in one beer may be totally acceptable in another style of beer. "Bad beer" is a very relative term. Every brewer paints the perfect beer with his own palette. Yet there are certain characters that most beer drinkers, including yourself, will want to recognize and avoid. Troubleshooting and learning to recognize problems are absolutely essential if you are going to continue to enjoy your homebrewing hobby. Learning these skills is easy and within the means of every brewer.

This section isn't comprehensive nor long—it's an introduction to common problems and the most likely solutions. The hints, tips, observations, and advice given here can help solve the most common problems and help make the difference between perfect beer and disappointment. Read this after you've made your first 3 or 4 batches. You won't regret it. For a more detailed discussion on troubleshooting and evaluating beer, see *The Homebrewer's Companion, Second Edition*.

It's easy to blame bad beer on ingredients, recipes, and the weather, but to try to find a reason and a workable solution to your problem may become one frustration after another. The problem usually emerges when you begin to wonder if your beer is the way it's supposed to be. To begin with, don't worry. Worrying is likely to spoil the taste of beer more than anything else you may have inadvertently done. Worrying does not contribute to a solution. My first recommendation is to become concerned. My second suggestion is to try to understand why your beer tastes or appears the way it does, and third, don't avoid your hunch—do something about it. Perhaps there is nothing seriously wrong with your beer, but you will have learned something through the process of discovery. Your tiny efforts will surely pay off with a vast improvement in future beers.

I'd like to assume that, if you have been using the procedures in this book, this appendix is unnecessary, but let's get real. Maybe I'd better not assume anything . . . so just in case, here is a list of the most common problems that homebrewers have:

1. cidery flavors
2. sour flavors
3. medicinal, plasticlike flavors
4. moldy beer
5. cloudy or murky beer
6. flat beer
7. overcarbonated beer
8. skunky
9. apparent prematurely stuck fermentation
10. poor or no foam retention
11. characters such as: sherrylike, paper/wet cardboard, green apples, astringent, sweet corn, butterscotch, grassy, husky/grainy, musty, solventlike, sulfur/yeasty, and others

One or more of the above may be what you perceive in your brew. Know immediately that it is quite easy to adjust your brewing techniques to rid beers of any one of the above if they are undesirable to you.

Let's address each of these problems and consider what may cause them.

CIDERY FLAVORS—Whether you mash or use malt extracts, cidery flavors are avoidable. Anyone who tells you differently has not addressed this problem appropriately. To my knowledge there are no known 100 percent malt extracts that should be faulted for cidery beers. The number-one reason why homebrewers may brew a cidery-flavored beer is that an excessive amount of corn sugar and especially cane (or beet) sugar is used. A homebrew kit that instructs the homebrewer to add sugar in the amount equaling 50 percent of the fermentable sugar is one to avoid. Some kits are well designed so that the combination of specialty malts and yeast provided will not produce a cidery flavor. But in general, if you have problems with cidery-flavored beer, substitute the sugar called for in the recipe with malt extract. Read the list of ingredients on the package. If there is no malt extract, start wondering and be concerned because there should be.

By all means, if you have problems, avoid cane sugar. That "Prohibition" flavor is the result of corn sugar or cane sugar, not the result of malt extract. I won't even let you blame cheap supermarket malt because I have brewed with it and made an excellent beer.

SOUR FLAVORS—Don't blame the ingredients. Face up to the fact that your procedures are not sanitary enough. Bacterial infection, often enhanced by warm brewery temperatures and sluggish fermentations, is to blame for sour beer. More on combating infections later. You might note that it is possible to brew beer that won't sour even in hot climates, as long as bacterial infection hasn't taken hold.

MEDICINAL, PLASTICLIKE FLAVORS—Ever smell a new Band-Aid? Does your beer begin to smell or taste like one? Then you've somehow introduced wild yeast into your fermentation. It could be dirty siphon hoses, or plastic brew buckets. It could be that your bottles aren't clean enough and need a good bleach-and-water soaking. It could be that you introduced wild yeast with your yeast culture, though this isn't likely if you are using prepackaged yeast cultures. Clean, clean, sanitize and sanitize.

In some cases your medicinal character may be a result of too much chlorine in your water source. Either integrate a simple charcoal filter into your water line or change the water source.

MOLDY BEER—"Egad! There's something growing in my beer!" Because of beer's acidity and alcohol content, there are no known pathogens that can survive in beer; therefore, you aren't going to die. But there are all kinds of molds that can contaminate your beer because of lax sanitation procedures. Sometimes infections do not perceptibly alter the flavor of your beer; other times they can be devastating. Your taste buds will tell you. Moldy beer is the result of inadequate

cleaning of equipment and undue exposure to microorganisms. Mold also is more likely to develop with inappropriate lagering techniques (aging) at temperatures above 60 degrees F (16 C).

CLOUDY OR MURKY BEER— Perhaps your brew never did clear or perhaps it was clear when it went into the bottle, but then—whammo!—3 weeks later a permanent haze developed. The problem is, again, another kind of bacterial infection. It isn't the fault of the malt or the sugars, and unless you are using very old or contaminated yeast, it isn't the yeast's fault either.

FLAT BEER—You've done everything right. Followed instructions just like you've always done. One week, 2 weeks, 1 month. . . . . . . flat beer! I don't know of a reason unless you've left an excessive amount of sterilant in your bottles or you are storing your beer at excessively cool temperatures. If so, try storing the bottles at room temperature. If that doesn't work, rehydrate some dry yeast in warm water, then uncap the beer and add a few drops of rehydrated yeast into each bottle and recap. That should work, but if it doesn't, then open the bottles again and add ¼ teaspoon (1.2 ml) of corn sugar to each 12-ounce (355 ml) bottle. If that fails, your final resort is to blend your flat beer with carbonated beer just before serving. It works every time.

OVERCARBONATED BEER—The simple explanation is that you've added too much priming sugar. An adequate amount is ½ to ¾ cup (120 to 175 ml) of corn sugar to 5 gallons (19 l). When kegging your beer for draft, ⅓ to ½ cup (80 to 120 ml) corn sugar per 5 gallons (19 l) is adequate. Sometimes, though, a seasoned homebrewer will experience a batch of aged homebrew that suddenly kicks into a mysteriously late fermentation in the bottle. This is usually the result of a bacterial or wild yeast infection that either ferments or allows the yeast to ferment otherwise unfermentable components in the finished beer. Almost all gushers are a result of bacterially contaminated beer. Again, keep it clean.

Here is another reason you may have foamy beer, despite all the cleanliness you can muster: iron! Yep, if there's iron in your water or rust that is originating in your hot water heater, iron will cause overdone, sudsy head retention and foaming. Seek water that doesn't have high-iron content.

SKUNKY—Does your beer or even other beers remind you of the smell of a skunk or cat urine? This is simple to avoid. Your beer has been light-struck. Sunlight is devastating, but even prolonged exposure to fluorescent lights will cause a photochemical reaction to occur with the bitter hop compounds in almost all beer, resulting in a skunky flavor and aroma even in the best of beers.

APPARENT PREMATURELY STUCK FERMENTATION—More often

than not, you're worrying. Many malt extracts are designed and produced to have a dextrin (unfermentable) content. This gives body to the beer. Some very fine all-malt extract beers will begin fermentation at 1.038 and finish as high as 1.013. Other high-gravity recipes will begin at 1.055 and be ready to bottle at 1.028. Aeration of the wort and choice of yeasts will make some difference, but usually minimal. Roll with the punches and bottle when fermentation has stopped or is negligible.

POOR OR NO FOAM RETENTION—More often than not, poor head retention is the result of a dirty glass, with residual grease, wax, soap, or detergent left unrinsed. Wash your glassware with detergent and water, and rinse well with lots of hot water. Households with hard water will have a more difficult time rinsing residuals from glassware. Sanitize your bottles and fermenters with bleach and cold water soaks and rinse well with hot water.

When you are sure the problem isn't your glassware, one likely solution is to take a look at your recipe and recall how fresh your hops were. Old and stale hops will diminish the head retention. Good-quality, fresh hops will definitely enhance head retention, especially with flavor and aroma hopping. Use the best hops, and freshest hops, in all your recipes. Hop oils enhance head retention.

CHARACTERS SUCH AS: SHERRYLIKE, PAPER/WET CARD-BOARD, GREEN APPLES, ASTRINGENT, SWEET CORN, BUTTER-SCOTCH, GRASSY, HUSKY/GRAINY, MUSTY, SOLVENTLIKE, SULFUR/YEASTY, AND OTHERS—Space doesn't permit a complete review of additional characters you may be encountering. A more comprehensive treatment of flavors, aromas, appearances, and origins can be found on pages 398–404 in *The Homebrewer's Companion, Second Edition.* An additional resource can be found at the Beer Judge Certification Program's Website: www.bjcp.org.

## BACTERIAL INFECTIONS

What are they? What do they look like? How do they taste? Where do they come from, and what kinds of situations do they like?

Bacteria are microorganisms that can be beneficial (and necessary) to the processing of many types of food (e.g., yogurt, pickles, soy sauce, sauerkraut, etc.). In the case of beer and homebrewing, there are a few types that are more troublesome. That's because they are common and they will "pickle" your beer in 24 hours, if given the opportunity.

Lactobacillus is probably the most common bacteria encountered by home-brewers. It sours beer by producing lactic acid. Pediococcus is another very common bacteria that loves wort and produces nasty flavors and aromas. Ace-tobacter is a less common problem with beermaking, but it is responsible for making vinegar from the alcohol in your beer by producing acetic acid. Bacteria will form hazes, promote gushing, form molds, alter flavors, and produce strange, bizarre, and undesirable aftertastes.

**BEST TIP:** One of the best and simplest ways to recognize whether or not your beer is contaminated with bacteria is to take a look at your used empty or filled bottles of conditioned beer. Look at the surface of the beer where it contacts the inside of the bottle. Is there a deposit ringing the neck? Every gusher, hazy beer, sour-smelling and sour-tasting beer I've had the pleasure of evaluating invariably has a "ring around the neck"—a sure sign that there is bacterial or wild yeast contamination. Sometimes a bottle will have two or three ring deposits, all from different fill levels of different batches of beer; the contamination is perpetuated in the bottles until they are properly cleaned and sanitized. And if the bottles aren't properly sanitized, then it is likely that your siphon hoses and fermenters aren't either. Don't despair. It is no big deal to do it right.

The sources of bacterial infections in homebrew are usually easy to track down because bacteria are everywhere. Hands, countertops, porous surfaces, scratched surfaces, grain, and grain dust (don't grind your grain in the brewhouse!). So if you have problems, it is likely that something unsterile came in contact with the unfermented wort.

Bacteria love malt. As a matter of fact, they probably prefer your wort over anything else in your home. Research labs at hospitals use malt extract and gelatin as a culture medium for bacteriological studies. And bacteria love warm temperatures. You are asking for problems if you don't take care especially when brewing a batch of unprotected beer in the heat of the summer. Protect it and you'll be fine.

## SOLVING THE PROBLEM

Here are a few simple, effective tips that will ensure excellent beer.

1.  Inspect your bottles for stains and bacterial deposits in the neck. Soak bottles and fermenters overnight in a solution made of 2 ounces (60 ml) of household (chlorine) bleach to 5 gallons (19 l) of cold water. This will remove all stains and kill the bacterial infection. Some proprietary special cleansers available at your local homebrew store may also do the job. Consult with your homebrew supply store. You can always count on common household (chlorine) bleach to assure a thorough job. Rinse well with hot tap water.
2.  Siphon hoses should never appear stained or discolored. Sanitize them in a bleach-and-water solution or other sanitizing solution. If the stains cannot be removed, retire the hose from beer-siphoning purposes.

3. Maintain sanitation throughout the brewing process, especially when wort temperature falls below 160 degrees F (71 C).

4. Scratched surfaces on plastic brewing equipment harbor bacteria. Discard worn, stained, and scratched primary fermenters and siphon hoses.

5. Do not immerse anything in the cooled wort except sanitized glass, stainless steel, or enameled utensils. Wooden spoons, plastic stirrers, or hands will be a disaster.

6. Do not suck on siphon hoses; rather fill the hose with water in order to begin siphoning. If you're a traditionalist, then gargle with brandy or a good single malt scotch before sucking.

7. Clean secondary fermenters immediately after each use.

8. Remove stubborn stains and residues with a bottle brush and with an overnight bleach-and-water solution.

9. Use a fermentation lock correctly; keep it filled with 1 inch (2.5 cm) of water.

10. Avoid undue lagering at temperatures above 60 degrees F (16 C). Two to 4 weeks is usually adequate for secondary fermentation at room temperature.

11. Rinse bottles after each use—immediately.

12. Boil priming sugar with a small amount of water.

13. Boil bottle caps or soak them briefly in high-proof vodka.

14. Cool your wort and pitch yeast as soon as possible.

15. Aerate your cooled wort in order to enhance fermentation.

16. Siphon quietly. DO NOT AERATE OR SPLASH YOUR BEER ONCE FERMENTATION HAS BEGUN.

17. Never add ice to your wort in order to cool it.

18. Avoid using low-grade plastics for secondary fermentations. They are difficult to sanitize and oxygen will pass through the plastic into the beer.

## SOME FINAL COMMENTS

If you are brewing great beer already, you're doing fine. Most beginners don't have drastic infection problems because malt-loving bacteria have had no reason to "hang out." But eventually sloppiness may catch up with you. The preceding outline of problems and solutions is presented especially for those who have experienced frustration in brewing good beer and for new brewers to use as a future resource. Remember, it's easy to make good beer.

For an advanced discussion on beer evaluation and quality, see "Beer Evaluation: What Am I Tasting and Why Is It in My Beer?" in *The Homebrewer's Companion, Second Edition*.

# APPENDIX 7

## BEER APPRECIATION: TASTING BEER— PERCEIVING FLAVOR

If the only kind of beer you've ever tasted has been light American lager, you haven't really experienced beer. However, as a homebrewer or as a beer enthusiast in pursuit of a variety of beers, you have undoubtedly tasted an overwhelming complexity of beer flavors. This section is meant to be an introduction to developing your skills for perceiving flavor. For a more comprehensive discussion on the art and science of evaluating beer, take a look at "Beer Evaluation: What Am I Tasting and Why Is It in Beer?" in *The Homebrewer's Companion, Second Edition*.

There are different reasons why individuals drink beer. The most significant reason is enjoyment. Our perception of enjoyment will vary with the mood we are in, the food we are eating, and the environment in which we drink. The beer that we remember enjoying on a hot summer day at the ballpark may not be as pleasing as an after-dinner beer. Likewise, that sweet stout that so wonderfully complements the finish of a meal or that warmingly full-bodied doppelbock just may not suit the mood you're in after a long drive home from work (or maybe it does).

The more you know about beer, the more you will appreciate beer flavors and understand what it is you prefer; choosing the right kind of beer for that special mood and situation lends more enjoyment to your life.

It is not really justifiable for anyone to say, "I don't like beer." There are so many different kinds of beer that surely there must be a style of beer for everyone. I do allow someone to say, "I don't like *this* beer" or "I don't like to drink beer," but to generalize and say, "I don't like beer" is like saying "I don't like food."

Through experience and our perception of flavor and other beer characteristics we discover what we enjoy in a beer (no one, NO ONE, can tell you what you like or should like, even though some people and brewing companies may try). By summarizing all the things that we experience when we taste beer, we can form an opinion of the beer's overall enjoyability.

As already suggested, enjoyability is influenced by many things, one of which is the perception of flavor. Beer flavor is a complex science for some. Let's not go off the deep end here, so for this introductory discussion, I'll simplify the science and complexity and perception of beer flavor. Relax. Don't worry. Have a home-brew and let's begin your cultivation of beer appreciation. What follows is an outline that will assist in determining the character and flavor of any beer.

## BEER FLAVOR PROFILE

There are four major categories that you should consider when fully appreciating the taste of beer.

1. Appearance
2. Aroma
3. Taste
4. Overall impression

In this section we are not judging beer (we'll introduce what's up with judging in the next appendix); therefore, numerical values have not been assigned. The purpose here is to help you more fully appreciate the flavor of beer.

### 1. Appearance
- *Head retention and appearance*—A certain amount of head retention is desirable in most beers but is largely a matter of preference. Generally speaking, no head or an excessive amount of head (that interferes with drinking) is undesirable.

   The ingredients and techniques used in brewing influence head retention. Generally, the more dextrinous the beer and the presence of certain types of protein (developed in the mashing process), the better the head retention. All barley malt beers and those that use a lot of hops and the freshest of hops tend to have creamier heads.

   Head retention suffers greatly in the presence of oils and waxes or when beer is served in a dirty glass or poured from dirty draft beer taps.
- *Clarity*—Some beers are not meant to be clear. More often than not, the clarity has little effect on the flavor of the beer. Beer that is normally clear at room temperature may develop a haze due to protein in the beer when chilled. This haze, called a chill haze, has very little influence on flavor. Hop oils can develop hazy beer, particularly if you use use dry hopping techniques. Certain styles like German Hefeweizen (wheat beer with yeast) are purposefully infused with suspended yeast when serving. However, some hazes that may develop in beer are due to bacterial or wild yeast contamination and will not go away at room temperature. If bottle-conditioned beer is being considered for its clarity, a careful pouring is important so that the natural yeast sediment is not disturbed.

## 2. Aroma

The careful perception of aroma must be made within the first three or four sniffs; after that perception is dulled and not as acute, even though the aromatic presence may still be there.

- *Aroma*—The aroma of beer can be first defined as the smell of beer relative to the malt, grain, and their fermentation by-products. Malt contributes directly to many aromatics that we can perceive. The most common aromas are those of malty sweetness, caramel, toffee, roasted, toasted, or chocolate. Malt contributes indirectly to many other aromas that are the result of fermentation. The most significant and noticeable aromas are those contributed by esters. Esters may give beer a fruity aroma reminiscent of apples, raspberries, strawberries, bananas, pears, grapefruit, and other fruits. Esters are often desirable to some degree and are particularly noticeable in ales and stronger beers. Butterscotch (from diacetyl) aromas are also a by-product of yeast metabolism and can be detectable in many beers.

    The aroma of beer can also be described as the aromatics that hops contribute to beer. The hop aroma will vary to a great degree. When it is present it can be described as floral, spicy, earthy, fruity, pungent, herbal, etc.
- *Odors*—Let's attribute odors to defects in the beer. Defective beer can be the result of mishandling (extreme temperature changes or agitation), bacterial contamination, oxidation or being "light-struck." Some of the more common odors associated with defective beers can be described as acidic, skunky (light-struck), garbagy, wet cardboard, winey, and sherrylike.

## 3. Taste

The actual flavor of beer is quite complex. Everyone has his or her own way of describing flavors and their importance in the overall perception. I will explain

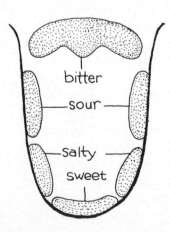

some things about the perception of flavor, things that are known and not arguable. Then I will present an outline that can serve as a means of helping you summarize the taste of beer.

Your tongue perceives four different tastes. They are *bitter, sour, salty,* and *sweet.* These four elements are perceived all over the tongue, but bitterness is *mostly perceived* on the back of the tongue. Sourness is *mostly perceived* on the sides of the tongue. Sweetness is *mostly perceived* on the tip of the tongue and saltiness is *mostly perceived* just to the rear and on either side of the tip of the tongue. There is one more elementary flavor that the tongue perceives; that is called *umami*. I discuss that in detail in *The Homebrewer's Companion, Second Edition.*

As you taste, the beer should be moved to all parts of the tongue in order to experience maximum flavor. The tongue sends all of its messages to the brain and it is there that we combine the taste experiences into an overall balance of flavor.

Beer contributes a variety of taste sensations to the tongue. The degree to which the four main sensations contribute to the flavor of beer is influenced by many factors. Here we discuss how different ingredients and by-products of fermentation influence flavor and aroma. The following outline summarizes how beer can affect the sensations of taste:

*Bitterness*—The degree of bitterness can be influenced by:

   Hops—The most assertive influence on bitterness in beer; often a dry bitterness.
   Tannins—Tannins from husks and grains can contribute an astringent sensation, intensifying bitterness in beer.
   Malt—Roasted malts can contribute to bitterness.
   Minerals—Mineral salts can influence the extraction of bitterness from hops and malt, influencing flavor.

*Sweetness*—The degree of sweetness can be influenced by:

   Malt—Malt has the most influence on the perception of sweetness. It can contribute unfermented sugars and unfermentable dextrins. The dextrins give beer a fuller body that can help perception of sweetness.
   Hops—The flowery and floral nature of hops can sometimes be interpreted as sweetness or can alter the perception of other factors of sweetness.
   Esters—Esters are by-products of fermentation. They are fruity in nature and can lend to the perception of sweetness.
   Diacetyl—Diacetyl, a by-product of fermentation, is, generally speaking, butterscotch flavored and can lend to the perception of sweetness.

*Sourness*—The degree of sourness is proportional to the acidity of the beer and can be influenced by:

   Carbonation—Carbon dioxide when dissolved in beer takes the form of carbonic acid. An excessive amount of carbonation will contribute an acidic flavor to the beer.
   Contamination—Bacterial and wild yeasts can produce acids such as acetic acid (vinegar) and lactic acid.

Fruit—If you're enjoying fruit-flavored beer, natural fruit acids can contribute to the sensation of sourness.

*Saltiness*—The degree of saltiness is influenced by:

Minerals—An excessive amount of certain minerals can contribute to a salt flavor in beer. Calcium, magnesium, and sodium are usually the culprits.

## SUMMARIZING YOUR IMPRESSIONS

Distilling your impressions into a meaningful summary can become an involved and absorbing process. What follows is a useful simplification that does not detract from the essential enjoyment that you should be experiencing.

### *Taste*
A. Bitter and Sweet—Malt/Hop/Fermentation Balance
  Generally speaking, most beers are made in a way so that fuller-bodied and sweeter beers are balanced with more bitterness. Likewise, a light-bodied delicate beer will not be as highly hopped (bitterness). A light-bodied beer that is excessively bitter will not be perceived to be in balance. A full-bodied sweeter beer that lacks hop bitterness (except in the special case of sweet stouts and the like) is usually not in balance.
B. Mouthfeel
  This taste is actually a sensation describing how the beer feels (literally) in your mouth. It can be described as being full-bodied or light-bodied. A particular style of beer will determine the appropriate fullness or lightness of body. The unfermented sugars and dextrins contribute to the degree of fullness. A low-calorie light beer would be classified as light-bodied. A German bock beer would be classified as full-bodied.
C. Aftertaste
  This sensation is experienced after the beer has been swallowed. (Beer drinkers don't spit it out!) Sometimes an otherwise good-tasting beer will leave an unpleasant aftertaste (bitter, sweet, sour, astringent, cloying). The aftertaste of a good beer should be clean and not linger unpleasantly. It should by all means encourage you to have another—either immediately or on another occasion.
D. Carbonation
  The tactile feel of bubbles in the mouth perceptibly determines the degree of carbonation. The feel of the bubbles

can also vary with the ingredient used. A big and explosive bubble feeling in the mouth may be due to the use of fermentable ingredients other than barley malt. A beer made with all barley malt will tend to have a smaller bubble feeling in the mouth (almost a creamy sensation). This phenomenon can be explained in terms of physics, surface tension, and bubbles, but need not be gone into in more detail here.

Over- or undercarbonation can also influence flavor. A highly carbonated beer will tend to be more acidic. As the carbonation diminishes rapidly and it goes flat, so does the flavor.

E. Overall Impression—Drinkability

This is the final "category" that you might consider when determining how you appreciate a beer. It is the most personal and subjective of the categories, but if you are taking notes it is probably the most important to consider.

The best way to use this category of perception is to determine whether or not you really enjoy the beer for what it is meant to be. Even if you don't particularly like a stout or a diet lite pilsener, you can still appreciate it for what it is meant to be for others. Keep this in mind.

## MAXIMIZING YOUR PERCEPTION OF BEER FLAVOR

The following hints will help in perceiving the most flavors from your tastings:

1. When tasting a variety of beers, begin with the lighter styles and finish with the darker, hoppier, and more full-bodied beers.
2. Do not smoke or be in a smoke-filled room when you taste.
3. Do not partake of salty or greasy food while tasting (greasy lips will devastate head retention).
4. Eat French-style white bread or saltless crackers to cleanse the palate between beers (unsalted matzoh crackers are excellent palate cleansers).
5. Do not wear lipstick or lip balm (the waxes will destroy head retention).
6. Use clean, spotless glassware that has been thoroughly rinsed of soap or detergent residues.
7. Serve the beer at the temperature it is meant to be served at; for example, light American lagers very cold, and strong ales at slightly chilled temperatures.
8. Relax. Don't worry. Have a homebrew.

## You, the Connoisseur

With a little knowledge of beer styles and the use of meaningful guidelines for tasting, you will be surprised at how much more you will come to enjoy beer.

Beer quality can be surprisingly determined and agreed upon by many; whether or not you prefer or like a particular beer will depend on the circumstances that you are in or on just plain unexplainable preference.

Beer is what you personally perceive it to be. Use all your senses. Look at it, smell it, taste it, feel it, and, above all as American homebrew pioneer Fred Eckhardt tells us, listen to it.

For an advanced discussion on beer evaluation and quality, see "Beer Evaluation: What Am I Tasting and Why Is It in My Beer?" in *The Homebrewer's Companion, Second Edition.*

*The best beer in the world is your homebrew. In this case I'll have one of mine.*
*Relax. Don't worry, and happy brewing. Charlie Papazian*

Judging beer is the process of assigning a numerical value to the variable qualities of beer. There are a number of reasons why one would desire to go through a process of judging beer. Three of them are:

1. Judging beer to help the brewer improve the quality of beer being brewed.
2. Judging beer to determine a winner in a competition.
3. Judging beer just for fun.

Your reason for judging beer may determine the degree of sophistication used in judging. For the purpose of an introduction for amateur brewers, two scoring systems are presented here. The 50-point scale is useful for focusing on the finer points of beer character. It is also useful for determining winners in large competitions. The 20-point system is essentially the same system but is simpler and more useful at informal beer tastings. The numbers are easier to add and the finer points of beer character are not so important to determine.

## THE 50-POINT SCALE

*Aroma* (as appropriate for style)          1–10 points_____
Malt (3)
Hops (3)
Other Fermentation Characteristics (4)


*Appearance* (as appropriate for style)          1–6 points_____
Color (2)
Clarity (2)
Head Retention (2)


*Flavor* (as appropriate for style)          1–19 points_____
Malt (4)
Hops (4)

Balance (5)
Conditioning/Carbonation (3)
Aftertaste (3)

**Body** (as appropriate for style)                    1–5 points_____

**Drinkability and Overall Impression**   1–10 points_____

**Total Points_____**

*Scoring Guide:* *Excellent 40–50; Very Good 30–39; Good 25–29; Drinkable 20–24; Problem <20.*

## THE 20-POINT SCALE

**Appearance** (15%)                    0–3 points_____

**Aroma** (20%)                    0–4 points_____

**Taste** (50%)                    0–10 points_____
Hop/malt balance (4)
Aftertaste (3)
Mouthfeel (3)

**Overall Impression** (15%)                    1–3 points_____

**Total Points_____**

*Scoring Guide:* *Excellent 18–20; Very Good 15–17; Good 12–14.*

# APPENDIX 9

## FORMULATING YOUR OWN RECIPES—
## ADJUSTING YOUR SPECIFIC GRAVITY

## FORMULATING RECIPES

The following information will be helpful in determining the influence various brewing ingredients have on the specific gravity of the wort. A more comprehensive table of ingredients and their "extract" or specific gravity potential is presented in *The Homebrewer's Companion, Second Edition.*

One pound (454 g) of the following ingredients and water to make 1 gallon (0.95 l) will (approximately) yield the specific gravity indicated:

| Ingredient | Specific Gravity | (Balling) |
|---|---|---|
| Corn Sugar | 1.038–1.044 | (9.5–11) |
| Malt Extract (syrup) | 1.033–1.038 | (8–9) |
| Malt Extract (dry) | 1.042–1.046 | (10.5–11.5) |
| Malted Barley | 1.025–1.030 | (6–7.5) |
| Munich Malt | 1.025–1.030 | (6–7.5) |
| Crystal Malt | 1.022–1.026 | (5.5–6.5) |
| Grain Adjuncts | 1.025–1.030 | (6–7.5) |

## ADJUSTING SPECIFIC GRAVITY

Whenever a recipe is followed or a new recipe is formulated, it is usually the intention to come as close as possible to a specified specific gravity. Sometimes we miss our mark. The easiest way to compensate for a discrepancy is to add more or less the next time and ferment whatever you have this time. But if you want to adjust the specific gravity of the wort, there are two options:

1. Add more sugars (malt or corn sugar) to the wort to raise the specific gravity.
2. Add more water to the wort to decrease the specific gravity.

## INCREASING THE SPECIFIC GRAVITY OF THE WORT

The addition of 1 pound (454 g) of malt extract syrup to 5 gallons (19 l) of wort will increase the specific gravity approximately 0.004 to 0.006 (1 to 1.75 B).

The addition of 1 pound (454 g) of corn sugar to 5 gallons (19 l) of wort will increase the specific gravity approximately .009. (2.25 B).

## DECREASING THE SPECIFIC GRAVITY OF THE WORT

Sometimes you may find that you've put too much fermentable sugar in the wort and the resulting specific gravity is too high. You can dilute the wort and lower the specific gravity by adding water. The rate of dilution and the change in specific gravity are not the same at various densities. For example: Adding 1 gallon (3.8 l) of water to 5 gallons (19 l) of wort that is 1.045 will decrease the specific gravity by about .006. But adding 1 gallon (3.8 l) of water to 5 gallons (19 l) of wort that is 1.060 will decrease the specific gravity by about .010. The following tables will help you make approximate adjustments within the ranges used by most homebrewers.

NOTE: The numerical value in parentheses represents gallons of water added to (specifically) 5 gallons (19 l) of wort. Metric conversions can be approximated based on 1 quart = .25 gallon = about 1 liter.

| FOR SPECIFIC GRAVITIES 1.035–1.048 | |
|---|---|
| 5% dilution or | (.25 gallon) more water decreases the specific gravity by .001 |
| 15% dilution or | (.75 gallon) more water decreases the specific gravity by .005 |
| 30% dilution or | (1.5 gallons) more water decreases the specific gravity by .010 |
| 50% dilution or | (2.5 gallons) more water decreases the specific gravity by .016 |

| FOR SPECIFIC GRAVITIES 1.048–1.053 | |
|---|---|
| 5% dilution or | (.25 gallon) more water decreases the specific gravity by .002 |
| 10% dilution or | (.50 gallon) more water decreases the specific gravity by .003–4 |
| 25% dilution or | (1.25 gallons) more water decreases the specific gravity by .010 |
| 30% dilution or | (1.5 gallons) more water decreases the specific gravity by .011 |
| 50% dilution or | (2.5 gallons) more water decreases the specific gravity by .017 |

FOR SPECIFIC GRAVITIES 1.055–1.060

| | |
|---|---|
| 5% dilution or | (.25 gallon) more water decreases the specific gravity by .002 |
| 10% dilution or | (.50 gallon) more water decreases the specific gravity by .005 |
| 25% dilution or | (1.25 gallons) more water decreases the specific gravity by .012 |
| 30% dilution or | (1.5 gallons) more water decreases the specific gravity by .014 |
| 50% dilution or | (2.5 gallons) more water decreases the specific gravity by .018 |

# Appendix 10

## Treatise on Siphoning
## by Professor Surfeit

Dedicated to Bernoulli, who, alas, never surmised that his thoughts would be passed on to the homebrewer.

The science of siphoning—the art of siphoning. What is the difference? One, you get it to work; the other, you get it to work for you.

The ancient problem of the homebrewer presents itself: How does one get the beer from one container to another without disturbing the sedimentary deposit? Only the marvel of the siphon endears itself in accomplishing this.

The siphon is a gravitational "pump" that avails itself to the homebrewer as a means of passing beer from one container to another without disturbing bottom sedimentary deposits.

Drop an apple and see what happens. It falls down. But if we place this apple at its own level on a table, it remains until the skin rots and is no longer able to gather itself.

Place a bucket of brew on a table. Surprisingly enough it remains there. Now take a cherry bomb and tape it to the base of the beer bucket. Light the fuse and run into the next room (you may snicker and chuckle if you wish, but be sneaky and enjoy yourself). When the explosion has occurred, run back into the room and observe the stream of beer. It flows out and down. Peculiarly enough, if we had punched a hole in the bucket above the level of the beer no fluid flow would have occurred. Why? The question may seem trivial, but with the answer the universe opens up before us (and after us). Once again, may I ask you, why? Because there exists no force that would bring the beer up to the hole and enable it to escape.

Thus, we are able to surmise that there must exist some force that "pushes" the beer through the bottom hole. "Gravity?" you say. Well, not quite true, for gravity is not force. Force in this case is: gravitational acceleration times mass ($F = mg$). Gravity is always constant at the point of departure. But the mass of the beer in the bucket decreases as it empties; thus, the force decreases. To prove this, watch the stream of beer empty itself from the bucket onto the floor. At first, the beer gushes out quickly, and then gradually the flow decreases to a slow trickle. So we see that the rate of flow is directly proportional to the height of beer above the hole and nothing more (to prove this, do the same experiment on a higher table).

Ten gallons of beer is heavy. Five gallons of beer is half as heavy. Refill your one-holed bucket to the 10-gallon mark and quickly place another cherry bomb halfway up and blow out another hole. Observe. The beer flows faster out of the bottom hole than the middle-of-the-bucket hole. Why? Well, of course, there is more pressure (pressure = force per area; pounds per square inch) exerted by 10 gallons of beer than by 5 gallons of beer. If you hesitate to accept this, do the following: Empty a 10-foot-deep swimming pool of its water and then re-fill the pool with beer. Immerse yourself in the pool of beer and swim to the bottom. As you swim to the bottom you will feel the weight (pressure) of all that beautiful beer increase upon your eardrums. The pressure is greater at the bottom of the pool than it is at the halfway point. A simpler experiment can be conducted. Drive up to the top of a mountain. Now drive quickly down the mountain. Your ears pop. Why? Because on the top of the mountain there is less atmosphere above you, and as you come toward sea level there is more atmosphere above you. The weight of this air above you presses against your eardrums until the air pressure inside your ears is the same as that on the outside.

Now where does that leave us? It leaves us standing in a puddle of beer with the knowledge that the greater the height of beer above the hole, the faster the beer will flow out.

$$e = mc^2$$

$$F = ma$$

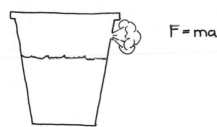

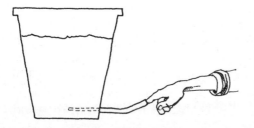

Now, my dear friends, let us proceed. You have a hole in your bucket. Let us stuff 2 inches out of 6 (sextipus) of clear plastic hose through the hole in the bottom of the bucket so that the only way the beer can come out is via the hose.

Place your finger tightly over the

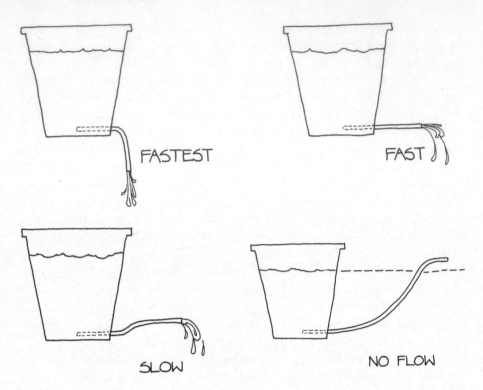

end of the hose. Fill the bucket with ale. Remove your finger from the end of the tube and watch the ale flow out. Lower and raise the tube and observe the various rates of flow. Guess what? Believe it or not (you better believe it), the end of that tube is a "movable hole" in the bucket. The more ale above the "end" of the hole, the faster your kitchen floor will get wet. If you raise the end of the tube above the level of the ale, you won't get any flow (like the hole in the bucket above the level of the beer).

You can bend and twist your hose into any shape, but the only thing that

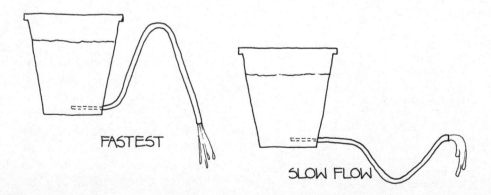

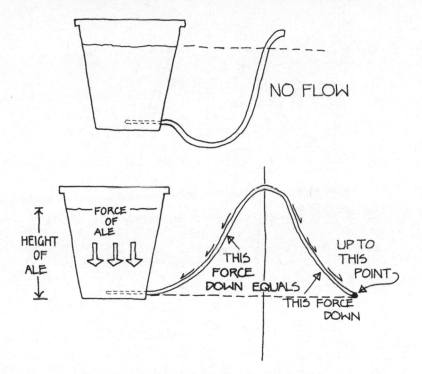

matters is where the hole (end of tube) is with respect to the top level of the ale. Amazing, eh?

Let us go one giant step further—let's reposition the tube as a siphon (see illustration above) and patch up our hole with sanitized chewing gum. Eureka!

We have the exact same situation as before. Once begun, ale flows out because of the distance between the end of the tube and the surface of the ale.

Aha! Now here comes a really amazing revelation. Let's bring the end of the tube, which is immersed in the ale, close to the surface.

So we see that it doesn't matter a goat's foot where the "X" end of the tube is in the ale. The flow remains simply a function of the distance between the surface of the ale and the "Y" end of the tube. So when siphoning beer, just concern yourself with not sucking the pasty sediment off the bottom.

If you want faster flow, have a greater distance between the "Y" end of tube and the surface of the ale.

Now here's a little trick. Let's say you want to pause in your siphoning to answer the telephone (there's always someone who is going to call you in the middle of siphoning, because it's just one of those kinds of things). Get a load of the diagram on page 444.

Now that we understand what a siphon is, how do we start one? The

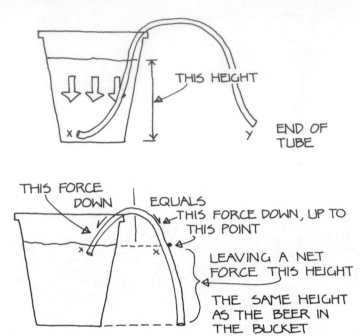

THIS HEIGHT

END OF TUBE

THIS FORCE DOWN | EQUALS THIS FORCE DOWN, UP TO THIS POINT

LEAVING A NET FORCE THIS HEIGHT

THE SAME HEIGHT AS THE BEER IN THE BUCKET

number-one thing to always remember is that you are not siphoning gasoline out of your neighbor's automobile. This is beer. Don't be afraid of it.

The only way you can start a siphon (for that matter to get a siphon to work at all) is to have a continuous flow of ale within the tube. Any large air spaces in your hose will halt the flow of ale or beer. As an air bubble travels through the tube to the end we have a situation which will reverse itself. Fill your hose completely full of water. Immerse one end into the beer and lower the other end at least to a level below the surface of the beer. Voilà, it's working.

Here's a final trick: You have one full bucket and one empty bucket. Siphon one into the other, and flow stops when each has the exact same height of beer.

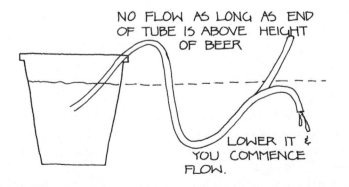

NO FLOW AS LONG AS END OF TUBE IS ABOVE HEIGHT OF BEER

LOWER IT & YOU COMMENCE FLOW.

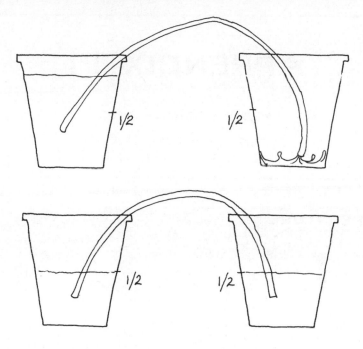

So remember: 1) It doesn't matter where the immersed end of the tube is in the beer. It's the distance between the surface of the beer (in the bucket) and the "out" end of the tube that counts. 2) The lower the "hole" or end of the tube is, the faster the flow (you can slow it down by pinching the tube, too). 3) Avoid air spaces.

Whatever happens, remember that you have mastered this art only when you are able to drink and enjoy your own homebrew—for only then does everything come into perspective.

The preceding science is real. The presentation is somewhat tongue in cheek. The implications are more than meet the eye. If you brew all-grain beer, think about how you might design a mash lauter system with a seesaw fulcrum that automatically regulates flow without any external forces. Relax. Don't worry. Have a homebrew.

# APPENDIX 11

## CONVERSIONS AND
## MEASUREMENTS

## TEMPERATURE

To convert degrees Centigrade to Fahrenheit:

$$(\text{degrees } C \times {}^9\!/_5) + 32 = \text{degrees } F$$

To convert degrees Fahrenheit to Centigrade:

$$(\text{degrees } F - 32) \times {}^5\!/_9 = \text{degrees } C$$

Here's a handy Fahrenheit to Centigrade/Celsius conversion chart:

| F | C | F | C | F | C |
|------|-----|------|------|------|------|
| 32.0 | 0.0 | 46.4 | 8.0 | 60.8 | 16.0 |
| 33.8 | 1.0 | 46.2 | 9.0 | 62.6 | 17.0 |
| 35.6 | 2.0 | 50.0 | 10.0 | 64.4 | 18.0 |
| 37.4 | 3.0 | 51.8 | 11.0 | 66.2 | 19.0 |
| 39.2 | 4.0 | 53.6 | 12.0 | 68.0 | 20.0 |
| 41.0 | 5.0 | 55.4 | 13.0 | 69.8 | 21.0 |
| 42.8 | 6.0 | 57.2 | 14.0 | 71.6 | 22.0 |
| 44.6 | 7.0 | 59.0 | 15.0 | 73.4 | 23.0 |

| F | C | F | C | F | C |
|---|---|---|---|---|---|
| 75.2 | 24.0 | 111.2 | 44.0 | 147.2 | 64.0 |
| 77.0 | 25.0 | 113.0 | 45.0 | 149.0 | 65.0 |
| 78.8 | 26.0 | 114.8 | 46.0 | 150.8 | 66.0 |
| 80.6 | 27.0 | 116.6 | 47.0 | 152.6 | 67.0 |
| 82.4 | 28.0 | 118.4 | 48.0 | 154.4 | 68.0 |
| 84.2 | 29.0 | 120.2 | 49.0 | 156.2 | 69.0 |
| 88.0 | 30.0 | 122.0 | 50.0 | 158.0 | 70.0 |
| 87.8 | 31.0 | 123.8 | 51.0 | 159.6 | 71.0 |
| 89.6 | 32.0 | 125.6 | 52.0 | 161.6 | 72.0 |
| 91.4 | 33.0 | 127.4 | 53.0 | 163.4 | 73.0 |
| 93.2 | 34.0 | 129.2 | 54.0 | 165.2 | 74.0 |
| 95.0 | 35.0 | 131.0 | 55.0 | 167.0 | 75.0 |
| 96.8 | 36.0 | 132.8 | 56.0 | 168.8 | 76.0 |
| 98.6 | 37.0 | 134.6 | 57.0 | 170.6 | 77.0 |
| 100.4 | 38.0 | 136.4 | 56.0 | 172.4 | 78.0 |
| 102.2 | 39.0 | 138.2 | 59.0 | 174.2 | 79.0 |
| 104.0 | 40.0 | 140.0 | 60.0 | 176.0 | 80.0 |
| 105.8 | 41.0 | 141.8 | 61.0 | 177.8 | 81.0 |
| 107.6 | 42.0 | 143.6 | 62.0 | 179.6 | 82.0 |
| 109.4 | 43.0 | 145.4 | 63.0 | 181.4 | 83.0 |

| F | C | F | C | F | C |
|---|---|---|---|---|---|
| 183.2 | 84.0 | 195.8 | 91.0 | 208.4 | 98.0 |
| 185.0 | 85.0 | 197.6 | 92.0 | 210.2 | 99.0 |
| 186.8 | 86.0 | 199.4 | 93.0 | 212.0 | 100.0 |
| 188.6 | 87.0 | 201.2 | 94.0 | | |
| 190.4 | 88.0 | 203.0 | 95.0 | | |
| 192.2 | 89.0 | 204.8 | 96.0 | | |
| 194.0 | 90.0 | 206.6 | 97.0 | | |

## VOLUMES

1 U.S. barrel = 31 gallons = 1.17 hectoliters
1 U.S. gallon = 4 quarts = 8 pints = 16 cups = 3.79 liters
1 U.S. quart = 2 pints = 32 ounces = 0.95 liter
1 U.S. cup = 8 ounces = 16 tablespoons = 48 teaspoons
1 British gallon = 1.2 U.S. gallons
1 U.S. gallon = .833 British gallons
1 liter = 0.26 U.S. gallons = 1.06 U.S. quarts
1 hectoliter = 100 liters = 26.4 U.S. gallons = 0.85 U.S. barrels
1 ounce = 30 milliliters

## DRY WEIGHTS

1 pound = 16 ounces = 0.454 kilograms = 454 grams
1 ounce = 28.35 grams
1 gram = 0.035 ounces
1 kilogram = 2.2 pounds

## MISCELLANEOUS

1 part per million (ppm) = 1 milligram per liter (mg/l) = 1 microliter per liter (μl/l)

# CONVERTING SPECIFIC GRAVITY (SG) TO PLATO

Formula:

Input degrees Plato          Output will be
(15.2, for example)          in SG

$$SG = 1 + \frac{P}{(258.6 - 0.8796P)}$$

Input SG in 1.0xx format          Output will be
(1.050, for example)          in degrees Plato

$$P = (463 - (205 * SG)) * (SG - 1)$$

Here is a handy specific gravity/Plato conversion chart, which is particularly handy when gravities exceed 1.060 (14.7). The chart is based upon the conversion equation given in the *MBAA Technical Quarterly*, 24(4):129 1987.

| SG | P | SG | P | SG | P |
|----|----|----|----|----|----|
| 1.040 | 10.0 | 1.050 | 12.4 | 1.060 | 14.7 |
| 1.041 | 10.2 | 1.051 | 12.6 | 1.061 | 15.0 |
| 1.042 | 10.5 | 1.052 | 12.9 | 1.062 | 15.2 |
| 1.043 | 10.7 | 1.053 | 13.1 | 1.063 | 15.4 |
| 1.044 | 11.0 | 1.054 | 13.3 | 1.064 | 15.7 |
| 1.045 | 11.2 | 1.055 | 13.6 | 1.065 | 15.9 |
| 1.046 | 11.4 | 1.056 | 13.8 | 1.066 | 16.1 |
| 1.047 | 11.7 | 1.057 | 14.0 | 1.067 | 16.4 |
| 1.048 | 11.9 | 1.058 | 14.3 | 1.068 | 16.6 |
| 1.049 | 12.1 | 1.059 | 14.5 | 1.069 | 16.8 |

| SG | P | SG | P | SG | P |
|---|---|---|---|---|---|
| 1.070 | 17.1 | 1.090 | 21.6 | 1.110 | 25.9 |
| 1.071 | 17.3 | 1.091 | 21.8 | 1.111 | 26.1 |
| 1.072 | 17.5 | 1.092 | 22.0 | 1.112 | 26.3 |
| 1.073 | 17.7 | 1.093 | 22.2 | 1.113 | 26.5 |
| 1.074 | 18.0 | 1.094 | 22.4 | 1.114 | 26.7 |
| 1.075 | 18.2 | 1.095 | 22.7 | 1.115 | 27.0 |
| 1.076 | 18.4 | 1.096 | 22.9 | 1.116 | 27.2 |
| 1.077 | 18.7 | 1.097 | 23.1 | 1.117 | 27.4 |
| 1.078 | 18.9 | 1.098 | 23.3 | 1.118 | 27.6 |
| 1.079 | 19.1 | 1.099 | 23.5 | 1.119 | 27.8 |
| 1.080 | 19.3 | 1.100 | 23.7 | 1.120 | 28.0 |
| 1.081 | 19.6 | 1.101 | 24.0 | 1.121 | 28.2 |
| 1.082 | 19.8 | 1.102 | 24.2 | 1.122 | 28.4 |
| 1.083 | 20.0 | 1.103 | 24.4 | 1.123 | 28.6 |
| 1.084 | 20.2 | 1.104 | 24.6 | 1.124 | 28.8 |
| 1.085 | 20.4 | 1.105 | 24.8 | 1.125 | 29.0 |
| 1.086 | 20.7 | 1.106 | 25.0 | 1.126 | 29.3 |
| 1.087 | 20.9 | 1.107 | 25.3 | 1.127 | 29.5 |
| 1.088 | 21.1 | 1.108 | 25.5 | 1.128 | 29.7 |
| 1.089 | 21.3 | 1.109 | 25.7 | 1.129 | 29.9 |

# APPENDIX 12

## BIBLIOGRAPHY OF RESOURCES

### Books

Brewers Publications. *Beer and Brewing Series*. Vols. 1–5 and 6–10. Boulder, Colo.: 1986–90.

Briggs, Hough, Stevens and Young. *Malting and Brewing Science*. Vols. 1–2. New York: Chapman and Hall, 1971.

Eckhardt, Fred. *The Essentials of Beer Style*. Portland, Oreg.: Fred Eckhardt Associates, 1989.

Editors of East West Journal. *Shopper's Guide to Natural Foods*. Cambridge, Mass.: 1983.

Fix, George. *Principles of Brewing Science*. Boulder, Colo.: Brewers Publications, 1989.

Food Learning Center. *Co-op Food Facts*. Winona, Minn.: 1980.

Forget, Carl. *Dictionary of Beer and Brewing*. Boulder, Colo.: Brewers Publications, 1988.

Foster, Terry. *Pale Ale*. Boulder, Colo.: Brewers Publications, 1990.

Gayre, Lt. Col. Robert. *Brewing Mead: Wassail in Mazers of Mead*. Boulder, Colo.: Brewers Publications, 1986.

Guinard, Jean-Xavier. *Lambic*. Boulder, Colo.: Brewers Publications, 1990.

Institute for Brewing Studies. *Brewers Resource Directory, 1990–91*. Boulder, Colo.: Brewers Publications.

Jackson, Michael. *The Pocket Guide to Beer*. New York: G. P. Putnam Sons, 1982.

———. *The Simon & Schuster Pocket Guide to Beer*, 2nd ed. New York: Simon & Schuster, Inc., 1988.

———. *The New World Guide to Beer*. Philadelphia, Penn.: Running Press, 1988.

———. *The World Guide to Beer*. New York: Exeter Books, 1977. Master Brewers Association of the Americas. *The Practical Brewer*. Madison, Wisc: 1946.

———. *The Practical Brewer*, 2nd ed. Madison, Wisc: 1977.

Kieninger, Dr. Helmut. "The Influences on Beer Making," *Best of Beer and Brewing*, Vols. 1–5. Boulder, Colo.: Brewers Publications, 1987.

Miller, Dave. *Continental Pilsener*. Boulder, Colo.: Brewers Publications, 1990.

Morse, Roger A. *Making Mead (Honey Wine)*. Ithaca, N.Y.: Wicwas Press, 1980.

*Proceedings of the National Homebrewers Conference*. Al Andrews (1982), Roger Briess (1982), Professor Dr. Helmut Kieninger (1983), Ron Siebel (1983). Boulder, Colo.: American Homebrewers Association, 1982, 1983.

Rajotte, Pierre. *Belgian Ales*. Boulder, Colo.: Brewers Publications, 1992.

Warner, Eric. *German Wheat Beer*. Boulder, Colo.: Brewers Publications, 1992.

### Periodicals

*The Amateur Brewer*. Fred Eckhardt. Portland, Oreg.: Amateur Brewer Publications.

*The Journal of the American Society of Brewing Chemists*. St. Paul, Minn.

*The Journal of the Institute of Brewing*. London, England.

*Master Brewers Association of the Americas Technical Quarterly,* St. Paul, Minn.
Narziss, L. "Types of Beer." *Brauwelt International,* November, 1991.
*The New Brewer Magazine.* Boulder, Colo.: Brewers Association.
Peindl, Professor Anton. From the series "Biere Aus Aller Welt." *Brauindustrie.* Schloss
    Mindelburg, Germany, 1982–1991.
*Zymurgy.* Boulder, Colo.: American Homebrewers Association.

## Individuals, Associations, Institutes, and Businesses That Provided Technical Assistance and Information for This or the Earlier Editions of This Book

The Adolph Coors Company, Golden, Colo.: Darwin Davidson, *Manager, Brewing Research;*
    Michael Mefford, *Manager, Engineering;* Gil Ortega, *Supervisor, Pilot Brewery;* Dave
    Schisler, *Microbiologist, Research and Development*

The American Homebrewers Association National Competition Committee

Birko Corporation, Henderson, Colo.: Dana Johnson, *Technical Representative*

Briess Malting Company, New York, N.Y.: Roger Briess, *President;* Mary Ann Gruber, *Director, Technical Services*

Coopers Brew Products—Cascadia Importers, Grass Valley, Calif.: Mark Henry, *President, Cascadia Imports*

Crosby & Baker, Westport, Mass.: Seth Schneider, *President*

Edme Ltd., Mistley, Manningtree, England: Richard Holt, *Director;* Dr. E. East, *Group Research Chemist;* A. R. Lansdown, *Production Manager*

Frankenmuth Brewery, Frankenmuth, Mich.: Fred Scheer, Brewmaster

The Great American Beer Festival[sm] Professional Tasting Panel

Lieutenant Colonel Robert E. Gayre of Gayre & Nigg, Argyll, Scotland

Havill's Mazer Mead, Rangiora, New Zealand: Leon and Gay Havill, *Owners and Mead-makers*

Hopunion USA Inc., Yakima, Wash.: Gregory K. Lewis, *Vice President and Technical Director;* Ralph Olson, *President*

Itona Products Ltd., Wigan, England: Jeffrey Hampson, *Director*

J.E. Siebel and Sons, Chicago, Ill.

Lallemand, Montreal, Quebec, Canada: Clayton Cone, *Technical Consultant,* Jim McLaren, *Production Manager*

Master Brewers Association of the Americas, St. Louis, Mo.

Muntons, P.L.C., Stowmarket, England: Michael Chaplin, *North American Sales Representative*

Gregory Noonan, Burlington, Vt.

Paines, P.L.C., St. Neots, England: Lance Middleton, *Director*

Premier Malt Products, Grosse Pointe, Mich.: Susan Hamburger, *Sales Director*

S.S. Steiner, Inc., Yakima, Wash.: Herbert Grant, *Technical Consultant*

Siebel Institute of Technology, Chicago, Ill.: Ron Siebel, *Director*

Ray Spangler, Erlanger, KY.

University of California at Davis: Professor Michael Lewis, *Food Science and Technology Department;* Jean-Xavier Guinard, *Graduate*

University of Saskatchewan, Saskatoon, Canada: Professor W. Michael Ingledew, *Department of Applied Microbiology and Food Science*

Wander, Ltd., Kings Langley, England: William Thorburn, *Industrial Sales and Marketing Manager*

Western Water Specialists, Boulder, Colo.: John Martin
Yakima Chief, Sunnyside, Wash.: Gerard W. Ch. Lemmens, *Sales Director—Craft Brewers*

Special thanks to the following friends during my early homebrewing days for the dedication and personal contributions they have made to teaching me and improving the quality of beer and beermaking in the United States:

Al Andrews, Riverside, California
David Bruce, Hungerford, England
Byron Burch, Santa Rosa, California
Fred Eckhardt, Portland, Oregon
George Fix, Arlington, Texas
Terry Foster, Milford, Connecticut
Paul Freedman, Washington, D.C.
Michael Jackson, London, England
Finn Knudsen, Evergreen, Colorado
Bill Litzinger, Boulder, Colorado
David Miller, St. Louis, Missouri
Greg Noonan, Burlington, Vermont

## ADDITIONAL READINGS AND RESOURCES FOR THE HOMEBREWER CITED IN PREVIOUS EDITIONS OF *THE COMPLETE JOY OF HOMEBREWING*

### Periodicals

*Zymurgy* magazine. American Homebrewers Association, P.O. Box 1679, Boulder, CO 80306.
    Telephone: +1-303-447-0816; www.homebrewersassociation.org

Of special interest:

1992 Special *Gadgets and Equipment* issue
1994 Special *Special Ingredients & Indigenous Beer* issue
1995 Special *Great Grain* issue
1997 Special *Classic Guide to Hops* issue
1998 Special *Magic of Yeast* issue
1999 Special *Lager and Lagering* issue
2000 Special *Brewing Up History* issue
2001 Special *Homebrew Packaging—Kegs to Bottles* issue
Summer 1995 feature article: "Kegging Basics" (highly recommended)
Jan–Feb 1999 *Kegging Basics* issue
March–April 2001 *Cleaning and Sanitation* issue
Nov–Dec 2001 *Hops* issue
Sept–Oct 2002 *Strangely Brewed; Offbeat & Experimental Brewing Techniques*

## Books

Brewers Publications. *The Dictionary of Beer & Brewing, 2nd edition*. Boulder, Colo.; Brewers Publications, 1998.

Buhner, Stephen Harrod. *Sacred and Herbal Healing Beers*. Boulder, Colo.; Brewers Publications, 1998.

Classic Beer Styles Series, Vols. 2–18. Boulder, Colo.; Brewers Publications, 1990–2000.

> Altbier
> Bavarian Helles
> Barley Wine
> Belgian Ale
> Bock
> Brown Ale
> Continental Pilsener
> German Wheat Beer
> Kölsch
> Lambic
> Mild Ale
> Oktoberfest, Vienna, Märzen
> Pale Ale
> Porter
> Scotch Ale
> Smoked Beer
> Stout

Daniels, Ray. *Designing Great Beers*. Boulder, Colo.; Brewers Publications, 1996.

Papazian, Charlie. *Home Brewer's Gold—Winning Recipes from the World Beer Cup*. New York, N.Y.; Avon Books, 1997.

Smith, Gregg. *Beer in America; The Early Years—1587–1840*. Boulder, Colo.; Brewers Publications, 1998.

## Associations

The American Homebrewers Association, Box 1679, Boulder, Colorado 80306. Telephone: 1-303-447-0816; www.homebrewersassociation.org

Activities include:

Annual National Homebrewers Conference
Annual National Homebrew Competition
Annual Great American Beer Festival
Annual Craft Brewers Conference and BrewExpo America

Publications include:

*Zymurgy* (magazine)
*The New Brewer* (for the professional craft brewer)
Brewers Resource Directory

# APPENDIX 13

## WEBSITE/INTERNET RESOURCES

There are thousands of Websites devoted to beer and brewing. They change and evolve every day. You will have no problem finding what you are looking for with keyword searches. The list below provides some of the most popular and authoritative sites on the Internet. Most of the sites listed under "Association and Homebrew Activities" provide portals and search engines linking you to the vast network of beer and brewing information.

### The Joy of Homebrewing Website
www.thejoyofhomebrewing.com

### Association and Homebrew Activities
Brewers Association and American Homebrewers
    Association—www.craftbeer.com; www.homebrewersassociation.org;
        www.brewersassociation.org
Beer Judge Certification Program—www.bjcp.org

### Hops
Barth Haas Hops—www.barthhaasgroup.com
English Hops—hopsfromengland.com
Freshops—www.freshops.com
HopUnion—www.hopunion.com
New Zealand Hops—www.nzhops.co.nz
Steiner Hops—www.hopsteiner.com
Yakima Chief—www.yakimachief.com

### Kegging
Party Pig keg—www.partypig.com

### Malt
Brewers Supply Group—www.brewerssupplygroup.com/malt
Briess Malting Company—www.briess.com
Castle Malt—www.castlemalting.com

Coopers Malt—www.coopers.com.au
Crisp Malt—www.crispmalt.info
Muntons Malt—www.muntons.com
Weyermann Malt—www.weyermann.de

## Mead
Talisman Farm (mead)—www.talisman.com/mead
Got Mead?—www.gotmead.com

## Software Homebrewing—Recipe Formulation
Promash—www.promash.com
Brew Wizard—www.members.aol.com/brewwizard

## Yeast
DanStar Yeast—www.danstaryeast.com
DCL Yeast—www.dclyeast.co.uk
Fermentis—www.fermentis.com
Lalvin Yeast—www.lalvinyeast.com
Red Star Yeast—www.redstaryeast.com
White Labs—www.whitelabs.com
Wyeast—www.wyeastlab.com

## Availability of Supplies and Shop Locators
American Homebrewers Association—www.homebrewersassociation.org
Brewers Supply Group—www.brewerssupplygroup.com
Cascadia Import—www.cascadiabrew.com
Crosby & Baker—www.crosby-baker.com
LD Carlson—www.ldcarlson.com
FH Steinbart—www.steinbart.com

# ACKNOWLEDGMENTS

Illustration by Joe Boddy appears on pages 316–317.

Illustrations of Mayahuel and Rabbit on page 276 and Beer on page 280 from the *Codex* Borgia.

Illustrations by Jamie Elliot appear on pages 13, 14, 29, 47, 90, 124, 140, 287, and 423.

Illustrations by Dave Harford appear on pages 184 and 358.

Illustrations by Steve Lawing appear on pages 11, 16, 41, 49, 52, 94, 101, 111, 157, 166, 167, 189, 197, 199, 201, 205, 209, 215, 221, 225, 226, 233, 235, 240, 243, 244, 247, 251, 261, 265, 269, 270, 286, 291, 323, 343, 348, 352, 359, 377, 378, 381, 385, 387, 391, and 415.

Illustrations by Peggy Markel appear on pages 17, 18, 56, 73, 146, 294 and 430.

Illustrations by Brent Warren appear on pages 8, 128, 153, and 424.

Photos by Michael Lichter appear on pages 22, 23, 24, 26, 30, 32, 33, 34, 36, 37, 38, 39, 40, 44, 58, 60, 61, 63, 71, 73, 139, 142, 311, 313, 320, 321, 322, 324, 325, 329, 337, 339, and 407.

Photo by Luke Trautwein on page 434 courtesy of the Brewers Association.

Photo on page 120 appears courtesy of the Adolph Coors Company, Golden, Colorado.

Photos on pages 327 and 409 appear courtesy of Andrews Homebrewing Accessories, formerly of Riverside, California.

Photo on page 410 appears courtesy of Quoin Industrial, Inc. (Party Pig®)

Photos by the author appear on pages 19, 55, 65, 418, and 420.

Lena on page 6 was the symbol and icon for wholesomeness and goodness for the now defunct Blue Ribbon Malt Extract that was ubiquitous, popular, and available at grocery stores during Prohibition and through the mid-1980s.

# INDEX